ART
WAS THEIR WEAPON

For Shaunagh, Charlie and Bridget

First published 2019 by
Fremantle Press Inc. trading as Fremantle Press
25 Quarry Street, Fremantle WA 6160
(PO Box 158, North Fremantle WA 6159)
www.fremantlepress.com.au

Copyright © Dylan Hyde, 2019

The moral rights of the author have been asserted.

This book is copyright. Apart from any fair dealing for the purpose of private study, research, criticism or review, as permitted under the Copyright Act, no part may be reproduced by any process without written permission. Enquiries should be made to the publisher.

Designed by Carolyn Brown, www.tendeersigh.com.au

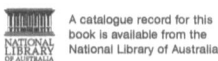
A catalogue record for this book is available from the National Library of Australia

Art Was Their Weapon: The History of the Perth Workers' Art Guild. ISBN 9781925815740 (paperback).

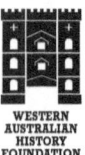

Assisted by a grant from the Western Australian History Foundation.

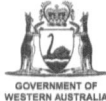 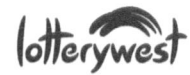

Fremantle Press is supported by the Western Australian State Government through the Department of Cultural Industries, Tourism and Sport.

Front cover images: *Top:* Egon Kisch addressing crowd on Esplanade, Perth, on his last day in Australia, 1935, Noel Butlin Archives Centre, Australian National University: J. Normington Rawling, N57-2353. *Bottom:* Harald Vike, *Perth Roofs (Suburban Perth)* 1939, oil on canvas, 44.5 x 54.3 cm, State Art Collection, Art Gallery of Western Australia, Purchased with Funds from The Carnegie Grant, 1941.
Back cover images: *Clockwise from top-left:* Ian Smith Asst. Stage Director for Effects with Model Stage, 1936, New Theatre Archives, Mitchell Library, SLNSW; Axel Poignant, Banner of the Amalgamated Engineering Union, oil on canvas, by Harald Vike, Labour Day March 1939, Perth, © Axel and Roslyn Poignant Archive, London; Phyllis Harnett with *Till the Day I Die* poster, 1941, Papers of Ric Throssell, NLA.

ART
WAS THEIR WEAPON
THE HISTORY *of the* PERTH WORKERS' ART GUILD

DYLAN HYDE

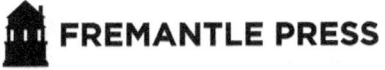 **FREMANTLE PRESS**

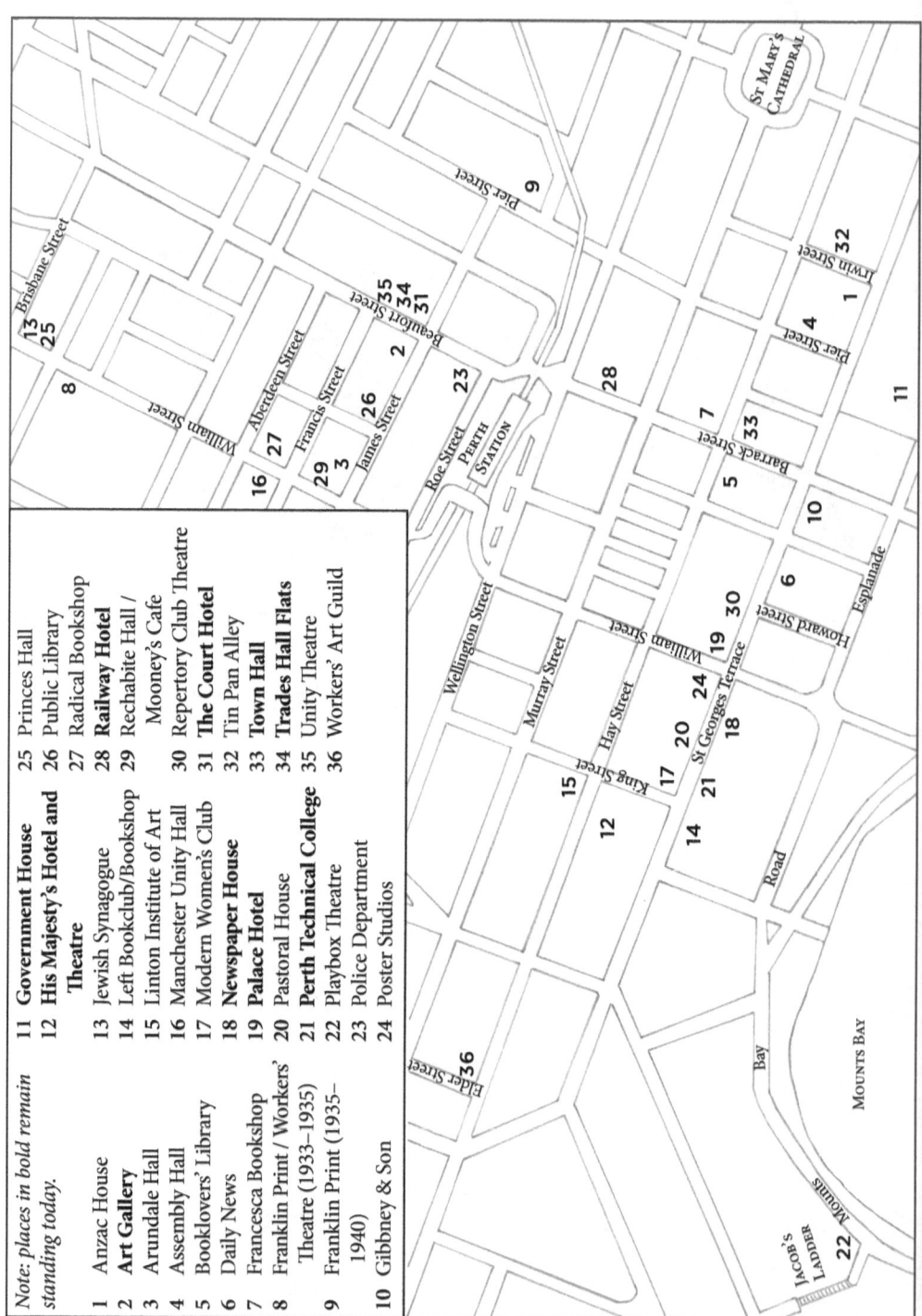

PERTH 1933–1941

Note: places in bold remain standing today.

1. Anzac House
2. **Art Gallery**
3. Arundale Hall
4. Assembly Hall
5. Booklovers' Library
6. Daily News
7. Francesca Bookshop
8. Franklin Print / Workers' Theatre (1933–1935)
9. Franklin Print (1935–1940)
10. Gibbney & Son
11. **Government House**
12. **His Majesty's Hotel and Theatre**
13. Jewish Synagogue
14. Left Bookclub/Bookshop
15. Linton Institute of Art
16. Manchester Unity Hall
17. Modern Women's Club
18. **Newspaper House**
19. **Palace Hotel**
20. Pastoral House
21. **Perth Technical College**
22. Playbox Theatre
23. Police Department
24. Poster Studios
25. Princes Hall
26. Public Library
27. Radical Bookshop
28. **Railway Hotel**
29. Rechabite Hall / Mooney's Cafe
30. Repertory Club Theatre
31. **The Court Hotel**
32. Tin Pan Alley
33. Town Hall
34. **Trades Hall Flats**
35. Unity Theatre
36. Workers' Art Guild

CONTENTS

Abbreviations used in this book		6
Introduction 'That Mad Little Era' in the West		7
1	The Red Witch of Greenmount	10
2	The Five Arts Club	22
3	Kisch and the Popular Front	35
4	The 'Living Theatre': Formation of the Perth Workers' Theatre	48
5	'A Man of Enterprise': Keith George and The Workers' Art Club	64
6	The Workers' Art Guild and the Party Line	76
7	'Bury the Dead'	85
8	Spain, Moscow and 'The Southern Cross'	99
9	'Offensive Epithets'	125
10	Standing Guard for the Party	138
11	Leading the Revolution on a White Horse	160
12	The War, and 'Blood on the Moon'	174
13	'The Fervent Years'	186
14	'Art as a Weapon in the People's Fight'	194
15	'The Surrealist Mob'	212
16	'The Faded Years': A Retreat to Provincialism	228
Appendix After the War		254
Endnotes		280
Bibliography		338
About the Author		346
Acknowledgements		347
Index		348

ABBREVIATIONS USED IN THIS BOOK

ABC	Australian Broadcasting Commission (now Corporation)	FAW	Fellowship of Australian Writers
ACTU	Australian Council of Trade Unions	FOSU	Friends of the Soviet Union
AEU	Amalgamated Engineering Union	IWDU	International Workers' Dramatic Union
AGNSW	Art Gallery of New South Wales	LBC	Left Book Club
AGWA	Art Gallery of Western Australia	MAWF	Movement Against War and Fascism
AIF	Australian Imperial Force	NAA	National Archives of Australia
AJA	Australian Journalists' Association	NLA	National Library of Australia
ALP	Australian Labor Party	PSA	Perth Society of Artists
ANU	Australian National University	SLNSW	State Library of New South Wales
ASIO	Australian Security Intelligence Organisation	SLV	State Library of Victoria
AWL	Australian Writers' League	SLWA	State Library of Western Australia
AWU	Australian Workers' Union	SORA	Studio of Realist Art
BBC	British Broadcasting Corporation	UN	United Nations
BPC	Budget Protest Committee	UNE	University of New England
CAWF	Council Against War and Fascism	UWA	University of Western Australia
CIB	Commonwealth Investigation Branch	UWM	Unemployed Workers Movement
Comintern	Communist International	WA	Western Australia
CPA	Communist Party of Australia	WIR	Workers' International Relief
CPSU	Communist Party of the Soviet Union		

INTRODUCTION

'THAT MAD LITTLE ERA' IN THE WEST

Someone called it an English village, he said. You should be warned.[1]

In the 'dissonant' early 1930s — a time described by Australian novelist George Johnston as 'that mad little era'[2] — Western Australia's capital, Perth, was a provincial frontier town with a population of just under 85,000. An isolated outpost on the edge of a fraying British Empire, it was bordered by a vast ocean to one side and a three-day train journey through inhospitable country to Adelaide on the other. Not until December 1933 would it be connected to Adelaide by overland telephone, and from there to the rest of Australia.

Socially, it was a place where virtually 'everybody knew everybody'.[3] Certainly it was small enough that 'one knew everyone interested in the same sphere, or knew of them'.[4] Social life was neatly compartmentalised, with the middle class belonging to respectable clubs and socialising almost exclusively within their own circles. 'Perthians' in general eschewed more intellectual pursuits, wrote John Graham in 1962:

> He avoids intellectual activity like the plague, preferring the more comfortable routine of social intercourse with his own kind and discussions on a parochial and highly-generalized level. Though his manners are informal, his sense of social convention is rigid and unyielding.[5]

It was also a place well insulated from international events. Journalist Bill Irwin noted at the time: 'a new idea has a long way to go before it reaches Perth'.[6] Whatever news, politics and culture did reach Perth came by sea. Ships docking at Fremantle — about twenty kilometres south of Perth and the first Australian port of call for most — were met by shipping reporters such as Irwin.

> In search of news we boarded freighters, smacks and mailboats, whale-chasers, shark-fishing motor-ships, and sailing vessels, those

decayed gentlewomen of the seas ... We interviewed the travellers on the mailboats. There was a missionary whose wife had been decapitated before his eyes by head-hunters in Borneo. (Such indignation was the missionary's!) There was the young New Yorker who had been with the whaling fleet in the Antarctic. There was the big-game hunter, pith helmet and all, bound for Darkest Africa. There were youths who had canoed through the waterways of Europe, and girls who [had] gone up the Amazon. There was casual talk of Hollywood Boulevard, Broadway, Piccadilly, the Champs Élysées. All over the world we travelled — up all those streams, along all those boulevards. But vicariously, always it was vicariously.[7]

Passengers' stories, and the papers and magazines they brought with them, provided news from Britain and Europe — though by the time of its arrival it was often months old and bore 'the quality of the light of a distant star'.[8] While Perth was connected to international cable services and radio broadcasts, to many the distant events 'could be given reality only by the fact of somebody talking about them'.[9] Perth's social and intellectual isolation was thus countered in some small measure by this tenuous maritime link to the outside world. British and European artists and entertainers travelling to Australia would break their journey in Fremantle after a long sea voyage, and would often preview east-coast performances at His Majesty's Theatre in Perth's city centre.

Australia's isolation more broadly had also begun to be diluted by those servicemen who had returned — in the apposite verse of W.B. Yeats, 'all changed, changed utterly'[10] — from the bloody conflict of the Great War. The nation as a whole had been transformed by its first global engagement, and its parochialism had started to fracture.

Although its size dwarfs the states and territories to its east, Western Australia's landscape, its climate and its geographical isolation invoke a sense of inertia — an impression of arrested time and 'the possibility that history might not continue precisely because, here, it has not yet begun'.[11] There is little sense of a fluid history in Western Australia, and 'a reluctance of West Australians to analyse conflicts in their history' for 'fear of recreating the very situation they are asked to recall'.[12]

Western Australia has always identified itself in contradistinction to the rest of the country. Perth arguably still perceives itself as a frontier town, teetering on the geographical edge and, despite its bluster, has always been an insecure and fragile society that does not easily deal with threats to its social order and cohesion.

The state, though, was not immune to the upheaval of the 1930s. The inter-war years were a time of rebellion against the old order, entrenched conventions and Australia's traditional subservience to Empire. Many of those coming of age after the Great War began to test the social, sexual, political and aesthetic margins. It was a decade of broad cultural experimentation. 'The generation that reached adulthood during the [Great] war,' wrote Michael Heyward, 'were arrogant' and 'at odds with the sluggish, philistine world around them.'[13]

The supremacy of orthodox movements in art and theatre, hotly defended up until the 1930s, were to be undermined. In Perth, the local tradition of landscape art 'as a place of comfort and nurture, a place of escape'[14] was increasingly challenged. Modernism arrived to undermine traditional art forms and liberate and legitimise new art practices. The movement shook the bedrock of the classical art establishment. Its arrival also troubled working-class cultural guardians — staunch defenders of the classic canon.

It was within this context, between 1935 and 1941, that the Perth Workers' Art Guild came into being, rupturing and rousing the city's social and political fabric — until the Second World War, ironically, re-established order. The Workers' Art Guild vitalised a city loath to stir from its heat-induced torpor. It became the most important artistic movement in Perth, attracting most of the young artists, writers and theatre people of the day.[15] In the fields of painting, architecture, photography and theatre, members of the Guild were in the vanguard: much of their work preceded developments that would later take place in the eastern states.

The story of the Perth Workers' Art Guild is an important one, and one that until now has been largely hidden from the public record.

1

THE RED WITCH OF GREENMOUNT

I feel myself ... a dreamer.[1]

Katharine Susannah Prichard was born in Fiji in 1883, as a fierce cyclone allegedly swept across the island. Her father, Tom Prichard, was editor of the *Fiji Times*. The family was by no means a wealthy one, Tom suffering ill health and frequent periods of unemployment, but during her later teenage years Prichard moved in a literate middle-class circle in Melbourne, where her family had by then relocated. A young woman 'full of romantic illusions',[2] she would sometimes walk from South Yarra to the city in animated conversation with the rapidly ageing prime minister, Alfred Deakin, a friend of her mother's and thirty years her senior, 'tall and stooping then, already worn and disillusioned', ravaged by the demands of high office, a role in which he was a reluctant but essential actor.[3]

Like Prichard, Deakin was a 'dreamer'.[4] He had been instrumental in the accession to power, and the undoing soon after, of the world's first national Labor government, which had governed Australia for four months in 1904, the year Prichard found her feet as a journalist. Prichard's political colours were somewhat different from Deakin's, but they were friends nevertheless. They shared a love of poetry and Deakin, like 'Kattie', had been a working journalist who aspired to being a great writer. When Prichard travelled to London in 1908 in search of work, Deakin would provide her with two important letters of introduction: one carrying the prime ministerial seal and addressed 'To whom it may concern'; the other an introduction to a literary idol of hers, eminent British author George Meredith.

Prichard had been troubled from a young age by the poverty and social discord she saw around her, in Melbourne particularly. Later, she would be appalled by the conditions of slum dwellers in London and Paris — 'the people of the abyss', as American novelist Jack London referred to them. But unlike many middle-class writers of the Left, Prichard was never 'romanced by poverty'.[5] Given her father's circumstances, her family had felt its sting.

It was in Paris, in 1908, that the then twenty-five-year-old Prichard had her 'first contact with socialist ideas' to graft onto her 'vague humanitarian philosophy'.⁶ Here she renewed an acquaintance with the Austrian socialist writer Dr Rudolf Broda. His interest in Australia stemmed from its international reputation, through the early part of the twentieth century, as an advanced progressive social democracy. Australia and New Zealand had been the first countries to legislate a minimum wage, in 1896. Early Russian revolutionaries and political theorists, including Lenin, had examined Australia as a social and political laboratory, admired by many for its advances and innovations in arbitration, its improved working conditions, its 'living wage' and its social welfare and electoral laws.

Broda and American academic Clinton Hartley Grattan, with whom Prichard would later become acquainted, took a particular interest in adult suffrage, working conditions, trade unions and education in Australia. The early formation in Australia of a union-affiliated Labor government, which came into political power within a relatively short time, was radically out of step with the rest of the world.

Broda was a cultured man and stimulating company for the curious Prichard. His political views impressed her, and she began to look into some of the social parity and political questions taken up by his investigations of social services, wages and international labour laws. It was at Broda's flat in the Latin Quarter of Paris that she first heard from Russian socialists-in-exile of the plans, then seemingly so remote to her, to overthrow the Czarist government in Russia and impose their own political and social system.

In 1912, after her return to Australia, Prichard resigned from her position in Melbourne as editor of the women's page of *The Herald*, and travelled to London for a second time to seek work as a journalist on Fleet Street. It was there in 1915 that she wrote her first published novel, *The Pioneers*,⁷ a work that won her the Australasian prize in the prestigious Hodder and Stoughton All Empire Novel Competition. This acclaim, along with her emerging political activities — she took up with the substantial suffragette movement in London, for which she wrote a one-act agitprop sketch — attracted the attention of the British and Australian intelligence organisations.

After the outbreak of the First World War, Prichard became an active campaigner for the anti-conscription movement and spent time visiting the war wounded in London hospitals. In late 1915, the now thirty-two-year-old Prichard met Lieutenant Hugo ('Jim') Throssell, still recuperating from serious wounds he had sustained with the Australian Light Horse.⁸ Throssell's bravery during a battle on the Gallipoli Peninsula, in which waves of men were cut down by Turkish gunfire, had earned him a Victoria

Cross.[9] Originally from the town of Northam in Western Australia, he was the prototypical 'digger' — the brave, handsome, affable Anzac larrikin later eulogised as a national archetype. He was described on Wills's cigarette cards as 'seven feet of gallant manhood'.

Prichard returned to Melbourne towards the end of 1916 to be feted as an internationally recognised writer. Between Cape Town and Fremantle she began a shipboard romance with Guido Baracchi, then Australia's leading socialist theoretician. The relationship lasted a little over a year. Baracchi's passion for Marxism proved contagious, and it was this encounter that escalated Prichard's politics. After her return, one Melbourne evening in 1917 while crossing Princes Bridge over the Yarra River, Prichard saw newspaper posters announcing the socialist revolution in Russia.[10] She would later write:

> It had happened. That dream of the exiles I met in Paris, so long ago, had come true. There was a gash of gold in the cloudy sky.[11]

Prichard immersed herself in the works of Marx and Engels, and became convinced that Marxism 'provided the only logical basis that I had come across for the reorganization of our social system'.[12] She joined a Melbourne group, headed by the dynamic Bill Earsman, that was planning the formation of an Australian chapter of the Communist Party.[13]

On her return from England in 1916, Prichard had moved into a bush cottage outside the town of Emerald in the Dandenong Ranges on Melbourne's outskirts.[14] It was here, between 1916 and 1919, among a literary circle of close friends that included Louis Esson and Vance and Nettie Palmer, that she applied herself in earnest to long-form writing. Her romance novel *Windlestraws* was published in 1916, and was followed by *Black Opal* in 1921.

When Hugo Throssell was medically repatriated back to Australia to great fanfare in April 1916, he courted a somewhat reluctant Prichard. He was eager to return to the fighting, however, and in February 1917 rejoined the battered 10th Light Horse in Egypt before its deployment to the desert campaign against the Turks in the Middle East. Throssell was wounded again during the Battle of Gaza in April 1917 (in which his brother was killed) and invalided back to Australia still carrying a torch for Prichard, and the pair fell into a spellbound romance.

On a walk from the Emerald cottage in November 1918, the couple saw the armistice flares sent skywards from the city, some fifty kilometres away, marking the end of the war and any impediment to their future together. They married in 1919 and spent their honeymoon at the cottage, from where they could see the glow of bushfires burning nearby.

Soon afterwards the couple moved to Throssell's home state of Western Australia, where he was feted as a hero. The Throssell family was a respectable fixture there, and Throssell was well provided for after his father's death in 1910. He was invited back to his hometown of Northam, around 100 kilometres east of Perth, as guest of honour for the town's Peace Day celebrations marking the cessation of the War. Almost five years earlier he had led a procession through the town's streets of the first eighteen local men to enlist, of whom seven, including his brother, were not to return. Now he led the Peace Day parade on horseback, dressed in full Light Horse uniform.

During his subsequent speech, Throssell's announcement to the adoring crowd that the War had turned him into a socialist and a pacifist was met with a bewildered silence. As Prichard later wrote to her friend Nettie Palmer:

> The Premier on the platform [was] an old friend of Jim's. You could have heard a pin drop. Jim himself was ghastly, his face all torn with emotion. It was terrible — but magnificent.

It was a shock to the crowd and humiliating to Throssell's family. His father, George Throssell, had been a revered figure in the town: having served as mayor, as conservative local representative in the state parliament and, briefly, as premier of Western Australia. He had also been responsible for the diversion through Northam of the railway line between Perth and Kalgoorlie. An intelligence report would later theorise that the probable cause of Throssell's purported political shift was either the meningitis he had contracted before his return or 'his mind perhaps having been affected' by a blow to the head at Gallipoli.[15]

In October 1920 the Communist Party of Australia (CPA) was formed in Sydney, and Prichard was immediately informed by means of a telegram from foundation head Bill Earsman that she was a foundation member. She subsequently established a short-lived CPA branch in Western Australia.

Around this time Throssell purchased two acres of hillside orchard land at Greenmount, about twenty kilometres east of Perth on the edge of the Darling Range. A Colonial-style house of jarrah weatherboard and corrugated iron was perched on the fairly steep and bushy block, overlooking the flat coastal escarpment on which the city somewhat uncomfortably sat and the Indian Ocean beyond. Surrounding the house was a verdant tangle of native bush and overgrown gardens, described many years later as:

> 2½ acres — of waving grass, gumtrees and wattles, old fruit trees, and creepers such as bougainvillea, honeysuckle, periwinkle and asparagus fern gone wild and creeping over fallen trees [surrounded by] grass-clad and bush-clad hills … green-and-scarlet kangaroo paw, flowering shrubs — white and purple and gold, spider orchids and enamel flowers in profusion.[16]

Here Prichard settled back into writing, albeit in a place where she felt she was 'taken more seriously as Jimmy's wife than as a writer'.[17] She felt keenly the seclusion of Greenmount and the isolation of Perth, and dearly prized her correspondence with friends in the eastern states and overseas, complaining in a 1927 letter to one such friend that she was 'very high and dry from all literary and intellectual associations' in Western Australia.[18] She wrote despondently to another friend in May 1930:

> There are so few people in the West who care … for intellectual adventure of any sort. Nevertheless, I love the country and my life here. Am by the soil — and don't wish to be otherwise. A good peasant, at best, probably — and fairly content if I can get the latest Russian & French books and 'the Modern Quarterly' occasionally. Or blow across to Melbourne and Sydney to yarn with Louis Esson, the Palmers, Hugh McCrae and Bill Dyson.[19]

To assuage this sense of intellectual isolation, Prichard was a frequent visitor to the city's Booklovers' Library, the literary and intellectual hub of sleepy Perth. When D.H. Lawrence stayed in Perth in 1922 he used the bookshop as his base there.[20]

Another consolation for Prichard was the freestanding dedicated writing room that Throssell had built for her in the orchard below their Greenmount home, overlooking its own stand of colourful Darling Range scrub. The writing of speeches, letters and political tracts here took up most of Prichard's time and helped allay her despondency at being so far out of the swim. Her detractors at the time would come to refer to her as the Red Witch of Greenmount.

In 1921, after the ill-fated initial iteration of the Western Australian CPA branch disbanded — principally, it seems, due to political differences among its organisers — Prichard founded the Labor Study Circle of Western Australia with the help of future Labor prime minister John Curtin. The group ran with limited success for about eighteen months until Prichard, heavily pregnant with her first and only child, Ric Throssell, was forced to pull out and the venture folded.

Curtin had earlier renounced his Catholicism and embraced socialism after turning to the comforts of the Salvation Army and alcohol to mollify his easily frayed spirit. As an active member of the Victorian Socialist Party — which had played a major part in the formation of the CPA — he had led the anti-conscription campaigns in Victoria during the First World War, for which he had been briefly jailed. Worry about Curtin's drinking had led Melbourne Labor figure Frank Anstey to organise what he'd thought would be a placid political sabbatical for Curtin in the barely bubbling political cauldron of Perth, to which Curtin moved in 1917 to take up the position of editor of Labor journal the *Westralian Worker*.[21]

In Perth Curtin continued his public opposition to conscription, and in the editorial pages of the *Westralian Worker* he continued to proselytise. 'Russia is a star of promise for the world, a beacon light for our future guidance', he wrote, and 'the democracy of tomorrow is the democracy of the workplace'. But he soon became convinced that the revolution had passed the Australian proletariat by.[22] Despite Australia's relative isolation, its advances in suffrage and social equity and its election of very early Labor governments had rendered the notion of a proletarian revolution superfluous.

Curtin could no longer support Lenin's dictatorship of the proletariat, and he began to concentrate on reform through more conventional means within the parliamentary Australian Labor Party (ALP), putting him at odds with many of his former socialist colleagues.[23] He publicly declared his opposition 'to every form of dictatorship', and for this the fledgling CPA derided him as a 'social fascist of the vilest type'.[24]

In 1928 Curtin was elected to the federal seat of Fremantle. He lost the seat in 1931 but was re-elected in 1934. In 1935 he was elected federal parliamentary leader of the ALP.

The Western Australian branch of the CPA was re-established in 1925, but it did not rise to any great heights until 1931, when its members became agitators in the rising anti-government activism that led to sometimes-violent demonstrations in Perth.

In 1929, as Western Australia celebrated its centenary of British colonisation, shockwaves radiated out from the economic collapse of New York's Wall Street stock exchange. The Great Depression polarised political opponents and created enormous social stratification, and Western Australia — as one of the country's poorer states — was severely affected. New populist movements in politics and the arts, intent on erasing the old order that had given rise to the devastation of the Great War and the Depression, were born in the years that followed.

Many sought solace in alternative systems of belief. Marxism became a political sanctuary to some, and the Communist Party offered an elaborate distraction from the discomforts of daily life. Party life was sustaining and all-encompassing. It was highly structured and rigid, with strict controls placed upon language and behaviour, but it also provided liberation from the repressive social mores of the time and offered itself as a source of spiritual nourishment.

> For a generation that had known only depression and war, Marxism provided both explanations and solutions. It provided a plan for living, not just for society but also for the party member. It gave many the radiance and utter conviction of religious faith, and it seductively offered intellectuals and artists influence and esteem. There was a purity of purpose for those who craved action, and it offered action immediately, the chance to make history. Above all, it spoke to people of high moral purpose, desperate to see an end to poverty, ignorance and war.[25]

The Depression also served to reconsolidate the notion, for many, of a 'working class'. Economic and class stratification created bitter resentments, but also cemented loyalties and camaraderie.

The Depression quickly began to bite into day-to-day life in Perth, as it did elsewhere in Australia and beyond. John Hepworth, a member of the Workers' Art Guild, vividly recalled its effect on Perth:

> The abrasive effect of the Depression was probably as vitalising an element as anything. Order had been taken away ... Death and war pervaded every Australian homestead. Then the economics of our society collapsed around us. [Perth] was a seething society. There was a great deal of ferment. The Depression led to a renaissance of thought and argument. Coffee shops and parks were places where politics was talked about all the time. Art is politics; whether you

eat or not is politics. The sort of class distinctions that you had in England were never manifest, perhaps, but the class distinction was still there ... It was a brutal time — not having enough to eat; not having clothes to wear; not having shoes to wear; not having anywhere to sleep was commonplace. There was no protection from Government as there is today. The difference in labour was enormous. The greater percentage of the people then lived by labour, many of them by manual labour, and the manual labour of those days was what today would be considered incredibly beastly, brutal in its physical demands. The master and man attitude still was in the workplace.[26]

Perth-born economist and later prime ministerial advisor Herbert 'Nugget' Coombs recalled the effects of the Depression on the city somewhat differently. Although Perth felt the economic effects 'just as bad as everywhere else', its social effects were, he recalled, somewhat less extreme.

You could go and catch fish in the Swan River, you could catch crabs and shoot birds along the banks of the river. Some young couples, who couldn't find a house, would camp in the bush, and the weather was so good, you weren't going to freeze, even in the winter ... Western Australia had that egalitarian feel about it.[27]

Coombs's view, though, was perhaps mitigated by the fact that he spent many of the Depression-ravaged years in London, where its effects were indeed brutal.

Financial relief for the Depression's dispossessed was minimal. The federal and state governments drastically cut expenditure during the Depression and social welfare was all but non-existent. With Australia attempting to trade its way out of debt, wages were also cut through the arbitration system and employers pared back working conditions. The high standard of living that Australia had hitherto enjoyed was arbitrated away during the early 1930s.

Perth's placid veneer and impression of social cohesion belied the stark reality of political conflict and social malaise. As the Depression bit hard into the community, it took a terrible economic and social toll on vast numbers of Western Australians. In 1930, the Western Australian Government dismissed 2172 of its employees, and in 1931 alone there were more than 100 suicides in the sparsely populated state directly attributable to the effects of the Depression. A consequent rise in revolutionary zeal and political activism led to a proportionate tightening of political control in an attempt to maintain social stability.

The Commonwealth Investigation Branch (CIB; precursor to ASIO), which was responsible for domestic security, concentrated its resources particularly on the CPA through the late 1920s and into the 1930s. Military-style right-wing groups that also sprang up in Australia during this time were left relatively undisturbed. The CPA posed a threat quite disproportionate to the forces gathered against it, its membership being relatively small. The threat that it posed was economic — the organised withdrawal of labour.

The federal government's *Crimes Act 1914* had been amended in 1926 to allow political organisations to be declared 'unauthorised', its primary target being the CPA. The Crimes Bill, though rarely invoked, enabled the jailing of participants in serious industrial disturbances and the deportation of participants not born in Australia.

By the 1930s Prichard's intense involvement in politics left her little time to devote to her fiction writing. The re-established CPA in Western Australia had become increasingly dependent on her, and she complained to her friend Vance Palmer in 1935 that she could only manage a day a month of writing since she was spending about eighteen hours a day on CPA affairs. Her high profile and popularity in CPA circles also brought her increasingly under the gaze of the police and intelligence agencies.[28]

The CIB had begun surveillance of the CPA and its members soon after the CPA's inception, with local police given responsibility for a lot of the surveillance work.[29] Simultaneous raids were made on Prichard's Greenmount home and premises associated with the local branch of the CPA in September 1932, and material confiscated. These would be the first of many such raids.[30] The CIB also infiltrated CPA conferences and meetings, and assembled lists of names and personal files on CPA members. The movements of CPA officials, including overseas travel, were monitored and their luggage frequently searched. British security agency MI5 also monitored visiting Australian CPA officials.

A series of major protests by the marginalised, some of which turned riotous, took place in Perth through the early part of the decade. Western Australian author Peter Cowan recalled these troubles as the 'expression of general discontent and anger rather than political belief and allegiance',[31] but increasing shows of defiance by growing numbers alarmed governments attempting to impose cuts in wages and working conditions, and the political response became increasingly fierce. Bert Moxon, the CPA's national secretary from 1929 to 1930, had encouraged attacks on police during these protests.

Left-wing activists led a number of the demonstrations, and the CPA saw this rise in activism as an opportunity to recruit the disaffected. Thirty-six-year-old John Ernest ('Jack') Stevens arrived in Perth in January 1931 to take up the position of local organiser for the CPA, carrying with him a letter of introduction to Prichard. He had been sent by the CPA's Central Committee in Sydney to oversee the growth of the CPA in Western Australia, and he quickly 'became a marked man in unemployed demonstrations'.[32] Within six months of his arrival in Perth, Stevens was convicted of vagrancy and jailed for six months on a charge of being a person of 'evil fame'.[33] He left Western Australia in the mid-1930s, travelling to Spain soon afterwards to fight with the International Brigade in the Civil War there.

The large unemployed group camps around Western Australia were fertile recruitment grounds for the CPA during the Depression. The state government, in an attempt to slow the growth of the CPA and fracture its influence, split these large camps into a number of smaller camps spread more widely across the state, but CPA members carried on their work in the smaller camps unencumbered, and demonstrations were organised within these camps by predominantly Communist agitators.

One of these camps was located at Blackboy Hill, below Prichard and Throssell's home at Greenmount. The facility had served as a military training camp during the First World War, but since then had stood relatively dormant until it was revived as a camp for unemployed single men in June 1930. Its wooden huts, built in 1915, accommodated unemployed men recruited in the 1930s to work on improvements to the nearby Greenmount National Park. This was one of a number of government projects initiated to provide a sustenance allowance to the large pool of unemployed, and to occupy what was seen as an increasingly menacing group by the government.

Within four weeks of opening in mid-1930, the community of makeshift dwellings housed 800 men from around the state, and by 1931 it had quickly filled to capacity, accommodating in cramped conditions 1000 men wearing ragged cast-off army coats dyed black to denote their station.[34] When near-starving and penniless men were turned away from the crowded camp, they sometimes made their way up the Greenmount hill to knock on Prichard's door seeking food and work. Prichard would serve ready-made soup, such was the frequency of their visits. The Blackboy Hill camp was closed in 1933 after the Labor Party won government in the state.[35]

In April 1933, Perth sweltered through its worst heatwave in recorded history and bushfires flared on the outskirts of the city. On the evening of 18 April, Prichard lectured students at the University of Western Australia on 'The Development of Communism'. The talk was presided over by the university's former vice-chancellor and professor of history and economics, Edward Shann. Known affectionately by his students as 'Inky' Shann and by his detractors as 'Bolshie Teddy', Shann had been a socialist in his younger days but was by no means a card-carrying member of the CPA. Like many of his liberal colleagues at the university, he was open-minded about the politics of the Left. He supported a number of causes that sprang out of the Left and he had addressed Prichard's Labor Study Circle in the past. His critics saw his support for left-wing causes as a dalliance with lunacy for a man of such standing in the community, but Shann mixed just as readily within Perth's conservative business community and was not given to entrapment by dogma. Historian Geoffrey Bolton would later write of Shann:

> few of his colleagues had thrown themselves more wholeheartedly into the Western Australian community. ... [He] had a lively mind given to keen enthusiasms, and stirred and stimulated his students by a mixture of charm, nervous energy and a spare lucidity of style.[36]

Shann was an unorthodox man of broad vision who had 'predicted, unthinkable in 1929, that one day Australia would look for her trading partners in South and East Asia rather than the British Empire'.[37] His presence at Prichard's lecture was appropriate for a political discussion of Marxist doctrine that preached as integral the symbiosis of history and economics.

On this balmy April evening, Prichard 'traced the evolution of the Marxian doctrines, their embodiment in the Communistic manifesto, and the application in Soviet Russia of the plan laid down in the manifesto'. She presented 'a picture of improvements in Russia', notably Moscow's reduced death rate, and in particular its infant mortality rate. Like many political activists before and since, 'she deprecated the apathy which existed among university students in connection with social problems'.

Prichard joked with her audience that she was unable to fully prepare for the lecture as 'all [her] papers having reference to Communism ... are in the hands of the police' as a result of the early-morning CIB raid on her Greenmount home in September the previous year.³⁸ She wrote to a friend of the raid:

> The police arrived in force the other morning before I was awake, 'to search the premises'! Can you see the criminal, sitting up in bed … passing the time of day with the inspector in charge of the job, herself in yellow silk pyjamas & a black silk gown embroidered with golden dragons? It looked like the first act of a play — the verandah hung with wisteria, & long sprays of dog roses. The only protest I made was that none of your letters, or Hilda [Esson]'s should be read, as they were entirely personal. The which [sic] was respected. But the days have been strenuous, & it looks as if you'll be hearing of an arrest, before this reaches you. My Communist activities, of course, the cause. But so long as I fight the good fight, what does that matter?³⁹

On 22 May 1933, Prichard left Fremantle for London on the steamship *Baradine* to flee the turmoil. Her departure came after a particularly draining time in Perth. Tensions had arisen within the CPA and some local members had levelled an official complaint against her of 'conduct unbecoming a Communist'. There were also more pressing personal tensions. Her marriage to Throssell had become strained, the family was suffering from financial difficulties and Prichard had written to her friend Nettie Palmer some eighteen months before her departure that she was 'worn to a frazzle … not sleeping and trying to work … Jim with no job and colossal debts, having to be sheered … off nervous breakdown all the time working myself to keep things going'.⁴⁰

Prichard sailed towards a continent undergoing much more political tumult than that which she left behind. From London she was to travel through to Berlin. By 1932 National Socialism had become a mass movement in Germany, and in January 1933 Adolf Hitler had come to power as leader of the movement's National Socialist German Workers' (Nazi) Party. Prichard intended to be away for about twelve months, and her passport contained visas for the British Empire, France, Italy, Belgium, Switzerland and the Dutch East Indies (now Indonesia). She kept authorities from knowing that she was also to travel to the Soviet Union, fearing that had they known they may have stopped her from leaving Australia.

2

THE FIVE ARTS CLUB

In the darkness he dropped from the slowing trolley bus near the end of Mounts Bay Road, and climbed the wooden steps of Jacob's Ladder up the face of Mount Eliza, a light rain like mist, and the lights of the ferry from the darkness below him. He cut through the Observatory grounds, the side streets empty.[1]

Since the turn of the century, theatre had provided *the* popular mass entertainment in Australia, and between the Wars the quality of much amateur theatre began to parallel that of professional theatre. Western Australia in particular, perhaps because of its isolation, had developed a vibrant amateur theatrical movement.[2]

In 1930, Sydney-born Dorothy ('Betty') Rowe[3] and her husband Arthur Miles formed the amateur Five Arts Club and Playbox Theatre in Perth. Not so much a company as a gaggle of itinerant but formidable actors, the Five Arts Club also encouraged local playwrights with one-act playwriting competitions and performances of their plays.[4] The small Playbox Theatre, the club's venue, was inside an old Scout hall on Mounts Bay Road, a kilometre or so from the city's centre. The building was nestled under Jacob's Ladder — a narrow staircase leading down the steep embankment of Mount Eliza to the Swan River below. One side of the ground floor was converted into the Playbox Theatre, seating about 100 people and with a small stage and proscenium, while Rowe and Miles lived in the other side.[5] Both audience and performers paid membership fees.

The Five Arts Club's chief dramatic director, Keith George, worked at the Playbox most nights alongside Rowe, who performed and maintained a controlling hand.[6] Rowe wrote musical comedies for performance every month or so, borrowing scores from well-known musicals and operettas produced by commercial theatre companies such as J.C. Williamson. The local agent for J.C. Williamson 'would appear from time to time on the doorstep and demand "£10 or the curtain doesn't go up" and we had to collect £10 between us', one of the club's principal actors, Phyllis Harnett (later Ophel), would recall later.[7] The club's repertoire, bankrolled by

Rowe's popular musical comedies, consisted mainly of 'serious' European drama such as Ibsen, Strindberg and Chekhov, so beloved, alongside George Bernard Shaw, of the 'moderns' and seldom seen on the Perth stage. It was to be many years before commercial theatres would present these plays.

Keith George was born in Western Australia in 1900.[8] He studied law at the University of Western Australia, where he also became involved with the University Dramatic Society.[9] He possessed a sparkling intellect and a flamboyant personality, and a lively and intelligent university coterie developed around him, attending open-house parties at his scenic, ramshackle farmhouse in Kenwick, some fourteen kilometres from the city, where he lived with several siblings, pigs and chickens.[10] George's parties were lively affairs where guests discussed drama and hotly debated 'ways of changing the world'.[11]

George was a gourmand[12] and what stood out most about him was his girth. Portly, short and balding, he resembled a cheerful Buddha. 'Everything about him was round,' remembered Ric Throssell. Actress Patricia Thompson described him in her memoir as 'a provincial Orson Welles with an authoritative manner, a sonorous voice, and a vivid creative imagination', adding, 'He would have looked at his best in a Roman toga; everyday twentieth-century garb rather diminished him'.[13]

George moved among Perth's professional elite, but was memorably relaxed about his personal hygiene and attire.[14] After graduating from law school he began work as a dishevelled solicitor's clerk with a city law firm, where he was affectionately known as the 'dirty clerk'.[15] He acquired a reputation for contempt of convention, a trait he also brought to the stage. Obstinate, sententious and fond of an argument, he spoke with a dramatic Shakespearian 'East Perth accent' and cast a spell on those around him. He took great delight in experimenting and making people think.[16] He was extensively active in radio drama, writing, adapting, producing and performing in many radio plays, alongside Phyllis Harnett, through the early 1930s. His overriding passion, though, was for the theatre, and he had directed plays intermittently through the 1920s for the Perth Repertory Club.

The conservative Repertory Club, although held in high regard, served the 'snobs and snobbery' of Perth.[17] Its repertoire was turgid and stodgy, predominantly English 'drawing room' drama, and its membership was restricted. The Five Arts Club and Playbox Theatre catered to a markedly different crowd: those with more 'modern' European tastes in drama that were not served by the establishment theatre.[18]

In early 1931, Phyllis Harnett joined Rowe and Miles in the Scout hall. Born in Sydney in 1907, Harnett was a descendent of English Middle Ages poet Thomas Yalden, and she grew up in a household in which *Das Kapital* 'lived in a trunk in the laundry along with the psychology of Havelock Ellis'. She was a daughter of the squattocracy, with a 'Protestant agnostic' mother and a 'Catholic agnostic' father who was a Marxist 'in his own way'.[19] In the latter 1920s, encouraged by the political literature given to her by a suffragette aunt, the writings of Fabian socialist George Bernard Shaw and an inquisitive mind, Harnett was drawn to left-wing politics.

Harnett's introduction to the theatre was through Doris Fitton, proprietress of the long-running Independent Theatre in Sydney.[20] Harnett fell in with a racy crowd, and her stern father did not take kindly to the news that his daughter was having an affair — her first — with a philandering author and newspaper man, the 'scandalous' Brian Penton. So when Rowe, a friend from Sydney, sent word that there was theatre work at the Five Arts Club in Perth, Harnett thought it opportune to move there.[21] She arrived in Perth just as demonstrating 'sussos' — people living on government 'sustenance' or unemployment benefits — who were marching for improved conditions of their enforced labour, were being beaten down by police batons.[22]

Harnett 'kept house' for Rowe and Miles at the Scout hall.[23] Although relatively inexperienced in the theatre, she was hailed in Perth as an 'establishment actress' from Sydney: 'It was always a great thing in Perth to come from somewhere else,' she would later observe.[24] She never became a practising Western Australian, however, unable to entirely adjust to life in Perth. She found the city stiflingly quiet after Sydney, and she was grateful for Keith George's presence at the Five Arts Club.[25] The theatre provided a focal point for Harnett and others seeking intellectual and social pleasures that Perth in the 1930s did not otherwise offer, and George was at its centre.

It was commonplace during the Depression to seek succour outside conventional realms, and Rowe suggested that Harnett, short of money, take up reading fortunes from the bottom of teacups. She found employment as a fortune teller in a fashionable city cafe, but would later lament that the role came with the 'unenviable experience of being thought to possess occult powers': 'For my threepence a cup, people bared their souls in an extraordinary manner to me.'[26] Her clever but increasingly desperate evasions only enhanced her reputation as a mystic. Rather than declaring the fraud, she solicitously retired from clairvoyancy to take up offers of leading radio drama roles on the strength of her being 'the actress from

Sydney'. Radio drama, like the occult, was a flourishing industry during the Depression. With fewer actors finding work on the diminishing professional theatre circuit, it was in radio that professional actors earned their keep while moonlighting with amateur dramatic clubs.[27]

However, neither radio drama nor mainstream theatre could initially compete with the advent of cinema in Australia. In the late 1920s and early 1930s cinema tickets were comparatively cheap, and theatre audiences dwindled. The arrival of 'talkies' — sound film — saw Australians take to the cinema in even greater numbers. Cinemas mushroomed in the 1930s as the Depression eased and taxes on professional entertainment contributed to a greater decline in commercial theatre audiences — along with a corresponding rise in audiences at increasingly relevant amateur theatre.

Harnett married artist, set designer, house painter and fellow Playbox resident Clement ('Clem') Kennedy soon after her arrival in Perth in 1931, retaining her maiden name, by which she was then well known in the theatre. In March 1932 they had a son, Gerard Kennedy, who in later years would make his name as a television actor. Clem Kennedy had a parochial sense of humour not shared by Harnett and, as Kennedy was an artist of the 'old school' and Harnett of the 'new', they 'fought to the teeth and blood' about art and literature, and their marriage was short-lived.[28]

George admired Harnett's acting, but their friendship was sealed by a mutual enthusiasm for the drama of Henrik Ibsen, and together they arranged a season of Ibsen plays at the Playbox. George directed Ibsen's *Hedda Gabler* in August 1931, and it was on this play that Harnett really cut her teeth as an actor.[29] The Ibsen season, directed by George, was lauded as being among the great amateur and professional theatre performances in Perth during the early 1930s.[30] Ibsen's plays appealed to the 'cultured' denizens of Perth and to those sympathetic with the suffragette and women's movements, Prichard among them. Prichard and Throssell regularly attended the Playbox Theatre, and Prichard came to greatly admire George's work. Her initial enthusiasm for the theatre was born of her contribution to the suffrage theatre of the Actresses' Franchise League in London, as well as her involvement soon afterwards with William Moore's Annual Australian Drama Nights in Melbourne.

Moore's initiative, established in 1909, was the earliest example of public theatre devoted solely to the presentation of Australian drama. Prichard's one-act play, *The Burglar*, was staged on the second of these Drama Nights in 1910. It shared the bill that night with the first performance of a play by Edinburgh-born, Melbourne-based dramatist Louis Esson, *The Woman*

Tamer, establishing a long association and a lifelong friendship between Prichard and Esson. (Esson would later marry Prichard's childhood friend Hilda Bull.) After the demise of Moore's Annual Australian Drama Nights in 1912, Louis and Hilda Esson formed a nationalist theatre group, the Pioneer Players, in Melbourne in 1922. Like the Drama Nights, the Pioneer Players staged only Australian drama, including Prichard's *The Great Man* and *The Pioneers* in 1923.[31]

Another of Prichard's delights in Perth was attending operas staged by Ercole and Anne Filippini, known as Count and Contessa Filippini. Ercole's title was inherited from his uncle, Count Michelangelo Tonti, a member of the Italian aristocracy who had adopted Ercole as a child. Ercole Filippini had sung baritone with Milan's La Scala Opera Company, where he had been engaged professionally for three years. He had arrived in Australia in 1916 and two years later married one of his Australian students, Anne McParland, a singer and conductor who had the distinction of being the first woman in Australia to conduct a symphony orchestra. He had also toured Australia with opera companies after the First World War, and in 1924 he and Anne formed the South Australian Grand Opera Company, embarking on successful tours of the east coast with productions directed by Ercole and the orchestra conducted by Anne. Known by then as the Italo-Australian Grand Opera Company, in 1926 the Filippinis moved the entire, fairly large, company of singers and musicians to Western Australia for a season at His Majesty's Theatre.

The Filippinis' company was feted in Perth, and their performances filled His Majesty's. In 1927, its reputation made in Perth, the company shifted to Melbourne for a season at the substantial Princess Theatre, where Nellie Melba attended every program, before it disbanded. The Filippinis returned to Perth in 1928 where they set up a school of opera, and in 1929 established the West Australian Grand Opera Company. They left Perth in 1932.[32] During the Filippinis' time in Perth, Prichard and Anne Filippini became firm friends and together they attended performances at the Playbox.[33]

The West Australian Grand Opera Company's key soprano was Lorna Sydney-Smith. She had sought the psychic counsel of Phyllis Harnett, whom Sydney-Smith knew as a Playbox actress. Harnett knew nothing of Sydney-Smith but was immediately struck by her fine elocution. Here was someone, Harnett thought, whose 'careful speech must mean something, and I made up this awful fortune … I said she was going to be very famous one day and she would have to leave Australia, and that she depended a great deal on her voice.'[34] Perhaps on the strength of this prophecy, Sydney-

Smith moved to Europe to study singing, where she did indeed find fame with the German soprano 'Lotte' Lehmann as her mentor.[35]

It was through the Filippinis that Keith George initially met Prichard. George had overseen the Filippinis' West Australian Grand Opera Company season in 1930, which Prichard had attended, but it was not until a later meeting — after a Playbox performance of Ibsen's *Ghosts* in October 1931 — that a friendship developed between George and Prichard. They discussed their enthusiasm for Ibsen in general, and his play *Ghosts* in particular, which was still considered risqué fifty years after its conception and which, George would later write, was a play that 'appealed to [Prichard's] feminism'. The pair also shared an admiration for the work of Irish playwright John M. Synge.[36]

Six months after George and Prichard met, two of England's greatest stage actors, Dame Sybil Thorndike and her husband Lewis Casson, toured Australian capitals with their masterful performance of *Ghosts* (as well as other plays), and George met and befriended Thorndike.[37]

The Five Arts Club and the Playbox Theatre were dissolved in 1933 when Rowe left Perth in haste. Her marriage had broken down and she had become pregnant to journalist and author Kenneth Seaforth Mackenzie. When Mackenzie spread news of Rowe's 'condition' around Perth, her position as proprietor of a 'respectable' theatre became untenable and she returned to Sydney.[38] Remnants of the Five Arts Club, including Phyllis Harnett and Clem Kennedy, went on to form the Little Theatre, in many ways a replica of the Five Arts Club. Its mission was 'to produce plays which would not otherwise be seen in Perth'.[39] It was constituted predominantly by a younger and more rebellious set and, like the Five Arts Club, it encouraged local playwriting and performances of locally written plays.[40]

On Boxing Day 1933, Prichard stepped off the ship at Fremantle. She had sailed from London at the earliest opportunity, having read of her husband's death in a London newspaper before she received the news by telegram. In the early hours of 19 November, two weeks after Prichard had left Moscow for a few weeks in London on her way home to Australia, Hugo Throssell, at the age of forty-nine, had put a gun to his head on the back verandah of their Greenmount home.

Prichard's father had also committed suicide, in 1907, and Prichard would later write to her son Ric of her husband's death:

> Think of me, alone in a London boarding house — reading that terrible news about Daddy in the morning paper! How I lived through the shock and grief, I don't know. And it was weeks and weeks before I could hear what had happened … I've never been able to understand how Daddy could leave me like that — despite all the mental distress and tragedy of his failure to cope with financial difficulties.[41]

Throssell's suicide followed a series of failed business ventures, the increasing strain of physical and psychological wounds sustained during the War, and consequent pressures on his marriage. 'I can't sleep,' he wrote in a suicide note. 'I feel my old war head. It's going phut, and that's no good for anyone concerned.'[42]

Throssell was one of a great number of men who had had a 'bad war' and were further afflicted with suffering through the Depression. Not only did he carry the physical and substantial psychological wounds sustained during the War, he had also been unable to provide for his family back in Australia for some time before his death. In the end he felt that his family's only hope was the war pension his death would provide. He was a victim of what historian Janet McCalman would later describe as a common male malady of the times.

> If, at the time, the Depression seemed hardest on mothers and it was the women who were pitied, it was more often the men who died. They could not cry, they could not drink, they could not go bush. Everything depended on the male burden to provide.[43]

While Prichard was away, Throssell had tried to sell his Victoria Cross to a pawnbroker in the city but was offered only ten shillings.[44] Every attempt to remedy the family's financial difficulties had failed and, with Prichard's absence, his depression had deepened.

Two weeks before his death, Hugo and Ric Throssell had huddled around the short-wave wireless at a Greenmount neighbour's home to listen to Prichard on an early-morning radio broadcast from Moscow. Her shrill voice modulating through the static filled them with immense pride, but it also compounded Throssell's feelings of isolation and his sense of inadequacy.

The day after her radio broadcast, oblivious to the worsening situation at home — which went unmentioned in letters between Throssell and her — Prichard attended a performance of Maxim Gorky's *Lower*

Depths at the Number One Art Theatre in Moscow, then presided over by Anton Chekhov's widow Olga Knipper. Russian theatre was then at its experimental zenith and Prichard wrote to her friend, playwright and *New York Times* journalist Spencer Brodney: 'So much to see here — the theatres would simply send you racing ... the magazines of the revolutionary theatre are marvellous'.[45] She organised for some of these Soviet theatre magazines to be sent back to Perth, and soon the Soviet-published English-language journal *International Theatre* was in stock at Perth's Radical Bookshop. Run by the CPA, the Radical Bookshop was in William Street, Northbridge, the political hub just north of the city, close to Trades Hall and the CPA's newspaper office.[46] As well as books it sold Lenin statuettes, left-wing newspapers and local and international journals including the *Moscow News* and *USSR in Construction*.[47] It was also the headquarters of the CPA in Western Australia. Rooms at the shop were also used for CPA-organised Marxist study groups, 'workers' study' classes organised by the West Australian Council Against War and Fascism, and meetings of affiliate groups.[48]

When Prichard returned to her room after the performance of *Lower Depths*, she wrote to her friend, Melbourne writer and illustrator Hugh McCrae, that she had 'never seen such acting or stage craft'. 'If only you could have been here,' she gushed. 'You would be crazy with the beauty & intense life.'[49]

The next day Prichard travelled with a writers' delegation into the autumn chill of Siberia for a month, where she was similarly overwhelmed by the landscape. She arrived back in Moscow in mid-October and left the Soviet Union for London in early November 1933.[50]

It was during this trip that Prichard witnessed firsthand the vibrant workers' theatre movement in the Soviet Union, England and Europe. The movement, dating back to the mid-nineteenth century, was particularly strong in Germany at the time. It was significantly vitalised in the period of Germany's extreme impoverishment after the First World War and during the period of the Weimar Republic, but it did not survive the end of the Weimar Republic and Hitler's ascendancy to power in 1933.

The formal Workers' Theatre Movement coalition, born between the Wars, referred to the collective of political left-wing theatre groups that carried on an older tradition of agitprop political theatre. Unlike their socialist predecessors, the international workers' theatre movement had strong ties to the Communist Party and was forged in the Soviet Union in the period immediately after the Bolshevik Revolution. The movement, promoted particularly by the Workers' International Relief (WIR), formed a loose international coalition of diffuse political theatre groups ostensibly overseen by the Communist International — known as the Comintern — the body that represented and governed the international face of Communism. The WIR was formed in Berlin in 1921 initially to provide material famine support to the Soviet Union from international working-class organisations and Communist Party bodies, but later broadened to become a Soviet propaganda arm.

Moscow, as the heart of the international workers' theatre movement, hosted the First International Workers' Theatre Olympiad in 1933, attended by representatives of various international workers' theatre groups. British and American groups that formed in the 1920s had affiliated with the Soviet-centred International Workers' Dramatic Union (IWDU). One of these groups was the New York Theatre Guild, formed in the late 1920s. A precursor to the American Group Theatre (1931–1941), the New York Theatre Guild set up a school to train and develop its actors, and the New York Group Theatre, under the auspices of the Theatre Guild, staged its first performance in September 1931. A number of American workers' theatres amalgamated in 1932 to form the League of Workers' Theatres, which in turn affiliated with the IWDU. A group of British participants in the 1933 International Workers' Theatre Olympiad formed the Rebel Players theatre group in London on their return from Moscow. Moscow's influence on international theatre was extensive. The American Group Theatre adopted the use of Konstantin Stanislavsky's drama techniques and other elements of Russian theatre design and staging. Stanislavsky's 'method', in particular, soon became de rigueur among stage and screen actors across America.

As Prichard made her way through Customs at Fremantle, she was singled out for particular scrutiny, despite the authorities' knowledge of her husband's recent suicide. British and Australian intelligence agencies had closely monitored her travels. Her luggage was searched, and three novels written in Russian and an English edition of *International Press Correspondence* were considered incriminating enough to be brought to the attention of Customs superiors. Surveillance of Prichard resumed with greater intensity from this time, and her circulation of Soviet political material on her return intensified the suspicions of intelligence agencies that she was operating as a Soviet agent.

During Prichard's absence, the effects of the Depression had begun to subside in Perth. In 1933 half of Perth's male population was either unemployed or underemployed;[51] however, in 1934 increased gold production in the state saw the unemployment rate in Western Australia decrease more rapidly than in other Australian states. Gold reserves helped to buffer the state from the drawn-out effects of the Depression felt in other parts of the country. Western Australia had experienced an earlier gold boom in the 1890s, during which large numbers of people, impoverished by that decade's recession, had moved to the state's goldfields. The mines around Kalgoorlie and Wiluna were once again seeing a great influx of labour.

The economic recovery in Western Australia allowed commercial art studios to re-employ artists who had been amongst the first laid off when the Depression hit.[52] One small Perth commercial art business that managed not only to survive but to thrive during the Depression was Poster Studios. Established around the start of the 1930s by architects Harold Krantz, John Oldham and Colin Ednie-Brown, it was a means for the trio to earn a living during the lean years in architecture.[53] Its staff was hired from among the ranks of local and transient unemployed artists, many retrenched by the larger commercial art businesses. While the larger studios struggled to retain staff, Poster Studios became a substantial business, employing up to twenty staff.[54]

Krantz, a man of considerable business acumen, was well complemented by Oldham as the studio's principal artist and designer. Krantz had trained as an architect in Adelaide and moved to Perth in 1927 to work in his uncle Harold Boas's architecture firm, Oldham, Boas & Ednie-Brown, where he remained until work dropped off in the early Depression years. Krantz often came to the financial aid of struggling Perth artists offering small poster and art jobs, though some detractors accused him of opportunism in exploiting cheap labour.[55] Oldham, born in Perth in December 1907, came from a long line of respectable artistic forebears. Both of his grandfathers were 'very competent painters'[56] and his father, Charles Lancelot Oldham, was himself a well-known Perth architect until his death in 1920. In 1924, at the age of seventeen, Oldham was also employed as an apprentice architect at Oldham, Boas and Ednie-Brown, in which his late father had been a partner. He worked there under Krantz's uncle, Harold Boas, who had bought the firm after the death of Oldham's father. The following year Oldham began his formal studies in architecture by correspondence through the University of Melbourne's prestigious Architectural Atelier, also attending lectures at 'Tin Pan Alley', the fibro-and-corrugated-iron University of Western Australia campus in Irwin Street in the city. He developed a particular interest in the designs of Frank Lloyd Wright, Le

Corbusier and the Bauhaus. Modernist Bauhaus designer László Moholy-Nagy was a great influence in shaping Oldham's architectural design ideas and practice.[57] Oldham spent his final year of study attending classes in person at the University of Melbourne. Architecture was then a very traditional profession, and Oldham redeveloped existing rendering techniques. He introduced a new clear watercolour wash method that gave great depth and atmosphere to his renderings, and his services as a renderer became much sought after.[58] He returned to Perth in 1930 and took up watercolour studies at Perth Technical College under James W.R. Linton Sr. Inspired by Japanese woodblock artists, he also began to experiment with linocuts.

Poster Studios made Oldham, Krantz and Ednie-Brown a reasonable living for almost four years. The business designed calendars, cards and labels as well as local newspaper and magazine advertisements. Its artwork was printed from linocuts on a four-colour press that allowed for striking colour. Linocuts were a cheaper alternative to the traditional metal blocks used by most commercial printers at the time, and this gave Poster Studios a commercial edge in winning print contracts. The business designed eye-catching posters for the state government's 'Local Products' campaign, aimed at encouraging support of local businesses to counter the domination of eastern-states products in the Western Australian market during the Depression. Krantz secured funding from local businesses and Oldham designed a series of posters with the slogan 'W.A. First', displayed on public transport and on hoardings around Perth and in country towns. These posters represented a revolutionary break from traditional local designs, influenced as they were by contemporary Japanese prints and German posters, 'which were, in their turn, influenced by Toulouse-Lautrec and the French'.[59] The pre-Modernist distinction between commercial art and the traditional 'high' and 'low' fine arts was now an anachronism.

Poster Studios occasionally used the services of Gibbney and Son, a commercial printing and graphic art firm that employed local artists including Herbert McClintock, Harald Vike (who had worked at Poster Studios) and John Lunghi. Gibbney's produced most of the local newspaper and magazine advertising but, although grateful for the regular work at a time of few employment prospects, many artists quietly grumbled about the employment conditions there. The business shackled good artists for a low wage, and employees were required to sign contracts prohibiting the use of their work by other commercial interests. The company was, however, loyal to its employees, and this would prove beneficial to a number of those artists in days to come.

In April 1933 a state election had been held in Western Australia. Labor won office in a landslide from the Nationalist Party, and Philip Collier succeeded James Mitchell as premier. Mitchell had served two periods as premier (1919–1924 and 1930–1933), and in July 1933 would be appointed the first Australian-born Governor of Western Australia, a post he would hold for eighteen years.

Collier, Victorian by birth, had worked for John Curtin's mentor Frank Anstey in Melbourne before moving to Perth in 1904 at the age of thirty-two. The following year he was elected the Legislative Assembly member for Boulder, a seat he would hold until his death in 1948. An active anti-conscriptionist during the First World War, Collier had already served a term as premier (1924–1930).

Following the Labor Party's return to office in 1933, it remained in government for the next fourteen years (although Collier served as premier only until 1936). It was not a Labor government, however, that brought joy to the progressive political left wing in the state. Collier led a right-wing Labor Party dominated by Catholics, who were no friends of the Communist Party.

A secession referendum held in conjunction with the 1933 state election reflected the sense of isolation felt by Western Australians from the rest of Australia. Tensions born of the state's sixteen per cent unemployment during the Depression were attributed to the eastern states,[60] and almost two thirds of the state's voters cast a vote in favour of secession from the rest of Australia. On the strength of this result, members of the Dominion League of Western Australia travelled to London to present the case for secession to King George V and the British imperial parliament. The British government ruled the secession unconstitutional and rejected the petition.

A secession that did take place in Western Australia that year was one of aesthetics. Ructions had begun to appear in local art institutions as Modernism started to make its mark, and in 1933 this shift led the Perth Society of Artists to break away from the West Australian Society of Arts, an institution of some forty years' standing. The split was caused by the increasing rift between Perth's orthodox art establishment and the young rebellious Modernists, as illustrated in a speech by *The West Australian* art critic Francesco Vanzetti in 1933:

> One need not have much experience as an artist to be able to notice that art has its crisis no less painful than those affecting the political economy ... people are so concerned with the troubles

of civilisation that they have consigned to the lumber-room their culture or spiritual development. Culture alone can liberate us from the slavery and incubus of our modern materialistic existence.[61]

By 1934, architectural work in Perth had increased sufficiently for Harold Krantz to invite John Oldham — who by then had moved to Sydney — to return to Perth to join him in his architectural practice, offering Oldham a junior quarter-share partnership in the firm. Oldham accepted and, despite the lingering conservative nature of architecture in Perth at the time, the practice broke away from convention to concentrate on simple and relatively cheap designs, free of excessive flourish. One of its design revolutions was the use of bare internal brickwork — a cheaper finish than plastering and with a rough look that appealed to Oldham. The pair designed Perth's first blocks of flats, an interest of Oldham's stemming from his enthusiasm for workers' cooperative architecture and the designs of the Bauhaus.[62] Krantz bought shares in these flats, recouping healthy profits. One of the early blocks, the Chelsea Flats, was commissioned by local property developer and patron of the arts Joe Skinner and built into his Foy and Gibson building on St Georges Terrace.[63] Having made his wealth in real estate, Skinner, an enterprising and successful speculator, commissioned Krantz and Oldham to design single-room bachelor flats.[64] An amalgam of Art Deco and Bauhaus design, they comprised a combined furnished bed-sitting room and small kitchen. Oldham designed both the flats and the furniture,[65] and this proved a lucrative venture.

3

KISCH AND THE POPULAR FRONT

It's too good a day to argue, she said. You reform the world if you want to.[1]

In October 1934 the Duke of Gloucester, Prince Henry, visited Perth en route to Victoria's centenary celebrations. When he left Perth his entourage included a local private physician, John Holland, whose daughter Eleanor was one of the University of Western Australia's left-wing coterie of bright young things that included her close friend Ruby ('Ray') McClintock. She and McClintock rented Mouse Cottage, also known as Mouse House, 'a rather derelict old weatherboard cottage, with a corrugated-iron roof that was rusted and full of holes',[2] in the sand dunes of Cottesloe for six months of each year over spring and summer. The first autumn rains seeping through the cottage's leaky roof would signal the end of their seasonal tenancy.

During their stay at Mouse Cottage they would swim at North Cottesloe beach every morning before work and every afternoon on their return, and host social gatherings in the evenings and on weekends. McClintock recalled later:

> We invited friends to visit us there (to meals) & sometimes to stay the night — when they had to doss down on the floor — we didn't have any spare beds or mattresses — just our own two single Cyclone stretchers.[3]

Most summer weekends saw the cottage play host to the intellectual, social and sexual dalliances of Perth's left-wing social set, and it was here that the group that would later form the Workers' Theatre and subsequently the Workers' Art Club met. As well as Holland and McClintock, the main social group at Mouse Cottage comprised Ian and Montaigne (Monty) Smith, John Oldham, Leah Marks, John Hepworth and Betty Jones.[4]

At Mouse Cottage this rebellious cabal could play up, away from the disapproving sectarian glare of CPA cadres and the wider Perth community. Bohemianism was scorned within CPA circles; indeed, the term 'bohemian' was considered pejorative. To many within CPA ranks it equated to middle-class bourgeois excess and, given the CPA's predilection for puritanism,[5] there was the added risk in CPA circles of such antics leading to official sanctioning. Phyllis Ophel (formerly Harnett) recounted that she and Gordon ('Bugs') Burgoyne would sometimes walk long distances naked along the beach at night from Mouse Cottage, dipping themselves in the water, 'concerned only with the sea and the sand and the pleasures of it'. It was not a particularly conscious gesture of rebellion, more a practical measure to prevent their clothes from becoming soaked. Nevertheless, on their return to the cottage after one such walk, Burgoyne suggested to Harnett that they 'keep mum' about their antics for fear of being accused of bohemianism.

> So we robed ourselves discreetly and went back to the crowd, and a few sleepers turned over and said, 'Where have you been?' And we said 'We walked along the beach to City Beach.' 'Bloody bohemians!' came the response.[6]

Ray McClintock was born in Kalgoorlie in 1911, a time when the isolated goldmining town was home to a vibrant intellectual cluster. She was the daughter of a Labor man, Albert McClintock, who had been born in Sydney and mixed with the radical intellectuals of both Sydney and Melbourne Universities where he'd worked as a librarian in the late 1890s. At the time of Ray's birth, her father was the secretary of the Literary Institute and Workers' Library in Kalgoorlie.[7]

In 1930 Ray McClintock enrolled in an English degree at the University of Western Australia, completing her first year of study at Irwin Street's 'Tin Pan Alley' campus in the city before the university moved to its new Crawley campus.[8] She joined the politically meek University Labour Club, and was one of those wistful youths who shared Keith George's by then not-so-youthful escapades at the university.[9] McClintock and George were also involved on the periphery of the University Dramatic Society, both performing and directing plays, and McClintock wrote a regular satirical social column for the undergraduate student newspaper, *The Pelican*, which at the time was edited by Griff Richards. When journalist James (Jim) McArtney succeeded Richards as editor of *The Pelican*—despite the strong objections of many, including McClintock—McClintock and George joined forces with some others to launch what they called 'an illegal newspaper'—a roneoed news-sheet entitled *T.N.T*. The *T.N.T.*

group would meet under the cover of darkness in the law office where George worked and don rubber gloves — more for dramatic effect than necessity — to produce the paper for distribution the following morning.

McClintock later joined the editorial board of the university's annual literary magazine, *Black Swan*. She also began to contribute articles to *The West Australian* newspaper, including a series on prominent Australian women writers for which she interviewed local writers including Katharine Susannah Prichard, Henrietta Drake-Brockman and Mollie Skinner.[10] She soon secured a position with *The West Australian* as a cadet journalist, a prized occupation for women at the time, given that journalists and barmaids were the only female workers in the state who received wages in parity with their male colleagues. It was a progressive workplace and, despite its very respectable reputation, its reporters included 'a few bohemians in whom everyone else had an oblique pride'.[11]

Employment with *The West Australian* ascribed a certain social status, even to a lowly cadet journalist serving a three-year apprenticeship as the most junior member of the editorial staff.[12] McClintock was a gifted writer and rose rapidly through the ranks to become a senior journalist. In 1936, she married in secret so she could retain her job on the newspaper, its policy at the time being not to employ nor retain married women. Her husband had a country teaching post and the couple lived together only during school holidays and on long weekends over the summer at Mouse Cottage.

It was at Mouse Cottage in the summer of 1936 that McClintock met John Oldham, who had recently broken off an engagement and 'decided that his next affair was going to be an intellectual one'.[13] Oldham had already come to McClintock's attention as a name on the 'W.A. First' posters she had admired. Oldham pursued her, and a spirited relationship began.[14] While McClintock was notionally interested in left-wing politics, though reluctant to become politically active, Oldham was dispassionate and relatively ignorant of politics. They roused each other's curiosity and went in search of their politics. McClintock mentioned having met Katharine Susannah Prichard, and Oldham suggested they visit Prichard to broaden their political investigation. They did so several times, and Prichard was impressed by their interest and intellect.

Prichard often had enquiring youngsters drop in, including Gordon Burgoyne, who regularly hiked with a group through the hills around Greenmount.[15]

> We were always welcome and would spend an hour or two in absorbing talk before we caught the bus back to Perth.[16]

The 'taciturn pipe-smoking'[17] Burgoyne was, like his father before him, a journalist at *The West Australian* and an occasional playwright.[18] Geoffrey Burgoyne had been a regular contributor to the *Bulletin* and had helped to establish the satirical weekly *Gadfly* with C.J. Dennis. He had also been managing editor of the *Daily News*, as well as a leader writer and later chief subeditor on *The West Australian*. He was an old friend of Prichard's.[19] His son Gordon displayed the impeccable manners and behaviour that came of his elite school education, and would later confess that 'to people of my kind there was something a bit repellent about orthodox Communism: its authoritarianism, the jargon'. However, for the younger Burgoyne, Prichard presented an unexpectedly gentle face.[20]

Prichard's home also hosted a steady stream of visiting dignitaries, writers, artists, musicians and eminent Communists. She held an annual picnic and burn-off of the long grass on her bush block: a significant social event for local CPA members, mostly young, who visited to pay homage.[21]

Since the death of her husband, Prichard had found writing difficult. Work on her novel *Intimate Strangers* had become slow and painful. She had lingering concerns that Hugo's suicide may have been the result of his reading the manuscript of the novel, a thinly veiled autobiography in which the failed husband commits suicide.[22] In March 1934, she wrote a forlorn note to her friend Hugh McCrae: 'Write to me. I seem to be losing all contact with life.'[23]

CPA work was a welcome distraction, and Prichard busied herself penning an account of her travels across the Soviet Union the previous year. She also spoke about the Soviet Union at Perth's 1934 May Day celebrations, and in the following months at public meetings across the city and in country centres. 'I have seen the future, and it works,' she opined about the Soviet Union, echoing US journalist Lincoln Steffens's declaration on returning from a 1919 visit to Petrograd.

In October of that year, Perth's Radical Bookshop started selling her written account, *The Real Russia*, a series of articles that had been commissioned and published in serialised form by *The Herald* in Melbourne before it terminated the series without explanation.[24] Local CPA newspaper *The Red Star* trumpeted that *The Real Russia* was a response 'to the tripe peddled by notoriety hunters like Mrs Cardell-Olivier [sic] about the Soviet Union'.[25] Prichard and Florence Cardell-Oliver, a conservative foe, sparred frequently in public over their differing accounts of contemporary life in the Soviet Union. Cardell-Oliver had also visited the Soviet Union, and she presented her critical impressions at public meetings across Perth — meetings that Young Labour League members were encouraged to attend to heckle her.[26]

In October 1934 the still-grieving Prichard welcomed an opportunity to travel to Melbourne to be among old friends. She had been invited to be part of an official welcoming committee for Czech-born German journalist and writer Egon Kisch, who would be attending a national peace congress as the delegate of the international committee of the World Movement Against War. Kisch was a Jewish member-in-exile of the German Communist Party and an erstwhile associate of Franz Kafka and Rainer Maria Rilke.

The All-Australian Congress Against War and Fascism was a 'United Front' initiative organised by the CPA, the Council Against War and the Militant Minority Movement. It was to be held at Port Melbourne Town Hall in November 1934, to coincide with both Armistice Day and the Victorian centenary celebrations attended by the Duke of Gloucester. Prichard was a member of the congress committee, as were writers Vance Palmer and Bernard Cronin, poet Edwin ('E.J.') Brady, artist Max Meldrum, and federal Labor politicians Frank Brennan (attorney-general in the previous Scullin Labor government) and Maurice Blackburn (also a member of the Scullin government).[27]

The United Front was a policy directive of the Comintern. It was born of the Comintern's call to form an alliance of both Communists and socialists, to be brought together under the umbrella of the Communist Party, its mission being to oppose capitalism and defend the 'basic interests of the working class against the bourgeoisie'. The lineage of the United Front was traced to a thesis reportedly written by Lenin and published in 1921. It was a policy proposed and promoted by Lenin and Trotsky to effect mass collective action with the moderate left-wing flank. Stalin was a less enthusiastic proponent of the United Front policy and set about diluting its efficacy. He returned to the divisive singular rhetoric of bolshevism, branding social democrats — and indeed all of those on the 'left' outside the Communist Party tent — 'social fascists'. Many prominent political figures and academics were also expressing concern about the rise of fascism in Europe from 1933 onwards, and in 1934 the Comintern adopted an official policy of opposition to fascism. To combat the growth of fascism in Europe, it called for a 'United Front' against fascism by the disparate strands of the international labour movement and left-wing organisations, and directed its international affiliates — including the CPA — to this end.

The ship carrying Egon Kisch, the *Strathaird*, was to make its Australian landfall at Fremantle, and a lunch had been arranged for Kisch on arrival at Java Head, the home of the Jewry-establishment Masel family, where

Phyllis Harnett lived. It was to be a show of public support from the politically progressive local Jewish community.[28] Before Kisch was able to disembark, however, Attorney-General Robert Menzies declared him a prohibited immigrant — despite his having a valid entry visa — and refused him permission to leave the ship and had his passport confiscated. Prime Minister Joseph Lyons, leader of the conservative United Australia Party, labelled Kisch a Communist subversive. There was talk that the Australian Government had bowed to pressure from the German government in prohibiting Kisch's entry. When word of these events spread, a crowd built up on the Fremantle wharf beside the *Strathaird*.[29] Walter Murdoch, august professor of English at the University of Western Australia, and Professor Frank Beasley, dean of the university's law faculty, boarded the *Strathaird* while it stalled in Fremantle Harbour to offer their support to Kisch.[30]

A number of libertarian university academics were very prominent in the political and social life of Perth in the 1930s. Notable among these were Frank Beasley and Associate Professor Fred Alexander, head of the history department and an Oxford and University of Melbourne graduate who had also served as a temporary member of the League of Nations Secretariat in Geneva, and as a member of the Australian Government delegation to the 13th Assembly of the League of Nations.[31] Both men were regular contributors to radio discussions on international affairs.[32]

After enduring a long fallow period, school and university curricula had begun to expand during the 'intellectual stirrings' of the 1930s, and 'university staff began to enter public life with a new vigour and a sharpened political sense'.[33] The 1930s saw the emergence for the first time in Australia of a dissident intelligentsia. Into schools and universities came 'a new breed of young teacher who talked to their charges about controversial things and who encouraged them to read dangerous books'.[34] Liberal academics at the University of Western Australia in the 1930s included Professor Robert Cameron, foundation Professor of Education, and Alec King, who dragged the university's English department 'into the twentieth century after its long sleep in the mid-nineteenth century'.[35] While the urbane Walter Murdoch was in many ways a social and civic progressive, his literature syllabus was firmly rooted in the past.

The West Australian Council Against War had arranged a public reception for Kisch on the evening of his arrival at Rechabite Hall on William Street in Northbridge. The crowd assembled there, unaware of the events of earlier in the day, had built to about 200 before council secretary Augustus (Gus) Stagg informed them that Kisch was being prevented from attending, and tempers flared. Keith George arrived at Rechabite Hall in his capacity as president of the council (having been elected to the position only a few months earlier), where he organised the first public protest against Kisch's ban. The council was a United Front enterprise, conceived by the Comintern after the 1932 International Congress Against War in Amsterdam. Soon after its formation, Prichard was contacted by the congress organisers and urged to become active in the broad-based World Movement Against War. The Australian Council Against War was founded in 1933, with Prichard and Throssell as members of its executive body, and Prichard established a branch in Western Australia the following year.[36] The central and district committees of the CPA oversaw the Australian national and local branches of the Council Against War, a strong and well-organised body that became an institution in the 1930s and spawned numerous affiliates.[37]

The *Strathaird*, with Kisch ordered to remain in custody aboard, sailed on to Melbourne's Station Pier while his exclusion was being appealed by supporters through the courts. When it docked in Melbourne, Prichard boarded and spent the day with Kisch. When she left the ship in the afternoon and began her walk down the long pier, she heard a disturbance behind her and turned to see that Kisch had jumped from the ship onto the wharf below.[38] He was immediately set upon by officials and arrested for illegal entry into Australia. Bundled back on board with his leg broken, Kisch's travels continued with the ship sailing on to Sydney. Kisch had hoped that his leap would lead to his arrest for illegal entry and then to prison on dry land while the case against him proceeded. Prison held few fears for him — he had been held in Berlin's infamous Spandau Prison by Hitler's Nazi government after the 1933 Berlin Reichstag fire, where he had narrowly escaped the savage beatings and murders of some of his co-accused.[39]

Prichard's childhood friend Christian Jollie Smith, by then an eminent industrial lawyer in Sydney, had taken up Kisch's legal defence on behalf of the powerful International Labor Defence (ILD). She briefed a barrister to appear on his behalf in the High Court, where the government ban on Kisch's entry to Australia was overturned. The High Court found that the Australian Government had failed to properly comply with legal formality in its processing of Kisch's ban and Kisch found himself a free man on arrival in Sydney.

Having banned Kisch's entry, the federal government now scrambled to enforce the ban's legality to counter the growing public uproar. Under the Commonwealth's *Immigration Restriction Act 1901*, prospective immigrants could be required to pass a language test in any living European language. Kisch, who was well versed in a number of European languages, failed to pass the test set for him in Scottish Gaelic and consequently was again deemed a prohibited immigrant. He was arrested and subsequently released on bail.

The Melbourne peace congress went ahead in November 1934 with added fervour in Kisch's absence. In January 1935, Prichard and her then twelve-year-old son Ric caught the train from Melbourne to Sydney, where Kisch awaited his fate being determined by a subsequent High Court appeal against his ban. Kisch secretly attended a number of anti-war rallies, with Prichard and Ric as companions, before the full bench of the High Court determined that Scottish Gaelic was not a living European language as defined by the Immigration Restriction Act, and High Court Justice Herbert Vere ('Doc') Evatt ruled that the government had again failed to properly comply with legal formalities in banning Kisch. Menzies eventually offered Kisch the return of his passport and the reimbursement of his legal costs in return for his prompt despatch back to Europe.

During Prichard's stay in Sydney she met frequently with writer and fellow Communist Jean Devanny, and long and excited discussions between the two encouraged Prichard's enthusiasm for a workers' theatre group in Perth, talk of which had arisen before she travelled overseas. Both Prichard and Devanny had seen the workers' art and theatre movement in the Soviet Union firsthand, and were convinced that a local workers' theatre would provide a practical arm of the CPA. Devanny had also attended drama productions staged by the WIR at its world congress in Berlin in 1931, which she had attended in her capacity as national secretary of the WIR's Australian branch.[40]

On her return to Australia Devanny had set about organising a WIR workers' art and theatre group in Sydney. However, an almost immediate division between members and WIR organisers led to a split from the WIR and the formation of the Sydney Workers' Art Club in late 1932, to which Devanny then devoted her energies.[41] *The Sydney Morning Herald* reported that the Workers' Art Club had been established 'with the object of bringing within the reach of the working classes various advantages in the way of lectures, musical recitals, art classes and the exhibition of pictures'.

> Organisers have laid down for themselves a wide and ambitious programme. They have begun by providing a cheerful clubroom and small library where members may meet and hold discussions on various questions related to arts and craft.[42]

The group quickly expanded to include the performance of drama. The Workers' Art Club Players' first production, *The Ragged Trousered Philanthropists* — an adaptation of a notorious English working-class novel advocating socialism — took place at the Rationalist Hall in Sydney in April 1933, by which time the club had also formed a music section, a weekly art class devoted to 'working-class art', and a literary section that ran a weekly writing class devoted to 'working-class literature'. Public lectures, mainly CPA-political, were also held at the Workers' Art Club rooms above a wine bar at 36 Pitt Street near Circular Quay in central Sydney.[43] The club quickly came under the control of the CPA; the art and literature sections soon disbanded and the theatre came to the fore.[44]

At the end of 1931 a similarly oriented Workers' Art Club had been established in Melbourne. It declared itself 'a co-operative organization of students and workers' and adopted as its slogan, 'Art is a Weapon'. It did not initially include drama in its program — its public debut in April 1932 was an exhibition of watercolours by founding member Jack Maughan — but in August 1932 it staged its first theatrical performance, Ernst Toller's *Masses and Man*. This was followed by a number of outdoor political agitprop plays at factory gates, trade-union nights and shopping centres. The group was short-lived, however, disbanding some time in 1933.

In early 1935 the Friends of the Soviet Union formed the Victorian Workers' Theatre Group, presumably with the Sydney group as its model, after a proposal was put to the FOSU by ILD organiser-secretary Frank Huelin. Betty Roland, who had recently returned from a fifteen-month stay in the Soviet Union, was appointed the group's artistic director, and some members of the disbanded Workers' Art Club became involved in its early stages, when agitprop sketches were rehearsed and played at trade union meetings, factories and suburban halls. Like its Sydney counterpart, the group was kept informed of the wider workers' theatre movement through the monthly American journal *New Theatre*.[45]

Sanctimonious CPA functionaries regarded such cultural ventures with a good deal of suspicion, if not contempt, and the more sectarian members denounced the group as a predominantly 'petit-bourgeois' band of bohemian degenerates whose work did not, and could not, serve or reflect the aspirations of the working class. The Communist Party organisation was instinctively sceptical about art being a useful political tool, and regarded the workers' art movement's often satirical approach to politics with jaundice. Rank-and-file CPA members were discouraged from outlandish shows of expression or indulgence, and the arts brigade typically did not submit to the sort of internal discipline that the cognoscente preached.

Neither Devanny nor Prichard shared these criticisms of culture as a weapon in the political armoury, and thankfully the CPA was not as rigidly censorious of the 'artist' as was the Communist Party of the Soviet Union.[46] There was no firm CPA line on cultural matters, and the party-political line on these things 'wobbled around quite a bit' under Stalin's rapidly changing edicts.[47] Under Stalin himself, however, the experiment was over. 'Modern Art' was politically unacceptable in the Soviet Union by the mid-1930s and Modernism, despite thriving after the period of the Russian Revolution, was deemed individualist and bourgeois, and Stalin finally crushed it there in 1935. The last gasp of Soviet Modernism was seen in 1935 in the photographs and photomontages of Aleksandr Rodchenko and Varvara Stepanova. Cubist and Futurist art, deemed unintelligible to the masses, was also forbidden in the Soviet Union. One of the last vestiges of Russian Modernism was to be Australia's first real experience of live Modernist theatre, when the remnants of the renowned Ballets Russes toured Australia (with the exclusion of Perth) in 1936 and with it the stunning Modernist costumes, sets and repertoire inherited from Sergei Diaghilev's original company.

The West Australian began to report on the Stalinist purges at this time — the arrests of Czarist and White Guard 'elements' in the country for their supposed terrorist crimes against the state. The utopian well had patently been poisoned, but local CPA newspaper *The Red Star* savagely attacked these reports, and the 'journalistic prostitutes' who wrote them, as indicative of an intrinsic hostility in the mainstream press towards the Soviet Union.[48]

In May 1935 the federal government again invoked the Crimes Act against the CPA, banning the transmission by post of CPA newspapers. A letter was also sent to the Radical Bookshop notifying it that the *Moscow News* had been banned and that copies of that newspaper destined for the bookshop had been seized by Customs. Within days, however, the *Moscow News* ban was lifted after the CPA took out a writ against the government, and the newspaper was again on sale — although the journal *Soviets To-day*, the organ of the Australian FOSU, remained on the list of banned publications.

The federal government had more sinister plans in train. It was seeking a High Court judgement banning the CPA. There was no concerted push for an immediate hearing, as the government was aware that it stood little chance at the time of winning the case: it was content to leave the threat hanging. Rumours of a potential ban left the CPA feeling vulnerable but the legal case, for now, did not proceed. Justice Evatt set down a High

Court hearing for May 1937, in which the government's case for an application before the High Court for a banning of the CPA was to be heard. Evatt rejected the government's application for a further hearing before the High Court. Attorney-General Robert Menzies, aware that the government now stood little chance of prosecuting the CPA, then settled with the CPA and lifted the postal ban on CPA newspapers. This was to be the first in a long line of clashes between Menzies and Evatt over the former's legal attempts to thwart the CPA.

The CPA in Western Australia had other more pressing local problems. Membership was dwindling and the state branch of the party was in a dire financial position. It was in an almost constant state of suspended animation, forced to undertake continuous funding drives. Had it not been for the philanthropy of, in the main, Perth's Yugoslav community, the CPA would have found it difficult to endure in Western Australia.[49] The local branch of the CPA was reluctant to expel any of its members, despite some of the rank and file having returned greatly affected by the horrors of the First World War and finding CPA behavioural strictures difficult to abide by. In early 1935, when its paid state members numbered just 130,[50] the Western Australian branch expelled Comrade Reginald Smith 'for bouts of drunkenness over a long period', despite conceding that Smith's 'mental balance' had been destroyed by injuries he suffered during the War. The CPA 'takes up neither a sectarian nor a wowseristic attitude towards drink', came the statement from branch headquarters, but 'it insists that its members must be able to preserve their self respect'.[51] Reginald Smith was later readmitted to the CPA.

Egon Kisch left Australia in March 1935, sailing from Sydney and stopping over in Fremantle in less hysteric circumstances.[52] Prichard by this time was back at Greenmount and, accompanied by Keith George and Gus Stagg as representatives of the newly named West Australian Council Against War and Fascism, she met Kisch when his ship docked in Fremantle.[53] Kisch walked from the ship with a 'slight limp' and embraced Prichard. He was taken to lunch at Prichard's Greenmount home before later addressing a public gathering of about 400 people on the Perth Esplanade at which he 'appealed to all present to assist the W.A. Council Against War and Fascism to build a mighty movement in Western Australia'.[54] He sailed for Europe that evening.[55]

Just prior to Kisch's departure from Sydney, discussions between him, Prichard and Devanny had led to the formation of the Australian Writers' League (AWL), of which Prichard was elected inaugural president. The

AWL was formed as a distinctly left-wing political lobby group to encourage a national literature movement in Australia and, at a time of broad censorship, to 'rally writers to a defence of culture against reaction' through 'independent thought and expression'. It was also to be a forum for the nurture and development of young up-and-coming working-class writers by the older established writers of the league.[56] It operated both collaterally and cooperatively with the Fellowship of Australian Writers (FAW), a writers' union and political lobby agitating on issues affecting Australian writers. The conservative central body of the FAW in Sydney came under the control of its left-wing members after the Kisch affair, and it became more politically active. The AWL affiliated with Writers International, and state AWL branches were formed. The first, in New South Wales, had Jean Devanny at its head, and was followed soon after by a Victorian branch to which John Mewton Harcourt (author of banned 1934 political novel *Upsurge*, set in Perth during the Depression) was elected president and Prichard's friend Vance Palmer vice-president. Both branches were established in early 1935.[57]

In August 1935, Comintern General Secretary Georgi Dimitrov gave a long speech on 'The United Front Against Fascism' to a Communist Party of the Soviet Union (CPSU) Congress in Moscow, in which he 'laid down the ideological line for the period of the struggle against fascism'.

The United Front was moderated and broadened in 1935 into what was termed the 'Popular Front'. It was a shift from the notion of a political alliance to a broad-based progressive coalition. The implementation of the Popular Front also saw a moderation of the Communist Party's hitherto hardline rhetoric, and this had its effect on the workers' theatre movement. A variety of organisations were subsequently formed, under the auspices of the Communist Party, to attract support for the Popular Front. The Front was also a means of broadening the Communist Party's influence within the wider labour movement, and the CPA courted the Australian Labor Party (ALP) as a partner.

The Comintern had long been critical of the CPA's failure to make inroads into the ALP as a springboard from which to press for political reform. Discussion about the form of any relationship between the CPA and the ALP was a cause of division within the CPA for decades. The parliamentary arm of the ALP was a friend to neither the Communist movement nor the militant industrial branches of the trade union movement. Although the trade union movement had been established by the ALP, tensions between the parliamentary and industrial sections of the ALP had arisen early on. Alliances and affiliations between trade unions and the ALP had formed and failed.

Attempts to work with, and from within, the ALP had been the modus operandi since the CPA's infancy. A United Front proposal in the 1920s referred to affiliation with the ALP, but CPA affiliation would have been electoral suicide for the ALP.[58] From early 1933 the CPA had again sought a national united-front partnership with the ALP, but its overtures were again rebuffed. A courtship with the trade union movement was also inherent in Dimitrov's Popular Front proposal, and it necessitated a tactical change by the CPA in its dealings with the trade union movement.

Prior to 1934, the industrial arm of the CPA, known as the Militant Minority Movement, was hostile to both employers and trade union officials. Responsibility for industrial policy then returned to the centre of the CPA and the quasi-independent arm of the Militant Minority Movement was disbanded. From around 1934, the CPA began to work from within trade unions, and trade union 'fractions' were formed. CPA members joined ALP branches in an attempt to both influence and denounce ALP policies, but refused to sign anti-Communist pledges. In May 1935 the ALP protested against this form of CPA infiltration through the unions.

The Popular Front's opposition to fascism garnered a great deal of support from a broad base. The CPA 'recognised that it was very useful that leaders of such bodies as the Peace Council were not Party members', as it gave those bodies greater public credibility.[59] Keith George was one such example, but many in the Communist Party, abiding by its former 'class against class' maxim, were hostile to the idea of political cooperation with those outside their immediate ranks — particularly the middle class, who joined the anti-fascist fray in large numbers.

The Popular Front period eventually dissolved with the Soviet–German pact during the Second World War.

4

THE 'LIVING THEATRE': FORMATION OF THE PERTH WORKERS' THEATRE

It is rumoured that certain agents of the bourgeoisie, who have been unsuccessful in diverting the Party line in this State intend to form a 'workers party' or a 'workers club'. It is very doubtful, however, if these few disgruntled political illiterates have enough energy to get out of their own way, and do more than indulge in gossip on street corners.[1]

Self-consciously or unconsciously, the workers of the Left theatre do the same work as the scientist who exposes the facts of the impaired health of people of England's Depressed Areas, as the statistician who arranges the figures of England's six million people who live on less than four shillings each per week, as the economist who shows the inevitable occurrence of increasingly severe depressions and the inevitability of war arising from certain home and foreign policies, as the philosopher who shows the definite order of social changes, and who gives us a scientific view of our relations to others, and the way in which we can become aware of our power to direct history intelligently.[2]

The 1935 Comintern directive for a 'popular front' to broaden the political struggle, particularly against war and fascism, precipitated the formation of workers' theatre groups worldwide by members of the Communist Party and a disparate array of kindred political moderates. In 1935 the American League of Workers' Theatres responded to this edict by changing its name to the New Theatre League and transforming itself into a broader political church than its politically charged Communist Party predecessor. The group dropped its previously singular pro-Soviet charter and slogans and took up the fight against 'war, fascism and censorship'.[3]

At Greenmount, discussions were being held about the formation of a Perth Workers' Theatre. Keith George was one of those involved and, while he respected Prichard's motives and the experience that her long involvement in Australian theatre would bring to the proposed group, he was apprehensive about their ability to work cooperatively on the project. He was concerned about what form their alliance would take, what their respective roles would be, and whether they could amicably agree on the plays they would produce. Neither George nor Prichard was greatly given to compromise on matters theatrical or political. Apart from anything else, a generation gap also separated the two and this, George knew, was reflected in their aspirations for the theatre.

> You must remember that between the romanticism of Katharine's early theatre and mine lay a desert of a world war, a social revolution and a great depression. My world was confused but more astringent than the world of the early 1900's.[4]

To George, Prichard was still a member of drama's old school and her writing for the theatre somewhat anachronistic and overly sentimental. He acknowledged that Prichard, dramatist Louis Esson and theatre director Gregan McMahon[5] had been 'in revolt against the worst excesses' of the saccharin social comedies staged in Australia at the turn of the century, 'in which businessmen and their wives with their social fringe enjoyed the ephemeral satisfaction of playing out little roles as dukes, duchesses, and lords and ladies'. But he 'felt that they never quite freed themselves from its toils, particularly from its romanticism'.[6] He favoured a grittier, more confrontational contemporary drama.

George and Prichard shared a similar social background but their political expression differed markedly. George advocated a more literal interpretation of the brief of a workers' theatre than did Prichard. He was not a CPA member but he was a politically sympathetic 'fellow traveller' who strongly supported the idea of a theatre constituted by the 'working class', staging the best drama in all its forms, irrespective, by and large, of its politics.[7] Prichard, on the other hand, was insistent that the theatre be a political tool: a theatre that reflected what she saw as the vital political aspirations of the working class, and one that expressed political solutions to the social and economic maladies of the working class. This was a contrast between the two rather than an irreconcilable difference, and George had too much respect for Prichard not to listen to her ideas with an open mind. Nevertheless, for better or worse he felt compelled to put forward his ideas 'or the result would not have been a happy one' for either of them.[8]

Prichard's decision to recruit George to run the Workers' Theatre had no political chicanery about it. Her trust in George was absolute. He displayed a great talent and passion for theatre which 'she thought she could harness for her working-class interests'.[9] Prichard herself 'had a long history in the theatre and a great admiration for the theatre and would never have thought of putting anybody in charge of a theatrical enterprise who wasn't able to do it.'[10] Although George's acquaintances were initially surprised that he 'was willing to do the bidding of someone [like Prichard] completely devoted to a politic he didn't share',[11] it doubtlessly helped him to recruit a broad ensemble and a wide audience, while 'Katharine's prestige attracted the intellectuals and workers alike.'[12] The 'new theatre' was not necessarily to be a didactic theatre.

The primary appeal of the proposed venture to George was the opportunity to at last take the reins of his own drama troupe, frustrated as he had been by his lack of absolute control as he had been at the Playbox Theatre. George's and Prichard's respective roles were crucially settled on within a relatively short time, and we can assume from George's statements on the subject that there was a compromise reached between them over the brief of the Workers' Theatre.[13] It would be devoted to that rather indistinct and ethereal creature characterised in Communist Party idiom as 'working-class culture', with George as 'the driving force' and Prichard 'the unobtrusive adviser' who did not interfere in its day-to-day operations.

For both Prichard and George, the Workers' Theatre was to be an adjunct to the activities of the Western Australian arm of the Council Against War and Fascism (CAWF). George presumably saw the Workers' Theatre as a more direct means of expanding the outreach of the CAWF. The pair agreed that the Communist Party was not to have any control of the theatre group. George in particular was adamant about autonomy from the CPA after some unpleasant personal experiences of CPA intervention into the CAWF.[14] A contemporary of his reflected that he 'wasn't the type to submit to the harness being put on him'.[15]

George was comfortable in the role of benevolent autocrat within the Workers' Theatre. He did not believe in the possibility of successful production by committee and he would not entertain any prospect of it. He had resolute confidence in his ability to build and control the Workers' Theatre and he quickly galvanised those around him. He was a theatre maverick. His aesthetic vision was ambitious, challenging and unconventional and, while there were those who doubted his capacity to realise his plans for the theatre group, the political climate was favourable. 'Liberalism was fashionable,' he later reflected.[16]

In May 1935, Henrietta Drake-Brockman announced the formation of the Perth Workers' Theatre in her local column for national drama magazine *The Playbill*.

> A Workers' Theatre is soon to put in an appearance in Perth. This will be run on the lines of groups at present in existence in America and Japan. Indeed, it will be a new link in a world-wide movement ... These theatres are run, presumably, on something like the same lines as Soviet theatres.[17]

The Workers' Theatre group was already rehearsing three short plays under the direction of Keith George — *Who's Who in the Berlin Zoo*, *The Thief* and *A Bed-Time Story*[18] — and local CPA newspaper *The Red Star* put out a call for recruits to join the casts.

> The castings for these plays are as yet not complete so workers who are interested in the Workers' Theatre and desire membership are advised to get in touch with the secretary.[19]

Who's Who in the Berlin Zoo was a satire that ridiculed the German Nazi leaders. *The Thief* was a one-act play, written by Prichard a short time before the inception of the group, and based on an incident that she had observed in a Soviet law court in 1933.[20] The play documents the trial of a peasant girl, Masha, accused of stealing food, a blanket and a pair of shoes from her employers. The trial reveals Masha's theft and prostitution as her only means of providing for her impoverished grandparents. Her employers, who are found to have exploited the girl, are heavily fined and ordered to pay her back-wages, and Masha is sentenced to six months' detention in a women's penal colony to undertake literacy instruction and industrial training. The play was written in the Socialist Realist style; this new literary form favoured by the Communist Party had succeeded Social Realism, and Prichard had become aware of its pre-eminence during her visit to the Soviet Union. The first All Soviet Congress of Writers in 1934 officially prescribed Socialist Realism as the official writing style of the Communist Movement. Andrei Zhdanov, soon after his appointment as secretary of the CPSU Central Committee, decreed that writers should be 'engineers of the human soul' and that the new expression of the achievement of the workers and the Party should be in a spirit of 'revolutionary romanticism'. A close confidant of Stalin, Zhdanov told the 1934 congress that 'the truthfulness and historical concreteness of artistic description must be combined with the task of ideological transformation and education of working people in the spirit of socialism.'[21] Socialist Realism was a shift from the mere expression of the proletarian battle between capital and labour to a form that expressed a resolution to the struggle.[22] *A Bed-Time Story*, written by Keith George for the Workers' Theatre, was also stylistically unusual. While a narrator read the story, which was set in the goldfields of Western Australia, actors mimed the narrative.

There is no record, aside from a little anecdotal evidence, of these three plays having been performed. They do not seem to have come before the general public, but may have been performed at a CPA or CAWF function.[23] Early Workers' Theatre member Angus McGregor, who attended some of the group's meetings around this time, remembered plans being discussed for the production of *Who's Who in the Berlin Zoo*, and was one of a group of art students asked to produce papier-mâché masks for the actors in the play.[24]

Prichard's connections helped the Perth Workers' Theatre to obtain material for production. Her international Communist Party network, the Communist Party's links to the wider international workers' theatre movement, and Prichard's own connections with the international literary scene all ensured that she and George were aware of the great political plays of the period.

In early to mid-1935, Prichard's London publisher, Jonathan Cape, sent her a copy of Clifford Odets's play *Till the Day I Die*, which had been written earlier that year to illustrate the plight of Communists in Nazi Germany. She lent it to George, who was greatly moved and excited by it. 'It may not have been great literature,' he would reflect later, 'but it was good theatre — violent and topical.' *Till the Day I Die* had been written for the Group Theatre in New York, of which Odets was an active member, and had very recently been staged to great popular acclaim. George was a fervent admirer of the Group Theatre, which had largely inspired his drive to form the Workers' Theatre.[25] George and Prichard discussed 'ways and means' of producing the play with the Perth Workers' Theatre group.[26]

George thought it prudent to disassociate the ostensibly non-partisan Workers' Theatre from organisational politics, and he resigned from his CAWF position in August 1935 to devote his energies to the task of getting the Workers' Theatre up and running and directing its initial major production of *Till the Day I Die*.[27] His resignation from the CAWF was well received by Prichard: he would later recall that 'Katharine breathed a sigh of relief and accepted my proposition with somewhat transparent alacrity.'[28] The reason for Prichard's 'alacrity' was George's reluctance to adhere to what he described as the 'volte-faces of the Party line' imposed on the CAWF. George 'was strongly interested in the left, but he objected to organisation.'[29] He was a person of great intellectual power and staunch opinions, but he could not submit himself to a higher authority. He was anti-doctrinal and critical of all shades of orthodoxy and dogmatism.[30] He would not adhere to any party line and as he was not a member of the CPA, he was not subject to Party discipline. As the CAWF was, for all intents and purposes, a subsidiary of the Communist Party and ostensibly remained under the direction of the Party, relations between George and the Party hierarchy had become strained, despite the fact that his value to the Party was precisely the distance he kept from it. An organisation was less susceptible to accusations of being a CPA front or affiliate if people like George held official positions in them.[31]

Planning for the Workers' Theatre production of *Till the Day I Die* began only a matter of weeks after the play's premiere in New York, but under George's intensive tuition it would take a year or more to prepare for the stage. The group began arrangements for the production, making use of their mutual contacts in the CAWF and with the 'whole weight' of Prichard's 'charm, influence and organising ability behind the scheme'. The Workers' Theatre had initially run its operations from the Radical Bookshop in Northbridge, but when rehearsals for *Till the Day I Die* started the CPA allowed the group free use of its premises on the upper floor of the nearby Franklin Print building in William Street, the printing premises of the Party's local newspaper, *The Red Star* (renamed *The Workers' Star* in April 1936),[32] shortly before Franklin Print moved to premises rented from the Western Australian Railways Department in nearby Pier Street.[33] According to intelligence reports, Keith George put up some of the finance for the establishment of Franklin Print, and it was probably here that posters advertising the Workers' Theatre and its latter performances were printed.[34] Although there would be neither direct affiliation nor any official connection between the Workers' Theatre and the CPA organisation, a number of minor CPA officials and CPA and CAWF members — Prichard's contacts and people who could be relied on to enthusiastically support such a venture — were involved in the group from its inception.[35] In the more sectarian CPA circles of the eastern states, CPA functionaries were discouraged by the Party from becoming involved with ventures such as the Workers' Theatre. There was little room for dissent within CPA ranks in the 1930s — centralism and the Party line was all — but in Western Australia, under Prichard's substantial influence, the Party was more flexible and tolerant.

While Prichard was vilified by many in the literary establishment for her political affiliations and known to many in Perth as the Red Witch of Greenmount, she was still a prominent and respected author who maintained contact with a wide social network, and she was able to cultivate the support of many respectable moderates for the CPA's cultural organisations. She was an important CPA figurehead in Western Australia and a vital link between the Party and the moderate middle class. She was also an ideal agent for the CPA in its push for broader recognition and its drive for increased membership. The Party machine made frequent practical use of her mediating public profile, giving prominence to her image, writing, thoughts and activities through the CPA press, in which photographs of 'Comrade Mrs Hugo Throssell' often appeared above the caption 'World-famous Revolutionary Authoress'.[36] She was an influential and highly revered figure in local CPA circles and, although she was officially subordinate to state secretary Wilfred (Bill) Mountjoy, she took charge of CPA cultural activities in Western Australia in the 1930s, and many of Mountjoy's early published public pronouncements were written with Prichard's help. She certainly subedited and proofread material that Mountjoy wrote for *The Red Star*.[37]

Bill Mountjoy was a West Australian by birth, a bricklayer turned brickmaker by trade, and a committee member of the Federated Brick, Tile and Pottery Industrial Union of Australia in 1927 when he moved to Sydney, where he took up with the CPA. He served a prison term as 'one of the victims of the Clovelly frame-up'.[38] The Clovelly arrests came after the Unemployed Workers' Movement (UWM), having decided to embark on more militant strategies than previous peaceful protests, tried to prevent the eviction of a number of unemployed workers and their families from their homes across Sydney. A number of men, including Mountjoy, were arrested and jailed on fabricated malicious damage charges after one such incident in the Sydney suburb of Clovelly in July 1930.[39] Such was the inauspicious start to a long and relatively successful national campaign by the UWM against evictions of unemployed workers, a practice that continued through the Depression. Many tenants were saved from eviction because of the courage shown by UWM activists, who were often badly beaten and sometimes killed while physically defending the homes of the unemployed.

In March 1931, Bill Mountjoy stood as a Communist candidate in the federal by-election for the seat of East Sydney, and in November 1931 the

CPA central executive sent him back to Western Australia where he was installed as CPA district secretary and, shortly thereafter, elected CPA state secretary.

Mountjoy quickly stamped his authority on the Party in the West, and initially imposed strict organisational discipline. In this, he replicated the national organisation of the CPA, under instructions sent from Moscow, after the long fractious period within the CPA during the wayward 1920s when the CPA was not averse to differing points of view and polemical discussion and argument. Mountjoy established a CPA branch in Kalgoorlie in 1932, and stood as a CPA candidate for the goldfields seat of Boulder in the state election of April 1933, in which he polled a fairly minuscule 274 votes. Philip Collier, then state leader of the ALP, was the sitting member elected premier after the Labor Party took office at the election.

The practice of standing CPA candidates against ALP candidates in parliamentary elections was primarily a means of protesting against a political party branded as 'social-fascists' by the CPA.[40] It was also an attempt to force a shift in ALP policy away from its increasing centrism and to raise the profile of the CPA.[41] Mountjoy stood as a West Australian candidate for the Senate in the 1934 federal election and polled a respectable 2703 first-preference votes, a significant vote given that official CPA membership in Western Australia at that time was only about 100 and he had campaigned under the provocative slogan of 'social liberation of the toiling masses — for Soviet Power'.[42] Mountjoy was never elected to parliament.[43]

Keith George chaired the early meetings of the Workers' Theatre, of which the aim was to elect a committee, determine the group's structure and agree on a drama program. Prichard's influence on the operations of the Workers' Theatre was initially considerable, though her presence was scarce. She 'whistled people to her side' and assigned them positions within the group, and although 'she was being quoted a lot' she did not attend the early formation meetings.[44] George's role as art director was to oversee the Workers' Theatre and its activities, and direct its plays. The early committee included such prominent CPA members as Arthur Rudkin and Maurie Lachberg, who was appointed inaugural secretary.

Arthur Rudkin was a full-time CPA functionary, treasurer of the CPA's state committee and member of *The Red Star* staff. He joined the Workers' Theatre, he said, 'as a means of relaxation from [his] political labours, not on instructions from the Party, nor as a moral political "duty"'.[45] He was born in Leicestershire in 1908 and had been an outstanding scholar in his youth. Two years after the death of his mother in 1921, his father and sister had emigrated to South Africa, leaving thirteen-year-old Arthur at a Salvation Army training farm in Essex for a short time before he was sent to Australia, sailing steerage. He spent his fifteenth birthday at sea and arrived in Fremantle on Armistice Day, 1923. Five days later he was sent to work as a farmhand on a dairy farm outside Bridgetown in Western Australia's south-west. He sang in the local Methodist church choir and in 1930, now unemployed, was accepted into a teacher's training college, but returned to manual labour when the college was closed by the Depression. He took up relief work, building roads and quarrying, and read books borrowed from the Busselton Library. The works of Upton Sinclair, George Bernard Shaw and H.G. Wells, in particular, had a dramatic political impact on him and he joined the CPA in July 1931.[46]

> One of the things that attracted me to the Communist Party was [that] in any political discussion, whenever I'd put forward an idea which I thought seemed rational and humane and the best solution to the problem, some silly bugger was always sure to say: 'Oh, you can't do that, that's a nasty Communist idea' and so I came to think — well if the Communists believe all these things, I'd better look into the Communist Party and see what they really do believe, and I found that of course the Communists ... in those days, at any rate, were in the forefront of every progressive movement.[47]

In 1932, Rudkin organised a Communist Club in Bridgetown that included a number of migrant members. One had fought in the Russian Revolution, another had been a member of the British Red Army, and several others were political anti-fascist 'fugitives' from Yugoslavia.[48] Rudkin established CPA cells and branches around the south-west of the state and later that year moved to Perth where he worked part time at the Radical Bookshop.

Maurice (Maurie) Lachberg was born in London in 1905. His Jewish parents had fled Tsarist Russia for London at the turn of the century before moving to Perth in 1910. After a series of labouring jobs in his teenage years, Lachberg worked as a farmhand in the Western Australian wheatbelt and joined the CPA some time in the 1920s. Later, he undertook a carpentry and cabinetmaking apprenticeship in Perth, joined the Carpenters' and Joiners' Union in 1929, and was frequently dismissed from 'brief runs of employment' for politically inciting his co-workers, moving 'from job to job defending his point of view!'[49] He was a highly intelligent man who, like many of his generation, was almost entirely self-educated, spending much of his time during periods of unemployment reading in Perth's public library.[50] He was elected as the first full-time trade union organiser for the Carpenters' and Joiners' Union in Western Australia, and became well known as a fiery left-wing orator.[51] At the time of the Workers' Theatre formation, he was a member of the Metropolitan District Council of the ALP and the single father of a young son.

Other prominent early members of the Workers' Theatre included artists Leith Angelo and Harald Vike, and trade unionists Tom Wignall (Snr) and Albert Osterberg.

The Workers' Theatre organising committee was not so much elected as 'suddenly there', according to John Hepworth, and John and Ray Oldham suggest that 'there were probably not more than enough for a committee prepared to be on the committee.'[52] During its early meetings the committee drafted a constitution.[53] This document most certainly 'shows the hand of Keith's legal training' but, in the years that followed, his adherence to the letter of the constitution was loose.[54]

With a constitution in place, Keith George quickly set about recruiting a cast for *Till the Day I Die*, with Prichard most likely providing a list of CPA people to contact about joining the group. A few of the cast members, including Francis (Frank) O'Grady and Phyllis Harnett, had worked with George at the Playbox Theatre.[55] George wrote to Harnett in Derby in the state's far north-west, where she was working as a laundress and barmaid, telling her of his plans to direct the play and asked her to return to Perth for a 'wonderful part' he had for her in it.[56] She returned to the Masel household in mid-1935 and immediately started work on the play.

At this point the Workers' Theatre was subsumed by the Workers' Art Club, which was formed in mid-1935 and oversaw the activities of the Workers' Theatre, its centrepiece. While the Workers' Art Club's initial brief was limited to the theatre production of *Till the Day I Die*, in early 1936 the venture expanded beyond drama production to encompass instruction and exhibition in a wider range of arts, hence the name change.[57]

Although autonomous from its eastern states' counterparts, Perth's Workers' Art Club was modelled principally on the workers' art clubs already extant in the eastern states and, by extension, on their Russian and European (notably German) counterparts. The Five Arts Club was also a model, and Keith George had recruited key personnel from the Five Arts Club's Playbox Theatre to the Workers' Theatre and Workers' Art Club.

The Workers' Art Club was also to serve as a social hub for the unemployed and the political Left. It was to offer practical opportunities to those traditionally excluded from participation in the arts. It publicly declared its somewhat utopian design as 'a non-party organisation dedicated to working class culture'.[58] Like its eastern states' counterparts, it was to be a forum of the 'working class ... and the intellectuals who are in sympathy with this class'.[59] Its agenda was both progressive and propagandist.

While preparations for *Till the Day I Die* continued, the Workers' Theatre 'quietly' undertook some small-scale dramatic work 'to further its aims'.[60] At the beginning of August 1935 the group staged a performance of John Drinkwater's *X=O: A Night of the Trojan War* at the conclusion of an Anti-War Day rally at the Rechabite Hall in Perth. The play was a particular favourite of both George and Prichard, and George directed the production, by his own account, 'for Katharine'.[61] *The Red Star* commended both the strong anti-war message of the play and its performance.[62]

The CPA actively campaigned against the federal government's amendments to the *Transport Workers Act 1928* and the Crimes Act outlawing industrial action on the waterfront, and encouraged workers to defy new government work regulations, consequently warning its members in September 1935 to prepare for illegality.[63]

In October, when the Crimes Act was invoked to try to break the back of the CPA and outlaw the FOSU, Prichard wrote to Vance Palmer:

> Although Gord [sic] ... knows, whether I'll ever get another book done. One day a month is all I get sometimes and working 18 hours a day sometimes on Party affairs. It's devastating — quite impossible to get any co[n]centration. And I'll be stoney, motherless broke if I don't earn something soon. Summer coming too, and you know how one's brain boils in the heat. I'm weary, most of the time, too. Speeching [sic] knocks the devil out of me. The M.A.W. and F. [Movement Against War and Fascism, as the Council Against War and Fascism was now known] fighting well ... and many sliding away. But the Crime's Act [sic] gathering others to the fold. Goodness knows what will happen if it's ever put into operation. I'm beginning to think [jail is] the only place I'll ever get any peace to write in. So long as you all demand political rights for me, so that I can write. Dont [sic] forget, if it does happen, to stir up the craft for me on this issue.[64]

Prichard was under contract to finish her novel *Intimate Strangers*. The manuscript was by now long overdue with her publisher but as 'the everyday demands of the movement keep intruding',[65] the novel was put aside.

On 7 December 1935, the Workers' Theatre made its first public appearance to a 'crowded house' at the Princes Hall in Brisbane Street, Perth, with a bill of three short plays: *Captain Pernot's Honour*, a play set in the Paris Commune; *Calphurnia's Claws*, a satirical anti-war play set in ancient Rome during the reign of Julius Caesar; and the one-act play *Forward One*, written by Prichard almost certainly to help launch the Workers' Theatre.[66]

Forward One was a vigorous agitprop play in the vein of Clifford Odets's *Waiting For Lefty*, with a simple but effective plot for its purposes. Set in a Perth 'frock shop' on a hot summer's afternoon, it dealt with the poor working conditions of the female sales assistants in the city's dress shops at that time, often without regard to the *Factories and Shops Act 1920* (WA), which governed their employment conditions. When an authoritarian manageress character refuses the shop assistants' prescribed rest periods, they walk off the job and set about organising the improvement of their conditions.[67] The overtly socialist realist play had the ineffectual Shop Assistants' Union in its sights. It was written to draw attention and support to the plight of these sales assistants, as well as to mobilise the wider trade union rank and file, and it was a precursor to later Workers' Theatre agitprops and 'Living Newspapers' — theatrical productions that portrayed contemporary political events and social issues from a partisan perspective. Not only did these plays serve a political purpose, they also had an exciting immediacy previously unseen in local theatre. *Forward One* was one of a number of 'fast episodic pieces' exchanged between Australian New Theatre groups.[68]

Prichard's son Ric felt that:

> [Prichard's] plays of the thirties were largely a matter of conscience, part of her political duty to the things she believed in and the people she cared about ... She did not regard them as significant work. Certainly they made no contribution to her livelihood as a writer, even though she was a good deal worse-off than the shop-girls and the miners she wrote for.[69]

The players in *Forward One* were relative unknowns, probably the middle-class friends and university acquaintances of Keith George in the main.

None of them, with the exception of Marjorie Smith (later Robson), performed in any other play with the group.

> They were interested for the same reasons that teenagers take to marihuana [*sic*]. Left wing politics were an even more adequate means of shocking their parents than they are today.[70]

Prichard was not exempt from Party press censure. The national arm of the CPA prescribed a rigid and unforgiving line and *The Red Star* found fault in the play's critical union line, the principal tenet of the play, observing that 'The dialogue is entertaining, but needs a sounder trade union line for its improvement'.[71]

Prichard would have bristled on reading this criticism. She objected strongly to attempts from any quarter to censor or manipulate the political line in her writing. In 1934, the national general secretary of the CPA, John Bramwell (J.B.) Miles,[72] had asked Prichard if the Party's Secretariat could vet the manuscript she had written about her trip to Russia, concerned at the possible adverse impression it might give of Soviet life. Prichard 'put up her hands in horror' and refused, and Miles was forced to back down, conceding that it was 'wrong to make such demands upon artists' (though he need not have worried about Prichard defaming the Soviet Union).[73] While Prichard was often attacked for combining politics with her literary practice, she 'would not equivocate on matters of principle for social comfort'.[74] She had, said Jean Devanny:

> that inward certitude that comes of a secure childhood, knit through with poise and balance derived from family and educational advantages … She would brook no dictation and once, when I told her that the district committee had refused me the time off to finish a book, she exclaimed angrily: 'I think it's disgraceful that you should be interfered with like this!'[75]

Miles probably had more understanding than most on the Central Committee of Prichard's work as a writer. He was engaged in a discreet longstanding affair with Devanny, and she probably tempered his proletarian scorn for such things. Miles himself was a devotee of pulp fiction.[76]

The fledgling Workers' Theatre had to keep its ambitions in check. Four days after the Princes Hall performance, Prichard wrote to 'Comrade' Frank Huelin of the Melbourne Workers' Theatre:

> Early in the New Year the Group must be put on a sound footing and I have written to Sydney for the Cons[t]itution and Principle[s] of the W.A.C. [Workers' Art Club]. I suppose you work on the same conditions. Our printing is due to friendly relations with the [Communist] press, hence the elegant paper and programme.[77]

By April 1936, the Workers' Art Club included a plastic and graphic art section, and by June a dramatic section had also been established, which ran members' classes in voice production, acting and fencing. Keith George tutored the drama classes and Maurie Lachberg taught fencing.[78]

The drama wing, under George's direction, was to produce challenging and innovative theatre informed by the Russian theatre of Konstantin Stanislavsky and Vsevolod Meyerhold. Like Stanislavsky and Meyerhold, George was strongly of the view that theatre should serve a useful social purpose.

Harald Vike oversaw the fine art wing, which provided facilities to members for etching, lithography, wood- and linocutting as well as general art and crafts. A popular weekly life drawing class was started soon after the art section's inception, conducted initially by German artist Ernst Dressler before Vike took it over.[79] The class, for which students were vetted given its use of a nude life model, ran for more than two years in the Workers' Art Club rooms in Hay Street, to the west of the city centre. It was 'carefully conducted to avoid scandal', recalled Bill Irwin later.[80] Perth was a puritanical town and few art teachers dared use life models; Vike, Dressler and James W.R. Linton were among the exceptions. Linton, having returned from London where the use of life models was commonplace, had wanted to use a life model for a drawing class he taught at Perth Technical College, but the college had forbidden it. He later used life models at the Linton Sketch Club, and police would sometimes visit the respectable Linton Institute of Art when it advertised for the services of a life model.[81]

Harald Vike had found his way to Perth by a circuitous route. He'd left his native Norway at age seventeen, joined the crew of an oil tanker named the *Perth*, and sailed with a whaling fleet to South Georgia in the South Atlantic. He went on to sail on a number of other tankers and whalers along the coasts of Africa and South America, working variously as a shark shooter and a stoker, emptying ships' boilers in the extreme conditions of the tropics and the Antarctic, and sketching and painting at sea, having taken up landscape painting as a teenager. In 1927 he sailed on a whaler-oiler to the Point Cloates whaling station at

Norwegian Bay in the north-west of Western Australia. Unhappy with the working conditions on the boat, he jumped ship with a friend and together they made their way to Perth. They spent six months clearing land in Western Australia's wheatbelt, with Vike selling sketches and drawings to farm workers before working his way back to Norway as a stoker at the start of the next whaling season.

Although somewhat romantically drawn to the myth of the seafaring Viking, Vike chose to pursue his art rather than continuing with life at sea. Western Australia's landscape and its clear, intense light had left an indelible impression on him, and he returned to Perth just prior to his twenty-third birthday in 1929 — the year of Western Australia's centenary of European settlement celebrations and of the Wall Street Crash that triggered the Great Depression. Speaking little English, the powerfully built but gentle Vike was employed briefly as a professional boxer, sketching and painting when he could.[82] The following year he met artist Leith Angelo while sketching in the city.

Angelo, born in the Western Australian goldfields town of Coolgardie in 1904, had worked as a drover and a mail truck driver in the state's north to save for art studies in Perth. He enrolled at Perth Technical College in 1927, under the tutelage of A.B. Webb,[83] and studied life drawing at the Linton Institute of Art. Vike and Angelo became drawing companions and firm friends. They rented a studio together in Beaufort Street,[84] just outside the city centre, where friends would drop by to paint and be regaled by colourful tales of Vike's Norwegian youth and his life at sea.

Vike also befriended the ageing curator of the Western Australian Museum and Art Gallery, George Pitt Morison, who had painted with Arthur Streeton, Tom Roberts and the Heidelberg School at their weekend art camps on the outskirts of Melbourne in the 1880s. Pitt Morison had studied at the National Gallery School in Melbourne and at the Academie Julian in Paris, and had been a companion of John Longstaff and Frederick McCubbin.[85] He encouraged and privately tutored Vike in oil painting and had a significant influence on Vike's landscape painting.

Vike and Angelo took up watercolour painting, making regular painting trips to the end of the Guildford train line, inspired in part by Pitt Morison's stories of the Heidelberg artists' camps. From 1930 to 1931 the pair also arranged a life drawing class, tutored by Ernst Dressler, that met in the upstairs studio of Greek-born artist Vlase Zanalis in Barrack Street, Perth.[86]

In November 1933, Vike, Angelo, John Oldham and William Thompson, who was to play a part in the initial Workers' Theatre production of *Till*

The Day I Die, exhibited at the annual West Australian Society of Arts exhibition. They received public praise for working in opposition to the classical styles espoused by the conservative WA Society of Arts in an exhibition dominated by traditional landscape painting.[87]

Defying tradition, Vike began to explore urban themes in his paintings and drawings. In 1934 he moved down Beaufort Street into the Trades Hall Flats (also known as the Trades Hall Apartments), adjoining the Trades Hall building and across the road from the public library, where he drew character sketches at night. A number of other Workers' Art Club members and Perth's left-wingers were also itinerant tenants of the Trades Hall Flats, and Vike was soon introduced to Katharine Susannah Prichard. He reluctantly joined the Communist Party, influenced by Angelo and other Trades Hall Flats tenants, and took up drawing political cartoons for *The Red Star*.[88]

5

'A MAN OF ENTERPRISE': KEITH GEORGE AND THE WORKERS' ART CLUB

At last Perth has a man of enterprise, ideas and a good deal of courage.[1]

By 1936, Western Australia's unemployment rate had fallen to five-point-six per cent — almost half the national average. The state election held early that year returned the Labor Government and delivered a poor result for the CPA, but Communist Party members could console themselves with brighter figures from the Soviet Union. Moscow was experiencing an increasing birth rate and a declining death rate — testament, no doubt, to the many wishing to enter the workers' paradise and the reluctance of many to leave.

In June 1936, a week before the Workers' Art Club went before the public with its first season of staged drama, the International Exhibition of Surrealism opened in London. The exhibition received considerable exposure in Perth's newspapers and, although the surrealist movement was by then more than a decade old, excited London like very little else had in recent times, with newspaper headlines declaring it 'a shocking art show' and warning readers about the 'girl subjects of surrealist paintings'.[2] As part of the event, Dylan Thomas served cups of boiled string and read a postcard aloud at a poetry performance attended by surrealist founder Paul Eluard, and Salvador Dalí gave a lecture in a deep-sea diver's suit, in which he nearly suffocated before fellow surrealist artist Roland Penrose was able to unmask him to allow Dalí to draw breath.[3]

That same year, Adolf Hitler opened the National Socialist Museum of Aryan Art in Germany.

And then there was Clifford Odets's *Till the Day I Die*, a watershed in theatre. Written the previous year for New York's Group Theatre, *Till the Day I Die* was one of the first plays to highlight the persecution of Communists in Nazi Germany. Set in Berlin in 1935, it depicted the cruelty and indignities suffered at the hands of the Nazis by underground militants working against Hitler's government. By mid-1936 it was playing in about fifty theatres across America, where it had 'created the greatest dramatic sensation in America in a decade'.[4]

The Workers' Art Club production of *Till the Day I Die* played at the Assembly Hall in Pier Street over two nights in June 1936. The Assembly Hall had been the St Andrew's church hall until it was converted into Perth's principal performance venue after His Majesty's Theatre, though it was uncomfortable and inferior to the Repertory Club Theatre.[5] There was no rake to the stage, and performers endured cramped conditions backstage.[6] People approaching the Assembly Hall to attend a performance of *Till the Day I Die* were met with the Salvation Army band performing on a nearby street corner.[7] Though both clarion calls of sorts, the sanctified music of the Salvos was in stark contrast to the highly charged play, which 'hit Perth like a bomb'.[8]

Keith George cut a serious figure during rehearsals, perpetually clad as he was in a dustcoat. He had spent close to a year preparing for these performances of *Till the Day I Die*, drilling his actors intensively — using Stanislavsky's 'method' technique — in an exacting choreography of poise, movement, dialogue and voice inflection. George was a commanding and, at times, fierce presence able to 'invoke' exceptional performances from his actors,[9] many of whom had never set foot on a stage before. Intense mental preparation of actors was integral to the method technique, which had found its way into Australian and American theatre through the international workers' theatre movement. Expedience played its part as well: the method lent itself to those with little theatrical experience.

While George was a method actor by nature and a student of Stanislavsky's writings, he never directly referred to the method when rehearsing a play and he departed from Stanislavsky on the issue of the script having primacy.[10] George was of the opinion that a theatre director's role was to 'interpret the word'.[11] Very little about the preparation and performance of a play was sacrosanct to George, something that irritated Prichard. '[George] has an idea,' she wrote to Louis Esson, 'that when he's producing, a play belongs to him, and the author is an unpleasant accident'.[12]

This difference in 'ideas of the respective functions' of the author and the director was an 'obstacle' between George and Prichard, to the point where he felt unable to direct plays written by her.[13] He was an advocate of the radical philosophies then sweeping the arts, as expressed in a 1931 publication titled *The New Movement in the Theatre*:

> The arts are ideal paraphrases of the social organisation of the world. As that organisation changes, either violently or imperceptibly, so also the arts change by abrupt or gentle degrees.[14]

Prichard's son Ric, who in adulthood would become a theatre acolyte of Keith George's, later observed that Australia had never before encountered theatre quite like that produced by George:

> Keith's method was wholly that of the 'marionette master'. He regarded his people as marionettes and he had the central creative, interpretive vision of a play, which he controlled throughout in all its aspects: its lighting, its sound and its staging, and in the performances. The result was stark realism and ... an imaginative approach to ... staging, lighting, sound and setting that had just never been seen before.[15]

Throssell described how George sometimes grafted a rigid 'mechanist' method of production onto a play, with the cast 'not using realistic acting' but rigid movement — 'a mannered kind of conventional acting'.[16]

The end result of George's work on *Till the Day I Die* was quite startling. *The West Australian*'s drama critic Paul Hasluck wrote of the first night's performance: 'There can be no mild words about the first major public show of the Workers' Theatre.'[17] Hasluck described the play itself as 'one of the most vital things that had ever punched America between the eyes', continuing:

> One came away from their play with the excitement of a prize-fight in the air [and] a large part of the audience which had crowded the Assembly Hall to the doors seemed to feel the same way.[18]

Paul Hasluck was a great fillip to Western Australian theatre in the 1930s. Born in 1905 into one of the state's respected old colonial families, he was raised in a pious Salvation Army household.[19] Robert Porter, in his biography of Hasluck, later observed that:

> while turning away from the religious aspects of his upbringing, the principal effect of his family environment was that it instilled in Hasluck as a young man a strong sense of duty and an obligation to work to relieve the suffering and distress of others ... The concept of duty — of seeking to do practical things to improve the condition of society and those within it — became an important and enduring feature of Hasluck's personality.[20]

Hasluck was widely read, and moved in a wide social circle, but:

did not become strongly attracted to theoretical beliefs of either a philosophical or a political kind. He was raised in an environment in which political doctrines were of little moment.'[21]

He joined the staff of *The West Australian* as a seventeen-year-old cadet reporter in 1922, and his initial experiences as a police and court roundsman were significant markers in his broad liberal politics.

> What I liked most was that newspaper work gave to me the chance to see events and people and to study facets of life I had never seen before ... I was eager for experience and curious about phases of life hitherto closed to me.[22]

As Trades Hall roundsman in the 1920s, Hasluck was:

> struck by the conservative nature of trade unionism. They were protecting the rights they had and ensuring that their members had a due share in the progress of an industry.[23]

He was sceptical of the 'great faith' of the trade union rank-and-file 'that the arbitration system would give them fitting returns for their labour', but he admired the devotion of many trade union leaders to the trade union movement:

> They were mainly self-educated and had great faith in self-improvement through education. They had an idealist faith in what education would do to make the working man a match for the privileged classes ... I discovered the humanity and the compassion for the weak and the dignity of labour that was in the mind of many trade union leaders.[24]

Hasluck's father often found fault with trade union officials' threats to withhold labour, but Hasluck himself 'appreciated the reasonableness of the claims they often made' and saw strikes as a reasonable response 'when labour was not reasonably rewarded'.[25]

This moderate view perhaps reflected the relatively benign industrial relations climate of the 1920s, before the increased trade union militancy that arose with the onset of the Depression. As a member of the Australian Journalists' Association (AJA) and of its district committee, of which his friend John Curtin was president, Hasluck was himself an active trade unionist, and he remained on the AJA committee, to which he was elected in 1924 as the cadets' candidate, for more than twelve years. He was intelligent, inquisitive and politically pragmatic and, at that time, ideologically a relatively free agent, and this made him an outstanding journalist and critic. In the mid-1930s he wrote a series of newspaper articles on the troubling plight of Australia's Aboriginal people, which he viewed as a social problem — a brave and extremely progressive view at that time.

In the late 1920s, Hasluck's interest in theatre led him to the Perth Repertory Club, and in 1933 he persuaded *The West Australian* to publish a regular theatre column, which he wrote under the nom de plume Polygon. He was one of very few serious-minded and erudite classical drama critics writing for the Australian press at the time, and is credited by *A Companion to Theatre in Australia* as a considerable influence on 'the development of theatrical taste in Western Australia'.[26] He was an associate member of the Workers' Art Club and often attended Workers' Theatre rehearsals.[27]

Of the Workers' Art Club production of *Till the Day I Die*, Hasluck wrote — displaying the sort of political objectivity that was a hallmark of his critiques — that although the play was 'frankly propagandist',

> the propaganda glows with such a fierce fervour and the play has such a tremendous passionate energy that, without regard to the facts, one is exhilarated by it [and] non-partisans in the stalls can surely be forgiven for the thrill and the elation they felt at seeing the precision of that strong, swinging blow.[28]

The production employed highly original and unorthodox theatrical techniques, paring down much that was traditionally associated with the presentation of contemporary theatre and breaking many technical conventions of staging, for which Hasluck praised George: 'At last Perth has a man of enterprise, ideas and a good deal of courage'.[29]

No curtain was used, and set changes were organised within the audience and carried out during blackouts between scenes.[30] Cast member Phyllis Harnett recalled that, in the style of the Russian theatre of Meyerhold, 'We were breaking down the front proscenium and rushing the sets up and down.'[31] The lighting, rather than being designed merely to reveal the action on stage, was elaborate and kinetic. A spotlight trained on cast members created what Hasluck described as 'bold pictures'.[32] George primarily used side lighting in his productions, rather than the traditional battens or footlights, and displayed a rich understanding and capacity for the design and arrangement of colour, texture and movement in his lighting.[33]

Another departure from conventional staging was the performance of part of the play within the audience. In a scene depicting a Communist Party gathering, players moved out into the audience and a platform speaker addressed both the audience and the players from the stage. This device, a feature of the theatre of Bertolt Brecht, was designed to magnify the play's impact by breaking down audience detachment from the performance.

The *Daily News* quoted an unnamed 'official of the Worker's Theatre' in describing this dramatic reformation:

> Modern methods of production aim at doing away with the illusion of the theatre and bringing the audience into the action of the play ... [The play] had no formal opening or end, but is [sic] presented to the audience as a slice of life ... The idea was not to settle the audience, by music or a formal opening, into the comfortable frame of mind which usually precedes a theatrical entertainment, but to keep them in a state of dramatic suspense from beginning to end. Similarly, it was hoped to send them away feeling they had seen a series of real events. To have broken up in a formal manner by singing the National Anthem or anything else would have provided an anti-climax. The method of production was so effective that members of the audiences voted during the meeting scene and when the prisoner's fingers were smashed by the Nazi captain a woman called out that she would leave if it happened again. Although the methods we used are new to this State, they are common overseas and represent a tendency in the contemporary theatre.[34]

The omission of the singing of the national anthem prior to performances of *Till the Day I Die*, as was tradition at that time, led to quite an outcry and the Workers' Art Club received particularly strong criticism from a quite unexpected quarter — Jewish newspaper *The Westralian Judean*. The paper praised the play's anti-Nazi line and 'the vigor of interpretation of the cast', but damned the lack of 'a passive appreciation of the symbol of British liberty and justice':

> Apparently the committee of the Workers' Theatre thought it a bourgeois act to sing the National Anthem. Though British rule

might, in their opinion be sadly lacking in comparison with that of Soviet Russia, they did have the opportunity of witnessing in the play itself, the type of government that obtains in Germany; and in comparison they might have at least paid some tribute to the democratic spirit of the British people that permits the production of such propagandist plays.[35]

A police siren howled aggravatingly at each change of scene in the Workers' Art Club production 'to create nervous tension for the next fistful of shocks'.[36] Odets had suggested creating this concatenating effect in the stage directions of the published play by means of 'shrill' whistles 'variously pitched, slowing with hysterical intensity'.[37] The siren was used instead as a narrative device to telegraph an impending police raid as well as a ploy 'to jangle the nerves' of the audience and maintain 'a spirit of tension' experienced by the characters portrayed on stage, living ceaselessly with the fear of Nazi arrest and torture.[38] And jangle the nerves it did. Prichard complained to Louis Esson that George 'insisted on having a siren blasting out before each act, until the [room] nearly [rose] from one's head.'[39] When she protested to George, who was fond of teasing Prichard, that the siren was driving her mad, his response was, 'It's intended to, my dear!'[40]

While the siren and spotlight effects were much discussed and drove some critics to distraction as well,[41] Phyllis Harnett felt that George's 'control of those sirens and his control of a thing like the metronome', which ticked incessantly through his next play, 'were part of his genius'.[42] Beryl Hearder (formerly Seward), a noted stage and radio drama actress of the time who attended a performance of the play, recalled that the flashing spotlight 'blinders' that George trained on the audience between scenes to screen the set changes caused the audience some difficulty in initially focusing on the subsequent scene; George also used a large gong which was struck at the end of a scene, creating such a noise that 'everybody lifted out of their seats'.[43] All in all, the production was a revolution, and Keith George fondly remembered the play many years later:

> In the first place the vitality and sincerity of a cast consisting of completely untrained actors, the long careful production with its minute attention to detail so different to the repertory club's slap-dash efforts … and finally the freshness and topicality of the play all combined to make it a success. Katharine was of course delighted and almost forgave me my sins.[44]

Despite their philosophical bickering, Prichard and George had developed a genuine respect and great affection for each other. Prichard had found in George the capable ringmaster necessary to make the Workers' Theatre a success, and he became increasingly devoted to her, later saying, 'Had she been advocating the introduction of voodoo, I'd have helped her with the same enthusiasm.'[45]

Despite George's 'capacity for making Katharine laugh',[46] his trademark theatrical 'sins' would continue to test Prichard, although she boasted to Louis Esson after the production of *Till the Day I Die* that George was 'the best producer, bar none'.[47] Prichard did not approve of George's use of gimmickry to garner publicity for the Workers' Theatre, however effective it may have been. She 'deplored this intensely', George later wrote, but 'I was arrogant and refused to yield'.[48]

George exploited the existence of the National Socialist (Nazi) Party of Western Australia (known locally as the Blueshirts), and encouraged a rumour that members of the group were planning to 'raid' a performance of *Till the Day I Die* — a rumour that gained a lot of currency. A Sydney newspaper reported that the play had a 'stormy season' in Perth and that its 'appearance coincided with the first public appearance of the Western Australian Blueshirts'.[49] This is certainly true, although whether, as the newspaper also reported, a small local band of Blueshirts attempted to disrupt a performance of the play from the theatre's gallery 'at the first words criticising Nazism, but were put out', is doubtful.

While George certainly created fresh and challenging theatre and was by nature flamboyant, he was also, by design, initially anonymous. He was not named on the theatre program — the production of *Till the Day I Die* was credited to the Workers' Art Club as a whole — and he performed in the play under the stage name Francis Juleff. Such was the philosophy of the 'new theatre'.

> The catchcry was 'the play's the thing' — an idea which did not prevail in commercial theatre.[50]

George's method, however, was far from collaborative. He refused to concede any control of a production to others, and his command of the stage ensured that he maintained the sovereignty he insisted on. To cast member George Wignall, George was 'the pivot' whence the 'force' and 'charisma came'.[51]

Despite the length and intensity of rehearsals for *Till the Day I Die*, Phyllis Harnett and the few other seasoned cast members had low expectations, given the inexperience of most of the cast, but it 'went absolutely perfectly'.[52] The cast relished 'the great thrill' of performances and 'agreed whole-heartedly with the spirit' of the play.[53]

Perth's middle class 'came in hordes' to see the play, with 'packed houses and cheering crowds' introduced to an otherwise sedate theatre scene.[54] People were turned away from the door on the second night, and the season was extended for a further four nights.[55] Prichard reported with delight that Keith George had 'created a sensation'.[56]

Despite its other glowing reviews, Paul Hasluck was critical of the pace of the performance of *Till the Day I Die* at times, as well as what he saw as the less than precise handling of the spotlight on players and the resultant shadow effects on stage.[57] Those rough shadows, however, were integral to the aesthetic of this and the group's later plays, and George had spent time carefully planning and experimenting with the shadows cast by players and the set into the depth of the stage.

Hasluck singled out Frank O'Grady's leading role in the play for special commendation. O'Grady's character, written to serve as a role model to political activists, was that of a Communist organiser tortured to breaking point by the Nazis in the hope that he would identify his Communist associates, and then released in the hope that he would lead the Gestapo to them. Fearing that he might inadvertently betray his friends, O'Grady's character takes his own life. O'Grady himself, son of a Kalgoorlie miner, was a fine actor and a Five Arts Club alumnus; Phyllis Harnett thought him an even better actor 'when Keith got hold of him'.[58] O'Grady also performed with Perth's Shakespeare Club and with the Repertory Club. Tragically, his role in *Till the Day I Die* would later play out off stage, with his life indeed imitating art.

Howard Smith, by day a draughtsman with the government's Lands Department, played the role of Carl Tausig, another member of the underground tortured by the Gestapo and sent back to his family 'broken and smelling of perfumed soap' to give the appearance of his collaboration.[59] Smith was a similarly imposing and talented actor and an active and influential figure in the Perth Workers' Art club, later to be its long-serving secretary.[60] Other leading players in the cast included commercial artist Ian ('Bob') Smith, then secretary of the Workers' Art Club, Phyllis Harnett and Maurie Lachberg. Harald Vike played the role of a Nazi stormtrooper and, with Leith Angelo's help, designed and built the set. Angelo also designed the striking modern poster for the play, which other members would 'run around town with paste pots at midnight and put up all over the place, being chased by police'.[61]

The Workers' Art Club took the play on the road. John Hepworth recounted a jam-packed performance for the Yugoslav community in a hall in the Swan Valley, outside Perth. During a scene set in a Nazi barracks, Nazi stormtroopers beat their Jewish prisoners, including Hepworth who played the role of a young Jewish boy. When Hepworth was being kicked, a voice bellowed from the audience, 'Leave the kid alone!', causing the actors playing the stormtroopers to back off a little, 'and coming down the aisle there's a phalanx of enormous fucking Yugoslavs, all brandishing their fists and salamis: "Leave the kid alone! Stop kicking the kid!", and the brutal stormtroopers pissed off out the back, leaving us in absolute possession of the stage!' Hepworth recalled.[62]

In the eastern states, the play encountered hostility of a different kind. The German consul-general complained to the federal government about the Sydney New Theatre's performance of *Till the Day I Die*, calling the play an affront to the German government and to the German nation. New South Wales Chief Secretary Frank Chaffey subsequently banned the play as 'unfitting for the preservation of good manners and decorum', opining that it 'did not truly represent conditions' in Germany, 'that it was insulting to some people, and that it tended to be prejudicial to good order in the community'.[63] Police officers asked to examine the offending script thought the play 'undeniably powerful and moving', but 'sordid and even brutal' in its characterisation of the Nazis.[64]

> It is frankly propagandist; there is scarcely a hint of objectivity … The Jewish question is an undercurrent throughout the piece … A German Nazi might particularly resent the description … 'a man like Goering' … There are also quotations from alleged broadcasts by Dr. Goebbels which show him in an unfavourable light.[65]

On the advice of federal attorney-general Robert Menzies, Prime Minister Joseph Lyons sent a circular to state premiers informing them of community dissension about *Till the Day I Die* and the fact that the federal government regarded the New Theatre League as a Communist auxiliary. The federal government had no power of control over the play's production in theatres and other venues licensed under state laws, 'but as the N.S.W. Government had decided to prohibit the play [Lyons] felt it advisable that other State Premiers should be in possession of the facts in case the matter came up for their consideration.'[66] *The Daily Telegraph* newspaper in Sydney reported that the Chief Secretary of Western Australia 'saw no reason to prohibit [the play], and the public showed their appreciation by packing the house every night.'[67]

There was widespread public denunciation of the play's banning in New South Wales, and Sydney's New Theatre defied the ban, announcing that it would stage the play again in late July 1936. Ten minutes into this performance a police officer went backstage and insisted that the play be stopped.[68] The audience showed its support for the cast and the performance continued uninterrupted despite the arrival of police reinforcements. Prosecutions against cast members were later prepared but not enforced.[69] Sydney New Theatre secretary Victor Arnold, however, was charged on summons with contravention of the *Theatres and Public Halls Act 1908* (NSW) but, as the ban had effect only on performances of the play in public venues for which admission was charged, Sydney's New Theatre staged another free private performance at its rooms in Pitt Street a week later without interruption. Uniformed police stood outside the doors and plain-clothed police in the audience took notes during the play. The audience included invited state and federal members of parliament, trade union representatives, university student organisation members, academics and members of the clergy.[70] By dint of publicity of the play's ban and of the subsequent prosecution of Arnold, *Till the Day I Die* continued to be performed widely to large audiences across the state. There were more than 150 private performances of the play in New South Wales before its ban was lifted in 1941, including weekly performances at the New Theatre.

There was also an official government ban in place in Victoria, and Melbourne's New Theatre found that all venues at which they attempted to stage the play were made unavailable. When the Mayor of Collingwood made the Collingwood Town Hall available for a performance, police surrounded the venue and the cast and audience were locked out. New South Wales and Victoria were the only places in the world where performance of the play was banned.

The West Australian published the following letter to the editor in September 1936:

> Sir, —
>
> 'Till the Day I Die' must be banned. I protest emphatically against the authorities allowing that Communistic play to be repeated at the Trades Hall tonight and tomorrow.

This play has already been banned in Sydney, and I call upon the proper authorities to prevent at all costs the re-staging of it here.

I have seen the play, and while I must admit the stage and lighting effects were excellent, I feel as a Britisher that the portrayal of Fascists as criminals and murderers is untrue. I believe that in this troubled world every attempt should be made to bring about understanding amongst nations …

Thousands of people's minds have been poisoned. The authorities have taken no action.

Finally, it reflects great shame upon our existing theatrical bodies when it is left to such an organisation as the 'Workers' Art Guild' to produce a play on such an excellent scale — but, unfortunately, a play not in the interest of freedom-loving Britishers.

Britisher (East Perth)[71]

Perhaps Keith George was the author of this letter.

6

THE WORKERS' ART GUILD AND THE PARTY LINE

The dogs may bark, but the caravan moves on.[1]

The Workers' Art Club production of *Till the Day I Die* was a great financial success. It left the group with the windfall of a £300 profit at a time when very few amateur theatre companies made money, and allowed it to continue its expansion. A literary section, which had been under consideration since the group's inception, was established in June 1936, and organised lectures on literature as well as classes in the writing of drama, poetry, short stories and journalism; it also included a writers' group led by Bill Darbyshire, a writer of high standing in Perth at the time.[2] From its early stages, the writers' group fixed on the idea of writing plays about local issues 'of social significance'.[3] The group held fortnightly meetings with Keith George as writing tutor, and initially explored the process of collaborative writing. One of its early activities, in mid- to late 1936, was an attempt to write a play on the social impact of the Group Settlement Scheme at Manjimup in the south-west of the state.[4]

There was a lot of public interest at that time in the Group Settlement Scheme, which had been established by the Western Australian state government in 1921, in line with the national White Australia policy. The scheme provided blocks of land in the state's south-west to groups of British immigrants, in the main, to be developed into farms in the hope of buoying the state's flagging agricultural economy.[5] The scheme was characterised as a charitable enterprise but it provided little reward. It was a disaster. Nearly all suitable farming land had been taken up prior to the scheme's introduction, and the land given over to the scheme was of poor quality. The migrant settlers were ill-prepared for the task. Groups of settler families moved into inhospitable conditions on ballot-allocated 100-acre blocks, many densely wooded with some of the tallest trees in the world, which they were expected to clear. The cost of clearing and developing the blocks far exceeded the financial assistance provided to the settlers by the state government, in the form of a thirty-year loan, in exchange for eventual freehold title. By 1924, forty-two per cent of the settlements had been abandoned. Many found themselves unable to meet the repayments on property loans, and the Depression put paid to the hopes of even the most resolute Group Settlers. What little income they earned derived from the production of butterfat from dairy cows, and when the price of butterfat collapsed during the Depression their fate was sealed. The Agricultural Bank, which charged exorbitant interest on Group Settler loans, foreclosed and evicted many. Others simply walked off their land, and by the mid-1930s the scheme was all but dead.[6]

One of these Group Settlers was invited to address the Workers' Art Club writers' group and provide biographical material for a cooperative writing venture about the scheme — a venture that also failed.[7] The collaboration was thwarted by the diverse politics of the writers' group members and by the lack of any 'plan for division of labour'.[8] To some degree Keith George's own cussedness 'stood in the way of the writing', but the CPA members in the writers' group, including Phyllis Harnett, John Hepworth and Gordon Burgoyne, must also have infuriated both George and Darbyshire with their interminable critical self-analyses of whether the material they were writing propagated the 'correct' Marxist line — an affliction common among CPA members.[9]

The Workers' Art Club was not a singularly political CPA enterprise, as evidenced by the involvement in the writers' group of 'respectable' Perth writers such as Bill Darbyshire and Gavin Casey. However, the challenge of writing within the prevailing Party line was stymieing and frustrating for people such as Phyllis Harnett, who later recalled:

> You were always being held up by somebody's opinions on what was Marxist and what wasn't and of course this applied more to the writers than anybody else ... I was unable to write for years because of my attachment to the Communist Party. I had this feeling that I couldn't really be a poet of the sort I was by nature because, I mean, it wasn't revolutionary. It had to be not only revolutionary, but really crude propaganda.[10]

John Hepworth later wrote of the 'Party line' impediment:

> the passionately turgid discussions of the CPA cultural committees trying to determine whether this or that line of verse, or note of music or blob of paint was essentially working class, or fascist, bourgeois or decadent, were as hilariously absurd in their way as

any medieval convocation of cardinals trying to settle the vexed question of how many angels could dance on the point of a pin.[11]

Bill Darbyshire did manage to cobble together a preliminary draft of the Group Settlement play, but it proved difficult to gather the four to six writers together at the same time to complete the project. Meanwhile Hepworth, a young but exceptionally gifted writer, was also working on the fringes of the group writing his own play about the Group Settlement Scheme, *We Are Hungry*, which he submitted to the West Australian Drama Festival writers' competition the following year.

Hepworth had been an early member of the Workers' Theatre group, and had begun to attract 'security interest' when he was arrested with sixteen-year-old George Wignall in June 1935 for pasting up Communist Party posters in the city for Gus Stagg[12] and the Radical Bookshop. At the time, Hepworth was just thirteen.[13] Born Alfred John Christmass in Pinjarra, Western Australia, in 1921, Hepworth was defiant from birth, growing up in a solid left-wing family and apparently joining the Communist Party at the age of twelve. He claimed to have been run out of Manjimup for being a 'dangerous agitator' while trying to organise a tobacco workers' union there as a thirteen-year-old.[14] He subsequently moved to Perth with his mother and stepfather, where he was educated for a time at Perth Modern School and the Perth Public Library — the latter in a self-driven capacity. Despite having little formal education, he had a great command of language and an impressive capacity to memorise and recite, by rote, long and complex passages of Marxist–Leninist theory 'in amended version'. This dialectic potential so impressed Party officials in Perth that plans were made to send him to the International Lenin School in Moscow to further his Party studies and groom him for greater things in the CPA — 'but fortunately', Hepworth later wrote, 'I discovered sex and alcohol about this time.'[15]

Hepworth lived in a ramshackle boarding house managed by his mother in Aberdeen Street, in lively North Perth.[16] The tenants, scathingly described by Keith George as 'lumpen proletariat', were an odd mix of Party members in the main.[17] In Perth's neighbouring red-light district of Roe Street, police turned a blind eye to illegal brothels where many workers, recruited in France, set about earning their fares home.[18] Perth's Greek and Italian quarters, and the James Street precinct of market gardens and opium dens where pre-federation Chinese immigrants resided, were also nearby.

Soon after joining the Workers' Theatre, Hepworth moved into the Trades Hall Flats in Beaufort Street where many of the founding members of the

Workers' Theatre were then living. Reportedly 'the cheapest accommodation in town', the Trades Hall Flats were 'crammed with comrades and itinerant actors', and must have been a lively establishment in the 1930s.[19] Tenants of the flats mingled with Labor Party and trade union figures at the adjacent Court Hotel.[20] Maurie Lachberg and Harald Vike were Trades Hall Flats tenants, as were Phyllis Harnett, Albert Osterberg and his later wife Irene Keiller, Dorothy Tangney (who would later become the first female member of the Australian Senate, on her election as a Western Australian Labor Senator in 1943) and artist Herbert McClintock.[21]

McClintock was born in Perth in 1906. His uncle Alexander McClintock was a landscape painter associated with the Heidelberg School, and in 1912 the family moved from Perth to Heidelberg on Melbourne's outskirts. At the age of about fourteen, McClintock started a process-engraving apprenticeship and in 1922, on his employer's instructions, he enrolled at Melbourne's prestigious National Gallery Art School where he met and befriended influential painter, teacher and art critic George Bell. McClintock painted, read Nietzsche, Schopenhauer and Dostoyevsky, and lurked around the hub of Melbourne bohemia — Fasoli's Cafe. In 1927 he moved to Sydney to begin work as a commercial artist at *The Sydney Morning Herald*, and it was here that he really learned the art of painting 'off old [William] Dobell by just standing around his studio up at the Cross', he would later recall.[22]

In 1929 McClintock returned to Melbourne and re-enrolled at the National Gallery School, where he studied with Roy Dalgarno, Noel Counihan, James Flett, Judah Waten and Nutter Buzacott, who later married McClintock's sister. McClintock later claimed that he 'had off and on been interested in left-wing politics', though he could not 'claim ever to have been an activist', but given the company he kept and the fact that his father had been a 'Wobbly' (a member of the Industrial Workers of the World, or IWW), he joined the Communist Party in 1930 and exhibited for the first time with Eric Thake and James Flett.[23]

In late 1930 McClintock, with Judah Waten, co-edited *Strife*, a one-off political journal published in support of unemployment relief which was seized by police as it was being handed out.[24] *Strife* advocated immediate revolution and the violent overthrow of the moribund institutions of the state, including art galleries.[25] McClintock and Waten were ordered by police to leave Melbourne within a day of the seizure of *Strife* and, when they did not, were charged with vagrancy.[26] Genuinely concerned about workers' conditions during the Depression, McClintock also worked with other left-wing artists as a sometime political cartoonist to expose their plight.

After two years spent wandering in search of work, he moved back to Sydney where he met and married Pat Carlon in 1933. The following year they moved to Perth, where his notoriety was assured. There, employed by commercial art firm Gibbney and Son, McClintock took charge of commercial art for the advertising department of the *Daily News*. He also took up professional singing, with performances on ABC radio. To protect his employment as a commercial artist and to differentiate his identities as a painter and as a singer, he took on the artist pseudonym of Max Ebert — a play on his nickname, Herbert Mac.

McClintock's Trades Hall Flats co-tenant Albert Osterberg was born in London in 1897. His French father and Swedish paternal grandfather were English crown jewellers for the coronation of King Edward VII. After his father's death in Paris when Osterberg was four years of age, his mother and siblings returned to poverty in London before moving to live with Osterberg's maternal grandfather, blacksmith Henry Morgan-Jones, in the Forest of Dean, near the Welsh border. Within a year, Morgan-Jones had also died.

At the age of eighteen, Osterberg was taken by his paternal grandfather to visit the grave of Karl Marx at Highgate cemetery in London, marking his introduction to socialism.[27] Osterberg's paternal grandfather, an influential figure in his life, had been a member of the Paris Commune. Hailed as the world's first proletarian revolution, the commune was a movement sacred to socialists. It had arisen following the French government's suppression of a popular insurrection in March 1871 during the long siege of Paris by the Prussian army.

After serving in the First World War, Albert Osterberg migrated to Western Australia in 1928, where he became active in the Amalgamated Engineering Union.[28] He was also a cheery and enthusiastic member of the Workers' Art Club, always around the theatre. He teamed up with Maurie Lachberg, with whom he worked at the Midland Railway Workshops, and they both gave the appearance of being 'working class to their bootstraps. They were ideologically intelligent and articulate and they were violently alive', but there was little about either of them that was authentically working class.[29] Osterberg married Irene Keiller; Lachberg married her sister Olive. Both Keiller sisters were members of the Workers' Art Guild.

In August 1936, the Workers' Art Club changed its name to the Workers' Art Guild, perhaps to differentiate or disassociate itself from the CPA-controlled Workers' Art Clubs of New South Wales and Victoria.[30] The precise reason for the name change is not known; however, in a report on the formation of Army repertory companies written by Keith George in July 1943, George referred to his admiration of the New York Theatre Guild, so perhaps this played a part.[31] The title of Guild was not uncommon for arts companies at the time.

In late 1936 the Workers' Art Guild moved into its own premises, above car and motorcycle showroom Mortlock Motors on the corner of Hay and Elder Streets on the city's western edge. The premises had previously been rented by a group of former students of art teacher James W.R. Linton, including Linton's deputy Betsey Currie, in order to continue their life drawing classes; it is interesting to note that Phyllis Harnett was under the misapprehension that the space had previously been the studio of Linton himself.

> When we got [Mortlock's], it had been Mr Linton's studio [sic] and it was heavily decorated with the plaster casts that all technical colleges used to teach sculpture at the time ... heads of Scipio and heads of Voltaire ... I had done my little time as a sculpture student at Sydney Tech and I was very familiar with these heads, but I resented them being around our Workers' Art Guild — my art ethos was something [quite different] and I felt enmity [towards] this kind of art that Mr Linton purveyed to Perth.[32]

It was to be art's new guard sweeping out the old, and this 'enmity' was shared by many of Harnett's peers.

There were at least three generations of James Linton who were artists: James Walter Robert Linton himself; his English father, Sir James Dromgole Linton, who had been president of the Royal Institute of Painters in Watercolours and was knighted in 1885 for his services to British art; and James W.R. Linton's son, James Alexander Barrow ('Jamie') Linton. Through the early part of the century until the mid- to late 1930s, James W.R. Linton commanded the arts scene in Perth, but to the new guard of the later 1930s he was an anachronism, regarded by those such as Harnett as a 'sacred cow who stood in the way of all art [and] prevented the West Australian artist from knowing what art was up to in the present'.[33] Linton had attended London's prestigious Slade School of Fine Art in its heyday, and had founded the Linton Art School in Perth at 636 Hay Street in 1901. From 1932 until 1938, the Linton Institute of Art—a partnership between Linton and his son Jamie—was located in a large upstairs studio above the Commercial Bank on the corner of Hay and King Streets, opposite His Majesty's theatre.[34]

Stairs on the left-hand side of the Mortlock Motors building led up to the large, open-plan Workers' Art Guild premises, which occupied the entire first floor. At the top of the stairs was a landing and a large noticeboard; the Guild rooms housed a worn-out piano and a small corner office.[35]

> There were a lot of easels piled up because Harald [Vike] had his art class. There were knockabout chairs all over the place ... But it couldn't have been plainer — there was no furniture, as such, there were pictures on the wall and posters, of course, before posters became an art form — these were political posters ... There was no stage. They'd rehearse on this big floor-space.[36]

The floor was partitioned. Vike had a painting corner and Tom Wignall (Jnr) had shelving in which his stage props were stored. Different Guild activities and classes took place each night. The Guild encouraged meetings and gatherings in its rooms and played an important social role as a place where 'people could expand a little'.[37] It developed into a significant cultural institution that hosted public addresses on often contentious social and political topics. Significant and eminent intellectuals, academics, authors, artists and visiting dignitaries spoke on such subjects as science, civil liberties, citizens' rights, anthropology and Indigenous culture.

Workers' Art Guild members were a disparate mix of the conventional and the not so. It was by no means a blue-collar institution. Many local small business identities, commercial art employees and journalists became leading lights. Social interchange within the Guild was sometimes fraught and class differences and antagonisms were not entirely subsumed. Some middle-class CPA members in the Guild enjoyed the companionship of working-class members and, indeed, endeavoured to 'proletarianise' themselves, but many found it difficult to dispel class prejudice. A number of working-class members had difficulty with middle-class professionals belonging to a 'workers' club', which they felt should remain their preserve.

Middle-class Guild figure Kathleen Beechey found the mix liberating, because she felt that 'working-class people had never really had that strict moral censorship over their lives that the middle class had.'[38] Outside Guild ranks, some middle-class Guild members were treated as pariahs by their peers who thought the Guild 'immoral, depraved and evil'.[39]

Membership of the Workers' Art Guild was ostensibly open to anyone for an initiation fee of one shilling and an ongoing fee of one shilling a month, but new members had to be nominated by an existing Guild member.⁴⁰ Despite its avowed liberalism, the Guild was somewhat constrained by contemporary conventional social mores and prejudices, and its management committee, to the horror of some Guild members, persisted in refusing membership applications to a member of the Council Against War and Fascism, simply because he was a known homosexual.⁴¹ The Guild did, however, include a high proportion of women in positions of influence, unlike the wider ranks of the Communist Party and its subsidiaries, in which women were largely marginalised.⁴²

The art and theatre of the Workers' Art Guild gave expression to marginalised social concerns and gave vent to a resurgent political movement. It had a contemporary relevance for many that was hard to find in any other forum. Despite this, there were some who thought the institution rather more exclusive than consensual. There was patently a hierarchy of prestige and influence in the Guild, with many of Prichard's and George's protégés on high.

The Guild continued to expand, and by November 1936 it included a producer's class with plans for tuition in fine and commercial art, as well as dance and music wings.

By late 1936, the Guild's children's theatre section, which appears to have been one of Keith George's pet projects, was up and running. The idea might initially have been Prichard's: she had attended the Children's Theatre in Moscow in 1933, and it was surely a concept borrowed from the Russian theatre. The section was initiated by Keith George and Phyllis Harnett, and was conducted on Saturday afternoons in the Guild rooms with the help of John Hepworth and Kathleen Beechey.⁴³ It was Harnett's role to coordinate the children's theatre, and Hepworth remembered it as a 'vigorous' wing of the Guild.⁴⁴ The children were to be the 'junior teams' from which the Guild would draw its future casts.⁴⁵

One of the group's leading lights was seven-year-old Rolf Harris, son of Agnes Harris, a Welsh immigrant who made her Guild debut in *Bury the Dead* alongside her twelve-year-old son Bruce—the first of many roles she played for the Guild theatre.⁴⁶

Gordon Burgoyne wrote a play for the Guild children's theatre. Entitled *Heil Jones*, it was a parody on Hitler and was performed in the Guild rooms over consecutive Saturday afternoons, with an entirely junior cast. John Hepworth recalled it as 'a good virtuous play politically, but also a rattling good yarn'.⁴⁷

Perth Repertory Club actor Henry Cuthbertson, a cadet radio announcer and an acquaintance of Phyllis Harnett's, invited Harnett to bring her fledgling children's theatre group into the radio studio for his program, but shifted uncomfortably in his seat when the children went to air reciting 'some violently anti-war poetry'.[48]

The children's theatre group proved very popular but was later hampered by increasing Guild sectarianism. Harnett and others on the Guild's management committee had suggested that, to keep the section viable, the children should pay a small fee to attend the classes. The fairly inconsiderable sum would be used to cover the costs of running the section properly, and to ensure that the group maintained some financial independence from the main body of the Guild. Keith George objected strongly, digging his heels in over an issue that seemed relatively inconsequential. A fierce verbal row ensued and there followed meeting after meeting to weigh up the pros and cons of charging the children. George won the day, and he and Harnett fell out over the issue.[49] The children's theatre section disbanded some time before June 1938.

7

'BURY THE DEAD'

A play about the war that is to begin tomorrow night.[1]

In October 1936, Nettie Palmer visited Prichard at Greenmount, after a year spent with her husband Vance in Barcelona at the heart of the Spanish Civil War. She wrote, somewhat concerned, to Vance that Prichard was:

> ... pretty ill — haggard and a bad colour — but game and energetic ... She does odd literary jobs when she can find time, but does four furious days' work a week for the [P]arty, organising, holding meetings, building up movements that will be spearheads, including a very flourishing Workers' Theatre.[2]

For Prichard, the Workers' Art Guild theatre was an integral arm of the CPA's Popular Front work.

John Oldham and Ray McClintock — by now a couple, though McClintock was yet to divorce — had arranged to see Prichard at Greenmount in August 1936 and, despite her concerns about potential public scandal at their relationship, Prichard encouraged them to join the CPA. Oldham and McClintock were vetted by CPA officials before their induction. They were interviewed by Gus Stagg rather than by district secretary Bill Mountjoy as was usual practice.[3]

> [Stagg] was supposed to be a middle-class person so they had him interview us to see if he thought we were genuine ... anyway, we passed the test ... and then ... Katharine suggested that we should work with the middle class and particularly in the cultural field where we had a ... background.[4]

Oldham's trials were not limited to his inquisition by Party officials. His political conversion led him to suffer the not-unexpected slings and arrows of his middle-class peers. His CPA membership made him, as he described it, 'a renegade from my class at the time'.[5]

Three days after their Greenmount visit, at which Prichard had also recommended they join the Workers' Art Guild, Oldham and McClintock attended a lecture given by Arthur Rudkin on 'Art, Literature and Communism', which included a discussion on the place of art in the 'class struggle'. They were subsequently appointed by Prichard to the Workers' Art Guild committee, with Keith George's approval, and immediately set about organising their own contribution to cultural debates through the forum of the Guild.[6] The couple prepared a series of Guild lectures examining 'The Origins of the Arts',[7] with McClintock speaking about music and Oldham about painting and sculpture. These lectures were delivered once a week in the Guild rooms, over at least six weeks, with the Bauhaus and the influential Bauhaus artist László Moholy-Nagy serving as 'the inspiration for our whole approach'.[8]

Oldham also set up an art and architecture study course in the Guild rooms, based on the contemporary ideas of Moholy-Nagy and the Bauhaus.[9]

> We were deeply interested in the contemporary movement ... and I felt that [the Bauhaus] was more appropriate to the Workers' Art Guild than just straight architecture.[10]

Oldham was keen to set up a library in the Guild rooms, an idea borrowed from the Russian workers' art clubs, and he managed to persuade a somewhat reluctant McClintock to donate books from her extensive personal collection.[11] They included English classics, more contemporary literature by writers including James Joyce, and Soviet novels *Man Changes His Skin* by Bruno Jasienski and Mikhail Sholokhov's *And Quiet Flows the Don*, so beloved of Communist Party members at that time.[12]

Oldham and McClintock were also 'full of' W.H. Auden, Christopher Isherwood, Cecil Day-Lewis, Walt Whitman and the modern writers of the Left.[13] They attended a UWA Adult Education course on poetry conducted by Alexander ('Alec') King, brother-in-law of Cecil Day-Lewis and a friend of W.H. Auden. As a lecturer in English at the University of Western Australia, King was an influential figure in the political and cultural education of many of his students. Raised in a conservative family, he was a liberal link to a politically progressive English culture, and he 'took a very personal interest in his students':

> He used to invite us down to his house for gatherings of an evening to discuss various writers and so forth [and] he used to

have gatherings of an evening in his study at the university [of] little groups who were interested. He would take an interest in any student who was attempting to write ... In those days the university was so small ... so it was very intimate.[14]

Although King held much of the literary canon in high regard, the literature that he particularly admired was that of a new and younger generation of 'modern' writers challenging the academy. He not only shared his enthusiasm for the works of T.S. Eliot and D.H. Lawrence, but also introduced his students to the literature of Auden, Isherwood, Day-Lewis, Ezra Pound, Stephen Spender, James Joyce, Browning and Irish playwright Sean O'Casey, before many of them were much known, as well as to a number of American writers then overlooked in Anglocentric Perth.[15] He would read poetry aloud to his students, revelling in the language and encouraging his students to discover poetry's sensualism. Writer Dorothy Hewett recalled her first lecture with King in 1941, at which he spoke on Wordsworth:

> He tells us that if we want to understand Wordsworth's relationship to nature, we should go out of the lecture theatre, take off our shoes, and feel the grass springing under the soles of our bare feet. I am the only student who takes him at his word, striding out across the green lawns, shoes in hand, rejoicing at Wordsworth between my toes.[16]

King was born in Dorset in England in 1904, and grew up there with Cecil Day-Lewis.[17] The pair attended Oxford University together, where Day-Lewis introduced King to Auden's celebrated Oxford poetry group in the 1920s. King read classics at New College, Oxford, before entering teacher training in London where he met his future wife, Catherine, daughter of Walter Murdoch. Day-Lewis was to marry King's sister, Constance. In 1929 King moved to Perth and married Catherine. His father-in-law helped him gain a position as classics teacher at the prestigious Guildford Grammar School on Perth's outskirts. In 1930, with the onset of the Depression, King was retrenched and took up an appointment at the University of Western Australia as foundation Professor of English. He 'thought literature and the life of the imagination more important in the end than political activism', and considered 'the imaginative life' imperative for an 'enlightened society'.[18] He supported the cultural endeavours of the Workers' Art Guild and later played an active role in the Guild with a number of his former students.

John Oldham's course on Moholy-Nagy would, in part, inspire Harald Vike's wonderful constructivist stage-set for the Guild's next theatre production, *Bury the Dead*, preparations for which had begun soon after the successful initial season of *Till the Day I Die*. With spirits around the Guild buoyed and its coffers brimming, plans were drawn up to design and construct an elaborate set for *Bury the Dead* and extensively advertise the play. Keith George 'went mad' with the £300 profit from *Till the Day I Die*, and the results were remarkable.[19] Vike shared John Oldham's interest in constructivism, and the play would provide an opportunity to fuse architecture and theatre, with the Soviet constructivist artists' recent experiments in this area as the model. Kazimir Malevich's 'architectonics' — the three-dimensional sculptural extension of his geometrical canvas paintings — and the work of Soviet architectural sculptor Vladimir Tatlin, who designed sets for the Moscow Art Theatre, were exemplars. Léon Moussinac had written in 1931:

> Architecture and the drama are the key-arts of American and Russian civilisation [and] they are ultimately related ... Architecture borrows expressive devices from the theatre, such as flood-lighting at night; and the theatre depends upon architecture for its concrete reality ... Corbusier has given us the conception of the house as machine to live in; we must learn to think of the theatre as a machine to act in. We must treat it simply as a construction designed to facilitate the action of the performers.[20]

This principle was applied to Harald Vike's design for the set of *Bury the Dead*.

The Workers' Art Guild's second season of drama opened on the evening of Armistice Day 1936, having been in rehearsal for at least three months. *Bury the Dead* was a powerful anti-war allegory, described by Paul Hasluck as 'an example of a significant movement in contemporary drama'.[21] Like *Till the Day I Die*, it was born of the New York Group Theatre and written by another member of that company, Irwin Shaw. The Guild production was played over eleven consecutive nights.

Ostensibly set in the American frontline trenches during the First World War, *Bury the Dead* represented no particular military campaign but the futility of all wars — it was 'a play about the war that is to begin tomorrow night'.[22] The central characters were a group of young soldiers killed on the battlefield who refused to be buried and instead each rose individually from the grave to deliver a stirring and stinging personal soliloquy against a war that had robbed them of their growing old. This play made an even greater impression on Perth audiences than *Till the Day I Die*. The spine of traditional theatre, the proscenium arch, was jettisoned and again no curtain was used. The drama, supported by intricate lighting, sound effects, music and 'the wonderful language of the play ... really, really shook them up', audience and critics alike.[23] Harald Vike's design created a 'new' stage placed within the space of the 'old', and a theatrical space new to Australia at the time.[24] A few years prior to the formation of the Workers' Art Guild, drama theorist Gordon Craig had written:

> both scene and 'mise-en-scène' have recently been called upon to do so much to bring people back to the theatre ... They have given a new appearance of life to the stage ... These 'externals', then — these lights, these colours, these fine new forms, these intelligent effects — though surface ones, have had the desired effect of very powerfully helping to attract crowds to the Theatre ... The curtain to-day rings up, not on that old back-cloth of 1860 ... but often on a really presentable spectacle. Sometimes it is beautiful; at other times it is expressive; sometimes it is both.[25]

This breakaway transcendent aesthetic is precisely what Harald Vike and Keith George brought to the theatre, and never more so than with the functional set design for *Bury the Dead*. Craig believed that the theatre director should be a 'monarch'. Truly successful theatre was achieved, he wrote, by a 'single great genius who will be able to determine each detail of his production himself'.[26] George was just such a 'monarch', and this is where he differed markedly from other auteurs such as Bertolt Brecht, who believed in the communal creation of theatre.[27] George believed that 'the desire to do the useful work meant that the [theatre] worker found the necessary and useful forms', and that form should be built around the message of the play rather than imposed upon a play.[28] The set for *Bury the Dead* was just such an 'architectural device for the promulgation of the lines the actors are going to say, not a representation of anything'.[29]

> It was a smashing set for our purposes. There was not the slightest fumbling or bumbling or wondering where you were ... Here's a prostitute under a street lamp; here are some people standing in a grave; here's an officer telling another officer off — and you were

never in the least confused ... It didn't have to be stated what it was. You knew by the words and the characters.³⁰

The set was a constructivist design despite constructivism being most certainly out of political favour in Stalin's Soviet Union by this time. A production of *Bury the Dead* by Sydney's New Theatre at the Sydney Conservatorium soon after the Guild production replicated Vike's set design, as well as the costumes of the Guild production. Dramatist and screenwriter Oriel Gray, a central figure in Sydney New Theatre, wrote of the Sydney set:

> the Russians had an awkward habit of suddenly bringing a style, or an art form, or a morality into the bright light of party approval, and Communist organisations throughout the world felt compelled to follow suit ... [however,] these innovations could fall into disfavour very quickly ... We were so far from the centre of things that an overseas theoretical/cultural journal, or a copy of 'The USSR in Construction' might find us numbered among the bourgeois goats. But as far as we knew at this time, constructionist [*sic*] sets were 'in'.³¹

The Vike set of raw wooden planks, informed by Irwin Shaw's suggestions, was made up of a number of bare levels with ramps and platforms that, Paul Hasluck reported, made 'not the least attempt to deceive the audience as to its nature'.³² The fixed, open set provided for battlefield graveyard, street corner, newspaper office, church and war office scenes. It also made possible an amalgam of theatrical and cinematic techniques on stage — with the ability to cut rapidly between scenes — at a time when cinema was imposing itself on the theatre. The set allowed for contiguous scenes to be played out on separate levels and areas of the stage, with lighting shifting from one area and sequence to another, dispensing with the need for breaks in the play for scene changes. The lighting also allowed the players to move to their next positions sight unseen.³³ Vike was not only responsible for the set but was also a cast member, and he won praise for his performance in the play.³⁴

Prichard was again at amicable loggerheads with George over his production methods. She wrote to Louis Esson in August 1936, while *Bury the Dead* was in rehearsal, that 'Keith says he's going to have a clock ticking all through the show. I threaten to walk out if he does.'³⁵ Despite her protests, the clock was part of the performance, as described by Arthur Rudkin:

The play opened in complete darkness with a trumpet playing The Last Post, mournfully and slowly, as from a great distance, and a deep, slow ticking as of a great clock, and a deep voice slowly and solemnly repeats the words, 'Bury the dead!' over and over again, with another voice replying in an angry stage whisper, 'They stink, stink, stink ...' (The script opens with one of a burial detail of soldiers at the front saying, 'Say, Sarge, let's bury 'em in a hurry. They stink.') The ticking goes on right through the play, with only one pause, very slowly rising in pitch and becoming almost imperceptibly faster, until towards the finale it becomes fiercely urgent. The voices speed up and rise in pitch more rapidly, and become louder, as a lurid purple light diffuses at the back of the stage, revealing the burial detail in silhouette as they dig the graves, while heavy gun-fire thunders and flashes in the background. The voices reach almost hysterical speed and pitch, piercing the background pandemonium in a fierce, penetratingly urgent tone, then suddenly fall silent as full stage lights come on and the dialogue starts, but the deadly clatter and flash of the guns continues unabated. Then, an instant before the dead stand up, there is a sudden deathly silence, broken only by the terrified scream of one of the burial detail as the first pitifully mutilated young head rises above the grave's edge.[36]

There was a structural complexity to the seemingly minimal staging and lighting of the play. Hasluck regarded the sounds and sights of the production as 'purposeful' rather than 'decorative'.[37] The main setting of the play, the battlefield graveyard, was situated on a platform high up towards the back of the set. The six buried soldier 'corpses', individually lit, stood in a wooden box in the 'graveyard' with their feet below the platform floor and their backs to the audience, itself unorthodox, their heads 'almost lost in the ceiling'. The burial detail, and the women addressed by the corpses, stood on this higher platform behind the graves, facing the graves and the audience.[38] Other scenes took place on smaller platforms below and on the flat of the stage. The portion of the stage where action took place was the only area of the set lit at a given moment during the performance, while the rest of the set remained in virtual darkness. The lights would drop at the end of a scene and light up another part of the stage where, after a short blackout, the next scene would take place. Floodlights intermittently blanket-lit the auditorium and loud speakers on the auditorium walls broadcast incidental music, intermittent laughter, rattling gunfire and battlefield explosions. A homemade smoke machine was used for effects, as well as smokeless fireworks.[39] At various points in the play, the actors and audience peered through a haze of smoke and 'dust'. The use of coloured lights was another important feature of the play's design. Blue floodlights lit the wings and blue spotlights lit the graveyard, with overhead lights filtering green 'moonlight' onto the scene: 'The density of the light was intended to give and support an eerie spectacle'.[40]

Bill Kidd was responsible for the play's lighting. A working-class teenager employed in a metal foundry, he was also responsible for the lighting of most of the Guild's subsequent plays.[41] *Bury the Dead* was almost entirely side-lit, with no battens or footlights, then quite a novelty in stage design. Side lighting was rarely used in the theatre at that time, but it would become commonplace in George's productions.[42]

> Later [in the play], the ticking and the gun-fire resume, the tick-tock continuing to rise very slowly in pitch and speed, the gun-fire with remorseless intensity in all the scenes at the front, suddenly dying away to a distant rumble in the scenes at military headquarters. The gun-fire was not mere recorded sound, but produced, amazingly realistically, from a selection of improvized apparatus, among which I remember a battered old bass drum and a sheet of corrugated iron, beaten nearly flat and suspended from a wooden frame. The operators, clad only in swimming trunks and sand-shoes, and bathed in sweat, were undoubtedly the hardest worked members of the cast and crew! The amateur and relatively inexperienced cast did not let Keith down. I have said the production was the most powerful and moving spectacle I have ever seen on any stage, and I can add with even more confidence that the most powerful and moving performance I have ever seen by any individual player was by Phyllis Harnett as the mother of one of the slain young men, as she led the drama to its shattering climax with her call to her son to 'tell the bastards all to stand up!' Right at the end, the same trumpet that played The Last Post at the beginning is heard again, but much louder, playing a stirring Reveille.[43]

At the end of the performance, the corpses rose from their graves before moving slowly down a curved ramp towards the audience to the repeated chant of 'Bury the dead!'[44] The actors playing these corpses were covered with grey-dyed calico shrouds and the sight of these resurrected corpses was too much for some in the audience, who screamed, ran from the theatre in fright or fainted as the shrouds slowly descended.[45] The actors playing the corpses witnessed the audience's response through peepholes in their shrouds and, on reaching the flat of the stage, made their exit underneath the ramp and off-stage.[46]

Perth newspaper *The Mirror* praised the play as 'one of the finest pieces of dramatic production ever seen in Perth — amateur or professional'.[47] Paul Hasluck also wrote glowingly of the performance, purposefully avoiding any political analysis of the play. Echoing Hasluck, *Daily News* drama critic 'John Doe' wrote in his review (under the headline 'War's Futility Exposed in Brilliant Play'):

> Whether its polemic is well directed or whether that message is to be approved, is no concern of the critic; they are controversial matters ... In these days when the theatre is too often occupied by emasculated plays of escape, it is refreshing and even thrilling to see drama which attacks current great problems with skill and courage. 'Bury the Dead' ... is such a play. It is a withering attack on war; and it carries a message so effectively presented that it rings in the ears like a bugle call ... the play is brilliantly produced and, considering its large cast of 33, acted with efficiency ... The play mounts to a triumphant climax when the last, half-retrospective scene echoes with the words: 'Mankind is standing, and climbing out of its grave.' The producer (not named on the programme) is to be congratulated for courageous innovations which could be accepted by all who do not consider that play production should be static, confined within conventional limits of 3 or 4 acts and nicely patterned curtain. The play goes straight through its 24 scenes ... loud speakers hurled words and satirical laughter down from the sides of the hall on to the somewhat astonished audience; the smell of cordite drifted across the footlights in the first battlefield scene.[48]

Perth's theatregoers turned out in droves to see the play, with Hasluck estimating that 'a good deal more' than 1200 people saw the play during its short season.[49] Despite this, the play was a financial loss for the Workers' Art Guild. George was able to cut some costs thanks to the donation of spotlights, floodlights and sidelights from the lighting technician at His Majesty's Theatre, but the Guild spent a lot of money on the production and its costs were not recouped. In fact, when *Bury the Dead* finished the Guild was significantly in debt.[50]

George had organised extensive advertising for the play, including enormous poster advertisements designed by John Oldham that were displayed along the sides of trams.[51] Posters were also pasted on hoardings and vacant walls around the city, and advertising was chalked on footpaths.[52] The Guild's plastic and graphic arts section handprinted Oldham's posters from a linocut master.[53] The unique poster, described by Oldham as an evolution from his 'W.A. First' tram posters, featured 'the corpse-like face of a soldier with staring eyes'.[54]

> Its menace expresses the mood of the play ... Oldham's poster must have excited attention on the streets of Perth in 1936.[55]

On the final day of the *Bury the Dead* season, when the temperature in Perth rose close to 100 degrees Fahrenheit, the film adaptation of H.G. Wells's prophetic novel *The Shape of Things To Come*, with a theme not dissimilar to that of *Bury the Dead*, opened in Perth. It was a powerful anti-war film that depicted a devastating conflict breaking out in 1940 in which London was bombed by enemy aircraft. It was a thoroughly Modernist film with sets by Moholy-Nagy, who had influenced the design of Vike's set for *Bury the Dead*.

By early December 1936, when the Workers' Art Guild would present the first night of its return season of *Till the Day I Die*, the public of Perth was awash with news of King Edward VIII's abdication and subsequent exile from the British Empire. Schoolchildren around Perth sang 'Hark, the Herald Angels Sing; Mrs Simpson's Pinched our King!' A report was carried on the front page of the *Daily News* on 12 December 1936 that Edward Windsor had left England that day by sea for 'none knows where'. Even *The Workers' Star* editorialised about events, despite criticising the hysterical coverage by the 'capitalist' press. The Communist paper declared that 'the sympathy of right-thinking people, so far as they trouble to think about such a storm in a teacup at all, will probably be with the King [Edward VIII]. It is a bit tough when a man has to tolerate degenerates like [Prime Minister] Baldwin butting in on his love-affairs', although the report did refer to King Edward's well-known 'fascist sympathies', adding:

> The whole episode serves once more to illustrate the fact that it is high time we put an end to a system which produces a class of idle exploiters who can find nothing better to do than to steal each other's wives.[56]

The reprise of the Guild production of *Till the Day I Die* was played over two December nights on the great expanse of stage at His Majesty's Theatre, one of the largest theatres in Australia. The 2584-seat venue was a three-level auditorium with a very large fly-tower stage measuring twenty by twenty-three metres. Its wooden shell created fine acoustics, although trams rumbling down Hay Street outside the theatre would sometimes interrupt performances. There were a number of cast changes from the original Workers' Theatre production, but the three central players remained the same and the production style relatively unchanged.[57] Two young Jewish philanthropists who had appreciated the power of the play to the Jewish cause and the Guild's rendering of it underwrote the season. The play had received considerable publicity since its initial June performances and its theme was now more poignant than ever given the alarming rise of anti-Semitism in Europe — of which most Australians, including many Jews living in Australia, remained unaware.[58]

Phyllis Harnett had begun to read something of the Jewish persecution in the literature that passed through the Lotus Library and Bookshop in Fremantle, where she worked. She had also heard firsthand accounts. Australian writer John Manifold had visited her at the bookshop, having returned from studying at Cambridge University. Manifold had spent his summer holidays working in Germany, and he shared some alarming accounts of the brutal treatment of Jews at the hands of Nazi soldiers. Harnett's sister had also travelled to Germany to stay with an English girlfriend, and the woman's German husband was shot dead by Nazis on his doorstep while she was there.

Harnett found these stories almost unbelievable, but 'they were just presages', she later said, 'of what everybody nearer to Europe knew a great deal about'.[59] It was this horror that was enacted in *Till the Day I Die*, with the final scene of the play encapsulating the atrocity it portrayed. The play's main character, Ernst (played by Frank O'Grady), captured by the Nazis, is forced to ride with them during their raids. His companions assume he has betrayed them, and he is ostracised by them after his release by the Nazis. Terrified that the drugs he was given during interrogations may have induced him to reveal information that could jeopardise his comrades, Ernst takes his own life while visiting his brother Carl and his lover Tilly (played by Phyllis Harnett). After a shot rings out offstage, Tilly lets out a blood-curdling scream, the force of which would cause Harnett to collapse into the arms of Carl (played by Howard Smith). Tom Wignall stood backstage with one of the theatre's old hands, ready to pull the curtains at the end of the performance. The stagehand rattled off a list of the names of the great and famous Australian and international actresses who had appeared on his stage — 'I've seen 'em all, and not one of 'em could hold a candle to her,' he said of Harnett's emotional performance in the play.[60]

When Harnett left the stage at the end of the second night's performance, she asked one of the men who had funded the production why he had done so. Somewhat evasively, he replied, 'When you screamed tonight, we got what we were paying for.' The anti-fascist labours of the Communist Party were greatly admired by the Jewish community 'because at that time Communism and Jewishness hadn't separated'.[61]

The much-discussed spotlight technique and siren effects from the play's original season were used again, and Keith George's handling of the production was again praised by the *Daily News* drama critic, who wrote that 'highly dramatic scenes, which in less expert hands would approach perilously close to the brink of bathos, are played with passionate intensity and convincing fervour.'[62] Unlike earlier Guild performances, George did use a curtain that dropped at the end of the play, leading *The West Australian* theatre critic 'Socio' to comment in his theatre column:

> It was regrettable that the producer did not follow his practice in his first production of the play and forbid a final curtain. Final curtains are a common sin, but to be reminded that the characters have been other persons posturing on the stage, lets down the final tension.[63]

The year 1936 had been an auspicious one for Keith George, and the success of the Workers' Art Guild's first two major theatre productions had elevated him to messianic figurehead within the Guild.[64] There was a widespread feeling in a hitherto very conservative Perth that 'only the Workers' Art Guild gave a view of contemporary drama — or a view of the modern world, difficult to find in Perth at the time.'[65] The plays 'had great vigour', and they presented a 'strong sense of the time'.[66] Ric Throssell was surprised that 'the people who came to see the Guild included the conservatives of society'; indeed, the audiences at Guild productions were, by and large, the entrenched middle class.

> I think probably the reason why the conservative, middle-class audiences would turn up to the Workers' Art Guild [was] that the revolutionary message was directed elsewhere, not at home.[67]

The Guild did play to working-class audiences at factories, halls and trade union functions, but those who attended its public seasons at the Assembly Hall and at His Majesty's Theatre were those who also regularly attended Repertory Club productions at the Assembly Hall and chamber music performances at His Majesty's. Repertory Club performances attracted a steady and established audience, but not in the numbers that were now attending the Guild plays. John Oldham considered this large mixed audience the Guild's 'greatest accomplishment'.[68] For the first time, Perth saw not only demonstrative theatre but equally demonstrative audiences. Heckling was rare, but engagement with the action quite common. Although some of the middle-class Guild audience were 'casting about', most who attended were not particularly political but simply drawn to compelling theatre. To others, the Guild plays went some way to expressing or giving vent to their disaffection.[69] The plays had initially been spoken about behind cupped hands, and opinions about the Guild had been a measure of one's radical social and political credentials.

The year 1936 had also been a relatively productive one for Katharine Susannah Prichard. In the middle of the year she had sent the long-awaited final revised manuscript of her novel *Intimate Strangers* to her London publisher. She had completed the rough draft before her trip to the Soviet Union in 1933, but the death of her husband and her subsequent political labours had meant she was unable or unwilling to revise the manuscript in the intervening years. The original conclusion to the novel — which described the breakdown of a marriage due to the tensions arising from a wife's thwarted creative career, on the one hand, and the strains on her returned-soldier husband who loses his job during the Depression, on the other — depicted the husband committing suicide. Prichard, 'fearing that it might be mistaken as an autobiographical account of their marriage', amended the ending in the final draft, excising the suicide.[70] She had sent a copy of the revised manuscript to Louis and Hilda Esson, and they had written an encouraging response. Prichard wrote gratefully to Louis Esson at the end of August 1936, after arriving home from a Spanish Democracy Rally at Arundale Hall in the city:

> It was good of you to write & comfort me about 'Intimate Strangers'. I was utterly depressed about [it]. Hilda's verdict, & yours, changed the face of the world. Can't tell you how difficult it was to write at all, in the midst of ... newspaper controversies,

meetings, financial worries, & doing all my own domestic chores. I despaired, over & over again, of ever getting any time to think two thoughts together.[71]

Prichard did have nagging doubts about the amended conclusion to the novel but, with the manuscript despatched, at the end of 1936 she took what had become an almost annual pilgrimage across the country and returned to the sanctuary of friends and family in the eastern states. A few months earlier, she had written bleakly to Hugh McCrae:

It's been a woeful year — living alone & working so hard … I say I'm too busy to be lonely. But you know what that means. There's nobody I want to come into my mind, anymore. Ça, c'est fini. Only necessary to tie off the ends. Good to think it'll be all over some day.[72]

The Guild had become a welcome distraction for Prichard. Since Hugo's death she had thrown herself into Party work, and the Guild was a forum in which she could combine the political and the creative, and to which she could also contribute her skills as a writer.[73] She was greatly respected there as a patron, with George Wignall remembering that on occasions she 'descended to see one of our rehearsals or something' and there would be a murmur that 'the great lady has arrived' and 'everyone paid homage'.[74]

Prichard stayed with her sister in Frankston, south of Melbourne, over Christmas, and soon after Boxing Day 1936 she left for Sydney.

8

SPAIN, MOSCOW AND 'THE SOUTHERN CROSS'

'So you're from Australia?' he asked us. 'Well, well. I bet you thought that all Americans wore horn-rimmed spectacles.'
'I bet you think that all Australians say "bastard".'
'Whereas,' retorted Groucho, 'they only say it when they're talking about Americans. You know, it always annoys me that people in other countries should get such absurd ideas about us. Now take that "Sez you!" business. I expect you thought all Americans said "Sez you!" at every opportunity. But tell me — have you heard a single decent American say that yet?'
'No,' we admitted.
'Sez you!' said Groucho, and returned to his own table.[1]

In July 1936, the CPA had been buoyed by the victory of the Republican Party in the Spanish elections, following the Communist Party's political success in France, where a left-wing Popular Front government had been elected. But the Party's initial euphoria — along with the fragile peace that had held in Europe since Armistice Day 1918 — soon dissolved. Spain's new Republican government was toppled in a right-wing revolt led by Army General Francisco Franco. A ragtag left-wing Loyalist–Republican coalition then rallied against Franco's forces and his equally diverse body of supporters in a civil war that lasted almost three years.[2] It was a battle with widespread international significance, as it also pitted the fascist governments of Italy and Germany, on Franco's side, against the Soviet Communist government, on the side of the Republicans. Reports of the Spanish Civil War crystallised support for the Left, and the CPA formed a subsidiary, the Spanish Relief Committee, to provide material support to the Spanish Republican movement.

In August 1936, news of the first Moscow show trial was reported in the Australian press. A purge was being conducted within Party ranks in the Soviet Union, and Stalin ordered affiliates of the Comintern to similarly rid themselves of Trotskyite sympathisers and 'wreckers'. 'Counter-revolutionaries' appeared before a Moscow public gallery to confess and seek absolution before being sent, in nearly every case, to the Gulag prison camps or to their deaths. The mainstream media carried reports of the Stalin show trials by British correspondents posted to the Soviet Union, but the Party press initially declaimed such reports as mere mischief-making on the part of the capitalist press. Reports of the Soviet purges had appeared in *The West Australian* as early as March 1935, though Party members did have reason to be sceptical of such reports in the mainstream press given their distinct anti-Communist bias. The Communist press acknowledged the trials but insisted that the Soviet government was of necessity dealing with 'traitors' and 'spies'. *The Workers' Star* claimed it was publishing the 'facts about the Moscow show trials that the capitalist press did not print' through its independent cable sources in Moscow.[3] In early 1938, 'Latest Soviet Purge' reports were published weekly in *The Workers' Star*, but Party stalwarts remained in relative ignorance about the atrocities being committed in their name.

> It was several years into the 1930's before we [in Perth] began to see any ... 'literature' ... that [was] at all critical of Stalin ... How could we, in this far-away little settlement, really know what was going on in the Soviet Union.[4]

One of those caught up in the Soviet terror was theatre director Vsevolod Meyerhold, a protégé of Stanislavsky who had taken charge of the theatre division of the People's Commissariat for Education, which was set up by the Bolshevik government after the revolution. He was arrested and imprisoned in 1937, and shot a few years later. Many Party members subscribed to the view expressed by André Malraux that 'just as the Inquisition did not affect the fundamental dignity of Christianity, so the Moscow trials have not diminished the fundamental dignity of Communism.'[5] It was a difficult proposition to sustain, but the CPA held public lectures to counter adverse publicity and reassure the rank and file.

There were also stark local reminders of the Spanish Civil War, both by way of the crowded Spanish Democracy fundraising and relief rallies, and the presence of Australian partisans who disembarked at Fremantle before their long voyage to Spain to sign up as foot soldiers and nurses. About fifty Australians, travelling relatively anonymously, joined the Republican International Brigades as political mercenaries during the Spanish Civil War, and almost half of them would die in Spain.[6] A typical Spanish Relief Committee evening consisted of 'speeches about the war, a play or a film, and an almost evangelical appeal from the platform for money', usually kicked off by a bogus donation.⁷ Money, watches and jewellery were donated and the proceeds were provided to the defenders of the vanquished Spanish government for the purchase of ambulances, food and medical supplies for relief work in government-occupied territory.⁸ The Workers' Art Guild also threw its support behind the Spanish Relief Fund. In June 1937, Phyllis Harnett organised a fundraising evening of poetry and music. Spanish government posters adorned the walls of Arundale Hall, the home of the Theosophical Society and the Temperence League, where Harnett recited poetry written for the occasion by Ray McClintock and fifteen-year-old John Hepworth. Keith George read letters from Australian nurses serving in Spain, and a poem by Prichard's friend Frank Wilmot (who wrote under the name Furnley Maurice) was recited by a 'verse-speaking choir' of children from the Guild children's theatre wing.⁹ There was also widespread support for the Spanish Relief Committee outside the Communist Party, and screenings of newsreel footage and films documenting the Civil War were well attended.

In October 1936, responding to a public appeal by the Spanish Relief Committee, four Australian nurses — Mary Lowson, May McFarlane, Agnes Hodgson and Una Wilson — sailed from Fremantle to serve with the Republican forces. A year later, Perth received its initial firsthand accounts of the Civil War when Western Australian Mary Lowson returned from Spain and spoke at the Workers' Art Guild as part of a nationwide speaking tour to appeal for support for the Spanish Relief Committee and the Red Cross medical units serving in Spain.¹⁰ Lowson had been transporting medical supplies to the frontline and she spoke of the long siege of Madrid, the air bombing of Barcelona and the use by Franco's forces of German and Italian troops and arms. The Republicans were ostensibly backed by the Soviet Union but Stalin, like Hitler and Mussolini, used the war as an extension of his domestic political program. During the 1937 purge of Trotskyites, Stalin's targets included the socialist POUM (Workers Party of Marxist Unification) militia, who were fighting in Spain alongside the Communist PSUC (Unified Socialist Party of Catalonia), the Anarcho-Syndicalist CNT (Confederation of Labour Unions) and the International Brigadiers. The vanquished Republican government began 'hunting down' the POUM.

The Spanish Civil War had led to a major rift within the ALP. The Catholic influence within the ALP was strong, and mainstream Catholics took a very strong line against the socialist forces in the Civil War. The

Catholic Church directed its followers to support Franco against the Republicans; the Catholic Church was no friend of the Communist Party and, indeed, no friend of the Workers' Art Guild. John Oldham recounted that the strongest opposition to the Guild 'came from the Catholic Church in the guise of the Right Wing faction of the ALP'.[11]

In June 1937, Catholic Archbishop of Perth Dr Redmond Prendiville informed clergy in his archdiocese that it was the wish of Pope Pius XI that the fullest publicity be given to the encyclical letter 'Divini Redemptoris', in which the Roman Catholic position in relation to Communism was spelt out. It was an edict from the pulpit to fight against Communism.[12] The ALP's left wing, however, remained steadfast in its support of the Republican side in the Spanish Civil War. John Curtin, as leader of the ALP, narrowly averted a split within the Party over the Spanish Civil War that would have put paid to any hopes of the ALP winning government.

Throughout 1937 the Spanish Civil War received extensive, almost daily, coverage in *The West Australian*. *The Workers' Star* also published regular reports from a member of the International Brigade through 1938. Another prominent journalist reporting from Spain at the time was intrepid 'lefty' Rupert Lockwood; having spent time in Germany witnessing the Nazi military build-up there, he was now reporting for Melbourne's *The Herald*.[13]

Bill Irwin — who had recently been appointed assistant editor of Perth's *Daily News* by his friend, the newspaper's newly appointed twenty-four-year-old editor James (Jim) McArtney — kept staff of the *Daily News* and *The West Australian* up to date on events in Spain, and many felt the Civil War's sting personally when *The West Australian* journalist John Hill was killed while fighting with the International Brigade. Jack Stevens, former Western Australian CPA leader, also died in fighting with the International Brigade, in June 1937.[14]

Irwin, as leader writer at the *Daily News*, was assigned to write the newspaper's initial feature on General Franco's attack on the Spanish Government that had led to the Civil War. Knowing little about Spain, he consulted *The Encyclopaedia Britannica* and John Gunther's influential *Inside Europe*, a contemporary portrait of European political leaders by the European correspondent for the *Chicago Daily News*. Influential local Catholic journal *The Record* attacked what it saw as Irwin's partisan 'plain man's guide to Spain', and the *Daily News* was pressured to publish an article giving an alternative point of view on the Franco issue.[15]

Irwin was a member of the ALP and, moved by what he had seen of the Depression's ravages on his travels, he joined the Communist Party.[16] He was a gifted journalist and discreet in his political activities, but McArtney, as his editor, was called on to protect Irwin's tenure on many occasions when Irwin came under political fire.[17]

South African born, Edward (Bill) Irwin had arrived in Western Australia in 1910 as a two-year-old. In 1927 he was employed as an office junior at West Australian Newspapers. Later, as a shipping reporter, he dreamed of sailing out through the Fremantle breakwaters, and in 1930 he resigned from his position as a cadet reporter on *The West Australian* and, with fellow shipping reporter Ivan Goff, and with fares paid only as far as Sydney, worked his way across the Pacific to the United States and England.

> We'd never seen any other city, but we thought it likely that Perth and Fremantle were as grand as any of them. Though London of course was older … We had a hundred pounds, four suitcases full of new clothes, a portable gramophone and some jazz records, and letters of introduction to a Denver traffic cop, a snake charmer in Los Angeles, and to President Hoover, who once had been a mining engineer on the West Australian goldfields.[18]

The trip was subsidised by intermittent payments from West Australian Newspapers' rural weekly newspaper *The Western Mail*, for a travel column by Irwin and Goff entitled 'The Innocents Abroad', a title lifted from a Mark Twain novel. Having stowed away on ships across the Pacific and jumped freight trains across Canada at the height of the Depression, the pair arrived in Hollywood close to penniless. During a dinner with film director Frank Capra, 'eating peas at five cents a pea and swallowing mushrooms by the dollar', Irwin was introduced to fellow traveller Groucho Marx, and the pair struck up a long conversation about left-wing politics and literature, with Marx recommending that Irwin read anti-war novel *Death of a Hero* by Richard Aldington. Irwin worked intermittently as a journalist in America, and one of his great scoops was to be an interview with gangster Al Capone, but Capone was arrested the day before their planned meeting. Goff, two years younger than Irwin, stayed on in Hollywood and sold articles to London newspapers before becoming the Hollywood correspondent for London's *Daily Mirror* in 1936. He later became a prominent Hollywood film and television producer and screenwriter. Irwin passed through London, where he worked as a journalist, before returning to Western Australia in 1934 and rejoining West Australian Newspapers.

Despite the injustices she must have witnessed during her time in the Soviet Union in 1933, Prichard's faith in the Communist Party did not falter. John McLaren, in his biographical history *Free Radicals*, posed the vexed question:

> First, how could so many people invest their hopes in a Soviet Union where, as far back as the Show Trials of 1936, it was clear that the revolution was devouring its own? Second, how could otherwise imaginative, sceptical, intelligent people submit their thoughts and actions absolutely to the dictates of the inflexible bureaucracy of the Communist Party of Australia?[19]

Prichard had once told Contessa Filippini that she believed 'the end justifies the means', by way of explaining her oft-stubborn belief in the sanctity of the Party line.[20] Any flaws she saw in the system, or among its supporters, did not undermine her overriding political conviction, commitment and submission to Party principles nor her belief that socialism would allay many of the social crimes and economic injustices of the world. She freely admitted that for her it had 'always been difficult not to idealise Communists: to forget that they have weaknesses, bad habits and temptations like other men and women.'[21] Prichard's adherence to the Soviet Party line was sacrosanct, sometimes prevailing over close friendships. She split with her one-time lover and dear friend of twenty-four years, Guido Baracchi, the man who had 'introduced' her to Marxism and a fellow foundation member of the CPA, when he sided with Trotsky against Stalin. They would not reconcile until shortly before her death twenty-five years later.[22]

Prichard's writing had been reasonably prolific before 1933, presumably underpinned by her initially comfortable married life at Greenmount, but it slowed considerably after her husband's death. *Moon of Desire*, described as a 'slight' novel, was published in 1941, but it was not until the first book of her goldfields trilogy, *The Roaring Nineties*, was written in the early 1940s that she returned to more regular writing.[23] There were a number of reasons for this hiatus — Hugo's death, the increased political work resulting from the Spanish Civil War, her anti-fascist activism and the subsequent Second World War among them. Her writing style also came under increasing self-censorship after her trip to the Soviet Union, where she had learned of the prescriptive style of Socialist Realism, which made her a more self-consciously political writer than she had earlier been. She came to identify 'herself with the Party as much as she identified herself as a writer.'[24]

Prichard's involvement with the Workers' Art Guild probably allayed some of her frustration through this fallow creative period, and perhaps this accounted in part for her great enthusiasm for the Guild. She wrote in *The Real Russia* that 'the writers of Russia and Siberia must become the shock brigades of the world.'[25] In Perth, if her work as a writer was not to be at the frontline, then the Workers' Art Guild would serve as her 'shock troops'.

In January 1937, Prichard caught the train from Melbourne to Sydney where she attended a Sydney New Theatre performance of her play, *Forward One*. The national CPA women's journal, *Woman Today*, described the agitprop play as a 'clarion call' for improved working conditions for shop assistants, then predominantly female.[26] Prichard must have been grateful that the play was well received outside its Perth setting. She addressed a large function of the Writers' League for the Defence of Culture in Sydney, where she spoke about the dangers of fascism and the censorship of writers within Australia. After a fortnight in Sydney she returned to Melbourne, staying with Louis Esson at his South Yarra flat and addressing a meeting of the Melbourne branch of the Association of Writers for the Defence of Culture, before sailing back to Perth at the end of January to launch into another busy year.

In August 1936, Louis Esson had sent Prichard a copy of a play he had written about the characters and events of the Eureka Stockade. Esson had written *The Southern Cross* between 1926 and 1927, and dedicated it to Prichard. She had been a great supporter of his and had defended him as a significant Australian playwright when his work had come under attack. He had entered *The Southern Cross* into the *New Triad* play competition in December 1927, where Prichard's *Brumby Innes* had won first prize (for best Australian three-act play) and Esson's did not receive a placing.

When the script for *The Southern Cross* arrived at Greenmount, Prichard excitedly read it to her son, Ric, home from boarding school, and to the visiting Henrietta Drake-Brockman. She wrote in response to Esson:

> I was tremendously impressed with the play itself — the dramatic graph & rhythm of conflicting forces ... you have achieved a piece of dialectical materialism in dramatic form! 'The Southern Cross' is Marxist in essence, — and would be appreciated in the Soviet Union, I'm sure.[27]

Esson had undertaken many revisions of the play over the years to formulate the right mix of the personal, the political and the historical, but there had been little interest shown in performing it. Prichard was keen for Keith George to read the script and consider a Guild production and, although George admired Esson's writing for the stage, Ric Throssell believed that his mother probably 'sooled' George into considering a production of *The Southern Cross* because she felt both guilt and an obligation towards Esson.[28] Esson's reputation would have been enhanced by a Guild production of his play, and it was uncharacteristic of Prichard to weigh so heavily into Guild matters, indicative of her motives one way or the other.

After reading the play, George agreed to direct it in Perth if Esson allowed him to make script changes. The dialectical materialism that Prichard saw as a great virtue of the play troubled George, who was 'primarily interested in the ebb and flow of emotional action and reaction'.[29] George was also concerned about the cost of a possible production, but Prichard leaned heavily on him to produce the play and asked that the script go before the Guild reading committee, 'on which my word has some weight'.[30] It is unlikely that George discussed his plans for production of *The Southern Cross* widely. It seems he may by then have been subject to the constraints of a Guild reading committee, but there is little doubt he still reigned reasonably unfettered. He would not accede to the growing calls for shared responsibility and control of the Guild's theatre activities. Any suggestion of that infuriated him.

Just prior to Prichard's arrival in Melbourne to visit Louis Esson that summer, Esson had received a letter from Keith George fleshing out his proposal for a Guild production of *The Southern Cross*. George told Esson that he liked the play's 'feeling for the period and a fine sense of the deepest sociological meanings underlying superficial incidents', but felt that the play was too weighed down by its reliance on actual historical events (despite the fact that the play was based on the written accounts of Rafaello Carboni, a participant in the Eureka Stockade).

> My criticisms which Katherine [sic] will explain to you in detail were made with considerable diffidence and essentially from the viewpoint of a producer ... It is always a little difficult to reconcile the point of view of the dramatist and the producer. We are a lazy crowd for the most part with a desire to adapt the cruder theatrical means in preference to sublte [sic] characterisations ... I hope however you will allow us to produce the play. It is the best handling of one of the most vital dramatic incidents in Australian history. If you will trust the handling of the initial production to me I would like to have a copy of the play as soon as possible.[31]

George's criticisms of the play's structure echoed the criticisms of others. He wanted to make major narrative changes — namely, to start the play with the Eureka 'diggers' meeting with the governor, Sir Charles Hotham, to put forward their political demands, rather than with the diggers clashing with troopers on the goldfields as Esson had begun the script. Prichard felt this was too great a compromise of Esson's play, of the history on which it was founded and of Esson's integrity as a playwright. As Prichard had struggled against interference into her own writing, so she stoutly defended the integrity of Esson's script and reported back to Esson that she believed she had 'argued [George] out of that'. The Eureka Stockade, she wrote:

> [could] not have arisen without the digger events. They created the atmosphere which was responsible for everything else. And your contrast of characters provides all the colour and variety of emotion stirred to the age-old struggle for freedom ... I didn't feel 'documents' at all with them.[32]

This reference to 'documents' was made, no doubt, in response to criticisms by George and others of the play's overly literal examination of the Eureka Stockade events. Author Leslie Rees supported this view many years later in his 1973 book *The Making of Australian Drama*:

> To my mind, Esson's play too literally follows established facts; it is a purely objective presentation of the main events leading to the stockade fight ... and at the end one does not feel that the author has included anything of himself, except some technical skill. He has not created any people, only copied them from history and from ... Carboni. Even apart from this, Esson's version takes a narrow view of the whole Eureka affair, suggesting none of the political undertones and ramifications, the growth of the Reform League, with its list of Chartist demands, and so on. Esson seems to concentrate only on the physical facts of Eureka.[33]

Keith George's proposal for script changes seems reasonable in light of this criticism, and Prichard herself had suggested to Esson that she 'now and again had an impulse to ruffle up the talk of the miners'.

> I understand your intention to give the speech of the period; but we have only got it in the written word, and not as she was spoke at the time. I'd rather their speech was broken more.[34]

Despite George's enthusiasm, his failure to gain Prichard's and Esson's support for his mooted changes to the play probably put paid to any chance of his producing *The Southern Cross*, and in the end plans for a Guild production were shelved or swamped by other events. Peter Fitzpatrick, in his 1995 biography of Louis Esson, acknowledged that 'Prichard's considerable influence with the Workers' Theatre Group in Perth almost carried it to the point of production in 1936', though it's unlikely that Keith George 'agonized about doing the play for several years', as Fitzpatrick also wrote.[35]

While Prichard was staying with Esson during the summer of 1936–1937, the two of them discussed the possibility of a Guild production of *The Southern Cross*, but Esson did not disclose the full contents of his letter from Keith George. In it, George had revealed that he was 'severing my connection with the Guild in April next and I am anxious to make this [*The Southern Cross*] my last major production'.[36] George had told few people of his plan to leave the Guild, and his decision seems somewhat puzzling given the Guild's successes in 1936. He sought Esson's assurance that Prichard, one of George's closest confidantes, would not be told.

> Will you please not mention my devision [sic] to retire from the Guild to Katherine [sic]. She will immediately imagine things are about to collapse here. We shall have our re-organisation established before she returns. She worrys [sic] so much that I am anxious to avoid even unimportant matters that may interfere with her holiday.[37]

Confiding in Esson, whom George did not know personally, did seem strange. He was probably prepared for Prichard to hear it from Esson, perhaps even hopeful of it, thus saving him the embarrassment of breaking it to her himself. It was probably Prichard's reaction that George feared most.

George also confided in John Oldham, who was dumbfounded. The Guild depended almost entirely upon Keith George. He was the only person then competent to direct the plays. He seemed pivotal to the stability and continuing success of the Guild and his departure was sure to create, at best, great instability, if not the Guild's demise. On a visit to Mouse Cottage, George and Oldham went for a long walk along the beach, during which Oldham tried to dissuade George from leaving.

> He just wouldn't listen. I said that we would give him complete freedom and make every concession ... I feel, as a result of that

hour or so, that he didn't really want to go on, that he'd decided that he'd reached his peak. I think he was a person of enthusiasms, you see. He'd be wildly enthusiastic about something for maybe three or four years and then, having reached what he reckoned was a peak in that, he swings to something else ... There was no threat to his position ... nobody else could take over.[38]

But it seems George felt threatened. Temperamental, he felt undermined by increasing confrontations with politically intransigent CPA members within the Guild. He admitted this some years later when he confessed that he 'was pretty arrogant in those days and this must stand as the real difficulty.'[39]

The first ructions had appeared the year before. After *Bury the Dead*, some Guild members had wanted to stage a production of Miles Malleson and Harry Brooks's *Six Men of Dorset*. The play dramatised events surrounding the Tolpuddle Martyrs' formation of an English trade union of agricultural workers, for which they were transported to Australia. It was English actress Sybil Thorndike who encouraged the Guild to stage this play. When she had toured Australia with her husband Lewis Casson in 1932, to perform in productions of *Macbeth* and the play for which she is best remembered, *Saint Joan*, she had become friendly with Keith George.[40] He had kept in correspondence with Thorndike, and she was probably influential in convincing George of the worth and usefulness of the theatre of the Left. According to Phyllis Harnett, she encouraged the Guild to stage *Six Men of Dorset*, in which she had made a name for herself as an actress. It was a play with obvious connections and appeal to an Australian audience, as well as being a useful vehicle for the Australian labour movement, and it had already been widely performed by other workers' theatres outside Perth. Thorndike herself was about to tour Britain in *Six Men of Dorset* in the English spring of 1937. However, George, again for reasons perhaps known only to him, refused to direct the play. It is possible that he already had it in mind to direct *The Southern Cross* when *Six Men of Dorset* was suggested. The plays were thematically quite similar, and maybe he thought the Guild could practically only produce one or the other and he favoured the production of an Australian play. He may have also favoured *The Southern Cross* over *Six Men of Dorset* in deference to Prichard, but Phyllis Ophel felt that George was not interested in the drama of *Six Men of Dorset*.[41]

The struggle between those who felt the Guild should be producing politically earnest plays and George's impulse to straddle politics with his interest in narrative experimentation had intensified, as illustrated by Ophel's assessment that George 'would have always been right theatrically, but we [the Party members] would have always been right politically'.

> Keith wasn't on the same side as us in the revolution — he was not a [political] revolutionary.[42]

Another struggle along these lines took place around this time. John Oldham and Ray McClintock wanted the Guild to stage a production of W.H. Auden and Christopher Isherwood's play *Dog Beneath the Skin*. However, either those 'in charge of Marxism' at the Guild at the time did not approve of the play or George did not want the play.[43] George was extremely wilful and given to quite arbitrary stances. 'He wouldn't explain them and he didn't,' remembered Oldham.[44] Despite his political moderation, he opposed some plays because he believed they were not revolutionary enough. His obstinacy led to a fierce exchange with Oldham and McClintock.

Since joining the CPA, Oldham and McClintock had become increasingly sectarian and, although McClintock's close friendship with George had preceded her joining the Communist Party, their relationship changed when McClintock 'got political'.[45] She and Oldham were keen to see a democratic broadening of the power base within the Guild. The Guild was ostensibly 'non-political' and 'non-sectarian', but they believed it 'should be subject to Party guidance'.[46] Tom Wignall recalled, 'There was a feeling about the place that [Party members] should take a stronger line.'[47]

The CPA had 'fractions', or Party cells, within the trade unions and Popular Front organisations at which Party members, with varying degrees of influence, discussed internal affairs, concerns and the organisation of these groups relevant to the CPA. The Workers' Art Guild fraction was described by George Wignall as being 'very loose' and meeting on only 'a couple of occasions' to discuss 'serious decisions'.[48] It did not have the 'rigid overlordship of the Guild's activities' as did other Party fractions, and was often thwarted, as mentioned previously in relation to the writers' group, by the folly of 'interminable discussions as to what was really Marxist'. Phyllis Harnett recalled:

> those days and nights and fortnights when we fine-combed a play and each of us had a different idea [of] what was really Marxist.[49]

With time, this 'berating' of things that were not 'properly' Marxist intensified within the Guild fraction and the wider ranks of the Guild.

None of us knew what we should be doing, and we became victims of the people who put it in the strongest terms.[50]

Increasingly frequent and fiercely contested discussions took place about the type of plays the Guild should present. George was furious when Oldham and McClintock challenged him.[51] He refused to concede any of his authority and the dispute was further inflamed when he told Oldham and McClintock that he was the Guild's indispensable 'dictator'. The couple was furious at George's use of what was then an abhorrent term 'because of its connotation with what was happening in Europe', and a heated argument ensued. George refused to apologise, stormed away and announced his immediate resignation from the Guild.[52]

These confrontations gave George's decision to leave the Guild some impetus, but he may have been looking for a relatively honourable justification for leaving rather than being seen so soon to abandon a project he had himself so enthusiastically initiated: perhaps he played a part in orchestrating the conflict. Oldham felt that George's 'enthusiasm for theatre was waning'.[53]

The split, however, was short-lived. Oldham and McClintock recanted, convinced that their semantic dispute with George had almost cost the Guild very dearly.[54] When tempers had cooled, George returned with the support of the rest of the Guild committee. Oldham and McClintock were informally disciplined by the Party for their confrontation with George, if not by Prichard herself then almost certainly at her behest. She remained a great devotee of George, whose battles were not unlike those she had endured with forces in the CPA over accusations that her writing was not 'socialist realist' enough. Prichard held strongly to the view that her work as a writer was not to be compromised, or manipulated, by what the Party deemed appropriate (notwithstanding her own self-censorship), and she later came into conflict with the Party in relation to one of her novels, *Golden Miles*.[55]

Phyllis Ophel later came to the view that George's insistence on autonomy was justified.

> There has never been a good producer living that didn't believe firmly that the only way a theatre could succeed was by being in the hands of a dictator. To let one man have his head and conceptualise a theatre, you get good theatre ... I know you couldn't possibly run the theatre on democracy and get the show on.[56]

In 1937, the locus of the workers' theatre movement shifted from the Soviet Union to the United States. Workers' theatre groups worldwide were integrated under the umbrella of the American New Theatre League and became known, henceforth, as New Theatre League affiliates. The association between New Theatre in the eastern states and the CPA was officially consummated in late 1936 or early 1937 with the de facto affiliation between the Party machine and the Sydney New Theatre, after which a formal CPA branch was established within the Sydney New Theatre. The link between the CPA and New Theatre had historically been close and, although the CPA did not subsume New Theatre nor did New Theatre act as a formal cultural conduit of the CPA (New Theatre fractions were sometimes at odds with the Party line and Party cultural groups generally retained an autonomy from the Party machine to varying degrees from state to state), from this point on there was a more rigid adherence to the Party line within New Theatre.[57]

There was no overt control of the Workers' Art Guild by the CPA. The Guild remained a relatively broad church, autonomous of the New Theatre League and of the CPA central committee, but the Guild fraction tried to ensure that the work of the Guild broadly reflected the shifting political lines and cultural policy of the Communist Party.[58] Guild members in mid-1937 numbered 200, about the same number of registered members of the Communist Party in that state.[59]

The Guild worked in unison with a broad range of left-wing political groups in Perth — the Movement Against War and Fascism (formerly the Council Against War and Fascism), the Left Book Club, the Spanish Relief Committee and the Modern Women's Club among them. Prichard played a leading role in most of these organisations, and all were steered by members of the Workers' Art Guild. Despite this, the Guild continued to raise the ire of Communist Party zealots, to whom Guild members were an ill-disciplined rabble who did not adhere to the asceticism required of Party members. Life in the mainstream of the Communist Party was ruled by a strict set of principles, language and conduct. The Guild was attractive to young Party members precisely because its constraints were significantly fewer than those of the orthodox CPA. The Guild was also an escape from the conventional strictures of Perth society at the time.

For George Wignall, involvement in the Guild provided respite from the social restrictions of home. It opened up a world hitherto unknown and denied to him.

A lot of the working-class people were very austere morally, and it was quite exciting for young people like me to mix with these — [as] my father used to call them — 'Bohemians'.[60]

The Wignalls discussed most things around the dinner table, but there were things spoken of in Guild circles that went unmentioned at home.

George Wignall's father, Lancashire-born Tom Wignall (Snr), had emigrated to Western Australia in 1912.[61] He'd worked on farms in the south-west for a short time before taking up the long-held dream of owning his own land at Katanning, only to be ruined in 1914 by a drought that decimated farms across the state.[62] His Methodist wife had left England in 1916, married him a few weeks after her arrival and died in 1927, leaving eight young children.

Their daughter Mairi (also known as Molly) left school at the age of thirteen, three years after the death of her mother, to run the family household, leaving time for little other than her participation in CPA branch activities and the Young Labour League. Hers was a rather more puritanical, working-class view of political duty than that of her brothers, and she 'somewhat despised the Workers' Art Guild as not being in the front line of the struggle.'[63] Mairi and her father saw themselves as attending to the rough and tumble of the political frontline, 'every day facing the enemy', selling *The Workers' Star*, attending rowdy political meetings and talking up the Party in often antagonistic situations, and they looked upon members of the Workers' Art Guild as political dilettantes abrogating their political responsibilities to self-indulgence.[64]

Mairi's younger brother Tom was employed as a carpenter in the maintenance section of the Railways Department at Midland, where he became an elected officer of the W.A. Railway Employees' Union, a CPA stronghold, and its delegate on the Metropolitan Council of the ALP. In 1931, following the sometimes violent unemployed street demonstrations in Perth that year, he joined the CPA and became a leading member of the Labour Day Committee.[65]

George, a year younger than Tom and two years younger than Mairi, was a member of the Young Communist League. Tom Jnr and George both joined the Workers' Art Guild in 1936 and became prominent members. While George performed in almost every Guild theatre production, Tom's involvement was principally backstage. In his teenage years Tom had also helped with the handset printing of *The Red Star* after school, riding his rusty bike to Voigts Linotype Press in a laneway off Murray Street, where the (then) news-sheet's linotyping was done, and then wheeling the material back to the printer.[66]

In May 1937, after a break of eight years, Perth's Labour Day street parade was revived. The equivalent Eight-Hour Day procession had been held only intermittently during the 1920s, the last time being the centennial procession of 1929. The CPA and the Workers' Art Guild put great stock in the 1937 Labour Day parade, with the Guild's art section producing socialist-realist floats as well as agitprop displays, street theatre and banners, and it was a substantial public event for Perth, with thousands lining the city streets to watch. At the head of the parade rode the Chief Marshal, Maurie Lachberg, cutting a fine figure atop a white horse. John Oldham and Ray McClintock were among those on a Spanish Civil War float produced by the Guild, dressed in military and peasant costumes to rally support for the Republican cause.

A fortnight later, McClintock, now divorced, married Oldham under a characteristic 'aura of scandal'.[67] Divorce was neither common nor accepted in Perth society at that time and, as such, divorcees were 'commented upon' though not openly spoken about in polite company.[68] It was then so titillating a subject that Perth's *The Mirror* newspaper remodelled itself as a tabloid concentrating on divorce reports and sexual gossip about town, immediately increasing its circulation by fifty per cent.

As a married woman, having taken her new husband's surname — perhaps to avoid the scandal that Prichard feared might reflect badly on the CPA — Ray Oldham lost her job as a features writer on *The West Australian*. This expedited the couple's move to Sydney soon afterwards, where Ray joined the *Australian Women's Weekly* and became editor of national CPA publication *Woman Today*. John was employed by large architectural firm Stevenson and Turner, and designed banners, pamphlets and posters for the trade union movement. In 1938 he was appointed associate editor of Sydney journal *Communist Review*, and became a founding member of the Australian arm of the Modern Architectural Research Studio. On Prichard's recommendation, he also joined Miles Franklin, Frank Dalby Davison, Betty Roland and Guido Baracchi in the Sydney branch of the Fellowship of Australian Writers.

After Menzies's attempt in May 1937 to outlaw the CPA was abandoned, the federal Labor opposition appeared more conciliatory in its public statements on the Party. In an election address in July 1937, opposition leader John Curtin 'rejected the philosophy of Communism as a working formula for

Australia, as it sought to do things which could be better done by adherence to Labor's own methods and practices'.[69] Although the Labor Party and the CPA differed markedly in the methods used to achieve their aims, here was an acknowledgement that these aims were not entirely divergent.

The threat to ban the CPA had not helped the Party's membership drive. In February 1937, *The Workers' Star* reported that an increase to 4100 'active' members nationally was insufficient, and well short of the 10,000 hoped for.[70] The CPA was also a victim of the federal government's extreme literature censorship policy. Australia was one of the most censorious countries in the world in this period, and by the time the government had established the Literature Censorship Board in 1937, 5000 publications had been prohibited as either 'obscene' or 'subversive', a large proportion of which was Communist Party literature.[71]

The ALP had also begun to wrestle with CPA subsidiaries, and in December 1936 the Western Australian ALP executive ruled that the Movement Against War and Fascism (MAWF) was a Communist organisation. ALP members were forbidden from joining the MAWF, and MAWF members were to be expelled from the ALP. As a result, a group of thirteen women, including Prichard, formed the Modern Women's Club (MWC) in Perth in April 1937, appointing prominent ALP member Margaret Green as its inaugural president.[72]

The establishment of the MWC was an intensely satisfying personal project for Prichard, and she took to referring to it as 'my club'. It was ostensibly formed to further the work of the MAWF among women and to agitate for the improvement of working conditions, recreation and housing for women. It was also a political body that became involved in a broad range of political issues, including Aboriginal citizenship rights as well as International Women's Day and women's rights in general.[73] The Club masked Communist Party activity — increasingly later, after the banning of the CPA — but it also served as an important social hub for women and it quickly developed a respectable reputation, though this failed to allay the suspicions of police who kept the premises under regular surveillance 'should any illegal activity commence'.[74]

The Guild's next drama season, with Keith George still at the helm, was a double bill of *Where's That Bomb?* and *Waiting For Lefty*, in July 1937. The performances took place at the Assembly Hall over three nights, and again Perth's middle class 'came in hordes'.[75] The season was extended, by public demand, to three further performances.[76] The 'reputation' of the Workers' Art Guild was now bolstering ticket sales, reported *The Mirror*.

> The Workers' Art Guild has produced several roof raising plays for enthusiastic Perth audiences. Sensational, tense, emotional, gripping dramas that roll tradition into little mud balls and throw it back at the audience.[77]

Paul Hasluck wrote in *The West Australian* that the large opening-night audience 'went into rapturous applause, stamping and whistling as well as clapping' at the performance's end,[78] and *Daily News* drama critic 'John Doe' could not remember 'such a hearty tribute to a local production ... of the high quality we have come to expect from the Guild productions'.[79]

Where's That Bomb?, though a satirical farce, was a very political and purposeful attack on capitalism. 'It packs punch like Joe Louis,' wrote Doe, referring to the world heavyweight boxing champion, 'yet a Joe Louis wreathed in smiles'.[80] The play was written by London taxidrivers Roger Gullan and Buckley Roberts, and was first performed by London's left-wing Unity Theatre in November 1936. The Workers' Art Guild performances were the first in Australia.[81] An agitprop comedy in two acts, it depicts a young poet sacked from his day job for writing socialist poetry, and subsequently commissioned to write a respectable capitalist narrative — on toilet paper — for the British Patriots' Propaganda Association. The characters in the story he writes — a kindly boss and a dutiful employee — subsequently come to life and rebel against their restrictive typecasting. The sinister Communist character of 'Bolshie', with his bomb, becomes the hero of the play.

The Guild took on the play 'in an effort to bring our message to a wider audience, and especially a working-class audience'.[82] Keith George's production was a fast-paced fusion of ballet and theatre, with a very simple set.[83] Maurie Lachberg played and danced the main role of the euphemistic ogre 'Money Power' (an evocation of Faust's Mephistopheles), which added 'immeasurably to the total effect of the play'.[84]

The Guild had already performed *Where's That Bomb?* at the annual social event of the Amalgamated Engineering Union in May 1937, and then toured it across suburban Perth before its July season at the Assembly Hall.[85] The University Labour Club invited the Guild to stage the play in the university's Guild of Undergraduates' building, the proceeds from which were to be donated to the Spanish Relief Committee, but objections by right-wing Catholic members of the Labour Club led to the executive committee banning the play's performance on campus. This ban was later overturned by the committee, subject to 'some expressions which might offend young ladies being replaced by more innocuous ones.'⁸⁶ *The West Australian* reported the incident in late June.

> Members ... considered that the prestige of the Labour Club would suffer in the public mind through any association of the club with performances such as those sponsored by the Workers' Art Guild. The previous play presented in Perth by the guild — 'Bury the Dead' — was blasphemous. Members of the Workers' Art Guild are indignant at what they term the 'discourtesy' shown by the University Labour Club.⁸⁷

The references in the play to a novel written on toilet paper, in a toilet, were considered improper by some, but made a political point that was integral to the play. It was presumably these references, which it was 'thought might possibly shock young women', that were excised from the Guild's university performance of the play.

In early August 1937 the Guild put on a Friday-night performance of *Where's That Bomb?* at the university refectory, after which *The Workers' Star* theatre critic 'Backseat' sniped that 'the audience showed no signs of corruption, either political or moral', as it left the venue.⁸⁸ Police suspicions about the Guild were heightened when Phyllis Harnett sent Agnes Harris, a member of the cast and an analytical chemist by trade, a telegram announcing a change of time and venue for a Guild rehearsal of the play. The telegram, which read 'Bomb. 7.30. Higgin's Bootshop', was delivered to Harris by the police.⁸⁹ Despite the disruptions, the Guild continued to perform *Where's That Bomb?* in city and country centres through August and September 1937.

The decidedly proletarian *Waiting For Lefty*, written by Clifford Odets, had become a popular vehicle for the workers' theatre movement internationally.⁹⁰ It was a 'play with a purpose', depicting events during an actual 1935 taxidrivers' strike in New York brought about by deteriorating pay and conditions for taxidrivers during the Depression. It was initially performed to raise funds for the striking taxidrivers, and the strike itself is the central focus around which many episodic sociopolitical vignettes are woven. The strike is the impetus for the play's final call for a political revolt against the existing social order, and the play itself is a call to strike for improved conditions.

The play opens at a meeting of the taxidrivers' strike committee with their union secretary, who enjoys a cosy relationship with the drivers' employer. The union secretary directly addresses members of the theatre audience (proxies for the union rank and file), urging them to vote against a strike. The personal consequences of the strike on the drivers are characterised through individual soliloquies. As members of the committee silently address the meeting, awaiting the arrival of their rank-and-file leader 'Lefty', events leading up to the meeting are played out on the stage, with interjections from cast members within the audience and a physical struggle in the stalls. News arrives of Lefty's murder, and the meeting erupts into angry demands to strike.

Waiting For Lefty is distinctly American and the dialogue includes a lot of American slang, but its political point was universal. First performed by the Theatre Guild of New York in 1935 and later that year by London's Unity Theatre, it was the Workers' Art Guild's first pure agitprop play, and it gave Perth audiences 'a hell of a shock'.[91] The Guild's first night of *Waiting For Lefty* was technically shaky, with lighting problems somewhat blunting the production, but the performance itself was enough to overcome this.[92] Actors rushed through the auditorium and audiences were 'absolutely galvanised by it. They were stunned, excited and bowled over by it.'[93] Reports filtered out that police had been 'called in to quell an incipient riot triggered off by an excited woman member of the audience who attacked a member of the cast.'[94] Paul Hasluck wrote of the Guild performances of *Waiting For Lefty* and *Where's That Bomb?* that the plays 'cannot be considered apart from the emergency into which they break with harsh intensity, and what the beholder thinks of the plays really depends on what he thinks of the emergency.'[95] The 'emergency' to which he referred was the financial and social distress still echoing from the Depression. Paul Herlinger described Odet's 'cinematic technique with its sharp juxtapositioning of realism and expressionism' as 'a dramatic revelation for audiences conditioned to accept so-called realism of the conventional drama of the thirties'.[96]

Peter Cowan portrayed something of the feeling of a Guild performance of *Waiting For Lefty* and *Where's That Bomb?* in his semi-autobiographical novel *The Hills of Apollo Bay*, and later reflected:

> The plays were seen by a character [in *The Hills of Apollo Bay*] as a view to a new and important world beyond a repressive local society — Perth, alas, in the thirties.[97]

The novel's main character, a writer undergoing a political awakening, and his lover, a painter, attend a Workers' Art Guild performance of the plays at the Assembly Hall in which a friend of the protagonist is performing.

> The first play [*Where's That Bomb?*] started abruptly, people still in the aisles, talking, then members of the cast moving from among them, the unexpectedness carrying to the bare stage, the few effects, the sudden energy and humour, the play riding hard its social satire.

The novel goes on to describe the performance of *Waiting For Lefty* after the interval.

> The hall darkened, to the bare stage, the semi circle of men, seated, the gunman by the door. The light fading and the men in shadow, the spotlight centre of the stage and the couple in the first of the episodes. The play moving to strength and conviction, a raw force, the episodes forming from the light and shadow, the group of men half hidden, the centre stage clear, the rise to tension and at the end the lighted space of the stage filling with the presence of the men, arms lifted, voices shouted in belief.

After the performance, the couple in the novel leave the theatre and 'in the street the shop windows caught the light of cars, the buildings dark'.

> He said: I've never seen anything like that. And how can it be here. How could you write that.
> It reminds me of 'Upsurge'.
> In a way. There was something here. For someone to get. I think it's impossible now.
> Whatever there was there's no way that play could have come out of it.
> There has to be.[98]

The reference to *Upsurge* relates to Perth journalist John Mewton Harcourt's novel set in Perth between the two Wars, which portrays a city ruptured by social conflict and political upheaval and occupied by decadent pagan passion. (Katharine Susannah Prichard would present a similar contemporary political view of Perth in her novel *Intimate Strangers*.) Originally published in 1934, *Upsurge* was a literary and political watershed. Considered Australia's first 'red' novel, it was the first Australian novel to employ the literary technique of socialist realism, and its publication led to the Investigation Branch of the federal Attorney-General's Department opening an intelligence file on its author. The novel predicted a cataclysmic revolutionary 'upsurge' against the prevailing conservative political forces that held sway in Western Australia at the time. *Upsurge* was deemed obscene and politically incendiary. It was banned soon after its initial publication — the first novel banned by the Commonwealth Book Censorship Board — and Harcourt was the subject of police prosecution.[99]

To Peter Cowan, the salutary dissonance of *Upsurge* was comparable to that of the Workers' Art Guild performances. Cowan 'never forgot' the personal impact of this particular Guild performance:

> I suppose you could see 'Waiting For Lefty' in terms simply of political assertion, and that may have had some effect on its impact. For me it seemed an assertion of the possibilities of modernism in writing/drama, something I was groping towards in a community where even the books of the modern Americans and some Europeans were or had been banned — and were still banned widely in the years after 1945. There it was — defiant, vibrant, quite shattering on that stage. You went out into the street — and into what?[100]

Arthur Rudkin, aged twenty-eight, caked in thick make-up to play a sixty-four-year-old medical superintendent in *Waiting For Lefty*, performed alongside Guild debutante Marjorie ('May') Berry, who would become a staple actress in future Guild productions.[101] Berry had been a member of the Independent Players' theatre group — which had formed from the remnants of the Five Arts Club and Little Theatre — and was a regular at the Lotus Library and Bookshop in Fremantle where Phyllis Harnett worked. Harnett had suggested that she try out with the Guild.[102]

Harald Vike and Leith Angelo again created the play's sets. This would be Angelo's last official contribution to the Guild before his move to Bunbury, south of Perth. As the CPA organiser for Bunbury, Angelo had the onerous task of establishing a CPA branch there and building up the Party stocks in the town, as well as acting as a CPA contact for a greater part of the state's south-west.[103]

In September 1937, the Guild played both *Where's That Bomb?* and *Waiting For Lefty* at the Midland Junction Trades Hall. Four days later the CPA's national leader, J.B. Miles, arrived in Perth to attend the Party's state conference, to be held at Prichard's Greenmount home, and to address town hall meetings in Fremantle, Perth and surrounds. Great deference was shown to Miles as Party leader. According to historian

Stuart Mcintyre, there was a 'similar cult of the leader' engendered in CPA ranks to that of Stalin in the Soviet Union—though Bill Irwin, no shrinking violet, maintained that there was also an element of obligatory Australian egalitarianism about the relationship Party members had with Miles that was unlike the relationship the rank and file in other countries had with Communist Party leaders, where there was 'terror at the very idea of challenging' them.

> We young people in the Guild would look up J.B. Miles and demand to be talked to.[104]

Prichard returned to Perth just before the state conference, worn out from having spent nearly two months in the Western Australian goldfields researching a novel she planned to set there. The trip included countless political addresses to miners and residents of Kalgoorlie, Boulder and Wiluna.

A Guild performance of *Where's That Bomb?* and *Waiting For Lefty* also took place at the RSL Hall in Collie, a coalmining town south of Perth, on a Saturday night in late September. Communists were proportionately plentiful in the metal industry unions in the late 1930s, and the coalmining industry was constituted by far-and-away the most militant group of workers in the country at a time when there had been few industrial strikes. *The Collie Mail and W.A. Coalfields Miner* reported on the Guild players' impending arrival:

> Six car loads of players and a lorry load of property will arrive in Collie during Saturday afternoon, the road transport being necessary on account of the players participating in the forthcoming drama festival and most of them will have to be back in Perth in time for rehearsal on Sunday morning.[105]

The night of the performance coincided with the opening carnival under lights of the Collie Cycle Club track season. Australian endurance cycling champion Hubert Opperman, a Depression-era sporting idol to rival Don Bradman, was also due in Collie within days, from where he was to attempt to break the Collie-to-Perth cycling record before cycling from Fremantle to Sydney. Collie's local duty policeman Sergeant Herrick had left town on annual leave a week before the Guild performance, to be replaced by Sergeant Brody from Perth—perhaps a reinforcement of the garrison with the arrival of the Workers' Art Guild imminent. George Wignall, who was born in Collie and took part in the Collie performances, later described them as 'very successful ... The people down there loved it.'[106]

The 'forthcoming drama festival' referred to in *The Collie Mail and W.A. Coalfields Miner* article was the inaugural West Australian Drama Festival, the first such major festival in Australia, to be held in Perth in early October 1937. Initiated by Paul Hasluck and sponsored by West Australian Newspapers, it was to be:

> a season of plays in His Majesty's Theatre, with a new programme each night for 7 nights, a round of plays presented by country repertory societies in their local halls, a conference on the drama, and prizes for original plays.[107]

Thanks to the Workers' Art Guild, 'there was now an audience for art plays and those of an experimental nature.'[108]

A number of leading Guild members, including Phyllis Harnett and Keith George, were co-opted to sit on committees and judging panels for the Drama Festival. Harnett was also preparing to direct an Independent Players' performance of Eugene O'Neill's *All God's Chillun Got Wings*, with a cast including Guild actors Gordon Wignall and John Gilchrist.

The principal of the Independent Players was James Quinn, an active member of the Five Arts Club from its early days.[109] When the Five Arts Club folded, Quinn had helped to form the Little Theatre in Hay Street with a similar repertoire to that of the Playbox Theatre. The Independent Players was co-located with the Shakespeare Club in Howard Street in the city. The Shakespeare Club, formed in 1930, staged only one or two of the bard's plays a year. Joyce Mortlock, a gifted actress and the only child of the Mortlock Motors family, joined the group in 1931, having been a Repertory Club member since 1923, and by 1936 she was overseeing the Shakespeare Club.[110]

The Director of the Repertory Club, Esmond George (no relation to Keith), was appointed secretary of the Drama Festival Committee, and Keith George was appointed festival organiser and stage director. The festival was to stage not only original Australian plays but also 'four of the most striking full-length-plays of recent years', giving Perth 'an unequalled chance of seeing modern stage work'.[111] The associated Australian playwrights' competition for one-act stage plays and for radio plays — with the best six from each category to be staged and broadcast on at least three of Perth's radio stations — had been advertised widely both nationally and across the 'Commonwealth'. Seventy-nine stage play entries and eighty-four radio play entries were received.[112]

The Guild's Phyllis Harnett won first prize and the considerable sum of £15 in the one-act stage playwriting competition for her play *I Am Angry*, ahead of seasoned playwrights Alexander Turner and Henrietta Drake-Brockman.[113] *I Am Angry* also won a 'special prize' for the best play by a Western Australian, for which Harnett was nominally qualified.[114] The play was a social critique that exposed the difficulties of motherhood and the employment abuses meted out to young 'nursemaids' looking after children.[115] One of its intentions was to illustrate 'the rotten way in which the "professional" class could treat the working class'.[116] It was a play, wrote Paul Hasluck, 'with one challenging idea, clearly expressed [and] the real merits of saying something that was worth saying and saying it plainly'.[117]

The social plight of domestic workers, labouring under extreme exploitation without the protection of a trade union, was of some public concern in Perth in the 1930s. A murder trial in Perth of a live-in housemaid at that time brought the issue into the open. Having hidden her unwanted pregnancy from her employer to avoid termination of her employment, the housemaid had given birth at her employer's house and smothered her newborn baby.

Sixteen-year-old John Hepworth also entered the festival's one-act play competition, with his play on the Group Settlement Scheme titled *We Are Hungry*.[118] This play was less conventional than Harnett's and required complex changes of scenery, which probably prevented its staging at the time.

Before *We Are Hungry*, Hepworth had written his first notable play, *Yellow Ticket*, which he also submitted to the Drama Festival competition. *Yellow Ticket* was an ostensibly autobiographical piece set in a Perth boarding house, 'fundamentally a slice, a thin slice, of the life of myself, my family, and my friends', Hepworth wrote at the time.[119] It was, characteristically, a play about prostitutes and venereal disease purportedly written, according to Hepworth's introduction, to dramatise 'the effects of the Roman Catholic church whose sexual teachings have created more neuroses than any other single factor in this city'.[120] Harnett would later reflect somewhat sarcastically that Hepworth was 'apt to be overcome with the sorrows and worries of women', and that when he read about the stigmatic 'yellow ticket', a licence required to be carried by prostitutes in Russia and parts of Europe to regulate prostitution, 'it swept into his mind and he wrote a play'.[121] Given its risqué subject, the play probably 'wouldn't have been considered for five minutes' for production at the Guild, but the script enjoyed widespread underground circulation in Perth.[122] It was around this time that Hepworth took up a graded journalist's position on the *Daily News*; his great command of language and his delight in word play then found professional expression in his newspaper columns.[123]

Despite his youth, Hepworth was a gifted poet, actor and raconteur, described by Gordon Burgoyne as 'a teenage prodigy in the Workers' Art Guild days'.[124] He was also precocious, boorish and intemperate and, not surprisingly, he fell in with Herbert McClintock, who had an established reputation as an art rebel. Despite McClintock's apparent shyness, this iconoclastic pair cultivated their rebellious characters modelled on the rogues of the European Dada and Surrealist movements. They were both extraordinarily talented and indulged artists. McClintock took Hepworth under his wing, and their close but antagonistic association included an arcane Dada venture that they undertook together, probably in 1939.[125] This apparently consisted of a stage performance and a small art exhibition at the Workers' Art Guild. One of Hepworth's installations, titled *The Nightmare of a Very Young Egg*, was a saucer with spilt yellow paint into which he had stuck a drawing pin. McClintock attempted to hammer a poached egg to the wall.[126] The associated performance had both men on stage reciting random stream-of-consciousness utterances and interjections that each had independently penned. Hepworth later described the performance:

> I can't remember much of the script now except things like: 'Pink, pink, pink — this is a rhapsody of uncertain colours — each of them determined by the relative propensity of Henry the Fourth and a mountain with hair no longer than a newborn pup.' Good stuff, you know. Deep, significant stuff ... The audiences were there — still and quiet [but finishing] to tumultuous applause and ... what really threw us [was that after the performance] we were being buttonholed by people saying: 'Now that's great, but what was the exact significance of that bit?' Significance was not actually what McClintock and I had set out to achieve.[127]

The venture was an expression of their love of Dada and, importantly for them, an exercise to mock conservative Perth.

9

'OFFENSIVE EPITHETS'

We present this play not for your entertainment, but for your chastening![1]

Six thousand people attended the 1937 West Australian Drama Festival. The Workers' Art Guild produced two plays for the event — *Private Hicks* and *Hinkemann* — which were described by Perth performing arts journal *Music and the Drama* as 'characteristic choices' given that 'social drama of wide significance is the special field of the Workers' Art Guild'.[2]

Private Hicks was another politically confronting play. Written by young American dramatist Albert Maltz, it is set in a factory storeroom in an industrial city in the American Midwest during a 'present day' strike, and portrays a young American National Guardsman who refuses to fire on unarmed strikers. Paul Hasluck had some reservations about the play itself, but strikers in America were indeed being fired upon by soldiers attempting to quell industrial unrest, and Hasluck applauded the play for moving 'with the tempo of these troubled times'.[3] The Guild's Howard Smith played the eponymous lead role, with Keith George (again under the stage name Francis Juleff) also playing a leading part and Marjorie Berry taking the female lead. *Private Hicks* was also probably the first Guild play directed by Howard Smith. The Guild production won the £15 first prize in the Drama Festival's performance competition for one-act plays, with the competition's adjudication panel of Prichard, Alec King and 'Miss G. Pendred' describing it as:

> marked by minor faults (noticeably defects in voice production, inaudibility, drowning of the voices on the stage by crowd noises), [but] it was just the rhythm and movement of this play, rising through a climax that swept the audience to sympathy and emotion, that marked this play out from the rest. Ingenuity of setting, variation of the rectangular background, reduction of stage space to the requirements of the play, grouping and lighting, but above all the atmosphere, spirit and speed, of the performance.[4]

The choice of Ernst Toller's *Hinkemann* was described by *Music and the Drama* as the Workers' Art Guild 'turning from the "empty trifling" which it sees in old fashioned drama'.[5] The bleak, stark and melancholy two-act play presents an entirely reasonable reflection of its Berlin setting and of the weighty period and matters with which it deals. Clearly Toller had written the play 'to purge the soul with pity and fear', and 'in attending to the souls of his potential audience he has not spared their stomachs' in 'swiftly changing scenes of undiluted horror'.[6]

Hinkemann was written between 1921 and 1923, while Toller was in prison. Political though not partisan, it depicts a grim and impoverished post–First World War Germany whose people were brutalised by the War and by the hardships resulting from the subsequent imposition of the Treaty of Versailles. It was the type of play, according to one newspaper, 'intended to replace the old, impossibly romantic dramas, which veiled the misery of the modern world beneath a cloak of happiness, and … dealing with the hitherto unspoken problems of sex, society and married life'.[7] It had something of the feeling of the grotesque anti-war illustrations of German artist George Grosz.

About a thousand people attended the Guild's single heady His Majesty's Theatre performance of *Hinkemann*, directed by Keith George, with 'the breathless stillness of an audience which must have been largely unaccustomed to such devastating frankness'.[8] Again the curtain did not drop between acts, and the audience sat both stunned and mesmerised through nearly two hours of this most powerful and assaulting anti-war play, impressively rendered by the Guild cast.

The large central cast numbered about thirty and, not content with merely playing the expansive stage, George increased the depth by stripping the stage bare, pulling out all scenery and backdrops and dismantling the back facade of the stage to expose the rough brick wall at the back of the theatre.[9] He then 'piled up any rubbish or anything that was around, and left it in sort of shapes and shadows,' and played spotlights into 'the wonderful depth' from the front to the back of the stage, signalling scene changes by adjustments of colour and shade in the lighting.[10] Not for the first time, George's sparse set was enhanced by the suggestions of these cunning lighting effects, and 'a few modernist circus posters formed his only "scenery"'.[11] *Music and the Drama* applauded George's 'modern production methods':

> The different settings were suggested by the barest essentials, which were boldly moved on to the stage between scenes within

full view of the audience. There was nothing incongruous in this method, and the settings were thoroughly effective.[12]

Paul Hasluck wrote in *The West Australian* that 'one cannot imagine any better way to play *Hinkemann* than it was played last night.'[13] Another article in *The West Australian*, however, criticised that which Hasluck had found so laudable:

> There is one school which goes to the ... extreme of stripping accessories to bare bones even, indeed, if one bare bone be permitted. The Workers' Art Guild subscribes to the beliefs of this school ... scorning even a back cloth.[14]

The curtain rose at the beginning of the play on 'an enormous darkness',[15] with the exception of a single light shining on a rickety table and chair. Phyllis Harnett, playing the role of Hinkemann's wife, stood alone on stage, wiping out the inside of a dish with a rag. It was a moment she would remember almost sixty years later as perhaps 'the most thrilling moment of my life ... the depth, the knowledge of what the setting was like, and Keith's voice.'[16] Like a sermon from the pulpit, Keith George's disembodied voice boomed out over the speakers, intoning, 'We present this play not for your entertainment, but for your chastening!' followed by an excerpt from Beethoven's Ninth Symphony, a particular favourite of Prichard's. This grand sweep was characteristic of George. He also played the tragic figure of Eugene Hinkemann, a German soldier having returned from the Great War, physically emasculated by a bullet, to an impoverished home and a suffering wife, with great 'stature'.[17] Hinkemann's wife begins an affair with a neighbour who comforts her after Hinkemann's return. Illustrating his misfortune, Hinkemann flees to join a circus, unbeknownst to his wife, where he performs as a strongman, biting the heads off live rats to demonstrate his absolute degradation. Attending the circus one night, Hinkemann's wife and her lover witness Hinkemann's performance in horror. She and her husband are both driven to suicide.[18]

Bill Irwin found Keith George's performance as a castrato, singing in a shuddering falsetto, both disturbing and compelling.

> Holding onto his loins and not being able to walk properly, and then coming out singing like that — it was climactic and terrible![19]

Music and the Drama described George's performance as 'one of the most remarkable pieces of work in the Festival',[20] and *The Mirror* reported that the Guild 'won their bout at His Majesty's Theatre on Wednesday night by a technical knockout':

> The big audience came prepared for a fight with convention; but they hardly expected that playwright Ernst Toller packed sufficient punch to rock them back on their heels, sit them bolt upright in their seats, make them swallow hard like a man with tonsilitis [*sic*], gasp like stranded fish, and mop their brows like a Marble Arch miner … 'Hinkemann' is undoubtedly the crudest, most vulgar, most convincing, intensely dramatic, slang-studded and convention-wrecking play that has ever been introduced in this State. The one man who could have foisted it on to a hesitating public was playing the title-role, and his effort stamped him as one of the greatest dramatic actors ever seen in Perth. For two hours the audience received shocks such as Hitler's storm troopers would have been proud to inflict … You simply can't present a man who, through war injury, is greatly handicapped, seeing his wife lured away by another, and having it thrown up at him everywhere he goes, without treading on many people's aesthetic corns. Hinkemann trod on them, alright; and he couldn't have done it more effectively had he worn bluchers. To the strictly conservative the play was a glorious conglomeration of unadulterated immorality and filth. To the broadminded, tolerant and inquiring student of human nature and its place in this mad, modern world, it was a triumph … Gloves were off from the opening scene. No back-cloth, no side curtains, no stage trappings, no make-believe; nothing but stark reality, taking shams and convention by the necks and choking the artificiality out of them … Toller wrote it; Mr. Keith George directed and acted it; and in doing so proved himself undoubtedly the most courageous producer and finest dramatic actor Perth has known for many a day … The starched shirts of many of the male members of the audience must have been limp long before the finish of the play; the frankness (uncouthness, many will call it) with which matters of sex were discussed must have made many of the ladies feel almost naked. 'Hinkemann' is bound to leave a nasty taste in their mouths, although Russia and Germany have been educated up to accept such a play as ordinary fare. But you don't expect to serve up a hefty meal of strong meat to Australians,

used (dramatically speaking) to dieting themselves, without causing violent mental indigestion. A lot of people needed a good dose of bicarbonate of soda after Wednesday night.[21]

The production of *Hinkemann* certainly fulfilled the Guild's own brief of using theatre as a weapon rather than as mere entertainment. One festival adjudicator described the play as a 'coarse and vulgar piece of socialist propaganda' that 'should not have passed the first reading. Its object "To chasten" is absurd'.[22] But the production was widely applauded.[23] Harald Vike painted backdrops for the play's circus scene and Harnett proposed that the actors in this scene wear varying shades of pink and yellow, creating a kaleidoscope of colour when they moved across the stage, evoking a swirling carousel. It was by these means alone that the circus was entirely suggested on the stage.[24] A dream scene, in which 100 performers appeared on stage, was equally powerful. In this exceptionally lit scene, Hinkemann fell down on a 'suggested' bridge and the horror of the aftermath of war passed him by — the maimed, lame and starving.

> Everything that signified diminution and destruction and horror floated over the stage in a manner controlled very beautifully by Mr. George.[25]

Maurie Lachberg, George Wignall and Howard Smith played leading roles alongside Agnes Harris, who played Hinkemann's mother, and seven-year-old Rolf Harris, who played a young boy soliciting for his prostitute sister. The Guild required permission from the Child Welfare Department to have Harris appear in the play, and a member of the department was supposed to attend the dress rehearsal. Had they attended, which they did not, they would have been horrified.[26]

Mairi Wignall made her stage debut in *Hinkemann*, with her brothers Donald and Gordon also in the cast. Their brother Tom worked backstage on sound effects, which included being armed with a 38-calibre pistol loaded with blanks to be fired at appropriate moments during the play. At one point during the first act the gun misfired, and Keith George ordered Wignall back to the Guild rooms during the interval to pick up another round of blanks from the properties room. Wignall ran out of the theatre and up Hay Street, let himself into the Guild rooms and ran upstairs. Knowing where to find the blanks, he rushed to the props area without stopping to turn on the lights. He found the blanks and loaded the pistol with six bullets. Worried about facing George's wrath if the blanks again misfired, he decided to test the gun before he returned. He fired two deafening shots into the darkness and, moments later as he was reloading the gun, two policemen came bounding up the stairs and grabbed him. His hasty explanation did not convince them. He was in the middle of a performance, he pleaded, and had only five minutes to return to the theatre for the second act. The policemen agreed to drive him back to His Majesty's to corroborate his story, and thankfully the pistol did not fail in the second half of the play.[27]

George had spent a lot of time on the play's preparation, perhaps in the belief that it would be his swansong. However, the controversy it generated relegated *Hinkemann* to winning just third prize in the Drama Festival competition for full-length plays. Prichard made reference to this disappointment in a letter to Mollie Skinner a few days after the festival:

> I was just so rushed at Kalgoorlie & collapsed on all my jobs during the last week [and therefore] had nearly a week on my back … So snowed under with work, letters that must be done … Also, I've been laid out with one of those filthy heads yesterday & to-day. Too much drama festival & disappointment that 'Hinkemann' didn't get first place. Chiefly on Keith's account. Because of all the work he put into it.[28]

The public reaction in Perth to both *Hinkemann* and *Private Hicks* was polarised. *The West Australian* received a barrage of letters both attacking and defending each play. One correspondent wrote of *Hinkemann*:

> We go to the theatre to relax and be amused, not to be assailed by the crudeness which we shrink away from as we pass hotel doors … There is no denying that the Workers' Art Guild put fine work into their production, but why should they go to the gutters of Germany for a play when there are hundreds of first-class plays that Perth has never seen?[29]

The paper also published a reader's response to Hasluck's review of the Guild's performance of *Hinkemann*.

> Granting [Hasluck] his opinion that all drama should make people think (a premise which I do not hold with myself), one might reasonably expect at least some dilution of the unnecessary

horror of the tragedy and the unnecessary foulness of the comedy ... In addition, one would surely be justified in expecting at least some corrective criticism on the matter of filthy language and an all-pervading blasphemy ... [I]s it essential that the lesson should be couched in offensive epithets[?] ... If the average drunk who had been celebrating the Show were brought before a local magistrate for using any of a dozen expressions with which this play was interlaced, he would have been awarded 'fourteen days without the option'. Why then should they be tolerated in the theatre[?] ... [W]hat is the Drama Festival Committee about when they tolerate such a heterogeneous collection of obscenity and gratuitous blasphemy?[30]

Another correspondent wrote in support of the performance:

If the individual has lived his life in the smug atmosphere of convention, refusing to look upon the tragedies which are enacted before his very eyes ... then such a play as 'Hinkemann' would naturally receive adverse criticism from him ... If 'Hinkemann' has shocked people into at least a discussion of the problems facing humanity; if it has given them just a vivid glimpse of one of the consequences of war; if it has portrayed the bestiality which does exist, then it is a great play.[31]

The day after the Guild's performance of *Private Hicks*, the *Daily News* published an editorial on 'the theatre and the people'.

Perth people have never had much chance of developing the theatre habit. Occasionally professional companies have been brought over from the Eastern States, or we have been treated to productions by companies travelling to or from Europe. With the increasing competition of the cinema, these productions have been still more infrequent, until now it is hardly too much to say that no other Western city in the world of the same size as Perth, has been so starved by the commercial theatre. Nevertheless, whether this has been to our advantage is questionable; for one result has been a gratifying growth of dramatic activities in the city and in country towns. For this our isolation may not be the only reason; there has been a similar growth of the movement elsewhere. But, in Australia at least, it can be said that in no other state is the amateur theatre so thriving. One indication of this is the Drama Festival now in progress. Another might be found in the fact that, for a volume of one-act plays which has just been published in Sydney, a remarkable number of plays was submitted from W.A. The development of the amateur theatre movement in this State has led to hundreds of people becoming actively interested in the stage. And this is immeasurably more valuable than occasional visits to the theatre to watch professional performances.[32]

At the conclusion of the 1937 Drama Festival, a drama convention was held at the Repertory Club at which Keith George again spoke of his commitment to 'useful' theatre, opining that the theatre, and the arts in general, 'must serve a useful social purpose.' He observed that it was futile 'to talk of "creating" an Australian drama; that drama would create itself when it found a task to do and tried to do it.' It was another shot in the eternal Australian debate about a distinctive 'Australian drama'.[33]

With reference to the local revolution in theatre led by the Workers' Art Guild, *Music and the Drama* had published an article just prior to the Drama Festival noting that local dramatic groups had outlived 'the phase of merely banal drawing room pieces', from which:

> there arises the controversy between highbrows and lowbrows, the lovers of old stage conventions and those who yearn for nothing but symbolism, the reading committee members who despise any dialogue that is intelligible, and the very large and lively section who desire nothing but hearty laughter. Is the amateur theatre to be amusing or to aim at high and serious standards? Shall we plump for farce or fantasy, space stage and 'significant' cylinders, or merely a return to the polite world of Pinero by way of the more topical approach of Mr. Noel Coward? Every group has to solve its own problem, which is largely a question of whether the Moscow art theatre disciples or the light-minded are the most articulate and determined section of its committee.[34]

As the Drama Festival concluded, London's Unity Theatre, already publicly supported by Irish playwright Sean O'Casey and author H.G. Wells, announced that singer Paul Robeson, then a major international star, was to quit the London West End stage to 'throw in his lot with the left-wingers' of Unity Theatre and 'devote his life to plays dealing with working-class problems'.³⁵ Robeson pronounced West End theatre futile and 'decadent'; his preference, he said, was to perform for 'working-class audiences'.³⁶ It was a great fillip to the greater international left-wing workers' theatre movement.

Prior to the Drama Festival, new members of the Guild writers' group had cooperatively written an agitprop revue titled *The Lyons Bungles*.³⁷ The play consisted of three short satirical sketches lampooning the federal government led by Joseph Lyons — who was prime minister from 1932 until his death in office in April 1939 — 'drawn together by the device of flash backs to the breakfast table of a trade unionist who discussed with his wife and children the subjects which the scenes satirised'.³⁸ It dramatised a wide gamut of political issues, from the performance of the federal government to Lyons's defection from the ALP, as well as maternal mortality, censorship, trade delegations and questions of civil liberties raised by 'the Freer case'.³⁹

In 1936 the federal minister for the interior had acted to prevent British citizen Mary Freer from entering Australia. Freer had fallen in love with a married Australian soldier stationed in India, and planned to move to Australia to live with him. Her intentions — as reported in the newspapers at the time — sparked moral outrage among Australians, and the federal government interceded to stop the breakup of 'a perfectly good Australian marriage'.⁴⁰ To thwart Freer's immigration application she was set an Italian dictation test, which she failed, and her visa was thereby denied.⁴¹ Civil libertarians and members of the federal Labor opposition were critical of Freer's exclusion and of the process applied to exclude her, and Freer herself embarrassed the government by demanding that it publicly release the facts of the case, threatening legal action against the minister. One of the skits in *The Lyons Bungles* dealt with this controversial case.

Another skit in the revue, George Wignall remembered affectionately, referred scathingly to Lyons 'trying on his silk stockings before he went to the Coronation [of King George VI, in December 1936] — from a Tasmanian postman to a courtier, with, as it said in the skit, "very tolerable calves"'.⁴² Hell hath no fury like the Left scorned. Bitter about his having abandoned the Labor Party to enter the conservative political ranks, the poison pens scrawled for Lyons and he attracted further bile from the CPA, having declared, when elected to office, that he would crush the Communist Party of Australia. Although *The Lyons Bungles* was 'very fortunate in its authors', wrote Victor Arnold,⁴³ its performance, reported *The Workers' Star*, was 'no credit to the Workers' Art Guild'.

Obviously under-rehearsed, the casts [sic] did not do justice to the sound work of the group of writers.[44]

It was originally intended that the revue be entered into the Drama Festival, but the preparation suffered in the rush to ready it for the festival and it was withdrawn at the last moment. It was also sidelined because the Guild was preoccupied with preparations for *Private Hicks* and *Hinkemann*. *The Lyons Bungles* consequently had only one performance, on the eve of the federal election in October 1937, at a Young Labour League rally at the Manchester Unity Hall in support of the Curtin Labor Party. It received little publicity, being subject to a press ban on political advertising on election eve.[45]

The CPA had rallied behind the federal Labor Party, directing its branches to work more closely with the ALP, and did not field any competing senate candidates in the 1937 federal election.[46] The CPA was optimistic that the ALP would topple the Lyons government after recent left-wing electoral successes in Europe. Nevertheless, the Lyons government was returned. Five years later, in a university address on Australian drama, Prichard referred to *The Lyons Bungles* as 'a brilliant political review [sic] ... which unfortunately was presented only once and was seen by very few people.'[47]

The Unity Theatre, where *The Lyons Bungles* was performed, was located at the rear of the old Trades Hall building. It had been used as a vaudeville theatre after its opening in 1923, and later hosted boxing and wrestling bouts. Harald Vike had boxed in the ring there soon after his arrival in Perth.[48]

Towards the end of 1937, internationally renowned Yiddish actor Jacob (also known as Yankev) Waislitz visited Perth on the Australian leg of a world tour. Waislitz had begun studying drama in 1913 at Hazomir, an experimental Yiddish drama academy in Poland whose teachers included David Herman, an innovative theatre director at Peretz Hirschbein's Yiddish Art Theatre in Warsaw, itself modelled on Stanislavsky's Moscow Art Theatre. Waislitz had become an itinerant actor-director, initially touring a one-man show of Yiddish 'recitations' around Poland, and forming amateur theatre companies on his travels. In 1919, he and his wife joined the celebrated Polish collective theatre group the Vilna Troupe ('Vilner Truppe'), which had been formed in the Polish town of Vilna in 1916, with David Herman one of its inaugural directors. Its model was also Stanislavsky's Moscow Art Theatre, and its repertoire included both Yiddish theatre and the works of the renowned European dramatists.

The ensemble troupe had toured Poland and greater Europe, gaining renown for its fine 'method' drama and drawing both Jewish and non-Jewish audiences. Its great success led many of its actors to part company with the troupe to seek their fortunes in splinter theatre groups around the world. Waislitz, as one of its leading members, stayed with the troupe until the rise of anti-Semitism in Europe led to the demise of the Vilna Troupe in September 1935. Waislitz continued to tour solo shows of Yiddish poetry, literature recitals and one-act plays through Europe, Africa and eventually Australia, where he arrived in late 1937.[49]

Waislitz visited the Workers' Art Guild after being told he could borrow from there what he needed for a play he was preparing for the Jewish Theatre in Perth. He met Phyllis Harnett, who at the time was up a ladder arranging the props in the Guild rooms — this, she recalled, 'convinced Mr Waislitz that [she] was the proper theatre worker. Not just an actress, but somebody who did the dirty work.'[50] A friendship developed between the two, and Harnett threw her support behind a proposal by Waislitz and Guild member John Hector for Waislitz to take on a Guild production of *Professor Mamlock*, written by Friedrich Wolf as a serious attack on the Nazis' treatment of the Jews in Germany at that time.[51] Due to the interminable debates within the Guild about the appropriateness or otherwise of the play's value to Marxism, and George's antipathy to the idea, neither the play nor Waislitz's proposed role as a Guild director materialised. It was probably Keith George who proved the greatest hurdle.[52] He would have been aware of Waislitz's work and reputation, and his reaction to the proposal suggested professional jealousy.

Waislitz travelled to Melbourne in January 1938 to begin a solo tour of the eastern states, where his performances received high praise. He also directed performances of Friedrich Wolf's *Yellow Spot* and the famous Vilna Troupe play *The Dybbuk* ('*Der Dibbuk*'), which played to an audience of 1500 at Melbourne's Princess Theatre.[53] Waislitz publicly supported such left-wing causes as the Republican fight in the Spanish Civil War from the stage. He also revolutionised Yiddish theatre in Melbourne, introducing a modern repertoire at odds with Yiddish theatrical tradition. Like Keith George, he was a perfectionist, whose intensive rehearsals were 'lessons in literature and Yiddish history'.[54]

Waislitz left Australia at the end of 1938 before returning in 1940, seeking sanctuary from the increasing military tension and Jewish persecution in Europe. Another great expatriate Jewish actor, Moshe Berinson, met Waislitz's ship on his return to Fremantle. Berinson had moved to Perth in 1913 at the tail end of a great influx of Jews from

Eastern Europe through the last decade of the nineteenth century and into the first decade of the twentieth.⁵⁵ Berinson had founded a Yiddish theatre ensemble in Perth, though not its first, in 1919. Yiddish theatre was popular in Perth in the 1930s because of the city's significant Eastern European Jewish population — a population considerable enough to form its own enclave in the city. Princes Hall, the venue for the Perth Workers' Theatre debut where Berinson's drama group performed, was behind a synagogue in Brisbane Street just north of the city, and it became a focal point for Jewish social life in Perth.⁵⁶

On his return to Perth, Waislitz directed a play for Berinson's theatre group and presented a series of his 'word concerts' and lectures, before returning to Melbourne where he established the David Herman Theatre (an amalgamation of two existing Yiddish theatre groups). Waislitz continued to perform solo shows worldwide into the 1950s, and directed and acted in plays at the David Herman Theatre until 1962. Berinson remained Perth's leading Yiddish theatre actor, producer and director until he moved to Melbourne in 1945, where the two men later worked together again at Waislitz's David Herman Theatre.

Many of Perth's Jewish expatriates were, if not Party members, certainly sympathetic to the Communist Party's opposition to European fascism, and they brought with them a link to a rich European culture. Many frequented the Guild. Under the Australian Government's 'White Australia' policy, European immigrants were deemed more desirable than those from Asia. Australia's marginal immigration program was bolstered between 1933 and 1940, allowing 7000 European refugees, including many Jews, to enter Australia. Jewish immigration into Western Australia had grown earlier with the state's gold rush of the 1890s: from a population in 1891 of less than 100 Jews, by 1933 the state's Jewish population had increased significantly to a figure of 2100, and continued to grow. Still, this was a proportionately small number given the vast numbers of Jewish refugees fleeing Europe.⁵⁷ There was a substantial undercurrent of anti-Semitism in Australia at this time, with some distaste expressed about the new Jewish arrivals, and the federal government implemented a policy that saw Jewish immigrants having to pay five times as much for a landing permit as non-Jewish immigrants.⁵⁸

The wealthy Masel family had arrived among a much larger wave of Eastern European Jews in the period between 1890 and 1905, during troubles in the Turkish Empire, and by the 1930s the family was a pillar of Perth's Jewry establishment — members of Perth's Jewish 'royal family'.⁵⁹ The status and notoriety of families like the Masels was such that their activities were reported in the social pages of Perth's major daily newspapers.

Soon after her arrival in Perth, Phyllis Harnett met the family matriarch, Doris Masel, a sometime Repertory Club and Playbox Theatre actress, and moved into the spacious riverside Masel family home in Johnston Street, Peppermint Grove, before her move to Derby in the state's north in early 1935. On her return to Perth later that year, Harnett moved back in with the Masel family at their new Nedlands home before moving to the Trades Hall Flats.[60]

Harnett had periodically been employed in lucrative leading roles in ABC radio dramas until the offers started to go to Beryl Seward of the Repertory Club, who became Perth's staple leading lady in radio drama. Harnett was now a member of the CPA, having joined in early 1937.[61] Her involvement with the Workers' Theatre and the influence of Prichard had wooed her into the Party.[62] She worked at the Lotus Bookshop until she took up the job of managing the Radical Bookshop when she joined the CPA. By late 1937 she had formed a branch of the international Left Book Club (LBC) in Perth.[63]

The LBC, a left-wing publishing house established in Britain in 1937 by John Strachey and Victor Gollancz, became an important cultural player in the English-language book trade in the 1930s, and had widespread political influence through its distribution of weighty political literature. It was a significant alternative channel of information about international events (with a particularly left-wing bent), as well as being a locus for the distribution of workers' theatre plays. Although there was no official connection between the LBC and the CPA, it was an entirely plausible suspicion and an accusation the LBC was often called upon to counter.[64]

10

STANDING GUARD FOR THE PARTY

You should maybe join them, she said.
The Workers Art Guild?
They do get things done.[1]

Eminent Australian art and drama critic William Moore described the Workers' Art Guild in 1937 as 'the best organization of its kind in Australia'.[2] High praise, considering the large number of drama groups across the country at the time.

Despite — or perhaps because of — its heresy, the Guild continued to enjoy widespread critical and popular success in Perth. Academic Paul Herlinger was of the opinion that the Sydney New Theatre performances of the 1930s were sometimes compromised by political propaganda, and that both the Sydney and the Melbourne New Theatre groups were somewhat hamstrung by a conventional 'working-class' aesthetic.[3] The same could not be said of Keith George and the drama of the Workers' Art Guild, where George was innovative and form was paramount. The Guild aesthetic was contemporary if not in the vanguard, but the Guild theatre group was dormant through late 1937 and the early part of 1938. There was a break of eight months between performances and, although it is difficult to determine precisely what the cause of this was, the 1937 production of *Hinkemann* had certainly overstretched the Guild and exhausted some of its players. It had been a taxing year for the Guild, with the double bills of *Waiting For Lefty* and *Where's That Bomb?* in July and *Hinkemann* and *Private Hicks* for the Drama Festival in October, when preparations for *The Lyons Bungles* were also underway. The Drama Festival itself had been a major undertaking for Keith George and others in the Guild. The break may also have been a result of internal Guild tensions and ructions between George and others.

On the eve of the 1938 May Day rally on the Perth Esplanade, Labour Day celebrations were held at the Rechabite Hall.[4] Prichard and Arthur Rudkin addressed the 500 or so in attendance before 'The Internationale' and the dancing. Prichard's 'voice rang through the hall' when she spoke of the 'heroic struggle' of the Spanish loyalists, concluding her emotional speech to great applause by exclaiming: 'They will win — in spite of all, they will win!'[5] Two days later, the 1938 Labour Day parade was held. The striking Modernist banner of the Amalgamated Engineering Union (AEU) won the parade's Best Display award. The substantial prize money of £150 won by the union barely covered the cost of the banner designed, painted and stitched together by Harald Vike in his room at the Trades Hall Flats. Jack Newman, an AEU official, was the model for the strapping proletarian 'everyman' on the AEU banner, having posed for Vike in the Guild rooms. A photograph of Vike's AEU banner leading the Labour Day parade was published on the front page of the *Daily News*.[6]

Vike had held his first solo exhibition of watercolours and pencil drawings in September 1937, at John Brackenreg's gallery in Pastoral House on Perth's St Georges Terrace. The exhibition was opened by his mentor and curator of the Art Gallery of Western Australia, George Pitt Morison, who referred to Vike as 'one of the foremost of our West Australian painters'.[7] *The West Australian* art critic George Benson praised the exhibition as exemplifying 'genius', given Vike's 'study of the greatest of all masters — Nature'.[8] But Vike's art was shifting away from nature to urban imagery, some early examples of which were on display in this exhibition — notably, a large watercolour of Perth's '1937 Skyline'.[9]

Despite Modernism's intercession nudging art from traditional tranquil landscape to jarring cityscape, the Workers' Art Guild had expanded by June 1938 to include a landscape painting class. By the middle of 1938 a musical section had also been formed, overseen by pianist Leah Marks who taught Thursday-evening music classes in the Guild rooms. The musical section held regular meetings, performances, lectures and musical composition, appreciation and instruction classes, and included a choral section which met weekly in the Guild rooms.

Leah Marks's Jewish émigré father — 'The Workers' Watchmaker' and jeweller Morris Marks (formerly Markovitch) — had joined the CPA in 1935, and regularly advertised his Hay Street watchmaker's business in *The Workers' Star* in the late 1930s. He was also a casual contributor to the paper. Leah was a gifted pianist and a correspondence studies graduate of London's Trinity College of Music, as well as a music graduate of the University of Western Australia. She had taken up a position as music teacher at the School of Mines in Wiluna in 1935, and later started a kindergarten in the town. She left Wiluna to study musical composition at the University of Melbourne, and then decided that she 'should be doing something more than music'. She returned to Perth and joined the CPA and the Workers' Art Guild.[10]

Some of the music that came out of the Guild's musical composition classes accompanied their theatre productions or was performed at occasional public concerts. A Guild music quartet of Joan Kidd (violin) and brothers George Benn (violin and viola), Thomas Benn (cello) and Maurice Benn (piano and viola) played through some of the Guild's theatrical performances, with Hope Bath, and later Charles Gordon, providing occasional vocal accompaniment.[11]

Joan Kidd's first sight of the Guild had been at the June 1936 performance of *Till the Day I Die*. Her brother Ben Kidd was in the cast. She had lived a sheltered life in a working-class family but, having 'pretensions to being cultured', she attended night art classes at Perth Technical College to broaden her orbit. The sight of the handsome, worldly and celebrated local artist Harald Vike on stage in the role of a Nazi stormtrooper had her transfixed: the contrast between them fuelled an instant attraction, and she gravitated to the Guild.[12]

The Benn brothers were raised in a cultured Scottish migrant family. Little is known about George, who took his own life in 1939. Thomas (Tom) Benn was a blue-collar member of the CPA. Maurice, the most talented musician of the trio, was a formidable intellect enrolled in an Arts degree in German at the University of Western Australia.

Hope Bath was the daughter of a respectable Perth barrister. Although a member of the CPA, she was too respectable and 'well-bred' to publicly associate herself with the Guild, but she was an efficient backroom worker as Guild secretary until Phyllis Harnett took over the role in mid-1938.[13] Charles Gordon, a gifted baritone singer who had studied music in England for a number of years, also arranged music for the Guild and performed at Guild musical performances.

Keith George and the Guild had been toying with the prospect of producing Prichard's as yet unpublished play *Brumby Innes*, but George had quite bravely resisted producing any other of Prichard's plays since *Forward One* during the Workers' Theatre's infancy. He appreciated Prichard's plays 'as literature', but he and Prichard 'had certain fundamental differences on the subject of production that made cooperation [between the] author [and the] producer difficult.'[14] This was exemplified by their arguments over the production 'gimmicks' of *Bury the Dead*. George also felt that Prichard's politics interceded too much into her writing. He was keen to direct interesting plays irrespective of persuasion, and he felt that Prichard's politics too heavily compromised her plays.

> Her great gifts became clouded by the phoney fantasies of Marx and his pseudo-realism. She seemed to me at times to sacrifice her own sensitive reaction to truth to the need of making a polemical point. A point in which the premises were false.[15]

The other factor that made George wary of producing Prichard's plays was that, as a director, he felt her plays were 'slightly "off balance"'. 'They did not therefore create in me that excitement which made it imperative that I produce them.'[16]

By George's own account, he perhaps 'tried to compensate' by directing 'against [his] better judgement Soviet plays which [Prichard] admired, but the results were not very happy.'[17] However, there is evidence of only one of these 'Soviet plays' ever being directed by George for the Guild, namely *Inga*, which the Guild staged in June 1938 and of which Prichard was not terribly fond. She wrote to Mikhail Apletin, deputy head of the Foreign Commission of the Soviet Writers' Union in Moscow, that 'the play is not as good an example of Soviet drama as I should have liked the Guild to produce'. Prichard was a member of the Workers' Art Guild 'advisory board' and solicited appropriate plays from Apletin to present to the board for production by the Guild.[18]

While *Inga* was in its final stages of rehearsal and preparation, the Guild, without George's involvement, was also rehearsing a very direct one-act agitprop titled *Women of Spain*, written by Prichard in 1937 under the pseudonym Rita Martinez. This play was 'an appeal in dramatic form to the people of all lands from the unhappy women of Spain', and it was staged by the Guild to raise funds for the local chapter of the Spanish Relief Committee.[19] Set in 'the living room of a working class flat in Barcelona' during the Spanish Civil War, the play portrays a family whose members, one by one, are killed by the Civil War. The performance concludes with an appeal by the women in the play for help in their struggle to defend their democracy 'barely glimpsed'.[20]

Women of Spain was a very direct and abrasive agitprop — 'fiercely partisan', according to Prichard's son Ric Throssell — and was written in a form that Prichard had first employed in 1914 when she wrote the sketch *For Instance* for the Actresses' Franchise League in London.[21] Articles about the plight of women living in Spain were being published regularly through 1936 and 1937 in the CPA journal *Woman Today*, for which Prichard was the Perth correspondent, and it was probably these stories, as well as the firsthand accounts she heard from friends like the Palmers and the Civil War documentaries then screening around Perth, that inspired Prichard to write the play.

The most notable performance of *Women of Spain* took place at a Spanish Relief Committee public meeting at the Perth Town Hall on 27 July 1938. Joan Williams, who attended, wrote of Prichard's speech following the performance that evening:

> Could this small, rather colourless woman with straight greying hair cut short and clipped back from a high forehead be the witch of Greenmount who so shocked Perth people? She spoke slowly and simply, avoiding the padding and circumlocutions that wore out reporters, giving an impression of emotional commitment on a carefully reasoned basis. When the applause died down, she took up her cigarette in its ivory holder and calmly answered questions. But there was no opportunity to really get to know her.[22]

The Guild toured *Women of Spain* around Perth between June and August 1938 to assist Spanish Relief Committee appeals, perhaps as a fixed-stage performance at some rallies but almost certainly on the back of a truck at others.[23] In late August the Guild performed the play at another Spanish Relief Committee rally at the new Slav Hall in Osborne Park, where a considerable sum was raised for the Committee.[24]

The Guild's next major theatrical production, in June 1938, was that of *Inga*. Selected from a book of modern Soviet plays in the Guild library, it was intended to portray a less strident, polemic image of Communism. *The Workers' Star* described the play as 'a change from the turbulent drama by which the Guild has made itself known.'[25] Notwithstanding that he may have directed *Inga* to please Prichard, this appears to be the first occasion on which Keith George did not have complete supremacy over the choice of play staged by the Guild. George admired many aspects of Russian theatre, Stanislavsky and Chekhov not least, but *Inga* was not a play that appealed to him, though he directed it with great energy.[26]

Written by Anatole Glebov, who became a CPSU apparatchik after fighting with the Red Guard during the Russian Revolution, *Inga* was an expansive play of twelve scenes 'presented by the Guild as an example of the contemporary Russian Theatre',[27] despite the fact that it was by then ten years old and quite unrepresentative of late-1930s Soviet theatre. *Inga* was written in 1928 and had its premiere at the Moscow Theatre of the Revolution in early 1929.[28] The play, which takes place in a clothing factory during the industrial reforms of Stalin's initial Five Year Plan, portrays the conflict between the ideals of the old Soviet political order and the new. The character of Inga is the manager of a clothing factory. The character of Dmitri, chairman of the factory committee, is in love with Inga and leaves his wife Glafeera for her. Inga is compelled to renounce Dmitri's consuming affection to pursue the righteous path of a good Communist, increased factory output and the greater ideals of Soviet society. Glafeera disapproves of a woman running the factory but is eventually reconciled to it in deference to the new order, and is liberated from the shackles of her oppressive marriage to Dmitri. *The West Australian* described the play as being about 'the adjustment of the relations between men and women to the new ways of living, in particular the breaking down of prejudice against women in a position of authority.'[29] It was a propagandist play illustrating the contrast between the character of Glafeera, representative of the 'old' pre-revolutionary Russian woman, and the emancipated Inga, a cipher of the 'new' post-revolutionary Soviet woman — the 'capable, intellectual' Party prototype who is 'the equal or superior of any man around her'.[30] The play is, in essence, a socialist realist tale of redemption in which the anachronistic character of Glafeera is transformed and released from domestic constraints to share in the spoils of the new society.

Keith George thought the title role in *Inga* well suited to Phyllis Harnett, and asked her to play the part. But Harnett was closer to the character of Inga than she would have liked, and so was reluctant to take on the role. Fearful that her political life was beginning to consume her private life, she was concerned about taking on the mantle of the 'new woman' off-stage. 'I was so bloody scared it was going to happen to me that I wouldn't play Inga,' she later said.[31] In addition, the heavy workload required of her involvement in a great number of Guild plays, the Drama Festival and Perth's Independent Theatre (antecedent to the Little Theatre) had taken its toll — her role in *Hinkemann* had been particularly taxing — and she was close to physical and emotional breakdown. She was still struggling to support herself and, while Guild activities had slowed through the early part of 1938, she had been able to pick up radio drama work that paid well and was far less demanding than her stage work. She was also greatly given to falling in love at the time, and she wanted to pursue romance more and masquerade less. Inga 'was the part of a woman who had expunged sex from her life so as to be a good working comrade, and I wouldn't play her because I thought it might come true', she later said.[32] George grudgingly replaced her with popular Repertory Club actress Betty Campbell, a well-known stage actress in Perth who was 'lured' into playing the part of Inga by the Guild's standing 'and the good nature of the part', despite the role being 'really anathema to her. She was the most anti-Communist person'.[33]

Hasluck wrote in *The West Australian* of the difficulty of presenting a play such as *Inga* in Perth.

> Many of the types have no counterpart in Australian life and this made it hard, firstly, for the players to get into the roles and, secondly, for the audience to appreciate them. The consequence was that two or three of the types which were familiar, ... the fading man-provoker and the drunken wife-beater, were either better represented or more readily appreciated and stood out disproportionately to other elements in the drama. Moreover, one of the strongest points about the guild's acting has always been a sense of actuality and in several of the character studies ... this was not felt. Nevertheless, the performance was a striking one with a good rousing pace, and it frequently communicated a feeling of excitement, while there was always that concentration and that perfect drilling of everyone on the stage that marks the guild's work ... It is an unusually interesting play, done vigorously.[34]

Keith George's distaste for *Inga* was yet another point of dissension between him and the increasingly persuasive forces in the Guild gathering against him, and *Inga* may have been forced upon him by the ascendant CPA pressure group. Prichard was an influential, though undoubtedly reluctant, intermediary in George's brawls with the Party faction in the Guild. Her loyalty was primarily to George, and she tried to persuade those within the Guild who sought a more hardline political direction for the Guild — with or without George — of George's paramount importance to the Guild theatre.

Prichard also had to deal with spot fires elsewhere in CPA circles. A sanctimonious letter written by Bill Mountjoy to Prichard in April 1938 revealed internal ructions within the local branch of the Party. Middle-class Party members at odds with Mountjoy had been approaching Prichard with their grievances, and it seems Mountjoy had once again taken exception to the behaviour of a few such members, including Gus Stagg, and he urged Prichard to tackle them rather than taking him on. The letter made diplomatic yet blatantly patronising references to Prichard's standing as a woman of substance and influence in the Party *despite* her middle-class pedigree.

Dear Katharine,

Lindsay [Mountjoy's wife] has informed me that you want to see both of us for a 'straight talk'. She arranged to meet you on

Thursday next but that is the night I am lecturing on Communist Philosophy at the Arundale Hall. You can understand therefore that I am reluctant to injure something of value for something of very doubtful value — that is if I have anticipated your reasons for going to an unprecedented end to see me. Frankly if you want to argue with me and defend the comrades mentioned the other day and turn me from my proletarian path then you are wasting my time — but worse still wasting your own which is more valuable than mine because there are a number of capable Party leaders in Australia but only one Katharine, whose national prestige is extremely important ... In our Party people with a middle-class background are continually threatening the erosion of the shores of our Party and the proletarians are continually defending it ... I stand guard for the proletarian purity of the Party — there I stand or fall. You are not sufficiently acquainted with the inner workings of the Party to know all that is going on. If you were I would not be worried about you. It grieves me to see such a brilliant representative of the working class taking the side — even if unconsciously — with those who would wreck the Party — probably just as unconsciously. These are serious times. I am prepared to fight disruption to the last. And in any form ... I flatter myself that I can be hard when necessary and now's the time. Think for a moment who's who in this struggle and then ask yourself if you are not suffering from the ivory tower disease. I mean that ... Tell the people that come to you to see me. They can write to the [district branch] if they want and then if not satisfied also write to the [central committee]. But I will not take any blame for wasting the time of [CPA leaders] Miles, Dixon, Sharkey and Co. They are real proletarians and really over-worked ... The Party is neither a backscratching organisation, or a playground for political playboys, or a manoeuvring ground for born intriguers. I regard it seriously. I don't want my time wasted. My time is the Party's time. With my proletarian comrades I can solve the inner-Party problems and keep those with middle-class ballast in their make up in their place. Once again dear Comrade don't waste my time or your own and don't let the two of us be at cross purposes with each other ... Don't spoil our achievement over people who, at bottom, are merely ethereal individuals.[35]

Relations had always been strained between Prichard and Mountjoy, and would later come to a head in a confrontation between the two over

Mountjoy's drinking.³⁶ Prichard believed that Mountjoy ruled the local CPA too heavy-handedly, while Mountjoy resented both Prichard's middle-class pedigree and her influence in the CPA. Prichard spoke to Mountjoy about it and he reacted angrily. She was subsequently called to appear before the CPA Control Commission, where she was accused of deviating from the Party line in her writing. This was the result, they said, of her bourgeois origins that separated her from the workers — criticism that greatly hurt Prichard, given her often-trying fidelity to the Party.³⁷ At the time Mountjoy's letter was written, he was becoming increasingly concerned about CIB infiltration of the CPA in Perth and was attempting to weed out police informants — despite the fact that he, inadvertently yet recklessly, would become the Party's most prominent police informant. This distrust, near antipathy, of middle-class Party members was endemic among CPA functionaries. Mountjoy directed many of these middle-class Party members to appear before the Control Commission to be scrutinised and berated. The mainstream of the CPA in Western Australia was predominantly working class and deeply suspicious of, if not antagonistic towards, middle-class recruits. The distinctions between the working class and the 'intellectual' middle class were laboured on in Party circles in the 1930s.

Influential left-wing American journalist and cultural critic Clinton Hartley Grattan visited Perth in June 1938. Grattan had first visited Australia in 1927, after which he had written about the state of Australian literature. He had gone on to develop a particular interest in Australian literature, befriending a number of Australian writers, academics and intellectuals on his subsequent visits to the country, and had been corresponding with Prichard for a number of years. In 1936 the Carnegie Corporation of New York had commissioned Grattan to write a political, economic and cultural analysis of Australian society, and in it he had singled out Prichard for particular praise among Australian writers, describing her as 'the strongest of all writers of fiction in Australia' at the time.³⁸

Grattan's 1938 visit was his first to Perth, and Prichard had arranged for him to deliver a public lecture in the Workers' Art Guild rooms on the history of protest and dissent in American literature. Writing to Grattan afterwards, Prichard declared that his visit had been 'like a south-west wind after a long drought!'³⁹

Peter Cowan described Grattan's Guild lecture in *The Hills of Apollo Bay*:

The big room at the top of the stairs was already crowded. They sat at the back, he had not expected so many to come ... Though the speaker might not know how many, or how few, how very few it was likely, had read the books he talked of with such confidence. Such easy assurance. Books hard enough to find. To order. To wait for. Some forbidden as imports to this community held about the banks of its slow river, which the speaker could know so little. The vigour of American literature and criticism came through the words, confirmation of his own reading. A reading at least of some of the fiction. He had been able to find none of the critical books. A tradition of dissent, Grattan said. Established in America. And how should that arise here.[40]

The next Guild production was that of Henrik Ibsen's *Ghosts*. Keith George had directed a production of this play in earlier times at the Five Arts Club, but it was Howard Smith, rather than Keith George, who directed this production for the Guild. The production was well received, though quite conventional: George's flair was noticeably missing. Ibsen had been closely associated with the People's Theatre movement in Germany in the late nineteenth century, but *The Workers' Star* wrote a veiled criticism of the Guild's having taken on a play, though 'once contentious', written fifty-seven years earlier rather than a more contemporary 'problem play':[41]

> Its subject must be quite as unpleasant to the squeamish as was 'Hinkemann'. Its treatment of that subject is as artistic as 'Hinkemann's, and in its day it produced an uproar, beside which Perth's 'Hinkemann' controversy would look like an academic discussion. Now, as it is venerable with age, it is unlikely that a single dog will bark about the subject. The classics can say what they wish, but let a modern author be a little outspoken, and the shouting will start.[42]

The Workers' Star's drama critic, 'Backseat', previewed the play under the heading 'The Guild Goes Classic' as:

> an effective show-up of those who hide from unpleasant facts, still pertinent to-day ... After the 'Hinkemann' uproar, the Guild should enjoy reading the public this lesson.[43]

But 'Backseat', a hitherto steadfast supporter of the Guild's theatre work, also took a dim view of the Guild taking on this play and expressed the 'hope that the Guild will quickly return to drama with more immediate and urgent themes.'[44]

Hasluck referred to the Guild 'taking a short holiday from its gusty dramas of labour in protest', but acknowledged that the play was also a 'protest against the polite facade built in front of the more distasteful aspects of human life' and in that sense was still in keeping with the Guild's 'mission of presenting plays with a social purpose'. Indeed, Hasluck felt that the angry response to the recent work of the Guild had served as a reminder that these 'ghosts' of antiquated standards of respectability were not as obsolete as many believed.[45]

The annual exhibition of the Perth Society of Artists (PSA) opened in July 1938, marking the beginning of a year described by art critic Sydney Ure Smith as 'the most outstanding ... in Western Australian art — certainly the most glowing since the [First World] War'.[46] The PSA had been formed in 1933 as a more progressive breakaway group from the steadfastly orthodox West Australian Society of Arts, and it held an annual exhibition showcasing the art of its members. Its 1938 exhibition heralded the ascendancy of a new generation of local artists, among them Herbert McClintock, Harald Vike and John Lunghi, described by Ure Smith as 'freedom-loving, straight-forward and robust ... shunning worn-out paths' and keen to experiment with new painterly forms and styles 'without fearing conservative opinions'.[47] Guild fringe dweller John Lunghi was singled out for special mention in reviews.

Lunghi was not a fully committed member of the Workers' Art Guild, but he certainly helped Harald Vike on the set design for at least one Guild production, and he had an 'affection' for those in the Guild.[48] He was a descendant of the great Venetian painter Pietro Longhi (1702–1785), and had studied at the London Central School of Arts and Crafts with Hal Missingham and James Linton. He'd moved to Perth in 1937, where he was employed at Gibbney's and tutored evening drawing classes at Perth Technical College.

In August 1938, Herbert McClintock held his first solo exhibition at the Newspaper House Art Gallery on St Georges Terrace. McClintock had made the first and most dramatic break from the orthodox arts scene, working through a period of constructivist art before immersing himself in surrealism and establishing himself as Perth's foremost bohemian. During his 1938 solo exhibition an anonymous 'critic', probably at

McClintock's urging, wrote a letter to the editor of *The West Australian* bemoaning the fact that the Trustees of the Art Gallery of Western Australia had yet to buy one of McClintock's surrealist paintings for their permanent collection[49] — a rather fanciful plea given that surrealism was then 'as much argued about as it was painted', and McClintock was still in his infancy as an artist.[50] Within two years, though, the Gallery Trustees did acquire one of McClintock's surrealist paintings for the state gallery's collection.[51]

Surrealism, by then just over a decade old, was still very contentious and confronting. McClintock had read André Breton's surrealist manifesto, *What is Surrealism?*, and then set out to pen subconscious surrealist prose and drawings and devour all the literature on surrealism that he could find.[52] For McClintock, surrealism was yet another manifestation of rebellion, but his work was significant given that it was some of the earliest surrealist art created in Australia — all the more remarkable as he was working in one of the most isolated cities in the world.[53] McClintock was then 'the public face of Australian Surrealism'.[54]

Shortly after his exhibition closed, McClintock and Harald Vike staged a public debate on 'Modern Art' at the Modern Women's Club, just a few weeks before the opening of an exhibition of Vike's work in the Newspaper House Art Gallery.[55] Vike had dabbled a little in surrealist art but the pair expressed ostensibly 'opposite points of view'. Vike criticised the 'ultra-modernism' and 'extreme tendencies' of surrealism but 'spoke appreciatively of the impressionistic school of Cézanne and the back-to-nature school' of Paul Gauguin. He also argued that those who indulged in surrealism's 'flight from reality' could not, by definition, 'have anything worthwhile to say'. McClintock, in contrast, spoke of abstract art inventing 'its forms of expression'.[56] He quoted German 'Blue Rider' painter Franz Marc in claiming 'that artists today were "seeking behind the veil of nature's outward appearance hidden things" which seemed to them more important than the discoveries of the Impressionists'.[57] Vike's anti-Modernist line was that being almost universally touted then by the Communist Party.

In September 1938, Sydney New Theatre director Jerold Wells moved to Perth to take up a paid position as director of the Repertory Club. Esmond George had taken over as director from Cyril Riley in late 1936, but vacated the position to take up work on the West Australian Drama Festival. The 1938 Drama Festival — the playwright's competition in particular — was a great stimulus at a time when it seemed harder than ever for Australian playwrights to get their plays performed despite the thriving repertory movement.[58] Ticket sales for the 1938 festival, again held in October, 'considerably exceeded' those for the inaugural 1937 festival, and the 1938 event included a playwriting competition for full-length plays. The winning full-length play was to be staged at His Majesty's Theatre, its author receiving the substantial sum of £50 in royalties for the single festival performance.

Eighty entries were received, from which the festival committee chose Betty Roland's *Are You Ready, Comrade? The Workers' Star* could barely contain its conceit in announcing that 'for the second time a play from the Left has won the playwright's competition', following Phyllis Harnett's win for *I Am Angry* the previous year.[59] The fact that this very partisan political play won such an award again illustrates the lack of any real animosity towards left-wing theatre in Perth by this time.[60]

Are You Ready, Comrade?, written in 1937, was partly autobiographical but overtly propagandist. Although set in Australia, it was inspired by Roland's 1933 visit to the Soviet Union with Guido Baracchi, 'attracted there by the theatre'.[61] Their visit coincided with Prichard's and the trio had roomed together in Moscow. Roland wrote to Paul Hasluck about the background to the play:

> By great good fortune I managed to get a job there and thereby remained for 1 year and 3 months, living and working in both Moscow and Leningrad, where I had the happiest and most stimulating period of my entire existence ... I had become so convinced that the people of the Soviet Union had found the correct and only solution of the world's problems and injustices that I felt it was my duty to come back to Australia and try and convince others of the same thing. Not so easy.[62]

Set in Melbourne's recent past, it is a complex domestic love story about proletarian virtue. The play documents the moral crisis of a working-class woman, married to a wealthy middle-class industrial magnate, drawn back to her class heritage 'with the expressed intention of "joining the revolution"'.[63] *Music and the Drama* described *Are You Ready, Comrade?* as 'a play of modern city life in Australia'[64] — a euphemism, no doubt, for the rather charged sexual and political melodrama and the play's somewhat abrasive language. It was the sort of convoluted character-driven melodrama to which Roland was partial. Author Leslie Rees later wrote of the play:

'Are You Ready, Comrade?', as I saw it done by the Sydney New Theatre with the authoress in the main role, had individual scenes as electrifying and urgent as any so far written in Australian drama; but regarded as an entity it was confusing, because indigestible and too rabidly propagandist.[65]

There was no official 1938 Drama Festival entry from the Workers' Art Guild, but the festival committee had appointed Keith George to direct the production of *Are You Ready, Comrade?* and he chose a cast of predominantly Workers' Art Guild actors. The lead roles were played by Keith George and Phyllis Harnett, alongside Howard Smith, George Wignall, Maurice Lachberg and Marjorie Berry and some more recent Guild recruits in Walter Poole-Johnson, George McCorkill, Pat Howard (who had made her Guild debut in *Inga*) and Clifford MacDonald (who had appeared in *Where's That Bomb* and *Waiting For Lefty*). Dorothy Powell, a staple Repertory Club actress and a theatre veteran at the age of twenty-six, made her Guild debut in *Are You Ready, Comrade?* She had made her first stage appearance at the age of three and had hardly stepped off stage since then. Powell was essentially apolitical and served a variety of theatre masters. She had been introduced to the Workers' Art Guild crowd by Harnett and had made a number of firm friends among them.[66]

The performance of *Are You Ready, Comrade?* took place on the last night of the Drama Festival, and Hasluck described the play as 'something of a disappointment'. The audience of about 1400, he wrote, 'seemed interested but not gripped' in a play that lacked 'emotional drive' and 'did not speak to or for Australians'.

> That may have been partly due to the fact that the play expresses dissatisfaction with the present social order while a large part of the audience probably feel quite smug about it.[67]

Hasluck felt that Roland had 'over-reached herself in her eagerness' to make a particular political point. Her characters were extreme and 'improbable' political archetypes and, as if the polemic of the script had not amply made its point, the final curtain dropped to the accompaniment of 'The Internationale'. Despite his weighty criticisms, Hasluck described the play as 'by no means an unworthy representative at the festival'.

> It is all competently written and some of it is exceptionally well done. It is good, too, to see a dramatist tackling boldly an

important subject and this play, whatever its defects, is far worthier of attention than the imitative or sentimental stuff that is found in most Australian manuscripts.[68]

Both the play and its production by Keith George were a stark contrast to other, more traditional festival entries. The performance took place on two adjoining sets on the stage of His Majesty's Theatre. The stage was divided in half and while the action took place in one scene, the set for the following scene was prepared behind a curtain in the adjacent half of the stage, allowing the action to switch immediately from one scene to the next, eliminating often lengthy waits between scenes. But the divided stage meant that some of the audience had their view of certain scenes obscured by pillars in the stalls, and some of the dialogue was inaudible to members of the audience, particularly that of Phyllis Harnett in the role of Connie Boyd.[69]

The Workers' Star drama critic 'Ravel' praised aspects of Keith George's production but also had gripes about the performance.

> Went to see [*Are You Ready, Comrade?*] on Saturday and enjoyed Miss Pat Howard's line. It was the only one I heard. I paid 2/– for a seat in the gods and sat next to a machine, which, I was told afterwards, operated the spotlight. The din was terrific. I'm sure nobody else in the gods was able to hear either.[70]

The Repertory Club's new-found audacity under Jerold Wells was illustrated by its plan to stage the Elmer Rice play *Street Scene*, a social commentary about American slum dwelling, at the 1938 Drama Festival. The performance did not eventuate, but another, though milder, 'problem play' replaced it, in Sean O'Casey's *Juno and the Paycock*.

The Repertory Club was a significant institution in Perth and there had been a great amount of interest in the director position. Seventy applications had been received, and Jerold Wells had been appointed with the official blessing of the CPA Central Committee. He was carrying the committee's letter of introduction to Bill Mountjoy when, shortly after his arrival, he was caught in a compromising situation with Phyllis Harnett during a police visit to her room at the Trades Hall Flats.[71]

Given the Guild's impact, it was little surprise that the Repertory Club appointed an experienced New Theatre director to the position. There had been a push by the increasingly influential younger set in the Repertory Club to move the group towards a more left-wing repertoire and 'to get even more red blood' into the Club.[72]

Wells's inaugural Repertory Club production in November 1938 was of Henrietta Drake-Brockman's three-act play *Men Without Wives*, written earlier that year and set on a remote cattle station in the north-west of Western Australia. The play, greatly admired by Prichard, had won the 1938 national Sesquicentenary Prize for drama and was initially staged by the Sydney Players' Club in April 1938.

A broadening of the influence of the CPA's Guild fraction and the push for more CPA outreach work by the Guild was by now a fait accompli. In 1939 the Guild sent agitprop drama out into the community, and Guild performances took place at ALP branch meetings, in town halls and on the back of trucks in country towns as far afield as Geraldton. Later in the year the Guild opened its doors wider, allowing the public to attend its weekly Sunday-evening rehearsals — final dress rehearsals prior to opening nights having hitherto been the only Guild rehearsals open to the public — monthly 'rehearsed readings' and free performances of certain plays, including the American Guild Theatre's Living Newspaper *The Cradle Will Rock*, Emlyn Williams's *Night Must Fall*, and an adaptation of John Steinbeck's *Of Mice and Men*.[73]

Guild activities being discussed at union meetings outside the Guild was indicative of the Guild's broadening political front from late 1938, encouraged by the younger sectarian members that Keith George so objected to. Guild plans for the March 1939 state election included the staging of agitprops in support of Labor candidate Roy Neville, a solicitor and a member of the state committee of the Left Book Club.

Man Gets House was one of two Guild plays staged for Neville's campaign.[74] The play owed something to American Living Newspaper *One-Third of a Nation*, which addressed that nation's housing crisis, its title a reference to President Franklin D. Roosevelt's January 1937 inauguration address:

> I see one-third of a nation ill-housed, ill-clad, ill-nourished ... The test of our progress is not whether we add more to the abundance of those who have much; it is whether we provide enough for those who have too little.[75]

Man Gets House satirised Western Australia's Workers' Homes Board, the forerunner to the State Housing Commission, and was presented in support of an ongoing campaign by the CPA to secure housing and fair rent for the poor and an improvement in the quality of housing for tenants on and under the breadline.[76] Characters — or rather caricatures — in this 'knockabout turn'[77] included 'the worker', 'the landlord' and a rotund man perched on a chair representing the Workers' Homes Board.[78] A later Guild assessment criticised the *Man Gets House* performances as 'over naturalistic', having 'not [had] the good fortune of a producer with agit-prop experience'.

> Its exposition of its subject was clear, its humour perhaps a little too subtle for its purpose.[79]

The second play staged by the Guild for Neville's state election campaign was *Socko*, an agitprop about the financial emergency tax.[80] The federal *Financial Emergency Act 1931* was a measure forced upon the Scullin government, agreed upon at a conference of state premiers and introduced in 1931 to curb government spending in order to repay Australia's increasing foreign debt to Britain during the Depression. It cut salaries and pensions, and led to a massive split in the Labor Party that marginalised the ALP for a decade. *Socko*, 'with its burlesque characters and slap-stick action', was more popular than *Man Gets House*.[81] 'Backseat' reported in *The Workers' Star* that *Socko* was 'acted in vigorous style' and an 'effective bit of election propaganda' … 'Even taxation can be dramatised.'[82]

At the end of a particularly hot Perth summer, both *Man Gets House* and *Socko* played nights on the back of a truck around West Perth through the election campaign.[83] The shows were characteristically interrupted by some degree of public fracas: during one performance of *Man Gets House* a couple in the audience tried to take the chairs and table from the actors on the back of the truck while police stood impassively by.[84] The life of an agitprop player was fraught with peril, and Kathleen Hector, who acted in some of these agitprops, recalled that it was often 'a matter of fleeing before the locals got to you'.[85]

As well as *Man Gets House* and *Socko*, the Workers' Art Guild drama wing performed short political plays on the topics of unemployment and the Legislative Council in support of the ALP during the 1939 election campaign. These 'street dramatisations', written by the Guild, notably dramatised parts of the CPA's election platform.

In early 1939, a Sydney New Theatre party member visiting Melbourne suggested that Melbourne New Theatre follow Sydney's lead by setting up a formal CPA branch within their organisation.[86] Meanwhile in Perth the Workers' Art Guild remained steadfastly — constitutionally at least — unattached to any political party, but developments in the eastern states were discussed within the Guild and there was probably a growing, if subtle, push from some in the Guild to follow suit.[87] This evolution within the New Theatre certainly coincided with significant changes within the Guild, no doubt spawned by increasing CPA influence within the tent.

In late March 1939, the Guild staged *Floridsdorf*.

> After a silence of several months the dramatic section of the Workers' Art Guild made plenty of noise in the Assembly Hall last night. Cannon, machineguns, rifle fire and the shouting of excited men.[88]

Like *Till The Day I Die*, *Floridsdorf* was a powerful attack on fascism and an illustration of the personal misery wrought by fascist despotism. The play, written by German Communist Friedrich Wolf, is set in workers' flats in the Vienna district of Floridsdorf and documents the struggle of the Viennese trade unions and workers against Austrian leader Engelbert Dollfuss during his quasi-dictatorial rule of 1933 to 1934. It dramatises the violent and ill-fated struggle of the militia wing of the Austrian Social Democrats (Der Republikanischer Schutzbund) against their suppression by the Dollfuss regime. The Social Democratic Party, buttressed by the support of the working class, had been the initial governing party in Austria after the formation of the Austrian Republic in 1918, but a right-wing coalition government dominated by the Christian Democrats came to power in 1920. Austria, as elsewhere, lurched into a major economic crisis in 1930 and, like the Germans, Austrians scapegoated Jewish residents and threw their support behind the Austrian Nazi Party whose political stocks and influence grew. With the Austrian economy in tatters and the political stability of Austria foundering, anti-Semitic sentiment was rife and anti-Semitic violence erupted. The Christian Socialist Party formed government in May 1932 and Dollfuss, appointed chancellor, initially took steps to curb anti-Semitism. In May 1933, Dollfuss, now presiding over a conservative anti-Semitic regime and unable to form a stable government, instituted an authoritarian regime of rule by decree, with himself as its quasi-dictator, in a country placed geographically snug between fascist Germany and fascist Italy. Dollfuss outlawed the Austrian Social Democratic Party and its militia wing. In June 1933, Hitler ascended to power in neighbouring Germany, with plans to annex Austria. The National Socialists and Austrian independence posed the greatest threat to his rule, and Dollfuss dissolved the Austrian National Socialist Party, which now had the backing of the powerful German Nazi regime. He relied on Austrian fascist leader Starhemberg for support and Mussolini in neighbouring Italy for the preservation of an independent Austrian state and they, in concert, forced Dollfuss to act against the Social Democrats.[89] Dollfuss met a resultant Socialist uprising in February 1934 — in essence, a short-lived civil war — with bloody retaliation and suppression.[90]

It was these events that formed the background to Wolf's play, and it was *Floridsdorf* that gave flesh to the bare bones of what many in the Guild, Phyllis Harnett especially, had understood, up to that point, to be the socialist movement and what was meant, more particularly, by the term 'social democrat'. The German Social Democratic movement, which had formed in 1863 and ascended to political power with the formation of the Weimar Republic, stood at that time in stark and brave opposition to the National Socialists, and was brutally suppressed by the Nazis. Keith George, though he was not a member of the Communist Party, recognised the significance of the play as an illustration of the manifest importance of the socialist movement as a political counterbalance. His concerns in theatre were primarily dramatic and aesthetic rather than political. In his *Floridsdorf*, the political and the spectacle were entwined. For George, *Floridsdorf* was a rare and exceptional revolutionary play and he was determined to do it justice. He was not given to political dissertation when rehearsing a play, nor did he openly discuss politics when rehearsing *Floridsdorf*. He knew that the political punch in this play did not need to be recited. He 'took "social democrats" and "communists", as presented in the play, by two dramatic conceptions as you might take laughter and tears.'[91]

George directed the play and played the leading role with biting intensity. There were times when he was unable, given limited resources, to attain all that he wished in the production of a play, and he was loath to compromise or abandon plans, however overambitious.[92] His enthusiasms sometimes clouded his judgement, and this is illustrated by his extravagant plans for *Floridsdorf*. He was keen to spend up to two years rehearsing the play, but many of the cast were not so keen. The Guild was certainly 'at work' on the play in November 1938, and it seems that George spent somewhere between six months and a year rehearsing the play, with a number of cast changes.[93] This meant that some cast members in the final production had been in rehearsal for only a short time, and that 'there were very few people in it at the last, who had been in it at the first rehearsal.'[94] Guild veterans in the cast included John Bottomley, John Gilchrist, Clifford MacDonald, Howard Smith and Ian Smith.[95] John Hector made his first Guild stage appearance in the play.

Hector was born into a wealthy family in colonial Hong Kong in 1914, and orphaned at the age of twelve. He boarded at Scotch College in Perth, attended the University of Western Australia and then joined the *Daily News* as a copyboy and cadet journalist. His pedigree was genteel and apolitical, if not conservative, and although he maintained middle-class tastes and views on art and literature, he later rebelled against his upbringing. At university in 1934 he was editor of the guild of undergraduates magazine, *The Black Swan*. Critical of the journal for its 'popular fiction in the O. Henry style' and for its verse which he considered 'artificial, immature, and modelled after an effete tradition', he attempted to raise its literary and cultural merits.[96] Under Hector's editorship *The Black Swan* published more scholarly material and allowed for more experimental prose and ideas. Many of its contributors were future Workers' Art Guild players, including Ray McClintock, Harald Vike and Alec King.

In 1935 Hector was promoted to senior reporter and chief subeditor at the *Daily News,* followed by a stint working on newspapers in South East Asia before returning to the *Daily News* in 1937 as news editor and chief sports subeditor. Hector was also a promising actor and theatre director. He had performed with the Repertory Club and was a strong supporter of the Workers' Art Guild; indeed, his contemporary Joan Williams later wrote that Hector was 'such an enthusiast that I might have thought he was the main force' in the Workers' Art Guild.[97] His support for the Guild would eventually cost him his newspaper career in Perth.[98]

The critical response to *Floridsdorf* was mixed. *The West Australian* reported that 'the Workers' Art Guild went at the play with an energy that sometimes made them incoherent, and unfortunately some of the disorder and desperation in the situation they were staging seemed to communicate themselves to their work'.

> It was a fevered scramble ... The play opened well. The production, particularly the timing and grouping of the first act, was admirable. Then it became disorganised ... The merits are chiefly to be found in the acting ... in the cast of 28.[99]

The Workers' Star opined that 'the production by Keith George might have been cleaner'.

> Words became confused in the shouting. The prompter was needed at times. The timing was sometimes at fault.[100]

Guild stalwarts John Hepworth and Marjorie Berry played the partial singing roles of the young lovers in *Floridsdorf*, and critics praised their performances. Numerous gunshots were exchanged in the production, and during one performance 'Hepworth had the distinction of dying on stage when not a single gunshot was being fired.'[101]

A few days after the completion of the Guild season of *Floridsdorf*, seventeen-year-old John Hepworth married twenty-one-year-old stenographer Kathleen Beechey at the Registrar's office, witnessed by Bill Irwin and Beechey's father — a man of fortitude, having been crippled at Gallipoli, but whose daughter's marriage to Hepworth must have tested his mettle.

Kathleen Beechey was a respectably educated Church of England girls' college alumna, but found Perth 'extremely stultifying' and had gravitated to the Guild out of teenage curiosity and a 'desperate' craving for excitement. She found the Guild 'a breath of fresh air', became involved in its children's theatre wing and provided much-needed secretarial skills to its administration. Her father was broadminded and had been a member of the English Fabian Society, but her Catholic mother regarded the Guild 'as the root of all evil, practically'.[102]

The day before Hepworth and Beechey's wedding, CPA national secretary J.B. Miles arrived in Perth to attend the Party's state conference. He addressed a crowd of more than 400 loyalists and probably a few clandestine police at Perth Town Hall. The CIB often planted officers inside CPA organisations and among CPA gatherings. Most state branch meetings also had a police officer present to record proceedings and the identities of those attending. The CPA's practice of adopting its own nomenclature sometimes stymied this. Party pseudonyms, though little used at other times, were used to identify speakers at CPA conferences and meetings, and in correspondence and records of meetings, in an effort to mask the identity of members.[103] The CIB sometimes found it inordinately (and comically) difficult to match these Party names to their rightful owners. This distinctive vernacular extended beyond pseudonyms: it was the idiom of the Party that distinguished and ascribed exclusivity on its members. A uniformity of language in the Party also helped ensure a uniformity of compliance through the centralised CPA.

The CPA had struggled nationally through the early 1920s to increase and retain members in any substantial numbers. The Party had battled to gain a foothold in Western Australia particularly. The tiny 'black stump' town of Blackall in western Queensland had more CPA members in 1925 than did the capital city of Perth, boasting seven members to Perth's four (which included Prichard).[104] By 1928, of the CPA's 300 official national members, Perth accounted for only fourteen, with just four of these being 'active' members.[105] From 1929 to the end of 1931, though, national CPA membership reportedly increased from less than 500 to 2500. The Party's membership statistics were notoriously unreliable, with branches tending to inflate their membership figures and many members being inactive; nevertheless, there was certainly a proportionately large increase in member numbers at this time.

CPA membership in Western Australia grew only slowly in the early 1930s — to about 100 by 1934 and about 130 in 1935 — but numbers increased rapidly in the mid- to late 1930s in response to the rise of fascism, the Spanish Civil War and the crippling effects of the Depression. By mid-1938, though hardly a political force in the state, the CPA had 236 members in Western Australia, and four full-time Party workers. By the end of May 1939, state membership had increased to 348.[106] The Party was particularly strong in the mining regions of the state — notably the eastern goldfields — but found it difficult to rally support in great numbers in Perth. Another impediment to an active CPA branch in Perth was the city's agreeable climate and the pleasures that came with it.[107] Formal party membership was also risky, and official member numbers masked countless 'fellow travellers' who supported the CPA. Despite relatively low party membership in Western Australia, the circulation of *The Workers' Star* was close to 2500.

11

LEADING THE REVOLUTION ON A WHITE HORSE

These men of sinew and determination[1]

After Joseph Lyons's death in April 1939, Robert Menzies succeeded him as prime minister. Menzies's first visit to Western Australia as prime minister came in July 1939, and attracted large crowds including hecklers and placard-carrying protesters demonstrating against the newly passed *National Register Act 1939*. Federal politics had been preoccupied in the first half of that year by increasing unrest over the compulsory National Register, a federal government inventory of 'manpower' created in preparation for potential military and industrial conscription. The government had put Australia on a war footing, and amendments to the *Defence Act 1903* were passed to allow the government to declare war without reference to the parliament, and to compulsorily conscript for the armed forces should Australia embark on military conflict. The National Register Act legally compelled all Australian males between the ages of eighteen and sixty-five to complete registration forms detailing their address, family background, marital status, state of health and employment history; every holder of property valued at £500 or more was also required to record their holdings. Those who failed to do so faced the threat of a three-month jail term and a significant fine of up to £50. It was a means of determining the number of men eligible for enlistment and their potential allocation to military and civil needs. As such, anti-conscriptionists and civil libertarians loudly denounced it.

The CPA condemned the National Register as preparation for conscription to a war to be waged against the Soviet Union. The Party urged people not to fill in the required forms and organised the burning of National Register cards at demonstrations across the country. The ACTU supported a boycott of the National Register, as did the Perth branch of the ALP. John Curtin, jailed for his opposition to conscription in the First World War, also feared the reintroduction of conscription presaged by the National Register, but the federal ALP he led opposed a boycott, insisting instead that the legislation be fought constitutionally.

The day after Menzies's arrival in Perth, he applauded 'Signor Mussolini' as 'a man of first-class ability', telling a largely supportive audience at Anzac House in the city that he did not believe that a man of Mussolini's achievements would provoke a war in Europe. 'His efforts had restored order and development and no other Italian in the last sixty years had rendered his country more service,' Menzies said, reflecting poorly on either the quality of Australia's foreign intelligence or the gullibility of his audience.[2] Australia would be at war with Mussolini within two months.

Menzies's speech was eventually interrupted by loud and angry protests. He had previously spoken of Hitler as an inspiring leader, and when he told this public meeting that Hitler had 'accomplished remarkable things in Germany' and that 'history [would] label Hitler as one of the really great men of the century', he was met with howls of fury. A 'smartly dressed young woman' rose from her seat and denounced Menzies's comments: 'Any sensible, thinking person knew,' Phyllis Harnett cried, 'that Hitler's work was the work of a maniac.' Menzies tried to quell Harnett and, usually adept at crushing interjectors with his wit, became increasingly agitated when Harnett persisted. He eventually asked police to throw her out. Harnett was escorted from the hall, 'defiantly' shaking her fist at Menzies, reported *The West Australian*.[3] John McKenzie later wrote of the altercation:

> Menzies paused, appeared to listen politely for a time and then appealed to her as a sensible member of 'the fair sex' to sit down. But she talked on in good oratorical style. Menzies leaned over and said something quietly to the chairman. The speech was being broadcast [on local radio 6PR] and it came loud and clear over the airwaves, 'Throw that bitch out!'[4]

Harnett recalled that she had met her 'crowd' outside when she'd arrived late to the meeting, as 'they'd all been put out':

> I had an enormous felt hat and had [borrowed] a [blue tweed] coat that [gave] me a kind of style that wasn't really mine. When I went in, there were places made for me everywhere — I was obviously just a middle-class lady who must be looked after. It was a most unfortunate thing that [Menzies] was sitting near to the mic and ... had whispered: 'Can't someone get rid of the bitch?' and it had broadcast very nicely.[5]

After Harnett's ejection, other protesters, including Leah Marks and Bill Mountjoy, stood up waving anti–National Register placards and were also ejected. Menzies curiously condemned the protesters for 'speaking in some strange accent', claiming he 'did not see much that was Australian' about them. Harnett lost her job over the confrontation and the National Register went ahead.[6]

A short, ten-minute anti–National Register play written by a Guild member, sketching 'the main dangers to workers in the register', was performed at at least one protest meeting in late May 1939, but little is known of this play. It may possibly have been a play entitled *No*, referred to in a CIB report and attributed to Victor Williams, a later member of the Guild writers' group. A 'Backseat' review of the National Register play appeared in *The Workers' Star* in early June 1939:

> There were some good laughs to be found, and a good dramatic kick in the conclusion … It is simply planned, made to be played almost anywhere. Good as were 'Till the Day I Die', 'Where's That Bomb?' and 'Awake & Sing', it is these little agit-props on immediate issues that will make the Guild a social force.[7]

Hard on the heels of the Guild's push against Keith George to a more polemic repertoire, this comment about agitprops making the Guild 'a social force' was yet another slight against George and a reinforcement of the Party line.

In early May 1939, John and Ray Oldham sailed from Sydney to the New York World's Fair. The architecture firm for which Oldham worked in Sydney, Stephenson and Turner, had been awarded the contract to design the Australian display pavilion, and oversight of its design and construction was given to Oldham and Arthur Baldwinson, who had served in London as an assistant to Bauhaus founder and renowned Modernist architect Walter Gropius. The design committee included Modernist photographer Max Dupain and artists Douglas Annand, Adrian Feint, Margaret Preston and Russell Roberts. The 1939 World's Fair was to be the last significant international gathering of artists before the War, and it took place at 'the peak of the Modern contemporary movement' in architecture and at a zenith in architectural experimentation by the likes of the Bauhaus designers, Le Corbusier in France (who also designed a pavilion) and American architect Frank Lloyd Wright.[8] John Oldham was particularly taken by the work he saw in New York of South American landscape architect Roberto Burle Marx, and a lifelong interest in landscape architecture was born.

The Oldhams' visit coincided with Roosevelt's 'New Deal', an expansive and revolutionary government employment program that contrasted starkly with the demeaning sustenance projects undertaken in most other parts of the world, including Australia, during the Depression. One of the successes of the New Deal was the amply funded Works Progress Administration Federal Theatre Project, one of a number of government arts projects that provided employment to unemployed theatre workers. It spawned many left-wing drama companies and much groundbreaking theatre, and the Oldhams attended the tail end of these theatre performances in America. It was this project that brought Living Newspapers to the fore.

In July 1939, the Workers' Art Guild returned to the stage with satirical farce *Cannibal Carnival*, written by London taxidriver and BBC broadcaster Roger Gullan, co-author of *Where's That Bomb?*, under the pseudonym Herbert Hodge. The play is a social and political critique set 'yesterday, tomorrow or maybe today' on one of the tropical islands of the fictional Canna-Cary Archipelago, whose indigenous inhabitants are 'living in a state of primitive communism'.[9] The three sole survivors of a shipwreck — proselytising archetypes of capitalism, organised religion and the Western legal system — come ashore and set about trying to 'civilise' the island's 'natives'. The play satirises the imposition of their moral code and ideologies, shared by the audience, upon the island's inhabitants.

The characters in the play are pure cartoon caricatures, and the Guild's set design bore many of the hallmarks of a cartoon. Wire fences were put up around coconut trees, and a cave on the island was turned into a commercial brothel.[10] Under the influence of the new arrivals, 'the natives [*sic*] pass through various stages of social development [until] they at last see through the mumbo-jumbo which veils the anti-democratic nature of Big Business'. The leader of the 'natives' — the character of Egbert, an agent of the ideals of freedom and enlightened democracy — is the play's most agreeable character, but is disparaged as a 'Red' by one of the play's villains. Egbert leads a rebellion to liberate his people from the shackles of capitalism imposed upon them: capitalism is represented as cannibalism, embodied in the character of a business magnate named Crabbe, an exemplar, 'moved by profit only', of the ills of capitalism. The play derides the paternalism and hypocrisy of Western orthodox religion, represented by the character of Bishop Bartholomew Bumpus (though the Guild program was at pains to declare that 'it is not religion [per se], but his kind of religion, that the play attacks'), and critiques a 'system' responsible for mass unemployment and the promotion of anti-Semitism and anti-Communism. The dutiful but innocent enforcer, a London policeman named Joe, inevitably maintains loyalty with his class and questions the virtues of the system and institutions he serves, and the wealth and privilege of those benefiting from the status quo. He is reconstructed through the 'popular socialist' revolt that restores the local inhabitants' 'freedom' and metes out punishment on Crabbe and the bishop.[11]

An audience member wrote a furious letter to the editor of the *Daily News* damning the play and presenting the somewhat sweeping, yet prevalent, xenophobic view that:

> the only comment overheard in favour of the production was made by a man with a guttural accent. He was certainly not of British stock. If that play had been written or produced in his country the people who had taken part in it would have not again seen the light of day ... Many of the young people in the audience felt as I did on coming out to the clean, rain-washed streets. I had a strong desire to wash my eyes and ears with a cleansing lotion.[12]

This correspondent did acknowledge the 'undoubted talents' of some of the cast, but urged that 'something be done by the Church or Parliament to put a stop to such outrageous productions'.[13]

Keith George had refused to stage the play — hardly the sort of play that appealed to him — after yet another skirmish with fellow Guild members. There had been an ongoing struggle with George about which plays would be produced. His plan to stage a production of Shakespeare's *Antony and Cleopatra* was rebuffed by Guild members, who thought the play too orthodox and apolitical. While George 'was devoted to the theatre', others were, by their open account, more 'devoted to the message'.[14] George did not think *Antony and Cleopatra* orthodox, and his plans for the production, though little known in detail, were predictably anything but conventional. It is likely that George intended to direct the play at that time as a virulent satirical anti-war play rather than as a conventional Shakespearean romance.[15] George wanted to portray Cleopatra as a 'whore' rather than as 'a romantic figure', recalled Bill Irwin,[16] and some thirty years later George wrote of the play, in a letter to Ric Throssell:

[Antony] can be a rewarding character, but surely not as a hero ... To me, he more closely resembles a Sydney businessman with a private callgirl list letting his hair down in Perth.[17]

Harald Vike's sets and props for *Cannibal Carnival* were minimal. The stage was chiefly bare, with a few palm trees, a fence around the brothel and a table and chair where a policeman sat. Sydney Fison played both the policeman and the magistrate. Joan Kidd, who played a bra-clad island girl in a grass skirt, remembered the relatively straightforward rehearsals for the play taking place after work and on weekends over a couple of months.[18] Paul Hasluck thought the play 'fun' and was enthusiastic about its irreverence; he was critical of the 'stuffy ... politically brassbound and flabbily cosmopolitan' Perth audience who watched it.[19] The play was another critical and popular success for the Guild.

During *Cannibal Carnival*'s season, the Guild staged another play at a Perth Town Hall fundraiser to benefit Spanish Republican refugees. *What Are We to Do*, a play about 'the refugee problem', was written for the Guild by broadcaster and published poet John Thompson.[20] It documented the plight of the Civil War's Republican fighters, who had fled Spain to France as refugees and were being housed behind barbed wire in French concentration camps, 'waiting for time to pass'.[21] Thompson's wife, Patricia (Pat) Thompson, whose mother ran Perth's Patch Theatre, was raised in Sydney and had spent four years treading the boards with Doris Fitton's Independent Theatre before travelling to Europe. Arriving in London in early 1937, she met and married John. She had worked for Spanish Relief in the Left Book Club of Victor Gollancz's London publishing house and in a secretarial job at Australia House in London before taking a job in Geneva with the International Labour Organization of the League of Nations. Soon after their arrival in Perth in early 1939, the Thompsons became friendly with Axel Poignant, and it was probably he who introduced them to Prichard and the Guild crowd. Not given to modesty, she later wrote in her memoir that while her husband learned his craft on ABC radio, she 'blossomed out as a star of the Workers' Art Guild, the local left-wing theatre group'.[22]

Poignant was another prominent Guild fringe dweller: a friend to many in the Guild circle and an occasional stagehand and photographer for the Guild. He was born to a Swedish father and a British mother in Yorkshire in 1906, and moved with his family to Sweden in 1919. In 1926 he migrated alone to New South Wales, under a scheme to recruit British boys to work on the land, where he began a taxing stint as an itinerant bush worker.

He had developed an interest in photography at a young age, and after emigrating he cultivated a passion for Australia. A particular delight in the bush and a fascination with local history and Aboriginal culture emerged, and these became preoccupations in his photography. Eventually jobless, he made his way to Sydney where he camped at Frenchs Forest, above Dee Why beach; though penniless, this was a happy time during which he read widely about Australia, including the novels of Katharine Susannah Prichard.

In Sydney Poignant began to eke out a living as a portrait photographer, and was introduced to socialism, theosophy, Hinduism and counterculture.[23] It was through the Theosophical Society in Sydney that he met and married Perth beauty queen Sandra Chase. They moved to Perth in 1931, into an already crowded house of theosophists including Chase's mother, Perth journalist Muriel Chase. The Chase family's social connections enabled Poignant to work as a 'society' portrait photographer and publish his work in *The West Australian*. He was one of very few professional photographers using a Leica miniature thirty-five millimetre camera in the 1930s and he took to introducing himself to visiting celebrities and photographing them.[24] He also developed an interest in aerial photography. He worked for a year on an aerial survey for the Western Mining Company, and during the Duke of Gloucester's visit to Perth in October 1934 he photographed the Duke's arrival from the air.[25]

In early 1935 Poignant was invited to photograph the Russian Ballet Company during a performance at His Majesty's Theatre of the collaborative Michel Fokine–Igor Stravinsky *Firebird* ballet — a sublime ballet composed for Sergei Diaghilev's company some twenty years earlier. In May of that year he was similarly employed to photograph Percy Grainger during a series of music recitals and lectures Grainger gave at the Assembly Hall. Poignant's marriage broke down later that year, and he set up a photographic studio in Outram Street in West Perth.[26]

Poignant's primary interests were in flora and fauna photography, but it was commercial portraiture that established his reputation. Unlike other emigrants from the eastern states at that time, he did not feel any particularly acute sense of isolation living in Perth. He described Perth in the 'purposeful' 1930s as 'a warm and stimulating place', and photography journals kept him abreast of international trends and developments in photography, such as the Depression photographs of the American Farm Security Administration. With greater financial security he was able to branch out into more personal photographic projects and movie photography, having bought his first sixteen millimetre film camera in

1933.[27] In the latter 1930s Poignant moved his studio from Outram Street to the city's mock-Tudor London Court, where his main source of income was studio and home portrait photography.[28]

Sydney New Theatre had sent the Workers' Art Guild a copy of Betty Roland's short play *Workers Beware*, which the Guild performed through July 1939 at Labor Party branch meetings, Left Book Club meetings and the Fremantle Lumpers' Union Golden Jubilee celebrations at Fremantle Town Hall. The latter was attended by Labor premier John Willcock and by federal opposition leader and Labor member for Fremantle John Curtin.[29] Roland wrote *Workers Beware* in response to a 1938 amendment to the Transport Workers Act (known colloquially as the Dog Collar Act), which had been introduced by the Bruce government to break a 1928 waterside workers' strike. The 1938 amendment similarly required wharf labourers to be licensed or forfeit their right to work, to be replaced by licensed volunteer labour. Menzies, then attorney-general and minister for industry, had the Act invoked in November 1938 during a long-running dispute with Port Kembla waterside workers who refused to load pig iron for export to an increasingly militarised Japan, an act for which he earned the uncharitable moniker 'Pig-Iron Bob'.

Maurie Lachberg, secretary of the Labour Day Committee, again led the 1939 Labour Day procession of 'men of sinew and determination' atop a splendid white horse,[30] with floats for the procession designed by the Guild's art section.[31] Lachberg, then a state official in the Carpenters' and Joiners' Union, was also the model for one of the figures on the new union banner carried at the parade. Harald Vike, Lachberg's Trades Hall Flats co-tenant, had been commissioned to produce the banner featuring Perth's striking new Modernist 'monument', the Gledden Building. Vike's velvet and gold-braided banner, made at a cost of £130, was exhibited just prior to the Labour Day parade in the display window of Boans department store, then the city's retail epicentre, alongside his Amalgamated Engineering Union banner of the previous year.[32] The 1939 parade was to be Keith George's last hurrah with the Guild, and he and Poignant filmed the procession for a documentary commissioned by the Guild. The resulting film was shown as part of Cinesound newsreel screenings at Perth's Piccadilly Cinema through May.[33]

George had found himself increasingly preoccupied with placating political factions and discord within the Guild, and in early 1939 these frictions reached their zenith. An acrimonious rift had developed over the direction the Guild should take with its theatre. The question of how political its activities should be had polarised the Guild prior to the March state election. Heated committee meetings chaired by Howard Smith argued the issue. George remained defiant, insisting that the Guild should not be an appendage of the Communist Party, and again threatened to leave the Guild altogether if the demands of the increasingly orthodox young CPA members in the Guild were met. He resented the fact that his authority was now being undermined by what he saw as youthful naivety, and he was not the only one becoming impatient with the interminable discussions about whether the Guild plays propagated the 'correct' Marxist line. George's critics, Howard Smith and Phyllis Harnett among them, were becoming increasingly influential on the management committee with the encouragement of partisan younger members. George later reflected:

> The Guild was theoretically and constitutionally non-sectarian and when they tried to force the Party line on me I objected because it offended my logical sense. They formed a cabal against me, and decisions made at faction meetings of which I was not eligible to be a member were forced through Guild meetings by a block vote.[34]

There had always been a degree of political tension within the Guild, but the disquiet was more acute now.[35] Tom Wignall recalled that 'there was a feeling about the place that we should take a stronger line', and this reflected what was happening within the wider international Communist movement at the time.[36] Debates within the Communist Party about the relationship between the arts as a political tool and the broader sociopolitical aims of the Party were hotly contested then, and the Vike–McClintock 'modern art' debate of September 1938 was an example of this. A generational change was occurring in the Guild, and younger, more politically militant Guild members were making an impact.

The basis of the quarrel, in Phyllis Harnett's opinion, 'lay in the fact that Keith didn't have these politics and we'd acquired them very rapidly'.[37] Mairi Wignall felt that George eventually became tired of the 'command-ism' of the CPA increasingly affecting the work of the Guild: CPA members in the Guild adhered to the Party line and acceded to Party authority and this, according to Wignall, George found very trying.[38] In contrast, Arthur Rudkin, who was undoubtedly in the CPA camp against George, recalled that:

> Despite his genius, or perhaps because of it, Keith George was not easy to get on with. Knowing that the Guild, especially the

Theatre, could probably not get on without him, he made himself a little dictator by threatening to resign if any suggestion with which he disagreed was even discussed, let alone democratically carried as a resolution. He was also very careful to maintain his own indispensability by laying it down that he would regard as a motion of no confidence any suggestion that he should delegate any of his responsibilities, or accept any assistant director.[39]

Ric Throssell felt that the split occurred 'simply because others wanted [George] to do things in the way that the Party suggested'.[40] To this end, George himself wrote many years later that he 'was not prepared to compromise. Production by a committee was far beyond my experience or acceptance'.[41]

Whatever the exact reason or reasons for the split, it was decided, at around the time of the 1939 state election, that a meeting would be held at Prichard's Greenmount home at which the vexed issue would be resolved. Prichard chaired the crisis meeting. Harnett was trenchant in her view that the Guild needed to harden its political line. Others argued that being too political at that time might kill off public support for the Guild. Bill Irwin remembered the heated meeting as 'primarily a dialogue' between Prichard and Harnett that lasted all afternoon.[42]

When the vote was taken and George saw that 'the committee' had won the day against him, he angrily left the meeting and the Guild.[43] He later wrote that 'Katharine fought to protect me, I was told, to the limit of her deference to the principle of (much abused) majority rule'.[44] According to Bill Irwin, Prichard was 'a woman of strong opinions who was rather loath to push them onto other people' and she 'did not try to influence the decision', but she must have been bitterly disappointed with the outcome.[45] Ric Throssell later observed:

> She believed that [Keith George] was the soul of the Workers' Art Guild and it was transparent from what was done by him and what was done afterwards that there wasn't the same genius at work.[46]

George himself recalled the events some three months before his death, still with some sorrow and bitterness.

> Circumstances connected with my resignation from the Guild were painful and I consciously suppressed my memory of them ... I had come to the end of my period of effective work and above

all I felt that I was no longer a help but an embarrassment to Katharine though she never wavered or expressed any disapproval. I resigned. Katharine did her best to dissuade me but by this time I had a dramatic scene to myself. I was for a brief period the centre of attention. I wasn't yielding my upstage position on any pretext ... [Prichard] was the only member of the Guild faction with any understanding. The other members were simply a bunch of ostriches with their heads in the sand and a hammer and sickle tied to their tails.[47]

George did later concede to 'a number of mistakes':

I was over anxious to develop the ancillary arts of literature, painting, music and dancing quickly. With Katharine's approval I brought in a strong bourgeois element — mostly my university friends ... They soon became converts to the cause ... I was older and more cynical. I couldn't believe in any cause. I found the oversimplifications of the Party line in theory as unconvincing and indeed similar in many ways to Christianity ... My recruits became extremely orthodox.[48]

It was decided at that Greenmount meeting that Phyllis Harnett would take over as the Guild's theatre and art director, and she immediately began rehearsals for the Guild's next play, *Awake and Sing!*, at the boarding house where she was then living. Fortunately her landlady was sympathetic: her husband, she told Harnett conspiratorially, was 'a bit of the mind of your people'.[49]

The other Guild members rallied behind Harnett, and rehearsals soon moved to the Guild rooms where Harnett, a little lacking in confidence given the shoes she had to fill, spent a lot of time working individually with the actors.[50] 'It was a pretty terrible moment,' she remembered, as 'nobody knew whether I could really direct a play or not'.

Awake and Sing! was a markedly different play from that which Keith George was wont to direct.[51] It was, in fact, another play he had vetoed. It was a three-act play of abrasive American vernacular written by Clifford Odets two years prior to *Waiting For Lefty*. Set in New York, it portrays the disintegration of a working-class Jewish family enduring poverty and misery, having 'lost their aspiration because they have been too long in desolation'.[52] It is a play that cites political rebellion as a means of escape from the restrictions and hardships imposed on this emblematic family and, despite its rather bleak subject, the play itself is more redemptive than gloomy. The grandfather of the family lives with the regret of not having sufficiently acted upon the revolutionary literature he has read and the political fervour he has preached to his family. A political idealist whose dreams are shattered, he exhorts his grandson to rise up and rebel against the indignities of capitalism. The grandson, young and in love, has no wish to carry the mantle. The grandfather takes his own life. His grandson reads through the political literature left behind and takes up political activism, fulfilling his grandfather's dream.

The Guild production of *Awake and Sing!* was staged at the Assembly Hall in late May 1939. Howard Smith played the role of the grandfather and John Hepworth that of the grandson. The play proved especially popular with Perth's Jewish community, and *The Workers' Star* theatre critic 'Backseat' wrote, somewhat excessively, that *Awake and Sing!* was the Guild's 'most polished work to date'[53] — perhaps a calculated response in support of Harnett and the Guild's deposition of Keith George. George's imprint was certainly gone. 'Backseat' reported that the play did not include any 'startling exhibitions of stage mechanics' and mischievously suggested that 'the play didn't want them'.[54] Paul Hasluck in *The West Australian* singled out the acting of Ian (rather than Howard) Smith for particular praise, and summarised with usual elegance:

> It is surely one of the strongest justifications of the modern theatre that it should be here calling people to awake from a bondage not only of the flesh but also of the spirit and calling with a ringing voice that stirs the hearer. It is hard to remember a sermon, a newspaper article, a stump speech, a pronouncement by a statesman, or an annual report of a limited liability company that stirred the heart as did the final call, 'awake and sing', at last night's play.[55]

Phyllis Harnett, with characteristic modesty, credited the success of the production to Clifford Odets. Whereas Keith George tore up the author's stage directions for actors in plays he directed,[56] Harnett was faithful to both Odets's script and his stage directions. Odets 'accounted for all the shades of feeling and all the gestures', she later said of the play.[57]

In Western Australia a local solution was being sought to the grave Jewish humanitarian crisis of that time. In a scheme originally mooted by the Jewish Freeland League in London, then in search of a suitable area within the British Dominions to resettle Jewish refugees, a major campaign was launched in Western Australia in August 1939 to resettle 75,000 European Jewish refugees on a large tract of undeveloped land in the East Kimberley desert region in the far north-west of the state.[58] Australia was the country considered most preferable by the Freeland League for the establishment of a homeland for Jewish refugees, and as late as 1941, Dr Isaac Steinberg, who had been a member of Lenin's first Bolshevik government, travelled to the Kimberley on behalf of the Freeland League to consider the feasibility of establishing a Jewish homeland there. A member of the Western Australian parliament spoke of the 'Jewish settlers' having made 'wonderful strides in Palestine' and as 'the river flats in the Kimberleys [sic] required no cleaning and the climate was healthy', it would, he surmised, be an entirely suitable location.[59] (As well as the Kimberley proposal, another site in a remote part of south-western Tasmania was also considered.) There was an ulterior motive, though, given the increasing military threat to Australia's north: 'Whom are we going to have, Japanese or Jews?' *The West Australian* enquired in August 1939.[60]

A meeting to discuss the Kimberley proposal was held at the Workers' Art Guild, where proponents and opponents (including Phyllis Harnett) spoke passionately. The misery of the Group Settlement scheme in the state's south-west was still fresh in the minds of many Western Australians. The Guild meeting discredited the proposal and the Curtin government eventually scuttled the scheme.[61]

Despite the success of *Awake and Sing!*, the Guild had initially floundered after Keith George's departure, with Harnett unable to commandeer the control that George had earlier been able to. The Guild set about producing agitprop drama, mainly street theatre, such as those in support of Roy Neville's election campaign during the last days of Keith George, which were taken around Perth on the back of a truck 'from place to place in the suburbs, playing up to three times a night'.[62] These small-scale propagandist plays were basic, 'politically topical' morality tales that, more often than not, portrayed the battles of the defenceless proletarian pitted against the dark and unjust forces of capitalism, with the worker invariably triumphing.[63]

Although the Guild had performed some worthy earlier agitprops — including the 1937 production of *The Lyons Bungles* — it was not until early to mid-1939 that it began performing these agitprops in earnest.[64] Keith George later took credit for initiating the Guild's agitprop work, and it certainly began while he ran the drama wing. 'The street corner productions were my idea and were very successful,' he wrote, 'but my part in their production was largely advisory.'[65] Guild members including Phyllis Harnett and Howard Smith directed the Guild's later agitprops (George had directed *The Lyons' Bungles*), which were often played at political and trade union meetings.[66] These performances were also born of Prichard's accounts of the propagandist plays she had seen performed in factories and on the street during her visit to the Soviet Union — though Gordon Burgoyne felt that 'the rather strident tone of most agit-prop plays' was not entirely to Prichard's liking:[67]

> I can remember Katherine [sic] saying once that she wished the left had quieter, sensitive playwrights like Chekhov.[68]

12

THE WAR, AND 'BLOOD ON THE MOON'

There was a sense of nationalism, he said. A kind of realisation in this country, an awareness, coming out of the last few years. And now it's all going to find expression in war.
Is that bad? I mean, the way things are.
It won't find expression in writing. Art. Discussion. It'll be conveniently buried in war. A perfect bloody irony.[1]

In 1939 a large exhibition of French and British 'contemporary' art, including original works by Dalí, Van Gogh, Matisse, Gaugin, Chagall, Cézanne and Toulouse-Lautrec, toured Australia.[2] It was the first time most Australians had seen anything other than reproductions of modern European art. As a nation Australia was so little exposed to the new and somewhat shocking 'modern' art streams in Europe that the exhibition generated a lot of controversy, and fuelled the very public conflict emerging between the academy and the Modernists in Australia at that time. Three years earlier, James Stuart MacDonald, director of the National Gallery of Victoria and doyen of the conservative art establishment, had labelled 'Modern Art' 'the work of perverts' and completely 'foreign to this relatively happiest of countries'.[3] He similarly attacked this 1939 exhibition and refused to let it be shown at the National Gallery of Victoria.

> There is no doubt that the great majority of the work called modern is the product of degenerates ... if we take part by refusing to pollute our gallery with this filth, we shall render service to art.[4]

The exhibition toured every Australian capital except Perth — where a local 'Modern Art Group' exhibition, hosted jointly by the University of Western Australia's Adult Education Board and the Workers' Art Guild, was organised so that the debates raging elsewhere in Australia could also be aired in Perth.[5] The Modern Art Group exhibition was held in a room at Pastoral House for a fortnight at the end of August 1939, and it drew large inquisitive crowds.[6] It was both a celebration of modern art and an attempt to educate the public of Perth about overseas trends in art that were of social and political interest. It was almost certainly also arranged as a showpiece for 'Max Ebert' (Herbert McClintock), given that his wife, Pat McClintock, was its driving force.[7] His surrealist painting *Approximate Portrait in a Drawing Room* had been hung alongside works by John Lunghi and others at a Perth Society of Artists exhibition in July 1939, and the *Daily News* would run a photographic feature on McClintock in October 1939 under the title 'Here is a Surrealist at Work', concurrent with another exhibition by Max Ebert along with works by Harald Vike and John Lunghi.[8] The *Daily News* article was an instructive 'how to be a surrealist' piece in which McClintock chatted about the greater unconscious forces at work in surrealism.[9]

The crowds that attended the Modern Art Group events and the volume of newspaper coverage given to surrealism at this time were testament to the great interest in modern art in Perth, and to the curiosity about surrealism in particular.[10] *Daily News* correspondent 'Gossiping Hepzibah' wrote of the Modern Art Group exhibition:

> I found I was in good company when I was slightly bewildered by some of the modern advanced works. I ran into William Hatfield, the well-known Australian author, who informed me he was looking for Harold [sic] Vike, who has promised to explain to him just what this modern art was all about.[11]

The exhibition included Vike's finely crafted painting *Perth Roofs (Suburban Perth)*, a panorama of the city from the rear of the Guild rooms, as well as works by Australian artists Clarice Beckett, Nutter Buzacott, Colin Colahan and John Lunghi.[12] There were also prints by Klee, Picasso, Matisse and Monet as well as Van Gogh's *Sunflowers*.

A series of 'comprehensible and temperate language' lectures was held to coincide with the exhibition. These lectures, which also attracted large audiences, included one on 'The Social Significance of Modern Art' by Alec King, in which he proposed that art should return to being a more public presence in people's everyday lives rather than being corralled into galleries which should instead, he proposed, exclusively exhibit experimental art. Herbert McClintock, Elizabeth (Betty) Hamill and Phyllis Harnett spoke on 'Revolutionary Art and Surrealism'.[13] The former two essentially discussed the origins and importance of surrealism, while Harnett talked of Russian art and the education of its audience since the Russian Revolution. In his lecture, 'The Science of Appearances',

John Thompson discussed the differences between representational and experimental art — objective and subjective forms. Dr 'Kurt Rogers',[14] in a lecture titled 'Modern Art', barracked for the progressive and holistic 'constructivist' view of art in contradistinction to the 'productivist' school, and Brian Elliott discussed the importance of 'truthfulness' in art in his 'Imagination in Art' lecture. Elliott, a postgraduate English student at UWA, would later spend many years lecturing and undertaking research in Australian literature at the University of Adelaide, where he became a central player in the 'Ern Malley' poetry hoax.

At the end of August 1939, a week after the opening of the Modern Art Group exhibition, Stalin signed a non-aggression treaty with Hitler. The Russo–German pact was as hotly contested as Modern art itself. The CPA's initial reaction was perplexed silence, as arguments about Stalin's motives and the alliance's consequences flared. Some saw it as further deceit and betrayal by Stalin; others viewed it as a necessary counterpoint to the threat posed by Nazi Germany, rather than as an act of complicity.[15] Soviet sympathisers were of the view that Stalin and the Russian people were left with little choice after the appeasement of Hitler by Western powers, which probably increased the threat of military aggression on Germany's eastern border with the Soviet Union. British historian A.J.P. Taylor wrote of the treaty that 'the British feared for Poland; the Russians feared for themselves'.[16] Arthur Rudkin acknowledged that the alliance initially 'came as a very nasty surprise' to Party members in Perth,[17] but *The Workers' Star* observed that 'it could not by the wildest stretch of the imagination be described as an "alliance" ... and did not in any way affect our attitude either to the Soviet Union or to Nazi Germany'.[18] This was disingenuous, given that the Communist Party's view on the War was utterly proportionate to the Soviet Union's shifting relations with Germany. Phyllis Harnett and the Guild were caught in a slightly awkward situation, as they were rehearsing the anti-Nazi play *Blood on the Moon* when the announcement of the Russo–German pact was made — a month before the opening night of the play at that year's Drama Festival.

In September 1939, Australia entered the War on Britain's side against Nazi Germany and, as the Soviet Union was signatory to the treaty with Germany, Australia was also at war with the Soviet Union. The Comintern declared it an 'imperialist' war, a position seen by many Party members who had spent years prior to the War rallying against fascism in line with Communist Party policy as yet another politically expedient betrayal. At the time of the opening of *Blood on the Moon*, the Red Army was marching into eastern Poland and the Baltic states, and the CPA set out to publicly quell rank-and-file concern about these aggressive Soviet forays. *The Workers' Star* reported that the 'oppressed peoples' of the region welcomed the Red Army's 'crusade of liberation', and Party members on the stump took up the topic.[19]

The Guild production of *Blood on the Moon* was not one that would loom large in the collective memory of the Guild or its audience. Director Phyllis Harnett conceded later that she found it difficult to handle the size and technical complexities of His Majesty's Theatre, where the performance took place. The lighting system was complex and daunting after the smaller venues in which the Guild had more recently played, and a drunken spotlight operator made matters worse. Harnett did not feel entirely confident in the cast she had, and she did not possess Keith George's exceptional ability to handle multitudinous scenes. Nevertheless, 'nothing would induce [her] to stop.'[20]

International events also somewhat overtook the performance. Paul Hasluck's subsequent review of the production in *The West Australian* suggested that it 'was a little over three weeks too late.' The play's forewarning about the threat posed by Nazi Germany no longer had currency, he wrote, having been 'scooped' by Hitler's invasion of Poland three weeks earlier:

> Seeing the play was like reading yesterday's newspaper when tomorrow's issue is just going to press.[21]

Blood on the Moon, written by Paul and Claire Sifton, again illustrated personal stories of Jewish suffering at the hands of the Nazis after Hitler's 1933 accession to power. An erudite article about the play was published in the September 1939 edition of *The Australian Quarterly*, following the Sydney New Theatre's July 1939 production of the play:

> The temptation in a play written to trace the suffering of a one-quarter Jewish family in Nazi Germany is to let the suffering speak for itself ... Merely to paint Nazi brutality and human suffering achieves nothing in either politics or art, because in politics it tells us nothing we did not know already and converts no-one not already converted, and as art it traces only the aftermath of a drama, the stoning of the loser in a fight that is over when the play opens ... The drama of Nazi and Jew must be written, if it is to be written, about the conflict in ideas before the present regime in Germany. There is no drama here because it is a picture of the killing of caged and helpless victims.[22]

Another difficulty for Harnett was posed by a leading role in *Blood on the Moon* being played by Patricia Thompson. Despite Thompson proving to be very good in the role, the personal relationship between Thompson and Harnett was poisonous, and Harnett had been keen on having Dorothy Powell play the part.

> Every nice actress in Perth offered herself to me to play the lead in 'Blood on the Moon', and I really was quite heartbroken at not having Dorothy [Powell].[23]

Harnett was, however, very impressed with Thompson's performance in the play.

Albert Osterberg and a 'terrified' Irene Osterberg made their only appearances on stage with the Guild in this production.[24] Gwen Duggan, who would perform in virtually every Guild production hereafter, and Hope Bath also made their debuts.

Harald Vike was set an enormous task in designing the impressive set and backdrop for the play, a task aggravated by Harnett changing her plans for the set during dress rehearsals.[25] Other problems also dogged the play's preparation. People passing by the Guild rooms during rehearsals complained to the police of Nazi cries of 'Heil Hitler!', 'Perish the Jews!' and 'Long Live Germany!' The War had heightened suspicions, enmities and mistrust to near hysterical levels. Virtuous citizens were encouraged to be vigilant and police jumped at shadows 'in the enforcement of wartime restrictions and regulations', on guard for signs of 'malicious acts by hostile civilians' and 'spies'.[26]

Police were sent to investigate the activities at the Guild rooms and initial, cautiously distant surveillance led them to surmise that the meetings were indeed of a Nazi group 'run by aliens'.[27] Police certainly knew that the premises were used by the Workers' Art Guild, which should have allayed suspicions, but a police report, reflecting inaccurate and obsolete intelligence, referred to the tenants of the building as the 'Workers' Art Club'.[28] Events took an even more farcical turn when people in the street below began to throw stones at the upstairs windows of the Guild rooms during rehearsals 'when "Heil Hitler" was called out loudly', presumably because they objected to Nazis meeting inside.[29] Detective Sergeant George Smith had 'received information to the effect that a number of Foreigners thought to be Germans have a meeting place or Hall above Mortlock's [and] these people hold their principal meeting each Sunday night.'[30] A police informant stated that the meetings could 'plainly be heard from the street at [a] time when the meeting appears to become heated.'[31] Detective Sergeant Smith, obviously relishing his role in the political intrigue, suggested that rather than making enquiries at Mortlock's, the police should carry out surveillance at the group's next meeting. Police suspicion was further excited when they uncovered the fact that one of the group's principals 'is supposed to be known as Van Dyk', a common Dutch name (presumably referring to the Norwegian Harald Vike) that they clearly assumed to be German.[32]

Initially unaware of the increasing throng of police lurking in the dark outside and of concerned citizens gathering below the Guild rooms, Harnett continued to rehearse. Evidence that she was unhappy with a rehearsal is suggested by a police informant's statement that 'a womans' [sic] voice appeared to be speaking to the assembled company ... [She] did not appear to [be] satisfied with her audiences' [sic] effort but asked them to repeat ... phrases over several times.'[33] This occurred only weeks before the play's opening at what was to be the Guild's third annual performance in the Drama Festival, held at the same time each year, but police suspicions intensified when on their visit to the Guild rooms they discovered an enormous painted swastika on the floor. Vike had painted a swastika onto the large stage curtain that dropped between scenes, to be lit by a play of coloured lights. The curtain had been laid on the floor of the Guild rooms and paint had soaked through the material, leaving an imprint of the swastika. Police visits to rehearsals eventually put an end to the saga: Harnett was told by police 'that the place was becoming reputed as a Nazi Club and advised her to have those present proceed quietly'.[34]

Notwithstanding the criticisms of *The Workers' Star*, Harnett's production of *Blood on the Moon* included an inventive opening. The play was written 'for interludes of tremendous crowd scenes with people singing German songs' to express 'the upsurge of German Nazism', but Harnett was forced to be somewhat more economical in her expression of 'the enormous marches of people through Germany', as written in the script.[35] She designed an expeditious scene, with great impact, that played out before the curtain rose for the main body of the play. In front of the curtain, on a darkened stage, stood a line of some forty actors unseen until each was momentarily spotlit to perform a single swift violent act before the spotlights were extinguished and the curtain rose on the first tranquil 'drawing room' scene, in which the overture of *The Flying Dutchman* was played on piano.[36]

Hasluck was disappointed with much of the production, but he described the prologue as having 'all the promise of a good headline'.

His review of the play included the mischievous observation that 'one unforeseen result of the Nazi purge [in the first half of the play] was that it had left the more capable half of the cast on the stage.'[37] *The Workers' Star* criticised 'long delays between scenes, mechanical slip-ups' and the play's 'unpromising opening'.[38]

Such critical responses to the play, though not unexpected, stung Harnett. She had hoped to do this important Jewish story justice, in part as a personal tribute to the Masel family, though she realised she had been far too ambitious and stumbled in its preparation.[39]

Before the Drama Festival performance of *Blood on the Moon*, John Hector had organised a subsequent two-night season for the play at the Assembly Hall in early October. This proved a greater success, well patronised and well reviewed. Scenes that had not worked well at His Majesty's Theatre were trimmed, and the smaller venue probably also helped.[40] The *Daily News* described the reprise as 'a tremendous improvement' on the Drama Festival production.[41]

The rapidly shifting political climate of the time began to affect the theatre a great deal. The Repertory Club's initial 1939 Drama Festival entry was a production of the play *No More Peace*, to be directed by Jerold Wells. It was another anti-war play written by Ernst Toller, though a lighter satirical comedy that was not as politically charged as many of his previous plays. The program notes described *No More Peace* as a play that 'entirely lacks the bitterness that characterises some of Toller's early plays, such as *Hinkemann*, *Masses and Man*, and *Hoppla*, masterpieces though these undoubtedly are'.[42]

Written in 1936, *No More Peace* was Toller's last play. Having been forced to leave his native Germany, he had been living in exile in New York and hung himself in a New York hotel room in May 1939. His suicide was by and large not remarked on in the Party press, given that the Party looked unfavourably on suicide.

Wells and the Repertory Club players had rehearsed their planned Drama Festival performance of *No More Peace* until the last moment, but hastily cancelled the production, ironically, at the outbreak of the Second World War, replacing it with Emlyn Williams's 1938 play *The Corn is Green*. *The West Australian* euphemistically reported that the switch of plays was due to 'abnormal conditions in recent weeks'.[43] In fact, the decision by the Repertory Club to cancel *No More Peace* was both political and practical. On 3 September, France and Britain had declared war on Germany, and Menzies had duly announced that Australia was 'also at war'.[44] Repertory Club members immediately steeled themselves for national service, and apparently 'most of the male members of the cast were uncertain of their movements and did not wish to tie themselves to a play at such a distracting time.'[45] Wells had only recently directed a successful season of *The Corn is Green* for the Club, and it was decided that that production, with the same cast, would be repeated for the Drama Festival.

When the initial 1939 Drama Festival program, including the Repertory Club entry of *No More Peace*, was released in the first week of September, *The Workers' Star* reported that 'the trend towards the social play moves on'.[46] *Blood on the Moon* was the sort of political fare to be expected from the Workers' Art Guild, it declared, 'but when other clubs produce social plays as their festival entries — their show pieces for the year — things are looking up.'[47] After the program change was announced, however, an article appeared in the following week's edition of *The Workers' Star* under the headline 'No More Peace — No More':

> This week we take it all back. 'No More Peace' will not go on. It is understood that some members of the cast — a minority, but enough to prevent the performance — objected to the play in view of the fact that war was now on. Apparently they regard the drama, even the social drama, as no more than amusement. When it becomes too relevant to real events, it must not go on.[48]

The Repertory Club's production of *The Corn is Green* was staged on the opening night of the Drama Festival and according to Hasluck it 'was warmly received.'[49] Phyllis Harnett was by then having an affair with Jerold Wells, and she refused a request by her own cast members to hold a final dress rehearsal for *Blood on the Moon*, due to be staged the following night, because she insisted on attending Wells's production of *The Corn is Green*.[50]

Since Wells had taken over at the Repertory Club there had been a considerable shift from its traditional repertoire to a more left-wing polemic repertoire repertoire. Keith George and Jerold Wells had a close professional relationship in the brief time they shared the Perth stage, and between Repertory Club productions Wells encouraged the Guild to make use of the Repertory Club Theatre; likewise, George offered Wells the use of the Guild rooms and Wells regularly attended Guild rehearsals there.[51]

Before Wells's November 1938 Repertory Club production of Henrietta Drake-Brockman's play *Men Without Wives*, the Club had staged Sean O'Casey's 'problem' play *Juno and the Paycock*, an appropriate median between the Club's more traditional fare and its emerging political plays.[52]

In December 1938 the Club staged Wells's production of Bella and Samuel Spewack's *Boy Meets Girl*, with Frank O'Grady in the leading role of a theatre director working on a number of plays at the same time. Breaking further with tradition, the Repertory Club production was open to the public rather than being restricted to Club members, as had been the case until then. There are many references in 1939 Repertory Club records to this 'new policy' having been adopted by the Club in late 1938, probably initiated by Jerold Wells, and it was a significant change. There was not an absolute break, though, from conservative tradition. The new 'open door' policy did not apply to all productions. A number of traditional plays, mainly comedies, continued to be produced intermittently by a second rung of Repertory Club directors.[53]

The shift at the Repertory Club to a more gritty realist political repertoire was due primarily to the popularity of the drama of the Workers' Art Guild. Moreover, given that the heavy veil of the Depression had lifted, there was no longer the widespread craving for light escapist drama. In response to the changing times, there was a 'renewed sense of literature's social function', and in early May 1939, Wells directed a production of 1938 anti-war play *On the Frontier*, co-written by W.H. Auden and Christopher Isherwood.[54] This was Wells's first overtly political play at the Repertory Club, and it disturbed many establishment members. Responding to what was obviously a groundswell of criticism, a Repertory Club member wrote to the Club in June:

> Despite my official status in the Club (I gather that for a long time to come I shall belong to the species 'New Member') I am worried by what appears to be a narrow-minded attitude in the Club on the question of plays for presentation. Were it not for a natural diffidence I feel as a 'New Member', I would define the attitude as unintelligent and a little old-fashioned. On every hand I hear complaints about the dullness and dreariness of the Club's [new] plays. People have told me that they are propaganda; that they are harrowing and uninteresting, and that anyhow, they can read in the papers about the problems of their fellow human beings, and that they fail to see why they should be forced to think about them … that they come to the theatre to be amused. In other words, that they want to Escape. (Note the capital E!) I'm sorry to see this attitude. But anyhow, they have been amply catered for. Of the last seven seasons only four have been in any way 'Problem' plays, and of these, only two have had any trace of political colouring. I'd rather like to ask them … what are they grumbling about?[55]

Early in the month that followed, the Repertory Club's Junior Circle staged Valentine Katayev's 1926 Russian play *Squaring the Circle*, a comedy about the 'matrimonial mishaps' of four young Communists, and in November 1939 Wells directed a rare season of George Landen Dann's confronting Australian play *No Incense Rising*, which deals with family relations, suicide and women's issues. Wells's next production, in stark contrast, was John Murray and Allen Boretz's comedy *Room Service*, later made into a Marx Brothers film. Despite its inner and outer turmoil, the Repertory Club finished 1939 in a healthy state.[56]

The Corn is Green was not the only substitution of the 1939 Drama Festival. The normally politically adventurous Independent Players had planned a festival production of *Power and the Glory*, Czech playwright Karel Capek's condemnation of totalitarianism and war, but replaced their entry with James Lansdale Hodson's *Harvest in the North*, a slighter, though nevertheless political play about the struggles of a Lancashire cotton mill town during the Depression, which they had already staged some weeks earlier.[57] At the beginning of August, six weeks before the 1939 Drama Festival, the Independent Players and the Workers' Art Guild had performed some short plays together at the Modern Women's Club. A week later, in keeping with the cooperative times, the Independent Players had staged performances of *Harvest in the North*, directed by James Quinn, over two nights at the Repertory Club Theatre, with tickets sold at the Workers' Art Guild.

The Workers' Star praised the Independent Players' Drama Festival performance of *Harvest in the North*:

> The Independent Players become progressive with a drama of England's depressed areas that applies to any country under capitalism. It ends with a stirring call to action in the people's fight ... support will encourage the Independent Players to continue this type of production.[58]

Paul Hasluck was also effusive in his praise, describing the play as a humane antidote to the brutal jargon employed by the economic rationalists (even then) to debase the impact of the Depression.[59]

The Independent Players had already staged a performance of Auden and Isherwood's challenging and rather unusual play *The Ascent of F6* at the previous year's Drama Festival. This was the first time Perth had seen an Auden or Isherwood play, and it was well received. The 1939 Drama Festival, however, 'was little more than a brave gesture', with people's minds on the War in Europe.⁶⁰ Only eight plays were scheduled, initially without an entry from the Workers' Art Guild. With the late Guild entry of *Blood on the Moon*, the Festival was extended by a night.⁶¹ The reason for the Guild's tardiness in submitting an entry was perhaps the turmoil resulting from Keith George's departure. George had no involvement with the 1939 Drama Festival. His battle with the Guild had been a rancorous one, and it had taken a toll on him and others that would never be entirely erased.

In late June 1939, a short time after his break from the Guild, Keith George delivered a lecture on Modern Drama at a meeting of the Western Australian branch of the Fellowship of Australian Writers. In it, he contended that most amateur playwrights 'had not given sufficient thought to the theory and practice of their craft', in line with his view that 'the function of drama in society was to serve a useful social purpose'.⁶² The objective of drama, he said, was to express emotional aspects of life that could not be revealed by science. Theatre was most successful when it expressed 'vital' contemporary social themes, particularly social discord and conflict, and this was best expressed, he said, by the American New Theatre League productions, the likes of which were rarely seen in Australia because Australia had 'little consciousness of social purpose'. He concluded, though, by stating that theatre should not limit itself to the expression of 'emotional and material facts', and quoted a statement by Ernst Toller ('perhaps one of the greatest modern dramatists') that 'the function of the drama was not to present a thesis but to illuminate life'.⁶³

With the War came an increasing shift to the political centre by outliers such as the Workers' Art Guild.⁶⁴ The War levelled class stratification, and there was a retreat in Western Australia to its parochial isolation.⁶⁵ With Australia now at war, the political Left more generally, and the peace movement in particular, began to fracture. In December, the League for Peace and Democracy (formerly known as the Movement Against War and Fascism) dissolved due to dwindling support and the military enlistment of its members.⁶⁶

In late 1939, the Guild wrote to Jean Devanny requesting a copy of her three-act play *Paradise Flow*. The play portrayed a love affair on a sugar-cane farm at Innisfail in northern Queensland, against the backdrop of the 1933–1934 migrant cane workers' struggles and the political activism of the Communist cane cutters. In response, Devanny sent a copy of the play to Prichard in January 1940, suggesting 'pruning and alterations' to her script before a Guild production:

I know it is rough of me to ask you to send this in to the Guild, but I am worked off my feet these days and I have lost the [Guild] secretary's address.[67]

A Guild production of *Paradise Flow* was shelved with the onset of the War: a return to xenophobia meant such a play would not have been well received at that time.

The War arrived on Perth's doorstop in a very tangible way in November 1939, when a shot was fired across the bows of a Japanese whaling ship that had failed to use correct the signals when entering the port of Fremantle. Prichard was thus 'prevented' from travelling east at the end of that year.[68] In December she sent her greetings to Comrade Stalin on his sixtieth birthday, and spent Christmas in Perth.[69]

With increasing political tensions overseas, Radio Moscow at dawn followed late warm nights for many through that Perth summer of 1939–1940.

13

'THE FERVENT YEARS'[1]

I've seen the green hopes wither in young eyes,
Work-heavy days drag on the eager hands;
I've seen the sapling brains, fresh with surmise,
Grow gaunt and barren in these barren lands.
I've seen the old staunch settlers shrink and shake
As debts tread down the sap from every root:
Dead leaves, dead wood, then they decay and break;
Drought upon men, when will they come to fruit?

The storm is rising. Gusts of questioning
Stir tongues to whisper, anger lights the eyes
Weary with watching the deceitful mists.
Thunder of voices to the deaf skies ring,
And from the fields, swept bare by tricks and lies,
Springs up the challenge of ten thousand fists.[2]

The CPA in Western Australia was about to endure a period of uncharted political persecution, but state secretary Bill Mountjoy (referred to in local CPA circles by the nickname 'Das Kapital') held steady — though increasingly precarious — sway in local Party circles. He 'was inclined to be a bit bureaucratic and a bit dogmatic, as most Communists were in those days', remembered Arthur Rudkin, but he was accorded the respect of high office by most within the Party — for the moment.[3] As the CPA began to experience the strain of increasing bureaucratic harassment, however, Mountjoy began to falter. He was not a good man in a crisis, and he put off dealing with impending crises within local CPA circles.[4] Under pressure, he also had a tendency to 'get on the bottle', and he found a willing drinking companion in Detective Sergeant George Ronald (Ron) Richards of the CIB's Special Bureau and Aliens Office.[5]

The office, to which state police including Richards were seconded, was formed in 1939 during the lead-up to Australia's entry into the War. Its role was to monitor 'the activities of aliens' and those 'suspected to be anti-British', including members of the CPA. Detective Sergeant Richards, whose reputation as a police investigator was on the rise, was appointed head of the bureau in 1940.[6]

Mountjoy thought having Richards as a drinking companion would serve himself and the Party well, keeping him in touch with police moves on the CPA. But word of the bar-room friendship soon became the subject of gossip in Party circles, and those who knew Richards either personally or by reputation thought Mountjoy well and truly in over his head. Party members 'were used to the activities of police officers whose use of informers and plants was clumsy and ineffective', wrote historian Stuart Macintyre later, but Richards 'was a much more formidable investigator'. He was a cunning policeman who cultivated an extensive surveillance network, and he would learn a great deal about the CPA in Mountjoy's company.[7]

Richards plumbed where he could. He befriended Arthur Rudkin as Rudkin was delivering *The Workers' Star* across suburban Victoria Park: one of the regular 160 copies sold in the area went to Richards's home. It was some time before Rudkin discovered that Richards was a policeman, after which Rudkin admitted being 'careful' in his dealings. But the ever-wily Richards often gave Rudkin 'interesting tidbits of information':

> Once, when we published statistics of the number of CPA members in each State, he told me the W.A. Police Special Squad had over ten times as many names on its list of 'known Communists' as there were Party members in the State, and were amazed that such a small group of people could be so influential![8]

Richards was highly intelligent, slick and duplicitous. He was remarkably conversant with Party theory, he was flirtatious when required, and his charms entrapped Party members.[9] Rudkin thought Richards 'quite honest' unlike 'some of the other wallopers'.[10]

One of these 'other wallopers' was CIB Detective Hugh McLernon, who made his presence felt just as forcefully as Richards, though more heavy-handedly. McLernon was an active member of Catholic Action, which might account for his overzealous dealings with Party members.[11]

Richards's and McLernon's immediate superior was Inspector John (Jack) Doyle, head of Perth's Criminal Investigation Branch. Doyle, a fellow Catholic, was a former Irish policeman and a distinguished police detective of long standing in Perth, described by Paul Hasluck in the

1920s as 'one of the straightest and fairest men in the force'.[12] Conversely, such was Richards's reputation for dissembling and deceit that he became known as 'the black snake' within state CPA circles;[13] he would later play a central role in the defection of Russian diplomat Vladimir Petrov and the subsequent spy scandal that would ensnare Prichard and her son Ric.

Richards was to stalk the Prichard–Throssell family for many years. He made frequent appearances at police raids of their Greenmount home, and Ric Throssell believed that Richards 'operated a vendetta against' the family.[14] Richards also visited the Workers' Art Guild, albeit seemingly innocently. He was on friendly terms with Phyllis Harnett and others in the Guild circle and would chat, watch proceedings and compliment people on their work.[15] 'Richards had this way of working as a detective that he behaved like an incipient lover,' Harnett later said. 'I very nearly thought him charming!'[16] But Harnett was to be a more formidable adversary than Mountjoy.

In January 1940, Jean Devanny wrote buoyantly to Prichard:

> since the Red Army marched into Poland my spirits have been skyhigh ... The final tussle of strength is coming close. Who knows what 1940 will bring forth. The mountain is laboring but we dont [sic] look for a mouse. Good luck and my love, dear Comrade. Look after yourself. You simply must be here when the turn over comes.[17]

By February 1940, some members of the CPA had begun to experience physical intimidation. Gus Stagg, then manager of *The Workers' Star*, was attacked while speaking from the CPA stump at the regular Sunday speakers' forum on the Perth Esplanade, as police stood idly by. Official rancour was heightened by a CPA anti-conscription campaign. Under the umbrella of the federal *National Security Act 1939*, Prime Minister Menzies imposed media regulations in March 1940 that made Communist publications subject to censorship. All copy had to be submitted to the military censor for the excision of any references to the War, the Soviet Union, the Soviet government, criticism of the Menzies government, strikes in any Empire or allied country, or industrial unrest of any kind. It was also illegal, said Arthur Rudkin, then editor of *The Workers' Star*, for publications 'to leave any large blanks or blacked out passages to indicate *where* we had been censored', or even to report the fact that they were being censored.[18]

Police also targeted staff at *The Workers' Star*, and within a few months most were in prison having been charged with a variety of offences other than their involvement with the newspaper. In March 1940, in the hope of evading the new regulations, the newspaper changed its name to the *Star*. However, the newly named *Star* became one of nine CPA newspapers and periodicals made subject to censorship restrictions. In contravention of censorship regulations, it had made reference, in April 1940, to Menzies's restrictions of the Communist press. Again in early May, in an article titled 'Ban on Working Class Papers', the paper had defiantly reported that it would continue to be published, albeit in an abridged four-page format — though this would also be short-lived.[19]

By late May 1940, all named Communist publications had been banned completely by the Menzies government. The penalty for mere possession of these illegal publications was six months' imprisonment. In a renewed effort to evade the sanctions, the CPA in Western Australia immediately published an abridged news publication under the new title of *The Clarion*, exploiting a loophole in the censorship regulations that banned the *Star* by name but not an equivalent newspaper by another name. *The Clarion* was therefore, at least initially, neither illegal nor subject to censorship. However, the government closed this loophole within weeks and police raided the premises where *The Clarion* was being produced, though were persuaded to leave before the duplicator machine and copy were discovered.[20]

CPA member Bill Irwin was appointed acting editor of the *Daily News*, in James McArtney's absence — against the wishes of a senior board member. Coverage given in late May to the banning of CPA publications raised the ire of the newspaper's board, and Irwin was called to account for his 'error of judgement'. But Irwin had not been responsible: it was the work of the newspaper's chief subeditor. The heat, however, did not elude Irwin for long. Within days police began searching premises associated with the CPA and the homes of its members, including Irwin's.[21]

Speakers at CPA rallies and meetings became subject to increasing harassment and physical threats at around this time. While speaking from the CPA platform on the Esplanade in April, Mountjoy and William (Bill) Dean, the CPA state treasurer who ran the Radical Bookshop, had been heckled and threatened by a group of soldiers and Catholic Actionists 'intent on causing serious disruption'.[22] The CPA had not endeared itself to members of the Australian Imperial Force when it started to denounce AIF soldiers as 'five bob a day murderers'. A CPA bulletin encouraged members to support Party speakers but warned them not to 'get embroiled in arguments with hecklers'.[23]

Mountjoy's relationship with Richards gave the CPA little, if any, forewarning of its coming plight in Western Australia or of the forces that would be unleashed against it. A CPA state committee circular of late April 1940 predicted that it was 'unlikely that a frontal attack will be made on the Party' because of the 'many difficulties and doubts of the powers of the Crimes Acts'.

> Indications are that they will attempt a piecemeal destruction by the arresting of leading Communists, the arrests being on the basis of 'subversive' and 'disloyal' statements made from the platform ... Our speakers must be careful not to give unnecessary openings to the police ... Care should be taken in selecting places to meet and in the keeping of records — all that is unnecessary to keep should be destroyed.[24]

Over in the eastern states, support for New Theatre had dried up with the War, and in response it had broadened its repertoire. In January 1940, Jean Devanny wrote to Prichard: 'we shall have to do more with the Australian playwrights now that Australia will be more isolated from overseas contacts.'[25] In March, the Workers' Art Guild committee put in place an 'associate membership' plan to bolster flagging public support, and began to stage smaller-scale plays every Sunday evening in the Guild rooms, where a stage had now been installed.[26] The first performance was that of a Living Newspaper titled *Hold Your Wheat*, written by twenty-five-year-old Western Australian schoolteacher, farm labourer, poet and mostly absent Workers' Art Guild member Victor Williams.[27]

Williams based *Hold Your Wheat* on the industrial action taken by Western Australian wheat farmers in November 1939 against the federal government, which had taken control of the sale and export of their product to support the war effort. The title had been a slogan used when farmers withheld the sale of their wheat until a satisfactory price was offered, but in this instance its use was far more declamatory. Living Newspapers, by their very nature, were partisan polemic dramatisations of current affairs in abbreviated form. They centred on an axis of conflict, both for dramatic effect and to make their political point, and used dramatic shorthand to telegraph necessary narrative information. In *Hold Your Wheat*, Williams was 'looking for dramatic clash' and built the Living Newspaper on both the chronology of events and the main points of conflict.[28] He used two main characters to tell the story, exemplars of the two main combatants in the dispute: the wheat growers and the government.

A lineage can be traced from the theatre of agitprop and the Living Newspaper back to the medieval religious plays, or 'mysteries', performed by members of English craft trade guilds. These plays had developed from religious pageants and mobile performances that took place, usually outdoors, on a stage or stages wheeled along a processional route; alternatively an audience moved past stages on which performances took place. The plays later evolved into more secular drama, and from the fifteenth to the sixteenth centuries they became known as the allegorical 'morality plays', portraying the victories of virtue over vice.

The American Living Newspaper Unit grew from the Roosevelt government–sponsored Federal Theatre Project in 1935. Progressive writers and journalists then struggling to make a living initiated the Unit, and the material used for these Living Newspapers was based on news stories from American newspapers. Though conceived in the Soviet Union, the Living Newspaper is attributed to left-wing American playwright Elmer Rice and the American Newspaper Guild, which harnessed the skills of a number of unemployed journalists and press editors as dramaturges. An editorial team of journalists and subeditors, in place of the traditional theatre production team, produced the early, unadulterated form of Living Newspaper; an editor-in-chief replaced the traditional theatre director.[29]

Bill Irwin had introduced Victor Williams to a number of the American Living Newspapers from the 'Roosevelt Reconstruction' period, and Williams was excited by their political and dramatic potential. Williams had initially turned his hand to agitprop in the style of earlier Guild plays such as *Waiting For Lefty*, but when he learned of Living Newspapers he saw the possibilities of being able to dramatise a 'wide sweep', the whole dramatic development of something that was happening at the time'.[30]

Victor Williams had been brought up on his family's wheat farm at Wyalkatchem, north-east of Perth, but when the Depression hit and wheat prices plummeted, the family was forced to sell up and move, which had a profound effect on sixteen-year-old Williams. The economic collapse of 1929 decimated Western Australia's wheatbelt communities, and this led to increasing rural industrial militancy. A state Farm Labourers' Union, independent of the Trades Hall, was formed at Lake Grace in the state's south-west in October 1936 to secure fair wages and conditions for the state's farm workers, but its registration was rejected by the Arbitration Court.[31]

A staunch advocate of agrarian unionism,[32] Williams was of rigid, rebellious Irish stock. He had been catapulted into political activism after reading *The Nature of the Capitalist Crisis* (1935) by John Strachey, co-founder of the Left Book Club and a widely read British economics writer whose work was a Marxist critique of the economic crisis of capitalism in the inter-war years. It was Williams's eventual contact with the Workers' Art Guild that led him to join the CPA.[33] As a student teacher he had attended Alec King's English classes at the University of Western Australia, and King had encouraged him to write and steered him to the Workers' Art Guild. There, in late 1937, Williams found kindred spirits, although his contact with the Guild was limited by his work in the country. Soon after joining the Guild he moved to Victoria for six to eight months and it was there, in Ballarat in early 1939, that he joined the CPA. After returning from Victoria he resumed working in country Western Australia, before returning to Perth and taking up with the Guild again.

Williams joined the Guild writers' group and became one of its strongest writers. Australian writer Dorothy Hewett, who knew Williams well in later years, described him as 'a dark, saturnine proselytizer' who 'deliberately proletarianized himself'.[34] He identified himself strongly with the working class and did indeed, to some extent, fabricate his class.[35] Around the time of writing *Hold Your Wheat*, he began a broad reading of Marxist and Leninist texts and set about writing a 'positive' history of farming struggles, eventually publishing a CPA pamphlet titled *Farmers' Way Forward* in 1943.[36]

In 1939, the bushel price of wheat had dropped to a level not seen since the worst years of the Depression. When war broke out, the Menzies government had wrested control of the entire national wheat and wool stock from the farmers who had, until that time, sold their product independently to buyers for the best price they could negotiate. The government paid wheat growers a fraction of the price they had formerly received: for many, this was below the cost of production.

At the beginning of the November 1939 wheat harvest, Western Australia's wheat growers voted at a mass meeting of the increasingly militant Australian Wheat and Wool Growers' Union to withhold their wheat until the price paid by the government was increased to a reasonable level. Farmers stockpiled their grain rather than delivering it to central silos and railway sidings, and pickets were set up to prevent deliveries by errant farmers. The stand-off was abandoned at the end of November 1939 because of a lack of support from growers in the eastern states, but a compromise on the wheat price was eventually reached with the government and the dispute was resolved in January 1940.[37] *The Workers' Star* had published reports throughout 1939 of Menzies's attempts to limit the production of wheat, and had attributed the wheat growers' hold-up, rightly or wrongly, to the CPA.[38]

The wheat growers' conferences of the early 1930s were certainly a platform for the CPA, and the Party held up the organisation of wheat growers as a fine example of the successful implementation of 'militant policy'.[39] Williams was working in the country at the time of the wheat dispute, and he closely followed developments through the rural newspapers. It was these newspaper reports and those of *The Workers' Star* that provided the material from which he wrote *Hold Your Wheat*.[40] Much of the dialogue for the play, which included direct quotes from the government and from the Wheat and Wool Growers' Union, came from *The West Australian Wheatgrower*.[41]

14

'ART AS A WEAPON IN THE PEOPLE'S FIGHT'

It's not easy being a Communist in this place.[1]

In April 1940, the *Daily News* published a large feature on the Workers' Art Guild, promoting the theatre wing's next major public performance and its most mainstream stage production yet, *The Women*. The newspaper's news editor, John Hector, who was also the Guild production's business manager and a Guild enthusiast concerned about its uncertain future, wrote the extensive article. In it, the Guild declared itself, for the first time, a political (though 'non-party') organisation, and announced that its objective was to use 'art as a weapon in the people's fight'. Ironically, the article was advertising the Guild's least political production to date.[2]

Hector took a substantial political risk in using his position on the *Daily News* to publicly promote the Guild in this partisan piece, perhaps designed to shore up support ahead of a surprise appointment to the Guild. The fact that James McArtney was editor of the *Daily News* at the time, and Bill Irwin its assistant editor, might also have given Hector licence to write this article. In any event, Hector was called to front an irate *Daily News* board of directors. He knew the article would aggravate but, recently having received a substantial family inheritance, he was financially secure enough to risk the wrath of his employers.[3]

The Guild had been divided and in difficulties for some time. The progress of the War had become all-consuming: there was waning public support for theatre, and many Guild members had left to join the armed forces. In the prevailing political climate, the public was in no mood for political sermons from the stage.

Howard Smith had pushed for a production of Clare Boothe Luce's satirical comedy *The Women*. The play was something of a social sermon but diversionary light entertainment nevertheless, and would appeal, it was hoped, to a wider mainstream audience after popular seasons in England, America and Australia. The script was in other ways expedient to the times, written as it was for an exclusively female cast. With many of the country's men in the armed services or lying low, it had become increasingly difficult to cast male roles.

The April 1940 production of *The Women* was also illustrative of a now widening gap between the Guild and the Party line, with playwright Oriel Gray claiming that the Sydney New Theatre would never have considered the production of such 'bourgeois' theatre.[4]

The Women both lampooned and appealed to a respectable middle-class audience. The production also advertised Perth's 'haute' retail fashion outlets. For the first time, the Guild had corporate sponsorship; Hector had offered Perth retailers the considerable publicity that the Guild still attracted in return for material and financial donations to the production. Business and product sponsorships were advertised in Hector's newspaper article and on the play's program. Professional retail beauticians applied make-up backstage, and expensive jewellery, furs and 'magnificent frocking'[5] worn by the cast were supplied by local businesses and kept under lock and key between performances.[6] Perth department store Charles Moore & Co. supplied the handbags used in the production.[7] Another curious feature was the involvement of the J.C. Williamson Company — one of the world's largest professional theatrical companies — in 'sponsoring' this Guild production.

The Workers' Star conceded that the play was 'rather different from the usual run of Guild shows', and pitched *The Women* as a lesson in class-consciousness, dealing as it does with the 'gossiping', 'flirting' and 'mental vacuity' of 'the idle women of America's more prosperous middle classes'.[8] 'Backseat' was, however, disappointed in the performance itself.[9]

The play had previously been adapted into a film. Released in 1939, *The Women* was described as 'a film famous for its bitchy, vicious, gossipy dialogue and its portrayal of women as financial mercenaries and clawing back-stabbers',[10] but it 'lacked the punch' of Luce's script,[11] as much of her dialogue was deemed offensive and thus subject to censorship by the priggish American film regulation body. Australian police had also instructed the producers of an earlier Sydney theatre production of *The Women* to cut what was deemed to be offensive dialogue from the play for reasons of propriety, and monitored the performance for potential obscenities.[12] The dialogue was not, however, cut from the Guild production.

Another member of the middle class, albeit a class renegade, was the subject of an anonymous letter sent to Perth police during the season of *The Women*:

> Just a reminder of a very strong Communist that lives in Greenmount and has quite a number of visitors to her home. Mrs. H. Throssell, York Road.[13]

The Guild season of *The Women* was directed for the first time by Marjorie Berry, with the assistance of Howard Smith, the only male involved in the production.[14] The cast was a mixture of Guild and outside players, including Dorothy Krantz (formerly Powell), who had appeared in *Are You Ready, Comrade?*, Phyllis Harnett and Doris Masel.[15] Harnett had 'lured' Masel into the play, along with the entirety of her elegant lounge-room to dress the set. Other players included Perth Independent Theatre actress Doris Neughar, Pat Howard, who had appeared in *Inga*, *Are You Ready, Comrade?* and *Floridsdorf*, Hope Bath, Joan Butcher, Joyce Coombes, Gwen Duggan, Joan Mockeridge and a number of debutantes including Betty Hamill and Olive Lachberg (formerly Keiller) in her only stage appearance with the Guild.

The Women was another popular success for the Guild, and its three-night season was extended by a further two. The Guild's stocks seemed restored. Hector's labours also ensured that the production was a financial success. However, this came at a cost: the outcome of his meeting with the *Daily News*' board of directors was that Hector 'found himself without a job, and had to leave Perth' for Sydney (via Melbourne).[16]

Gordon Burgoyne also left *The West Australian* and moved in to Bill Irwin's Mounts Bay Road flat before heading to Sydney in June. Burgoyne and Irwin were prominent members of the local branch of the Australian Journalists' Association and had worked together on *The Workers' Star*. Burgoyne became an active member of the Guild, writing sketches for production, and formed a social trio there with Irwin and Phyllis Harnett.[17] Before he left, Prichard wrote him a letter of introduction to *Smith's Weekly* journalist Bartlett Adamson.

> This will introduce you to Gordon Burgoyne who I think is a brilliant young writer. If you can give him any help with advice or suggestions as to jobs in Sydney I know you will do so. G.B. has a very dry whimsical style & I attach great importance to his dramatic work — although on the press here, he has demonstrated all-round ability.[18]

The political atmosphere at this time was volatile, fuelled by suspicion, fear and innuendo. The tension was palpable when John and Ray Oldham returned to Perth in May 1940. After three months in New York, they had sailed back to Sydney in September 1939. A few days into the voyage, the Second World War was declared, and anxiety on board was heightened by sightings of periscopes and surfacing allied submarines. The Australian press mistakenly reported the sinking of the Oldhams' ship by an enemy vessel.[19]

On their arrival in Sydney, John Oldham applied for military enlistment but was rejected on medical grounds. Fellow Western Australian Herbert ('Nugget') Coombs, then a senior economist in the federal Treasury Department, helped tide the Oldhams over financially until John got a job with the Department of the Interior, working on protective measures for coastal defence.[20] But Ray Oldham was expecting their first child and the pair wanted to return to Perth. When they did, in May of the following year, John Oldham returned to work as an architect with Harold Krantz, and 'reacquainted himself' with the Workers' Art Guild.[21]

To counter the perceived insurgency of the CPA during this period, draconian laws and penalties were introduced and enforced ruthlessly in Western Australia. Police raids on Party members in Perth, on flimsy legal grounds, began well before the official declaration of the CPA's illegality. The first round of raids took place in late May 1940, before the Subversive Associations Regulations were proclaimed in mid-June. Arthur Rudkin was of the view that the CPA in Western Australia was not sufficiently abreast of the changing legal landscape and was disadvantaged by its distance from Canberra.

> The government would notify the W.A. political police in advance when new 'security' regulations were about to be promulgated, so that they were able to pounce on 'offenders' before they had any means of knowing that what they were doing was illegal.[22]

In May, Detective Sergeant Ron Richards and a police constable offsider arrested mine rigger Patrick ('Paddy') Troy — a longstanding Australian Workers' Union agitator and known Communist — and charged him with distributing a publication (CPA state committee circular *The Spark*) making reference to the War without lawful excuse, 'upon which was not printed in legible characters the name and address of the printer'. The name and address of the editor, Kevin Healy, did in fact appear on the publication but without the declaration 'Printed and published by'. Eric Knowles, a fitter workmate of Troy's, was also arrested by Richards and his offsider, and charged with the same offence.[23]

Troy thought the arrests merely part of an operation to flush out CPA members. He tried to allay Knowles's concerns, assuring him that possession of the bulletin did not necessarily implicate him as a Party member. Knowles need only tell the police that Troy had given him the bulletin and it would blow over, he said. Richards visited Troy at work to corroborate Knowles's account, and left telling Troy that there was 'nothing to it'.[24]

A week later, Arthur Rudkin, editor of *The Clarion* and former editor of *The Workers' Star*, was arrested and charged under the National Security Act with publishing information 'which might be useful to the enemy [and] likely to prejudice the efficient prosecution of the War'.[25] Rudkin, a senior air raid precautions warden, was also charged with possession of a document urging CPA members to become involved in air raid precautions, and of a letter to noted British scientist J.B.S. Haldane, through the Communist Party of Great Britain (of which Haldane was then a supporter and later a member), seeking advice on the improvement of gasmasks. Much of the requested material on gasmasks was publicly available; indeed, Haldane's book on England's air raid precautions preparedness had been promoted in Perth as the Left Book Club's book of the month in October 1938, but some of this information had become, unbeknown to most, 'classified'. Rudkin's criticisms of the inadequacy of air raid precautions in Australia and his attempts to pass such information through CPA channels cast him as a saboteur.[26]

Troy, Knowles and Rudkin were all accused at trial of being traitorous 'fifth columnists' providing aid to the enemy. Troy received a three-month jail term, Knowles was sentenced to one month's imprisonment, and Rudkin was sentenced to four months' jail with hard labour and served three months with remission for good behaviour.[27] The Defence Department's counsel for the prosecution stated that 'recommendations would be made for the internment of the [CPA] offenders for the duration of the war', so that they would not be released on expiry of their sentences.[28] Under the National Security Act, no trial was required to intern 'subversives'.[29] Gus Stagg, Leah Marks, assistant state CPA secretary Kevin Healy and *Workers' Star* publisher Henry Matson were subsequently arrested and charged with contempt, having given a clenched-fist 'Communist salute' to Rudkin in court after his sentencing, though these charges were later dropped.[30]

CPA state treasurer and Radical Bookshop manager Bill Dean was also jailed for three months for actions deemed prejudicial to the efficient prosecution of the War and a further three months for the possession of printed CPA material that did not carry the name of the printer. A former British army physical education instructor, Dean had attended a Guild course on public speaking run by Keith George.[31] Foolishly, it seems, he chose as his speaking topic Australia's defence and reasons against sending troops overseas. Police searched the Radical Bookshop and found extensive notes in Dean's hand on the Australian armed services, made in preparation for his speech, including what they suspected to be military intelligence codes.[32]

In June, following Italy's declaration of war, Italian clubs in Perth and Fremantle were closed down and a ship flying the Italian flag was impounded in Fremantle Harbour. The machinery and members of the CPA faced a similar fate. In late June the federal government was granted increased powers of control over Australia's resources, production, workforce and citizenry.

It was a time of great anguish for Prichard as she came under increasing strain with the CPA ban and the raids on herself and her friends. A few days after Rudkin was sentenced, Prichard wrote to the editor of *International Literature* in Moscow, Timofei Rokotov:

> [O]ne can scarcely breathe in Australia without being suspected of giving information likely to be of service to the enemy ... It is ludicrous of course that Communists in Australia who have opposed Fascism for years should on the most flimsy pretexts be accused of any such motive. I was to have given some addresses on the work of [Australian poet Bernard] O'Dowd, Furnley Maurice, and [Henry] Lawson at the University of W.A. this month. These, however, have been cancelled because I am a Communist. Several members of the Party have been arrested and imprisoned recently, so that if you do not receive this article for International Literature, you will understand why.[33]

This letter, enclosed with an article on Bernard O'Dowd that Prichard had written for the magazine, indeed never made it to Moscow.[34] On passing through the hands of the censor, it was confiscated. The Western Australian censor, who it so happened had been to school with O'Dowd, took it upon himself to correct Prichard's potted biography of O'Dowd before it was forwarded to the Chief Publicity Censor in Melbourne.[35] Rokotov, unaware of this, complained to Prichard about the infrequency of her correspondence, reproaching her 'for communicating with us so seldom':

> I feel you could have written to us more often … We know very little about Australia and now less than ever. As matters stand you are our only contact with the fifth continent and we count on your cooperation in bringing to our readers news on the literary and cultural life in Australia.[36]

The university addresses to which Prichard had referred were contributions she had been asked to give to a series of lectures on Australian literature at the University of Western Australia. Australian universities had received Commonwealth grants to establish short courses on Australian literature as a part of the English syllabus, and UWA had organised a series of ten lectures by speakers including Norman Bartlett, John K. Ewers and Paul Hasluck. The weekly lectures, which began in June 1940, included discussions of the origins and development of Australian literature. Shortly before Prichard was due to deliver three of these lectures, she was informed by UWA that her lectures had been cancelled, presumably because political pressure was brought to bear on the university. It was certainly a political decision, and Prichard was justifiably incensed. She wrote an angry letter to the university's Professorial Board.

> You are well aware, no doubt, of the implications of your action. That those, who should defend intellectual integrity, have thrown the first stone at me, is a matter for surprise and shame. But what I feel more deeply is, that by repudiating the value of my knowledge of Australian literature, for political reasons, you are destroying the principle for which the University is supposed to stand, and which is supposed to be the basis of your own work. To prostitute your power to the service of hysterical obfuscation, at a time like this, in my opinion is servile and cowardly. It remains for you, in any future incidents, to direct the tide of public opinion, either towards the defence of intellectual integrity, or for its persecution and immolation. I ask you, very earnestly, to consider the deeper issues involved, and to retrieve the impression that will be made by your action towards me, by resolutely and vigorously refusing to allow the University to be made an instrument for political oppression. I understand that there are those among you who may seek to acquire merit by this gesture; but I have the honour to stand with Milton, Voltaire, and the greatest writers of my day, against ignorance, turpitude and pusillanimity — and for truth and justice in human affairs.

> My life and work may not have been of very much worth, but at least I can serve my grail faithfully to the end.[37]

The Western Australian branch of the Fellowship of Australian Writers also protested, and successfully pursued payment for the cancelled lectures, which Prichard could ill afford to forgo. The outrage was amplified by the fact that the Fellowship of Australian Writers had voted Prichard 'Australia's leading writer' that year. Irene Greenwood, a noted feminist, peace activist and radio broadcaster, drew international attention to the university's actions later in the year when she spoke about the literature of Prichard on an international short-wave radio broadcast to a predominantly North American audience. The broadcast was, funnily enough, one of a series of 'propaganda' talks by Greenwood, funded by the Australian Department of Information, to try to win American popular support for the Allied war effort before America's entry into the War. Greenwood's talk made little reference to Prichard's political activities, but criticised the cancellation of her university lectures.[38]

Prichard was to come under particularly intense surveillance over the next three-and-a-half years, and police raided her home on a number of occasions. She stored potentially incriminating material in a large tin trunk that she secreted in a hedge near her writing shed,[39] and when national CPA official Harry Gould visited her at Greenmount, 'first thing on arrival [she] showed me a likely escape route for getaway in case of a police raid.'[40]

After the imprisonment of Troy, Knowles and Rudkin, more than a dozen other Perth CPA members followed. Also jailed were non–Party members simply found to be in possession of illegal CPA newspapers bought, in many cases, before the banning of the possession of such material. Party members imprisoned in the fairly brutal conditions of Fremantle Prison were denied permission to leave the prison grounds on working parties, as was common practice at the time for other inmates. A prison regulation stipulated that 'sexual perverts and Communists [were] not allowed out of the gates'.[41]

Rudkin, Bill Dean and Kevin Healy, who were also serving three-month prison sentences with hard labour for the possession of printed CPA material that did not carry the name of the printer, petitioned unsuccessfully to be treated as political prisoners.[42] They wanted to be segregated from the jail's criminal population, granted free association with other prisoners charged with similar offences and relieved of restrictions on their correspondence and visits. They also sought to be allowed books, newspapers, tobacco, their own food and the right to wear clothes other than the prison uniform. Their requests were denied by federal attorney-general William Morris (Billy) Hughes. The prosecution and imprisonment of these Western Australian CPA members were intended to serve as a warning to other Party members in the state and to frighten members out of the state, and many did leave.

The disproportionately heavy-handed constraint of the Communist Party in Western Australia was puzzling to many and somewhat unexpected. The CIB and Western Command Military Intelligence, according to John Oldham, 'regarded us as in a strategic position and they set out to smash the [Communist Party] in Western Australia and destroy any influence it might have.'[43] The authorities feared that the state branch of the CPA posed a far broader threat than its relatively modest size suggested. In fact there was less CPA influence on the trade union movement in Western Australia than there was in the eastern states. With the exception of the waterfront, there were not the powerful industrial unions in Western Australia that existed on the other side of the country. Yet the convictions of Communists in the eastern states were far fewer, and the penalties imposed much less severe.

Another possible reason for the heavy-handedness was the zeal of the Catholic-dominated right-wing faction of the ALP, then in political power in the state, to smash the CPA. The ascendant ALP right-wing 'troops' pulled deviants and heretics into line.[44] The Labor Party made a point of exposing as many CPA members in their ranks as possible, and it was often an unsavoury process. The ALP insisted its members sign a pledge stating that they were not members of the CPA, and CPA members in the ranks were called before the state executive–controlled ALP Metropolitan Council to account for themselves and their sins. In April 1940, Tom Wignall Snr, then senior vice-president of the ALP's Labour Day Committee and a member of the committee since the revival of the street parade, was sacked from the committee because of his affiliation with the CPA.[45]

On Empire Day, 15 June 1940, the CPA and allied groups, including the Friends of the Soviet Union, were officially declared 'unlawful' organisations under the National Security Act. An amendment to the Act meant that those fraternising with these groups could be arrested under Subversive Associations Regulations.[46] For many it came as no surprise, and indeed was 'almost a relief when it happened at last, freeing us from the everlasting tension of wondering when and how the blow would fall'.

An alternative leadership had been selected, and careful preparations made to ensure that publication of our paper and other Party work could continue uninterrupted. Unfortunately, some of the comrades entrusted with this task panicked and fell down on the job, so that the Party in W.A. had no State Committee and no official journal for about three months.[47]

Preparations for impending illegality in Western Australia had been made but not enacted, and Bill Mountjoy was blamed when the day of reckoning arrived.[48] Prichard supported calls for his removal. Mountjoy had been confident that he would be sufficiently warned by Detective Sergeant Ron Richards before any move was made to ban the Party, and had given little regard to doomsaying members of the CPA's state committee predicting peril. His relationship with Richards had only served to undermine his position, and he had become the subject of poisonous gossip within the Party.

After the CPA's banning, the Western Australian branch fractured into smaller cells and went underground. State committee members went 'into smoke' and Party functionaries effectively abandoned members who were prosecuted and jailed. Troy received little support during his prison term, and vowed to offer his own support to imprisoned members and their families on his release.

Immediately after the declaration of the CPA's illegality, raids on Party offices and members' homes took place across Australia. New South Wales and Commonwealth police also raided the premises of the New Theatre League in Sydney and confiscated a large number of manuscripts, including copies of *Forward One*, *The Lyons Bungles* and *Are You Ready, Comrade?* This was despite New Theatre secretary Freda Lewis's statement in Sydney's *The Daily Telegraph* that the theatre had 'no Communists in our organisation, and we are not connected with the Communist Party in any way.'[49]

On Sunday 16 June a second round of police raids took place across Western Australia. The homes of Prichard, Phyllis Harnett and Gus Stagg were searched, as was Mooney's Cafe in William Street, run by *The Workers' Star* publisher Henry Matson.[50] Harnett had recently moved out of Java Head and into the Cardigan Flats on St Georges Terrace. She was no longer working at the Radical Bookshop but was employed as Guild secretary, having just taken over the position from Hope Bath.[51] Harnett was also, by now, the medium through which confidential directives were transmitted from the CPA's central committee to the Western Australian branch of the Party, and police seized a large amount of CPA literature and correspondence relating to the Workers' Art Guild from her. This, and the other material confiscated in these raids, was taken to the Investigation Branch office for examination, which would sometimes last months and material was often not returned.

After the June raid on her home, Prichard wrote a letter of complaint to the Ministry of Information requesting the return of a red notebook 'containing extracts from newspapers':[52]

> In view of a recent announcement in the 'West Australian', I understand that it is necessary to make application for the return of books and papers taken from [Greenmount] by officers of the Criminal Investigation Department on June 16th. As a writer, I find myself hampered by the loss of some notes for work I was engaged on [including a] red note book containing quotations and extracts from Newspapers which represent references of about thirty years' gleaning. At the same time, I wish to protest at the removal of this material, and at the foolish attack which has been made on members of the Communist Party in Western Australia. Communists have always been the most active opponents of Fascism and Hitlerism. They still are. It is noteworthy that in Great Britain no such action has been taken as has been considered necessary in Western Australia. The situation, of course, is ludicrous.[53]

Prichard's letter was passed on to Perth CIB Inspector Jack Doyle, but supposedly no trace was found of her red notebook.

The raids disrupted Prichard's writing. Notes she had written for the lecture she was then preparing on Bernard O'Dowd, as well as a notebook with extracts from *Poetry Militant*, O'Dowd's 1909 address on the political responsibility of the poet, were taken. It would be four months before any of the seized material was returned to her. Prichard again complained to the Ministry of Information:

> [I]n Great Britain, Fascists have been prosecuted and imprisoned; in Western Australia, Communists — not Fascists … This fact could be interpreted as 'subversive activity' of a very serious kind.[54]

Police did monitor the relatively ineffectual right-wing fringe groups that surfaced for short periods in Western Australia at the time, but these groups were not seen as posing any significant threat to security and thus, by and large, were left undisturbed. There is no evidence of a conspiracy by Western Australian police to turn a blind eye to the activities of right-wing extremist groups; in fact, in the latter years of the War, Detective Sergeant Ron Richards was responsible for the arrest of four members of the Australia First Movement who were plotting to overthrow the state government and destroy major public infrastructure.[55]

On 17 June, Bill Mountjoy's house was raided and 'Communist literature and correspondence was seized'.[56] Mountjoy immediately went into hiding under an assumed name and very few people, including Rudkin and others on the state committee, knew where he was.

The events that quickly overtook Mountjoy came as a great shock to him. The CPA's central committee in Sydney thought it prudent to get him out of Western Australia as quickly as possible, and arranged his discreet return to Sydney in July or August 1940. He was booked into a Fremantle hotel and the next day smuggled aboard an eastbound ship by the Seamen's Union.

A replacement for Mountjoy was also arranged by the CPA's central committee. Gallipoli veteran John Spencer ('Jack') Simpson — whose real name was Maurice Flynn — was 'smuggled over' from Sydney to take over the running of the CPA in Western Australia.[57] On his arrival in Perth he took up residence in Cottesloe, posing as a retired farmer, and was paid a small living allowance by the Party.

The Wignall household was also raided twice in June 1940, and police again searched Bill and Dorothy Irwin's flat, which Gordon Burgoyne had only recently left. No incriminating literature was found, but police reported 'there is no doubt that same had been destroyed'.[58] Despite a police report stating that Bill Irwin 'has always been regarded as a leading intellectual member of the Australian Communist Party ... has expressed advanced communistic views ... [and] was in a position to spread the communist doctrine in places where acknowledged communists were not welcome', Irwin would frustrate their efforts to prove this. Police were never able to uncover evidence that tied him to any illegal activities. They were of the view that 'his position on the *Daily News* allowed him to allocate a considerable amount of space to Australian Communist Party activities', but Irwin was careful, given this position, to carry out his Party activities in a reasonably veiled manner. He consistently denied being a member of the CPA, in line with official Party policy for members at that time.[59]

As an experienced journalist, Irwin was very useful in helping with the publication of *The Workers' Star*, editing parts of the paper from time to time.

He would frequently subedit *The Workers' Star* on weekends and slot the finished copy into the Party office at midnight on Sunday, 'dead with fatigue' after the many rewrites that were often required.[60] He wrote a little for the paper but more often encouraged others to write. Irwin was not a member of a CPA fraction, and was initially not as politically active as many other Party members about town, unable as he was to devote a lot of time to CPA and Guild matters given his very long working hours at the *Daily News*.

It was a nerve-racking time — Irwin later said of that period that 'everybody was being raided' — and people looked suspiciously on anyone who was active in any way in marginal political circles.[61] It took more than a little courage to be politically outspoken, if not active, especially for those employed in the media or the public service. But despite being called on a number of occasions to front the directors of West Australian Newspapers and of the *Daily News*, who viewed him 'with dour suspicion and dislike', by luck or design Irwin eluded serious damage to his reputation.[62]

In an attempt to intimidate and embarrass Irwin, police took to collaring him at the *Daily News* office. On one occasion three police officers, including Richards, confronted him in the middle of the newsroom and escorted him back to his flat, which they then searched. The trio found the large amount of material on kindergartens in his flat suspicious, despite his wife's position as an organiser for the Kindergarten Training College, but overlooked a copy of American Marxist magazine *New Masses* and escorted Irwin back to the *Daily News* office — presumably to compound his humiliation. Irwin was subsequently called to a tense meeting with the *Daily News* board of directors; although some board members wanted him sacked, he was retained.[63]

Bill and Dorothy Irwin were both members of the Nedlands branch of the CPA during its illegal period, and were also involved in an array of legitimate and marginally legal political committees, including the 'Aid to Russia' campaign. The times called for extraordinary precautions, given that 'your typewriter became hot after one use', and the Irwins had a compartment built under the floor of their flat in which typewriters, a silk-screen and other potentially incriminating items were hidden. The following year they would move to the Berkeley Flats in Adelaide Terrace, where they would again be searched. Bill Irwin's brother Richard, a farmer at Maida Vale in the Perth foothills, also had his home searched by police.[64]

On 20 June, authorities stymied plans to publish an illegal edition of *The Workers' Star* when police seized plant, stock and printing equipment from Franklin Print after guarding the premises for several days to ensure that none of the equipment was secreted out by the Party. The recently upgraded printing press and linotype machine were among the items confiscated.[65] Bill Mountjoy had not yet paid off the linotype machine at the time of its seizure and it became the subject of a protracted legal battle between the Attorney-General's Department and its owner, Carmichael and Company, which lasted more than a year. The Western Australian Railways Department also made a fruitless claim against the Attorney-General's Department in respect of unpaid rent for the Franklin Print premises.[66]

The first illegal issue of *The Workers' Star* was not printed until late September or early October 1940, four months after the press ban was imposed. The newspaper started up again only a short time after Rudkin's release from prison in early September and, although Rudkin was not involved in the illegal publication, this coincidence aroused the suspicion of authorities and police closely shadowed him — indeed too closely to allow any involvement with the paper.[67]

Rudkin was unemployed on his release from prison and, despite the police reporting that he had 'curtailed his public activities', he was refused state government 'sustenance' in December 1940. He withdrew from the Workers' Art Guild at this time. He was blacklisted as a journalist during the period of CPA illegality but continued to distribute illegal Party literature around Perth.[68] The Rudkins' home was raided while an illegal Gestetner copier was operating in their loft, but police were diverted from searching the loft.[69] The Gestetner, used to print CPA material during the illegal period, was constantly on the move but an informant on the CPA state committee kept police abreast of the machine's whereabouts and the houses of members suspected of harbouring it were raided.

With Rudkin's withdrawal from the Workers' Art Guild, Leah Marks was propelled into a more prominent role in both the CPA and the Guild. In 1939 she was elected secretary-organiser of Perth's CPA metropolitan district committee, and she became increasingly influential as a Party functionary. She was also elected secretary of the Guild and of the Friends of the Soviet Union for a time, as well as managing the Radical Bookshop in 1940. However, for her own safety, and to maintain her usefulness to the Party, she soon followed Bill Mountjoy into exile. The CPA sent her to Melbourne for five months of literally 'underground' Party work. Unable to get a seat on the train as the railways were being used for troop transport, Marks was booked, under a pseudonym, onto a ship bound for Melbourne via Adelaide. Fearing arrest, she was told to 'stay out of the way' from the time she boarded the ship until it set sail, so she hid in the toilet. Concerned that authorities were keeping tabs on her movements, she then left the ship when it docked in Adelaide and caught the train to Melbourne, where she began work as a typesetter for an illegal CPA newspaper in the cellar of a house, the entrance to which was concealed by a bookcase. She would stop working when she heard an unusual noise upstairs or a visitor arriving, with the owner of the house signalling for her to stop and restart work by tapping on the floor above the cellar. Occasionally she would masquerade as a housemaid upstairs.

On her return to Perth in October 1940, Marks, with some diffidence, married Kevin Healy, then president of the CPA state branch.[70] As a CPA official of some standing herself, she feared that marriage to Healy might marginalise her. The couple moved into 'The Kremlin', a block of small flats in a house in Salvado Street, Cottesloe. Owned by local arts patrons Joe and Rose Skinner, the flats offered respite accommodation to Party members, officials and fellow travellers.[71]

The Guild rooms had also been raided by the CIB in June 1940.[72] Correspondence, a list of names of associate members, and internal minutes and reports were confiscated. A Special Bureau report following the raid stated that:

> This Club is composed of persons of the Bohemian student type, most of whom are recorded as [Communist Party] members or radicals — are allianced with the Little Theatre League [sic] in Sydney — (now banned) — Many complaints have been reported to the police regarding the habits of the members with regard to usual disorderly conduct, also the shouting of 'Heil Hitler' and other similar sounds during plays ... Most of the neighbours also complain — is of strong anti-capitalist views — has approximately 60 to 70 known or associate members. The Club is conducted 'in the interests' of the Communist Party.[73]

John Oldham was of the view that on his return to Perth in May 1940, the Workers' Art Guild was regarded by CIB and Military Intelligence as a very serious obstacle to their attempts to restrict the Left, because its activities gave members the opportunity to meet and politically organise.[74] Although the Guild itself escaped classification as an unlawful body, there appear to have been proposals to have it declared illegal.[75]

On 11 July 1940, Prichard's house was again searched. Correspondence and papers were taken that resulted in new intelligence files being opened on people yet to come to police notice. The following week, the National Security Act brought the national press, broadcasting and film industries under the control of the Director-General of Information.

In mid-1940 there were moves to force Phyllis Harnett to stand aside as head of the Workers' Art Guild. Her star was on the wane. She had become unpopular and had been relegated to the fringes of the Guild. The new centre of the Guild was the social group that revolved around Axel Poignant, including Victor Williams and Patricia Thompson, who disapproved of Harnett. The old Guild loyalties were gone and 'little jealousies and political uncertainties' began creeping in.[76]

Harnett was both disappointed and relieved. She had grown weary of the time and energy required to run the Guild and wanted again to reclaim her private life.[77] The Guild production of *The Women* had restored her fortunes as an actress, and radio drama work, which had dried up for Harnett with the rise and rise of Beryl Seward, was again coming her way. It was announced at a Guild meeting that Harnett would no longer hold office:

> The excuse was given that I was likely to go to jail because I was an acting communist and all acting communists were going to jail.[78]

The rationale was difficult to fathom, given that Harnett was to be replaced by a person with a much greater Party profile.

Harnett's loyal allies were indignant, and many of the younger Guild members, including John Hepworth, Tom Wignall and Gwen Duggan, strongly defended her. Harnett was 'staggered' by the way her ousting took place, but she submitted to the CPA fraction.[79] She was unaware that John Hector had donated a substantial amount of money to the CPA to pay for the appointment of a full-time Workers' Art Guild secretary to coordinate the Guild and direct its plays.

Hector had been orphaned at the age of twelve and was the beneficiary of a substantial inheritance held in trust until his adult years. He was to be a generous donor to the CPA, and perhaps his first act of philanthropy was to donate £300 to bring Victor Arnold over from the Sydney New Theatre League to the Workers' Art Guild.[80] The deal to pay Arnold a full-time wage was announced in Hector's April 1940 Workers' Art Guild article in the *Daily News*.[81]

Arnold had been paid little for his Sydney New Theatre work, so the financial inducement and the fact that his friend and colleague Jerold Wells was also in Perth were enticing.[82] Much of the success of Sydney New Theatre could be attributed to Arnold's popular five-year tenure as secretary there and, presumably, it was hoped that he would have a similar effect on the Guild. But his appointment drove yet another wedge through the Guild, with virtually nobody knowing that it was John Hector funding his appointment.[83]

Arnold was scheduled to arrive in Perth to take up his position in late May 1940, but he was delayed and did not arrive until late July. In May, long-running Sydney CPA newspaper *The Tribune* reported that Arnold would 'make a trip to Perth shortly to take up the leading post'.

> Members of the N.T.L. have granted Victor three months' leave of absence so that he can accept this position if the endeavours of the 'The Workers' Art Guild' are successful.[84]

Victor Arnold was born in London in 1905 and worked on ships crossing the Atlantic from the age of sixteen. In 1931 he sailed to New Zealand where he was employed on a sheep station. He moved to Sydney in 1933, joined the CPA and became secretary of the Sydney Workers' Art Club (the precursor to Sydney New Theatre) in 1935, taking up residence at the Club's rooms in Pitt Street, near Circular Quay. He and Jerold Wells directed most of the Club's plays,[85] but Oriel Gray also remembered Arnold as a fine actor:

> The first time I was asked to usher for a New Theatre play was at a performance given in the Australian Railways Institute. It was close to [Sydney's] Central Station, and trains went past at frequent intervals. Really expert practitioners like Victor Arnold or Jack Fegan could hear the train leave the station, raise their voice levels gradually as it drew closer, and lower them to normal as the sound died away.[86]

Arnold regarded his New Theatre work as important work for the Communist Party. He was a passionate advocate of 'theatre that was reflecting the times in which we lived' and believed that 'social plays can and must deal with values as well as events'.[87] He had been prosecuted after a December 1938 New Theatre performance in Sydney's The Domain of Betty Roland's agitprop attack on Menzies and BHP, *War on the Waterfront*.[88] The fact that New Theatre was so 'caught up in the maelstrom of events' of the 1930s, in Arnold's view, gave the theatre a 'sincerity [which] held the audiences at the time'.[89]

After the New Theatre production of *New Way Wins*, which he directed in early June 1940, Arnold left Sydney to take up his position at the Guild. On his arrival he moved into a flat in Howard Street in the city with John

Lunghi, and took over rehearsals from Phyllis Harnett of the next planned Guild play, *Love on the Dole*.

Arnold quickly won friends and respect within the Workers' Art Guild as a 'no nonsense' theatre director, but he missed Sydney and his partner, Ruth Pettersen, who eventually had her fare to Perth paid by the CPA.[90] Pettersen, an occasional secretary and performer at New Theatre, was known in Sydney circles as 'Vic's Blonde'.[91]

Arnold's 'slightly grubby' appearance did little to dampen the attraction of women. When he arrived in Perth, Harnett introduced Arnold to Betty Hamill and by the time Pettersen arrived in Perth shortly thereafter, Hamill and Arnold were a couple, and Pettersen found Axel Poignant.[92] Pettersen moved into a flat on St Georges Terrace, joined the Modern Women's Club and took up a typist's position at Penfold's Wine Store in the city. She also quickly came to the attention of police, who derided her as 'a typical radical bohemian' who drank 'a good deal'.[93] She did indeed drink a good deal and this problem only worsened at Penfold's Wine Store. Under stress, Pettersen became very depressed.[94]

15

'THE SURREALIST MOB'

You are surreal. But it's not something this town offers any welcome to.[1]

In 1940, leading members of Europe's surrealist movement fled to New York to escape the spread of fascism. In Perth in July of that year, a retrospective of the art of local surrealist 'Max Ebert' (Herbert McClintock) opened at the Newspaper House Gallery, as a joint venture of the Workers' Art Guild and the University Art Club. McClintock was soon to leave Max Ebert and surrealism behind him and return to more conventional art. By the time the exhibition opened he had already left Perth for Sydney, so it had largely been arranged by his wife, Pat McClintock.

McClintock's cheer squad, Alec King among them, sang the exhibition's praises, and four days after the opening an article about it appeared in *The West Australian*:

> From his seat at the lift controls Steve watches, with a shrewd appraising eye, the stream of humanity which flows up and down the arcade and in and out of his lift ... Steve is one of these men who, in the last war, remained unruffled when generals had the jitters, and it is not unnatural that he appraises men with no respect for rank and person ... Not that he is intolerant of art. If people like that sort of thing, well, it's harmless enough, and it's their affair anyway. But what puzzles him most is the surrealist mob who peer earnestly at weird daubs of colour set in deal frames and then talk learnedly about what it all means. He has his own ideas about what it means ... Therefore, when the exhibition was over I broached the matter with Steve as I went down in the lift alone. Maybe there was something to it, I said, but I did not profess to understand this form of art. 'Neither do I,' said Steve. 'Those pictures are like a German sausage—you know there's something in them but you don't know what it is.'[2]

Pat McClintock 'cultivated the press and people with influence to help further Mac's career', and financially supported her husband during their years together in Perth.³

The McClintocks had earlier lived in a studio next door to the Workers' Art Guild rooms in Hay Street, described by Joan Williams who sat for a McClintock portrait there:

> The scene took my breath away: swags of hessian in jewel colours draping the walls hung with portraits and abstract paintings, Mac striding around singing snatches of opera in a rich bass between roars of laughter and muttered imprecations at Perth philistines, Pat asking in her nasal twang if I'd like the coffee she was pouring into the striking Japanese blue and orange cups she had bought from Woolworths. Was I a philistine? I wondered, relieved at not being asked to pose in the nude. After an hour or so of painting, Mac said it was no good and tore it up.⁴

They later moved into a house in Applecross where they 'camped' among McClintock's paintings. The couple often had violent arguments and Pat threw plates with great accuracy, as her husband's scars attested. She would wait outside Gibbney's on pay night to snatch his pay packet before he spent it on drink. Her thrift was essential to establishing McClintock's reputation as an artist. He, though, showed scant regard for their marriage or for his wife's endeavours, and left her virtually penniless when he skipped town.⁵

During the continuing police raids in Perth, the CIB's Inspector Jack Doyle had issued a warrant to search John Hepworth's apartment at 180 St Georges Terrace 'for Communist literature or other literature of a subversive nature'.⁶ Hepworth was at that time a cadet reporter on the *Daily News* but, with both domestic and political tensions on the rise, he was looking to escape.

Hepworth's overindulgences led to his sacking in late June 1940.⁷ His philandering continued after his marriage to Kathleen Beechey, and the marriage did not last long before Beechey was rescued by John Hector. Hepworth devoted himself diligently and brazenly to the promiscuity of 'love and the Party line':

> Johnny led a life in which he was absolutely unreliable in every way … He not only made love to all the girls we knew, but to their mothers as well.⁸

Shortly after losing his job, Hepworth travelled with Herbert McClintock to Melbourne, staying initially in Warrandyte, thirty kilometres north-east of Melbourne, with McClintock's sister Winifred and her husband, artist and Melbourne Workers' Art Club co-founder Nutter Buzacott. Buzacott was part of an artist's colony at Warrandyte that included Penleigh Boyd, an aged Clara Southern and painter-sculptor Danila ('Daniel') Vassilieff, who would later marry the Guild's Betty Hamill.

McClintock left for Sydney in mid-September, where another Max Ebert exhibition opened at Macquarie Galleries, accompanied by a pictorial feature spread in *Pix* magazine.[9]

Her marriage over, Kathleen Beechey also left Perth, 'just to get out', travelling with her now-partner John Hector first to Melbourne and then to Sydney.[10] Gordon Burgoyne and Hope Bath, by then engaged, also left Perth for Sydney in June 1940, and the Perth branch of the CIB's Special Bureau informed its counterpart in Sydney that the five Guild members were on their way.[11]

Travelling in the opposite direction, Victor Arnold arrived in Perth in August 1940, just prior to the Guild's production of *Love on the Dole*. Arnold had directed a Sydney New Theatre production of this play in December 1938 and was intended to direct the Guild production, but his arrival in Perth was delayed a number of times so Phyllis Harnett reluctantly oversaw the start of rehearsals until Arnold's arrival.[12]

Love on the Dole, written by Ronald Gow and Walter Greenwood, is a moving domestic yet very political play set in the Depression-fractured industrial heartland of England's north in 1934. It was adapted from Greenwood's popular 1933 novel, and centred on the miseries and struggles of a family impoverished by unemployment, compounded by the British government's welfare cuts during the Depression. The novel was a powerful social and political allegory based on characters Greenwood had known, events he had witnessed and privations he had experienced when unemployed. The British Board of Film Censors considered the story too 'sordid' to be portrayed on film at the time, although it later would be.[13]

Set in the slums of Salford, Manchester's twin city, where Greenwood had lived, the play faithfully reproduces the language and struggles of the local people as well as the unemployed workers' movement that sprang from these struggles. It also records the brutal response by the government and police against organised demonstrations by the unemployed in England, a fairly universal theme of the Depression years.

The Guild production of *Love on the Dole* was staged in August 1940 at the Repertory Club Theatre, with a cast of seven women and seven men that included Rolf Harris along with leads Gwen Duggan and George Wignall. John Lunghi and Harald Vike designed the set, while Tom Wignall helped with its construction. After handing the production over to Arnold, Harnett helped backstage. Paul Hasluck praised the production as one of 'substance and significance'.[14]

Most of the truncated 1940 West Australian Drama Festival, ostensibly the state's last, was staged from late August at the Repertory Club Theatre, rather than in the grandeur of His Majesty's Theatre. Given the times, it was difficult to raise funds for the event and the smaller 1940 festival staged just seven plays over seven consecutive weekends.[15] *Penalty Clause*, a play written by Prichard in 1939–1940, was the Guild's 1940 festival entry. It was directed by Arnold and performed over three nights in September.[16]

Penalty Clause portrays an industrial dispute at the time involving miners on the Western Australian goldfields, who had formed a CPA stronghold and were striking in protest over the 'much-execrated' penalty clause inserted into the Mining Award to curb work stoppages.[17] Miner and Australian Workers' Union (AWU) organiser Paddy Troy, who had been party to the dispute, supplied Prichard with the material to write the play.

The state's Arbitration Court had approved the 'penalty clause' amendment to the gold mining award in 1937. It stipulated that for each day (or part thereof) that a mineworker was on strike, that worker would be docked an additional day's holiday pay. This applied to all work stoppages, including those that followed worker fatalities. Paid stoppages had until then been accepted practice after mine fatalities.[18]

The penalty clause was first invoked after workers walked off the job following a mine fatality at Youanmi, on the Western Australian goldfields, in May 1937. The area of the mine in which the accident took place was known to be unsafe, and the mine was operating counter to safety recommendations by the Inspector of Mines. The miners, led by Paddy Troy, who was also secretary of the AWU at Youanmi, insisted that the foreman responsible for ordering workers into that particular area of the mine be dismissed before they return to work.[19] Despite lacklustre support by the broader AWU, the miners remained on strike for more than a fortnight, during which a coroner's inquest implicated the management of the mine in the fatality. The AWU recommended a return to work, against the wishes of the workers, but successfully prosecuted the case that the penalty clause was being applied unlawfully in this instance, and work resumed.[20] It is on these events that Prichard's play is based, relying on dramatisation for political effect rather than mere reportage.

The main character in *Penalty Clause* appears to have been based on Troy himself, who later wrote that Prichard had accurately 'captured and portrayed the spirit and sentiment of the events':

> I was clearly able to identify the principal characters even though the fictitious names in no manner corresponded to the real ones … 'Penalty Clause' might even be regarded as a factual record of the events.[21]

The play attacks the antiquated safety conditions in the mining industry at the time that endangered miners' lives, and advocates that improvements would only be achieved through industrial militancy. The central characters are two miners working at a site knowing it to be unsafe; fearing employment repercussions, the pair is unwilling to refuse to work there. A rock collapse occurs in which one of the men is killed and the other seriously injured. The mineworkers call a stop-work safety meeting and the mine owners, threatened with escalating industrial action, promise to reinforce the mine. The workers return, but when the owners renege on their promise the miners walk off the job again. Despite union complicity and the owners' devious attempts to break the strike, the union rank and file remain steadfast and win the fight. As in her earlier Workers' Theatre play *Forward One*, Prichard had both the establishment and the union in her critical sights.[22]

Penalty Clause is a three-act play of eleven short scenes, and the Drama Festival performance included live music accompaniment by a Yugoslav string band. Simple scene changes and short scenes running into each other helped keep the suspenseful drama flowing, though this was stymied slightly by linear narrative shifts and switches between indoor and outdoor scenes.[23] The sparse stage setting of a grey drape suggested the underground mine and, echoing *Waiting For Lefty*, actors moved through the audience and spoke from the stalls, and an off-stage chorus among the audience participated in a strike-meeting scene. The device of breaking down the 'fourth wall' between the actor and the audience was a hallmark of Brechtian theatre, and Prichard cited Bertolt Brecht as key to the play's structure. The play concludes with the familiar declamatory call to 'smash the penalty clause!'[24]

Ric Throssell later described *Penalty Clause* as 'the longest and most successful' of Prichard's agitprop plays 'written for an audience of committed supporters' to extract the maximum possible amount of cash for the cause at rallies at which it played.[25] Paul Hasluck was more circumspect. He acknowledged that the play 'had emotional pull' and was impressed by its 'strikingly natural presentation', but he was critical of its partisan polemic.[26] Keith George later wrote that *Penalty Clause* had been written by Prichard 'in an effort to stimulate interest in the Guild' at a time when the Guild was struggling with the onset of the War and the loss of George, just as *Forward One* had been written by Prichard to help the fledgling Workers' Theatre.[27] Gordon Burgoyne was of the opinion that Prichard 'wrote those agit-prop plays ... more as her contribution to the cause than from any strong inner urge'.[28] The plays certainly served both a practical and political purpose.

Prichard was particularly proud of *Penalty Clause*, and disappointed that it did not win the prize for best Australian play at the 1940 festival. She wrote to Mikhail Apletin of the Soviet Writers' Union that she 'was informed that it was considered the "outstanding" play submitted' to the competition, but that the political climate probably hindered its recognition:

> The Workers' Art Guild accepted the challenge and made a most triumphant production ... It was really a thrilling performance, due to the splendid co-operation of all the workers in the Guild — some of whom had been miners and knew the realities of conditions they were portraying.[29]

The cast of *Penalty Clause* included motor mechanic Walter Harmsworth, who shared the stage with Yugoslav CPA member Yure ('George') Borich. Harmsworth had been expelled from the Party in 1934 'because of actions not in keeping with the dignity of the working class and its revolutionary vanguard'.[30] The CPA's district committee had found Harmsworth guilty of 'conduct unworthy of a Communist' when, in December 1934, he had attended a Yugoslav Cultural Clubs picnic at Point Walter on the Swan River with other Party members, where he had behaved 'generally in a manner inconsistent with Party principles'. Harmsworth had been drunk and had 'indulged in a contemptible chauvinist outburst', racially insulting some of the Yugoslav picnickers.[31] He was directed by the Party to confess his guilt and seek absolution — *mea culpa* was regular Party practice — but a long stand-off ensued before Harmsworth fronted the committee to acknowledge the error of his ways that had 'led him away from the revolutionary movement'.[32] The CPA had good reason to be concerned.

Perth's considerable Yugoslav community then formed a large proportion of CPA membership.

Yugoslav immigrants to Western Australia at that time hailed mostly from Croatia's Dalmatian Coast, and settled primarily in the grape-growing region of the Swan Valley just east of Perth. They had escaped the turmoil of a recently constituted country populated by an uneasy, more often warring, alliance of the disparate Serbian, Croat and Slovene population. Yugoslavs came in greater numbers to Australia after the United States imposed restrictions on immigration in the mid-1920s and, although the CPA's criticism of the government's White Australia immigration policy was equivocal, the Party set out to recruit new members from among the recent Italian, Greek and Yugoslav migrants with some success (most notably from among the anti-fascist Yugoslavs).[33]

The thick Yugoslav accent of George Borich in *Penalty Clause* was in marked contrast to that of Esther Missingham, recently arrived from London, who played the role of an old miner's wife and whose strong British accent struggled with the colloquial dialogue and flattened vowels of the play.[34]

Esther Missingham (formerly Long) had married Perth-born Hal Missingham in 1930, and her brother-in-law John Lunghi had introduced her to the Guild. Hal Missingham was by then a member of the Workers' Art Guild committee, having been elected around the time of the Guild production of *Love on the Dole*.[35] He had worked as an apprentice process engraver at J. Gibbney and Son and studied art under the influential A.B. Webb and James W.R. Linton. After his apprenticeship he worked his passage to Europe, where he studied at the Académie Julian in Paris before spending five years as a student at the Central School of Arts and Crafts in London, where he met John Lunghi. In 1930 he was awarded a three-year London Art Scholarship and took up photography, a passion he pursued for the rest of his life.

Between 1934 and 1940, Hal Missingham taught Art at London's Central School of Arts and Crafts, interrupted by a brief return to Gibbney's in Perth in 1937. He began exhibiting mainly landscape paintings from 1938 and returned to Perth with his wife in June 1940, re-employed by Gibbney's as a photographer and artist for a brief spell until he was put off during wartime staff cuts.[36] Harold Krantz introduced Hal Missingham to Axel Poignant, and with their shared passion for photography the two (both Leica enthusiasts) became friends.

In September 1940, CIB Special Bureau police constables William Basley and Harold Nevin searched John Lunghi and Victor Arnold's flat in Howard Street, and seized 'a quantity of Communist Literature'.[37] During the search Lunghi was questioned about his background and denied ever having been a CPA member or having any interest in the Party. After the search Basley questioned Arnold, who likewise denied ever having been a CPA member despite being 'very much interested' in the Communist Party.[38] Basley and his offsider Constable Bert Buzolic went to Gibbney's later that day to again interview Lunghi, this time at work, where Lunghi admitted that he was a member of the Workers' Art Guild and had read Party literature but again denied ever having been a CPA member.[39] Police described Lunghi as 'a definite sympathiser', but were not convinced that he was a card-carrying CPA member; they knew that Arnold certainly had been, and probably still was.[40]

On the night of Saturday 5 October, Constable George Standen from Perth's CIB Special Bureau 'proceeded to premises over Mortlock's Motorcycle Co. showrooms' to monitor a Left Book Club meeting at the rooms of the Workers' Art Guild, at which a Guild performance of the play *Plant in the Sun* was to take place. This American 'labour' comedy written by Ben Bengal in 1937, full of the vernacular of the Bronx, was a personal account of the effects of a strike on its participants, though it represented a departure from the Guild's earlier polemical trade union plays such as *Waiting For Lefty*. Victor Arnold's September 1939 Sydney New Theatre production of the play had won an award in Sydney's British Drama League Annual Festival, and it was probably his idea to perform the play at the Guild, and undoubtedly he who directed it.

Sergeant Hugh McLernon had drawn the meeting to Standen's attention after seeing an advertisement for the event in *The West Australian* that morning.[41] (A 'Loyal British Subject' who had also noticed the newspaper advertisement penned their grievances in a letter to police, insisting that they 'would rather listen to the jabbering of the monkeys at the zoo' than to the political speeches given at an event such as this.[42])

That evening Standen lurked outside the Guild rooms, recording the car registration numbers of those entering the meeting so that he could later make traffic office enquiries to 'ascertain the names of the owners'.

> When about 30 persons had entered the hall, I attempted to enter also, but was asked by the door-keeper if I was a member, and when I replied in the negative, he informed me that the meeting was not for the general public.[43]

Standen kept up surveillance outside for another forty-five minutes and saw another fifteen or so people arrive, 'most of them being young women of the student type, probably attracted by the fact that Alex [sic] King of the University was the main speaker'.⁴⁴

The following night there was a repeat performance of *Plant In the Sun* at the Guild rooms. Two days after this performance, the Guild's annual general meeting was held at its rooms. Proposed productions and amendments to its constitution were discussed, a new management committee was elected and Howard Smith was appointed Guild president.

At the end of November 1940, plain-clothed police officers Basley and Nevin, with colleague Patrick O'Neil confronted John Oldham at work at the Oldham, Boas & Ednie-Brown offices with a search warrant that granted them fairly sweeping legal powers to question and search, and rifled through his desk. Oldham also denied being a CPA member in Western Australia, though he did admit to having been a Party member in Sydney. He was served with a warrant to search his home at 32 Napier Street in Cottesloe, and the police asked him to accompany them there. Oldham was clearly exasperated but police warned him to 'be very careful' about what he said. At Cottesloe, Ray Oldham was equally evasive, but both admitted to being members of the Workers' Art Guild again.⁴⁵

In mid-November 1940, Guild performances of two one-act plays — *Rehearsal* and *Sub-Editor's Room* — were staged in the Guild rooms. *Rehearsal*, written by *Private Hicks* author Albert Maltz, deals with the 1932 demonstrations of Ford workers in Detroit, although the play itself is set during a rehearsal of the American Labour Theatre. Victor Arnold had previously directed a production of *Rehearsal* for Sydney New Theatre, winning the Sydney Eisteddfod drama prize.

Sub-Editor's Room, much admired by Prichard, is a social realist play about journalistic ethics written by former Perth journalist Leslie Rees.⁴⁶ Rees was a significant early advocate of Australian theatre and its writers as well as being an author, playwright, drama critic and radio drama editor. Arnold had directed *Sub-Editor's Room* for Sydney New Theatre soon after it was written in 1937.

Another significant performance took place at the Guild in November 1940. Victor Williams, author of *Hold Your Wheat*, had set about dramatising a sequel to the events covered in that Living Newspaper in another titled *Feed the Sheep*. Grain had been stockpiled after the wheat stand-off because the federal government had encountered difficulty exporting it. Wheat shipments were restricted, and grain exports had slowed to a trickle during the War. A drought had followed the wheat strike, and sheep on properties in the Western Australian wheatbelt were starving. Farmers who had withheld their wheat into the summer of 1940 were now without grain to feed their starving sheep. They demanded that the federal government-controlled Wheat Board release some of the wheat that was now deteriorating in storage to feed to their sheep, threatening to raid the wheat bins and recover their wheat by force if it was not released. Violent conflict was averted when the drought broke at the eleventh hour.[47]

Williams later wrote, albeit somewhat excessively, that 'despite [their] illegality, the words and ideas of Lenin were running down every bush track then'.[48] The CPA had long seen this increasing rural unrest as an opportunity to extend its influence outside Perth: in the early 1930s the Party had begun to tap into the disaffection of farmers and farm workers, actively encouraging them to join the CPA and organise themselves as an industrial force.[49]

In August 1940, Williams was working as a farmhand at the then isolated outpost of Lake Grace, almost 400 kilometres from Perth, when he was met by police with a search warrant. They seized books and receipts for literature purchased from the Radical Bookshop.

The grain dispute and subsequent stockpile had been and was still receiving widespread newspaper coverage, and Williams's dramatisation of these events attracted an audience. *Feed the Sheep* was written and performed simultaneously with the events it portrayed, and its immediacy was such that Williams, who was still working in the country, was required to update the play daily as new events in the dispute unfolded. If the wheat bins had been raided and there was a clash with the police, that was immediately relayed to the performances at the Guild rooms and in parks around Perth on the back of a truck.[50]

As the nation moved further into the fog of war, patriotic and fundraising performances were organised by what local talent remained in Perth, but there was little professional theatre. Wartime travel restrictions isolated Perth, and touring artists were unable to visit. British performer Noel Coward, then at the pinnacle of his talent and popularity, was an exception. He sailed in to Sydney in November 1940 to great fanfare and near hysteria, to embark on a frenetic seven-week Australian tour to raise funds for the Red Cross. His schedule included morale-boosting troop concerts and patriotic radio broadcasts back to Britain.

Coward took some interest in the state of drama in Australia on his travels, observing:

> I have read numerous plays while I have been here, but they all suffered from the same complaint. None of them was about Australia.[51]

He stayed at the Lodge as a guest of Prime Minister Menzies, and was mobbed by fans and fawned over by the press wherever he went — despite, characteristically, ridiculing his hosts. He flew in to Perth in December and attended a garden party at Government House with state governor Sir James Mitchell and a gathering of Perth society, presumably providing ample fodder for his biting satire. During his subsequent performances at the Capitol Theatre in Perth and Hoyts Theatre in Fremantle he mocked such social occasions.

> I was told publicly by an eminent gentleman in Perth that it was a great privilege for me to visit Western Australia. This was absolutely true, but it seemed strange to hear it said with such sublime complacency, rather like arriving at somebody's house and being told by the host how fortunate you are to be eating such delicious food in such distinguished company.[52]

After Coward's departure, the Guild returned to the stage with a production of Olive Popplewell's *This Bondage*. Betty Hamill and Phyllis Harnett, who remained on the Guild fringes, were both very keen on the character roles in the play, and they had strongly lobbied the Guild to stage it. Like *The Women*, *This Bondage* was a comedy with an all-female cast. Its politics, though, were markedly different from that of *The Women*. *This Bondage* chronicles the lives of four generations of militant suffragette women and their 'home-loving sisters' from a particular family over a fifty-year period.[53] It charts the suffragette movement of the 1890s and that of 1911–1914, contrasting these two periods with a portrayal of the vacuous 1930s 'modern girls' who mock the privileges won by the struggles of their suffragette predecessors.

Prichard was not happy about the Guild putting on this particular play, and she expressed her disappointment to Harnett for encouraging the production. Harnett was puzzled by Prichard's objections. She saw the play as a credible and virtuous story about the political achievements of the women who became suffragettes — women such as those with whom Prichard had associated in London. Prichard did not explain her grievances clearly, but she seemed to take exception to the manner in which the play portrayed the social flaws and sexual peccadilloes of the suffragettes, recalled Harnett:

That infuriated Katharine: that it was women rejected as women. It wasn't an anti-suffragette play, by any means, but it was about women becoming suffragettes and it did give [a] sort of psychological background to most of them.[54]

Towards the end, the play depicts the next generation of political agitators for women's rights, the inheritors of the vote, critically evaluating their predecessors' somewhat diffident attempts to secure women's suffrage. Harnett wondered whether this was what Prichard objected to.

When I look back on it now I can't really see that it was objectionable, except that when you're trying to found a revolution or a 'feminism' you can't afford that sort of [critical] inflection on the way up. You can [only] afford it after it's all over.[55]

Some relatively new Guild members, including Gwen Duggan and Joan Mockeridge, put on strong performances in the play. Harnett insisted on playing the demanding role of a character both in her youth and as an older woman, with some difficulty.

Howard Smith directed *This Bondage*, probably with the assistance once again of his partner Marjorie Berry. The pair made a very able team. Berry specialised in working closely with the cast, while Smith's talent was the technical side of production.[56] Paul Hasluck acknowledged that the subject was an interesting one, but thought the play disorganised and poorly written, and described Smith's direction as chaotic, having 'sacrificed clarity to pace'. He also thought the acting 'showy, exaggerated and self-satisfied', and wrote that the leading players 'came perilously close to the edge of burlesque' at times. He was particularly critical of the performances of Harnett and Hamill, whom he described as acting 'in aid of their own virtuosity'. In contrast to the excellent ensemble performances of earlier Guild productions, most of the actors in *This Bondage*, in Hasluck's opinion, 'had a tinge of amateur theatricals about them'. Despite these criticisms, Hasluck recommended that those with a serious political interest in the feminist movement see the production, in spite of its flaws.[57]

The next planned Guild venture was a performance of *Penalty Clause*, which was to be directed by Victor Arnold, at Kalgoorlie in the state's goldfields in late 1940 or early 1941. However, Arnold postponed this performance, claiming he was too busy working in support of James (Jim) Dinan, the ALP candidate in the federal by-election for the local seat of

Swan. Dinan, a Kellerberrin farmer and Gallipoli veteran, was a member of the Workers' Art Guild and an official in the Wheat and Wool Growers' Union who had taken a leading role in the wheat growers' dispute. He was a radical within ALP ranks, held in contempt by the ALP's right wing.[58]

Arnold rescheduled the performance of *Penalty Clause* for April 1941, after which he planned to return to Sydney. Prichard had heard gossip that Arnold was 'more interested in trotting round with one of the candidates for the by-election than working for the show', but she conceded that 'the election was so important' that she could 'quite understand other things having to be put aside'.[59]

Prichard seemed happy with Arnold's contribution to the Guild. She wrote to an ailing Louis Esson that Arnold 'really did an excellent job here', despite Keith George being 'critical' of the 'rhythm & tempo' of Arnold's performances for the Guild. Prichard had more pressing personal concerns. Her son was to attend teacher training college and classes at UWA the following year, and he would have to board closer to town, 'so that extra will have to be provided for'.[60]

Prichard arranged for Keith George to tutor a weekly drama class for her son Ric and some university classmates through the year at the Linley Wilson Dance School. The students underwent the same sort of rigorous training that the Guild actors had endured, with George not only coaching them in acting but also teaching them 'a great deal about the way in which a play is constructed'.[61] Ric Throssell later recalled George discussing in great detail the background and significance of the plays he was rehearsing. As ever, he retained directorial control.

> We did [a play] called *X=O: A Night of the Trojan War*, and he took us all through the history of the Trojan War ... and we'd do Pirandello and he'd give us the situation Pirandello was writing about. But when the rehearsals for the play itself began, there wasn't discussion backwards and forwards — Keith told you! Some of the later writers of the theatre referred to a director who used the technique of the 'über-marionette' — as if he was a puppet master. That was Keith's technique, and a technique that I used myself later.[62]

Keith George also helped Victor Arnold teach the drama course at the university's summer school over the summer of 1940–1941, occasioning Prichard to observe:

> [George] noisily declares he is finished with the theatre, but I can't believe it. He is the most disinterested — & unselfish person — but I think bitterly hurt by the treatment he got from some folk here. At the same time, a lot of the difficulty due to a sort of defeated arrogance. Maestro manqué attitude. Committing intellectual suicide rather than risk failure in any way — or stand up to criticism, I'm very fond of him — in the platonic way. The only real platonic, unique platonic, I shd say.[63]

By late 1940, Jerold Wells had returned to Sydney. In March of that year, with the Repertory Club in financial difficulty, its finance subcommittee had recommended that Wells be dismissed to cut costs. A decision on the matter had been deferred until a committee meeting in July, at which it was decided that Wells would go, despite his offer to take a salary cut.[64] Unlike Victor Arnold, Wells was keen to retain his post in Perth.

Wells's last hurrah in Perth had been a production of *Our Town* by American playwright Thornton Wilder, for the Repertory Club's twenty-first anniversary in August 1940. The influence of the Guild on the Repertory Club is evident in this production, in which there was no scenery nor curtain used; actors mimed, and a 'stage manager' addressed the audience and the actors from the stage.[65]

In early December 1940, Prichard sent the final draft of *Moon of Desire* to her London publisher, Jonathan Cape, despite not being entirely satisfied with it. An advance from an American publisher and talk of a Hollywood dramatisation of the novel briefly relieved her worry about financial debts inherited from her husband.[66] It was her first serious novel since *Intimate Strangers* in the early 1930s and she had been hard at work on revisions to the novel, which was to be sent to the American publisher 'before Xmas'.

> Wish I hadn't done the thing now. It's just a yarn, though has got a few decent bits. All the same, I feel I've let myself down on a concocted story. Just felt I had to do something to save the financial situation for next year. The situation has been acute latterly. But better now. The family sent me cheques for my birthday, & I managed to rake in £20, on a debt, long outstanding. So am all right … The [Commonwealth Literary Fund Fellowship] grant will be a blessing, if it materialises … Have been so utterly weary of this damned book, chiefly. Will be relieved to get it off my mind altogether.[67]

In late 1940 Prichard applied for a literary fellowship from the Commonwealth Literary Fund after Louis Esson sent her the application form. 'I'm afraid if you hadn't bustled, I wouldn't have done anything,' she wrote back to him. She sent off the application in December 1940, accompanied by 'a wonderful letter' of support from Walter Murdoch:

> Mrs. Throssell is the most famous of living Australian writers ... though she has achieved fame she has not achieved affluence; and in these times, so difficult for all who live by the pen, she is feeling the need for assistance. I can sincerely say that in my opinion she deserves all the assistance her country can give her.[68]

It was a brave gesture on Murdoch's part.[69] Prichard had been 'quite prepared for him to say he couldn't — "under the circumstances" etc. But really, he has made a most generous gesture ... An awfully nice letter came from [politician, poet and novelist] Leonard Mann too, so I enclosed that.' Prichard had also hoped for references from Vance Palmer and 'Furnley Maurice' (poet Frank Wilmot), but they had not arrived in time to be included with the application, and she was satisfied that 'the Murdoch buddy's letter ought to do all that's necessary'.[70]

When Prichard had begun research in 1937 on a novel she planned to set in the goldfields, Henrietta Drake-Brockman had written to their mutual friend Hugh McCrae:

> When & if she does a Kalgoorlie book, it should be magnificent — there won't be any need for her to colour it, the dust is red enough for even her![71]

The writing that eventuated was a trilogy of novels set in the goldfields: *The Roaring Nineties* (1946), *Golden Miles* (1948) and *Winged Seeds* (1950). Prichard's goldfields trilogy was criticised by Soviet journal *Novy Mir* ('New World') precisely because it was not 'red' enough. It was attacked for its lack of a socialist realist Communist hero, but Prichard later countered that there was no such person in the goldfields at the time and 'I do not believe a writer of socialist realism should falsify reality.'[72]

Prichard was obviously troubled by the Communist Party's public censure of her work. She had written apologetically to Mikhail Apletin in Moscow in September 1940 about her play *Brumby Innes* representing Aboriginal Australians as a 'vanquished race'. 'If I were writing it now,' she wrote to Apletin, 'I would emphasise their right to an independent existence.'⁷³ This view was perhaps at odds with her insistence with respect to her goldfields trilogy that 'an authentic sketch of life' did not require a redemptive narrative.

National Security Regulations had prohibited Prichard from sending her publications to the USSR. She was informed by the Chief Censor's Office that books could only be sent through a bookseller or newspaper office. She was under intense police scrutiny and the systemic harassment of local CPA members meant that she, as the state's most prominent Communist, was finding it difficult to find paid work and make ends meet — despite being named Australia's leading writer by *The New York Times* that year. Many of her proposed public addresses were cancelled, often at the last moment.

Police raids on suspected CPA members continued through the end of the year and into the next. Local sales of *Mein Kampf* were on the rise, with sales of *Das Kapital* on the slide. With the War grinding on, the public now had little appetite for serious reading on international affairs, nor for serious theatre. Wartime reading was largely 'light humour and detective novels', according to one Perth bookseller.⁷⁴

16

'THE FADED YEARS':[1]
A RETREAT TO PROVINCIALISM

May your noble shadows never grow less
— Yours, Katharine Susannah[2]

A New Theatre League conference in Sydney in December 1940, attended by representatives from both Sydney and Melbourne, discussed ways of reversing flagging public interest in the work of New Theatre. Plans were drawn up to dramatise more 'local political and industrial issues as they arise'.[3] The Workers' Art Guild again followed New Theatre's lead, and from early 1941 sought to rebuild its proletarian credibility and gain greater support from the 'practically unassailed fortresses' of local trade unions.[4]

The Guild went as far as attempting to affiliate with various trade unions, with Guild president Howard Smith writing in April 1941:

> the real future of the Guild must be linked with the Trade Union movement. With this in view, we have decided to concentrate our immediate activity upon the preparation and presentation of plays, agit-props etc. which are suitable for this objective.[5]

The Guild's stated intention was to 'approach' individual trade unions:

> with offers of assistance in the way of presentation of plays, firstly as a means of entertainment at their social gatherings, and later as a means of assistance in their campaigns, by the presentation of agit-props giving expression to their demands.[6]

Although the writers' section of the Guild appeared buoyant, the ranks of its drama wing were diminishing and buckling under some pressure. The Guild had taken on ballet and chorus work, which Victor Arnold reported 'was adding unnecessarily to our difficulties'.[7] The Guild's audience had evaporated, and it was under 'continual pressure from [financial] creditors'.[8]

Losses to military enlistment were damaging enough for the Guild, but the War also 'absorbed the energies of everybody' not in military service.[9]

Four days before Christmas 1940, a lower-house by-election was held in the federal electorate of Swan, on Perth's outer-eastern fringe, brought about by the death of the sitting Country Party member. Jim Dinan recontested the seat for the ALP.

Following the 1939 federal election, Menzies's United Australia Party, in coalition with the Country Party, held a very narrow balance of power with the support of two independents. The Swan by-election was, consequently, of vital importance to the federal government and its Labor opposition. Menzies and several of his senior ministers travelled to Perth for an intensive campaign, where federal treasurer Arthur Fadden, minister for commerce Earl Page and minister for aviation John ('Black Jack') McEwan all spoke at public meetings in support of the Country Party candidate.[10]

Dinan's involvement with the CPA tempered his support from the local Labor executive. 'Doc' Evatt, who had made a return to federal politics after his 1940 resignation from the High Court, briefly campaigned on his behalf. Opposition leader John Curtin reluctantly also made his way across to campaign, but fell ill en route and had to return east before reaching Perth; he was ordered to rest and not take any part in campaigning. The Guild had written some performance material in support of Dinan's run for the by-election, but the ALP's campaign committee refused to allow the performances, a slight referred to by Victor Arnold as 'a check from our enemies in the Labor Party office'.[11] Despite increasing the ALP vote in the seat of Swan, Dinan lost the by-election.[12] He publicly blamed Curtin for the loss, and was subsequently expelled from the ALP.[13]

The Labor Party was declaring war on the Communist Party on a wider front. In early 1941, Western Australian Labor journal the *Westralian Worker* branded the Budget Protest Committee (BPC) the 'Communist Party in a new disguise' and 'an organisation created for the purpose of injuring the Labour Movement and … therefore a thing to be shunned by every loyal Labourite'.[14] The BPC, established after the banning of the CPA, was ostensibly formed to organise protests against several provisions of the 1940 federal budget. Although not all its members were CPA members, the BPC was indeed a clandestine arm of the illegal CPA, used covertly by the CPA to carry on its public political work.[15] John Oldham, by then a senior member of the CPA in Western Australia, was elected chairman of the BPC in the state after his return to Perth in May 1940, and chaired a number of its public meetings.

Local BPC secretary June Carder issued a libel writ against the *Westralian Worker* and sought damages. The *Westralian Worker* countered in its defence that it 'did not mean, nor was it understood to mean, that the plaintiff (Carder) was a member of the Communist Party and was engaged in subversive activities'.[16] Criminal lawyer T.J. Hughes, who had previously represented CPA members prosecuted under the National Security Act, encouraged Carder to pursue the libel case and offered his services pro bono, confident that substantial damages would be awarded. The BPC backed Carder. The CPA was not in favour of running the legal case because it 'didn't regard being called a Communist as slanderous', but once Carder and the BPC had resolved to proceed and Hughes had offered his legal support, the CPA state branch dropped its opposition.[17]

The trial of 'the Carder case', as it became known, was to be held over thirteen days in May 1941 in front of a Supreme Court jury, but the proceedings dragged on. Carder effectively perjured herself by stating in the witness box that 'no member of the Budget Protest Committee in this State was a Communist'.[18] Like most CPA members, Carder was discreet about her political affiliation. She had only very recently moved to Perth but, damningly for her, she was a former employee of Ernie Thornton, the militant secretary of the Federated Ironworkers' Association in Sydney and a prominent member of the CPA central committee.[19] The jury eventually found that the article had not been defamatory and was therefore not libellous, though it did concede that the article had 'originated in malice', which left the door open for an appeal that Hughes was confident Carder would win.[20]

Oldham had been called to give evidence on Carder's behalf. He was a reluctant prosecution witness who skirted around any suggestion 'that being called a Party member was libellous'. Under questioning, Oldham denied being a Party member at that time, but he nonetheless used his time in the witness box to promote 'Party policy and programmes' and attack 'the idea of the Party being made illegal' as well as the conduct of police during a late-night raid of his home.[21] The day after Oldham took the stand, the *Daily News* reported the case under the headline 'Treated Like Criminal, Says Architect'.[22]

The police raid that Oldham referred to was one of a sequence of raids following the arrest of John Simpson, head of the CPA in Western Australia. On 2 April 1940, Detective Sergeant Ron Richards, accompanied by constables Basley and Nevin, had searched Simpson's room at the Railway Hotel in Wellington Street in the city, where he was staying under the assumed name 'John Campbell'. Richards found incriminating CPA documents hidden inside a chair, and Simpson was arrested. His arrest was a coup for police and a major blow to the organisation of the CPA in Western Australia, given that its effective running then depended almost entirely on Simpson.²³ It netted the police a prized head and a significant quantity and quality of information about the local CPA, its members and workings. An intelligence report on the confiscated papers described the material as 'up to date and authentic':

> Detailed reports of the organisation, structure and activities of most of the leading Trade Unions were included, and the methods to be adopted for white-anting the Unions are of special interest.²⁴

The raid uncovered plans by the CPA in Western Australia to 'capture' the trade unions in an attempt to bring about what the Party called 'the end of Trainer-Curtin rule' over the trade union movement. Percy Trainer was general secretary of the state executive of the ALP and a close friend of John Curtin's.

The CPA believed the ALP was more vulnerable in Western Australia than in other states, and it planned to take up positions within the Labor Party and the trade unions in order to build CPA influence. It was confident that this infiltration would fast-track change inside the ALP and the wider trade union movement, help maintain the legality of the CPA 'and provide [the CPA] with a scope for legal propaganda and agitation'.²⁵ Another significant document seized during the raid on Simpson, intended for distribution to senior CPA officials, urged caution during the illegal period and offered instructions on how to avoid arrest. Entitled 'WARNING', it advised:

> Be careful and subtle ... Seize upon issues affecting the masses according to the degree in which the issue could be linked with 'hindering the war' effort, subversive action, etc. At the same time mass work is to be increased, not lessened. Ensure that each member with any degree of freedom of movement is active in one or more mass organisations or movements. Check on the means of communication and transmission of documents. See that inner documents, such as this, are not issued when personal work is possible, that they are sent only to known safe places, that they are immediately used and destroyed.²⁶

The Simpson material, including Simpson's cash book and correspondence, also provided evidence that police had been looking for in order to move on a number of suspected Communists involved in the BPC, and confirmed police suspicions that the BPC was indeed a covert subsidiary of the CPA. Documents revealed the names of 'well known Communists in this Command, indicating that they are still active in the movement', including Prichard, Oldham, Kevin Healy and Maurie Lachberg.

> These persons are now under close Police surveillance and have had their premises searched.[27]

Police identified Oldham as 'one of the leading Communists in W.A.'[28] Oldham had been tipped off that Simpson was to be raided and went to Simpson's hotel room to forewarn him, but police had already arrived and 'invited' him in.[29] At 1.30 am the following morning, constables Basley and Nevin, with an officer from the military intelligence office, raided Oldham's home in Cottesloe, where Ray Oldham was nursing their five-month-old daughter, and questioned John Oldham about his relationship with Simpson. Oldham had endured an 'aggressive' Basley raid four months earlier and, although police were again quite hostile and thorough in their search, they found little aside from notes written by Oldham for inclusion in an upcoming edition of a BPC publication. A later police search of Oldham's home turned up a typewriter 'of a type that would be used for preparation of Leaflets and other matter', though again this was not evidence enough to lead to prosecution. The Oldhams had buried all incriminating CPA material in the sand dunes near their home.[30]

Oldham was at this time not only chairman of the BPC but also a member of the Workers' Art Guild committee. He was, in effect, deputy leader of the CPA in Western Australia during the War, second in charge after Simpson. Police were becoming impatient in their attempts to find the evidence required to jail Oldham, and police reports reflected this frustration.[31]

> Oldham's association with John Spencer Simpson is of vital interest in establishing his active association with Communistic activities ... Oldham is 34 years of age, well educated and sufficiently shrewd and clever to carry out underground working with the object of avoiding any evidence against him that might be actionable.[32]

In early June 1941, the minister for the Army was asked to approve a ministerial order from an application by Western Command Military Intelligence to impose restrictions on both John and Ray Oldham that would effectively place them under house arrest under the extraordinary wartime powers.

> It is desired to indicate that certain difficulties are being experienced in deciding upon the most effective action that can be taken against Communists in view of their clever underground working with the object of avoiding any evidence against them that might be actionable. Oldham's case comes under this category, and it is submitted that the restrictions proposed to be placed upon him should have the desired effect of restricting his activities without in any way affecting his employment or placing upon him severe hardship. The same remarks also apply to his wife ... It is known that Oldham has spoken of his intention to proceed to Sydney at an early date, and in a case such as his it is considered desirable that interstate travel should definitely be restricted.[33]

The proposed ministerial order would make it illegal for the Oldhams to 'associate or communicate with members of subversive organisations, or with enemy aliens or persons of enemy origin; change [their] place of residence, or travel beyond a radius of twenty miles of [their] present residence, without the prior permission of the military authorities; be in possession of a roneo machine or any other machine for the printing of books, pamphlets, etc.' and force them to 'refrain from any acts or utterances which directly or indirectly may be prejudicial to the safety of the Commonwealth or the successful prosecution of the war.' It was also recommended that John Oldham be banned from attending meetings of the BPC, Young Labour League, Council Against Unemployment or Council for Civil Liberties, and that he should not be allowed to attend rehearsals, readings or meetings of the Workers' Art Guild.

The application for restriction of association was denied, purportedly because it would also unfairly impede the Oldhams' 'beneficial' legal activities, 'namely the abolition of unemployment and the protection of civil liberties'. The minister had been 'in general agreement' with the submission but saw it as inadvisable 'at this stage at least having regard to the fact that Russia is now at war with Germany.'[34]

An earthquake shook the courthouse in which John Simpson was appearing on 29 April 1941. He had been charged with having in his possession material 'advocating unlawful doctrines'. Ron Richards took the stand for the prosecution and, under questioning from defence counsel Hughes, asserted that the doctrines of the CPA were traitorous and adverse to the national war effort. Richards testified that the CPA was 'actively engaged in creating disaffection in industry and industrial unrest, backing beer strikes, and backing Budget protest'. He made it clear to the CPA that he was well aware of its concealed work.[35]

Simpson admitted to being a member of the CPA and did not deny his service to the Party, but he denied being an organiser. He was sentenced to six months' jail and bailed to appear the following week to face another charge of breaching the National Security (Subversive Association) Regulations and the National Security Act, for which he was sentenced to a further three months' jail.[36] The additional charge was that Simpson had collected money for the CPA 'for the purpose of promoting doctrines which were advocated by that body' and deemed prejudicial to the defence of the Commonwealth and the efficient prosecution of the War.[37]

With Simpson's incarceration, John Oldham took over the running of the CPA in Perth. The political climate and Oldham's public involvement with the Carder case had closed employment doors to him, and his personal situation had become fairly dire. When he visited the federal government's Works Office to apply for work at the height of the Carder case, he had a newspaper thrown down in front of him referring to his evidence during the trial and was told, 'We don't want people like that!'[38]

The Oldhams could no longer afford the rent on their Cottesloe home and Joe Skinner came to their aid, giving them rent-free use of a flat in his West Perth home. Unable to find work and disenchanted with the CPA over its handling of the Carder case, among other things, John Oldham returned to Sydney in the middle of the year, where he was able to take up a job in the architectural division of the Department of the Interior. A federal ministerial application for the restriction order on him was still pending, and a military intelligence report dated 23 July 1941 stated that 'Oldham is now in the Eastern Command, which has been advised of the position.'[39]

Another Guild member with reason to be grateful to Joe Skinner for the roof over his head was Harald Vike, who rented accommodation and a studio from Skinner just a few doors away from the Workers' Art Guild rooms in Hay Street.[40] Vike was also in financial hardship. In the winter of 1941 he wrote Skinner a note regarding rent due on his Hay Street lodgings:

> I did not come in as I promised, due to no funds. Something may happen at end of this week, if so I will be in Re our arrangement of

coming up to see some work. Could you leave it to later. I ... sent 3 watercolours with a friend of mine to Melbourne. It was just to feel out my chances there. I will be doing some again as soon as weather breaks in a couple of weeks, I hope. I shall let you know. Thanking [you] very much for your patience with me.[41]

It seems that Vike had made an arrangement with Skinner to make part payment on the rent with some of his paintings. Skinner was acquiring a collection of works by local artists, which he eventually displayed in his Skinner Gallery.

Raids on CPA members were renewed with punitive vigour in April 1941, and Prichard wrote to Miles Franklin in late April:

> The nervous tension of these days is so exhausting. So many friends in trouble & it seems almost impossible to disassociate oneself from the grief & suffering. The woes of the world & the salvaging of humanity. I stand where I always did, of course, but is 'the pen mightier than the sword'? If only it were so.[42]

In May she wrote to Timofei Rokotov, editor of *International Literature* in Moscow:

> My Communist sympathies are well known and although it is not necessary for me to engage in active organisational work, so many of my friends have been prosecuted and are in prison, that I must help and defend them in any way possible. It is almost unbelievable that in this country which has always prided itself on its democratic traditions people could be imprisoned on such trivial pretexts.[43]

In late June 1941, Prichard wrote to Mikhail Apletin of the Soviet Writers' Union in Moscow:

> Prosecutions under the so-called National Security Regulations have been more numerous and vicious in this State than in any other or in any part of the British Dominions, as far as I know. No one of course is intimidated by these tactics; no one who attaches any importance to his convictions and personal courage, at any rate. It would be giving you a wrong impression however to imply

that the position is not very difficult, both for me and many others whose sympathies are well-known. I am not in the least concerned about going to gaol at any time. The experiences will naturally provide interesting material to write about some day.[44]

The names of Workers' Art Guild members came up repeatedly in military intelligence reports as 'active Communists'. Police scrambled to assemble the evidence to prosecute, and a number of Guild members were kept under 'close observation' with a view to 'internment or restriction', but in all cases to no avail.[45]

In June 1941, a few days before the final evidence was heard in the Carder case, an anonymous letter was sent to Detective Sergeant Ron Richards. The letter included a newspaper cutting advertising an upcoming production of the play *Robert's Wife*, which was due to be performed in late August at the Repertory Club Theatre,[46] and pointed out that Ric Throssell would be among the cast members.

> Many people have been wondering where [Prichard] was & what she is doing. This will serve to enlighten a few of those interested as for years past (while being relieved of the task of educating her son by old school pals of 'Hugo', who wanted to see the boy get a decent training for a start in life.) Relieved of this responsibility she had ample time on her hands to educate those unfortunates that came under her thumb. To say that she was successful is putting it mildly, as her pupils are now coming under public notice being fined, jailed, etc. and she is having a very nice time thankyou [sic] as the above will testify ... No doubt, some if not all the cast for 'Robert's Wife' is from the Workers' Art Guild as it was a well known fact [Prichard] was gathering in all the young people for plays, etc. They were most thorough in their organising, and it must have been a bitter pill for them to swallow when the Police put the thumb screw on them. To my way of thinking they are a bad 'germ' ... It is a thousand pities this [Carder] Libel Case had to be as it is such a fine advertising medium for the Illegals brought under notice of people who would have never heard of them. However the best of Luck with the huge clean up of this destructive 'Germ' in our midst — I first heard of it in 1935, and much unhappiness was the cause of my hearing of it.[47]

The letter concluded with the seemingly defiant yet curious statement: 'There will always be an England.'

While the CIB built a case for her prosecution, Prichard shuttled back and forth between Perth and Kalgoorlie though 1941 to research her goldfields novels, thanks to a Commonwealth Literary Fund Fellowship. It seems there was probably serious consideration given to jailing Prichard. Police were certainly preparing a dossier of her 'crimes', but her imprisonment would likely have created an international outcry and this, perhaps, is what prevented it. CPA women in Perth escaped jail terms probably because there was not suitable accommodation for them at Fremantle Prison and Perth was perhaps 'too polite a town' to send them there.[48]

Prichard was buoyed by the recent translation into Russian of her novel *Working Bullocks* and the production of one of her plays in Leningrad.[49] She had enrolled Ric in the Meyerhold Academy, an experimental theatre school in Moscow, but it had closed under Stalin's orders when constructivism fell out of favour, and Ric was unable to take up studies there. During his time attending teacher's college Ric had acted in, written and directed theatre. A security report on Prichard stated that:

> [Prichard's] son who is qualifying as a teacher at the University and Training College is also interested in Communism, and has no doubt come under his mother's influence.[50]

Axes tilted dramatically when Germany invaded the Soviet Union in the latter part of June 1941. British prime minister Winston Churchill subsequently welcomed the Soviet Union as an ally and, as such, the Soviet Union also became Australia's ally, 'turning Australian communists, who had formerly obstructed the war effort, into Australian patriots.'[51] The CPA reversed its previously strongly held stance opposing the War to one that now supported the War, and with the Soviet Union now an ally there was an almost immediate 'upsurge of interest' in the Soviet Union and its international political affiliates that led to a marked increase in CPA membership.[52] These developments, though, did not curtail police harassment of CPA members, and the Party remained an illegal organisation.

At the time of the Nazi attack on the Soviet Union, Prichard was in Kalgoorlie working on her goldfields novels, where the CIB Special Bureau kept close tabs on her. When she decided to take a break from her writing and attend a Russian Aid Committee meeting in Sydney, a trip that took nearly a week by train, a Special Bureau notice was sent to agents along the line informing them of her seat on the train so that she could be watched all the way.[53]

The West Australian carried reports on the march of the Nazi forces into the Soviet Union. In July, the German Army fought a bloody battle against the Red Army in the Russian town of Smolensk, south of Moscow, where Napoleon's troops had fought and failed, and the German Air Force attempted mass air raids on Moscow. Given the battering the Soviet Union was enduring, Prichard wrote a letter to Moscow journal *International Literature* in support of the Soviet people:

> [Australian] public opinion has veered from mistrust to applauding the Red Army ... My confidence in the soldiers and the workers of the U.S.S.R. and their great leaders is supreme ... Love and greetings to you all, splendid Comrades of the Soviet Union ... Soldiers and sailors, airmen, workers and farmers will be united in a fury of resolution to defend not only their country but all that it has given them under Soviet Socialism ... Cheers for the Red Army, and for the Central Executive Committee of the Communist Party, which has made the U.S.S.R. what it is.[54]

A public meeting was convened in Perth at the Assembly Hall in August 1941 to petition the Australian Government to renew diplomatic ties and recommence trade negotiations with the Soviet Union.[55] Vigilant police constables Basley and Buzolic attended, and their presence was brought to the attention of the meeting. Prichard, not long back from her ten-week stay in Kalgoorlie, addressed the crowd of about 200 and, at Phyllis Harnett's request, the meeting concluded with the crowd singing 'The Internationale' and cheers for the Red Army as well as the Australian Army. Basley and Buzolic 'particularly noticed that during the three cheers for the Red Army and singing of the "Internationale", the audience sang with more feeling and vigour than when singing the [Australian] National Anthem.' They also noted the presence of a number of Guild members as well as June Carder, whose legal challenge to her libel case would within a week be granted an indefinite adjournment.

Harald Vike had been planning to exhibit in Melbourne for some time. In late August 1941 he met Joan Kidd at the Perth railway station to board the choked train to Melbourne on which the couple planned to elope.[56] He had raced out of Gibbney's at the end of a day's work with a violin case in one hand and a painting under each arm, and been bowled over by a truck on St Georges Terrace, narrowly escaping serious injury. Shaken but unhurt, he picked up his violin case and paintings and arrived at the station shortly before the train pulled out.[57]

The train was crammed with German nationals being escorted to detention for the duration of the War, as well as those leaving Perth while they were still able. It was to be the last passenger train out of Perth before the city fell outside the 'Brisbane Line' — a supposed federal government defence demarcation separating Australia's populous south-eastern cities from the rest of the country, which would potentially be sacrificed in the event of a Japanese invasion.[58] All interstate trains from that time were requisitioned by the armed forces for use as troop transport.[59]

Vike and Kidd arrived in Melbourne on 4 September 1941 and were married four days later. The next day Vike was fingerprinted and registered as an enemy 'alien', given that he was a Norwegian national and Norway was then occupied by the Nazis. As his wife, Joan was also registered as an enemy alien. Vike was to sketch and paint through the remainder of the War while Joan worked to support them, but the arrangement was understandably not a happy one for her and Harald soon started work as a steel weigher in the BHP steelworks.

In September, a joint exhibition of photographs taken by Axel Poignant and Hal Missingham on their miniature Leica cameras was shown at the Newspaper House Gallery in Perth.[60] The arrival of Missingham in Perth had been a great morale boost for Poignant, who had worked for quite some time in relative isolation, though his photography compared favourably to that of many admired international photographers of the time. This exhibition was one of the earliest documentary photographic exhibitions held in Australia, at odds with the predominant formalist pictorial tradition of the time. The photographs 'caused quite a stir', Missingham later wrote:

> because of the unusual choice of subject matter, from extreme close-ups to aerial shots, but [also] because of the sharpness and clarity of the enlargements, almost unbelievable to most professional photographers, used to large format cameras with half-plate or whole-plate negatives.'[61]

In October 1941, Prichard left for Sydney, her fare being paid by the CPA central committee. She had been invited by the Australia–Soviet

Friendship Society to undertake a lecture tour of Australia's eastern states. For the next three months she travelled up and down the eastern seaboard and through Adelaide back to Perth speaking at innumerable gatherings about the need for better social, economic, cultural and sporting relations between Australia and the Soviet Union. She continued to lobby for diplomatic exchanges between the two countries and for the provision of aid to the Soviet Union. Her trip included meetings in Canberra with ministers in the new federal Labor Government, abetted by her old friendship with the recently appointed prime minister, John Curtin.[62]

In a tumultuous period in Australian federal politics, Robert Menzies had resigned as prime minister in August after a long riven period within the United Australia Party–Country Party coalition that had virtually paralysed the government. Country Party leader Arthur Fadden had succeeded Menzies as prime minister, only to be brought down himself within a month by a no-confidence motion. The great political chameleon and former umbrella repairman Billy Hughes had replaced Menzies as leader of the United Australia Party. Like Lyons, Hughes had been expelled from the ALP. Menzies, in later paying tribute to Hughes on his ninetieth birthday, mentioned that Hughes had astonishingly been a member of every political party represented in the federal parliament, to which Fadden interjected: 'Not the Country Party!' The still-feisty Hughes shot back: 'Had to draw the line somewhere, brother!'[63] In fact, Hughes *had* offered his services in 1929 as a possible leader of the Country Party, in one of his bids to topple then prime minister Stanley Melbourne Bruce — an act for which Labor member King O'Malley had labelled him a 'vicious little mugwump … capable of separating a cripple from his crutches'.[64]

In the first week of October 1941, after the defeat of the Fadden government, the notional Western Australian John Curtin was commissioned to form a Labor government. New attorney-general 'Doc' Evatt immediately put in train steps to end the political persecution of the CPA and its members and, with Curtin and the Labor Party's accession to power, the CPA moved towards more fulsome support of the War.

During his tenure with the Workers' Art Guild, Victor Arnold had been called away on a number of occasions, apparently on CPA duties probably related to New Theatre. In December 1940, six months after his arrival in Perth, Prichard wrote to Hilda Esson that Arnold expected to travel to Melbourne 'towards the end of April', and that if he did, he was considering directing a play for Melbourne New Theatre.[65] Freda Lewis, who had taken over as secretary of Sydney New Theatre when Arnold left for Perth, was convinced that Arnold had wanted to leave Perth almost as soon as he'd arrived, and that he may have been looking for an opportunity to get away.[66]

Arnold eventually left Perth in May 1941, travelling by train only as far as Adelaide, where he arrived two days later.[67] A few days before his departure, police had searched his city flat and discovered that he was to be involved in the organisation and production of a left-wing theatre in Adelaide. They believed he planned to return to Sydney New Theatre shortly afterwards 'to produce plays'.[68] The Western Australian military intelligence branch informed its South Australian counterpart of Arnold's plans and requested that it in turn 'advise [Melbourne and Sydney] Commands when Arnold leaves your State in order that his movements might be watched.'[69] Arnold was in fact planning to launch and oversee Adelaide's Labour Youth Theatre, which had been formed just days before his arrival.[70] It was, in all but name, a branch of the New Theatre League that initially concentrated on the performance of agitprop drama, an area in which Arnold had form.

After six or so months in Sydney, John Hector and Kathleen Beechey left for Brisbane. Hector was committed to funding Victor Arnold's term in restoring the fortunes of the national workers' theatre movement, and Arnold by now had apparently set the Labour Youth Theatre 'in full swing'.[71] He was happier in Adelaide than he had been in Perth, and in July 1941 Hector wrote to reassure Arnold that he would be 'sending a lump sum to cover your remaining six weeks of the originally suggested term'.

> I hope to be able to make available to the [New Theatre League] a sum of between £50 and £100 within two weeks and suggest that this amount be used to help develop the theatre movement in places such as Adelaide and possibly Newcastle by maintaining producers there long enough to get going properly. From what you say about Adelaide it appears that the Youth Theatre is starting off on the right track with activities among the unions the Keynote.[72]

Arnold remained in Adelaide, on and off, until at least March 1943.

At Sydney New Theatre, a writers' group was formed in early 1941. Sydney New Theatre was one of the few amateur theatre companies whose ranks were not decimated by the War, as many of its members were employed in essential service industries and therefore exempt from compulsory military training and enlistment. The writers' group was quite possibly formed at the suggestion of Gordon Burgoyne and John Hepworth, who had likely brought the idea with them from the Workers' Art Guild. Prichard had written to Louis Esson about Hepworth's arrival in Sydney towards the end of 1940, concerned that Hepworth might be a bad influence on Esson's son Hugh:

> Oh John Hepworth! He's got some ability — was ruined here, by too much flattery I think, at first. Became utterly irresponsible & decadent ... A thorough little swine where women are concerned — though if he pulls up he might still be a decent sort. Home atmosphere was pretty awful — & yet not sufficient to account for his goings on before he went to Sydney, weak, chiefly. Booze — & the rest, made a mess of him! [73]

Hepworth had arrived in Sydney from Perth with a companion, poet Douglas Wilson. His reputation had preceded him and there were great expectations of him, both socially and professionally. Wilson, like many others, 'drifted in Hepworth's orbit because that was where interesting and pleasing things were likely to happen'.[74]

Hepworth initially 'wrote a couple of good agit-props and took part in several [New Theatre] shows without turning up drunk',[75] but soon disgraced himself. Oriel Gray later recounted Hepworth's celebrity status within Sydney New Theatre ranks in her 1985 autobiography, *Exit Left*:

> A visitor from Melbourne New Theatre had been enthusiastic about Hepworth's performance for them in 'Awake & Sing', about an agit-prop play he had written at short notice, and his talent as a poet (of which, I suspect, she had some personal mementoes) ... [Hepworth] went quietly about the theatre, doing whatever was asked of him. He stepped into a part at a moment's notice; he went to work on an agit-prop sketch; he wrote a critical article for *The Tribune* which delighted the editor. At theory class he made good sense of our own situation in Australia, instead of quoting from interminable overseas texts. Although he was popular with the ladies, the men also liked him ... Hepworth did not have a job, and did not look for one, although journalists passing through might have helped him. He had come to Sydney to write the great Australian novel.[76]

Sydney New Theatre secretary Freda Lewis thought Hepworth 'talented' but 'utterly and completely mad'.[77] He was part of a small bohemian clique in Sydney that included Oriel Gray and her sister Grace. Relationships with the women around him were becoming complex, serious and more strained than Hepworth wanted. He married Oriel's sister and then began an affair with Oriel herself. Hector reported from Sydney that Hepworth:

> bludged for a couple of months, got a job for a couple of weeks, then sought an appreciative personal audience, got a girl in trouble, started to perform again in his worst style, and finally staged a suicide act.[78]

In May 1941, after an argument with his new wife the evening before he was due to appear in Sydney New Theatre performances of *Waiting For Lefty* and *Private Hicks*, Hepworth vanished to stage a melodramatic suicide attempt that was perhaps his finest dramatic performance. He wrote a cryptic 'suicide' poem in the style of the romantic poets he was then undoubtedly reading, and left it for his wife and her sister to find after his disappearance. Although he later described the incident as a serious attempt at suicide, accounts of the event, including his own published account, do not really bear this out.

> I decided that I would go with a certain theatrical insouciance — I would swim in the dark of night out into the middle of Sydney Harbour and be torn to pieces by a shark, no less! There was of course some slight delay while I composed my suicide poem, but pretty ripe stuff it was, as I remember, when I'd finally polished the stanzas to my liking.
>
> *Deepsea and green shall my death's kingdom be*
> *And let my death be swift and free —*
> *Wild and white and swift and free*
> *By clean cold fang with savagery, driven ...*
>
> Any ms would have had to be pretty stonyhearted not to have been affected by it. I was a trifle affected by it myself. 'That great talent,' I thought. 'What a loss!' Actually I made rather a cockup of the suicide poem because the two Mss who found it (both of whom later to their regret became, at different times, my wife), found eight other copies of it addressed to different birds in a

suitcase along with two pairs of silk pyjamas which were the only trousseau I then had in the world. They were not amused.[79]

So that his 'suicide' would not go unnoticed at Sydney New Theatre, Hepworth also slipped a note under the front door of the theatre describing where his clothes could be found. With preparations complete, he made his way in the evening from his Paddington flat to the harbour near Elizabeth Bay, 'a very prestigious area indeed for anyone thinking of knocking themselves off'. He undressed, but left his shoes on 'because the beach seemed to be a bit rocky', and started to wade out into water so cold that he decided to delay his plan. By his own account he then 'wandered starkers (except for shoes) as a Nederlands ballet dancer' along the harbour shore, before stealing a pair of trousers, a shirt and a jacket from a laundry, dressing himself and lying down in the Domain to sleep, 'waiting for a propitious change in the weather.'

> Came the dawn of course, the whole thing had to be postponed. The script called clearly for the thing to be done by dead of night. Whoever heard of anyone swimming out into the middle of Sydney Harbour to be torn to pieces by a shark in daylight? You'd look a right Charlie.[80]

Hepworth then ambled into a 'sort of shed' back in Paddington, where he was asked if he wished to enlist.

> I nodded and mumbled something amiable. 'Army?' he said. I nodded and mumbled again. 'Sign here,' he said. I seized the shaky pen and wrote in a firm schoolboy hand 'John Hale Davidson' ... and that's who I was for the rest of the war.[81]

The Investigation Branch of the Attorney-General's Department intercepted a letter from Hector making reference to Hepworth's enlistment, and a memorandum to the CIB in Canberra remarked that 'the A.I.F. might be interested in Hepworth and his ways.'[82] But enquiries proved fruitless, since Hepworth had indeed enlisted as 'John Hale Davidson' and given a false date of birth.[83]

News of Hepworth's supposed dramatic passing spread quickly around Sydney New Theatre. Some of the women were teary, many of the men sceptical and annoyed. Hepworth later turned up at Oriel and Grace Gray's flat in Paddington, dressed in slouch hat and uniform, to a very chilly reception.⁸⁴ He later sailed overseas with the 2/2nd Battalion of the Australian Imperial Force (AIF) 6th Division, after Germany's invasion of the Soviet Union and before his twentieth birthday.

In Perth, police had been taking a keen interest in the Workers' Art Guild. A CIB report on the Guild around April 1941 — prior to the Carder case and soon after John Simpson's arrest — stated that:

> this organisation is undoubtedly an offshoot of the Communist Party, which is using lawful bodies [of which the Guild was one] as a cloak for its subversive propaganda. Apart from producing plays of an emphatically 'left' nature, it affords ample opportunity for Communists to hold meetings in the guise of rehearsals, readings, etc. The graph of the Communist Organization operating within Australia discloses that movements such as the 'New Theatre League' and the Unity Theatre are definite offshoots of the Party, and the workers Art Guild [*sic*] appears to come under the same category. A great number of well-known Communists in Perth … are members of the Guild, and control its activities. It is felt that so long as this organisation is deemed lawful, Communist and subversive propaganda must to a certain degree, remain unchecked, and it is recommended that its activities be curtailed.⁸⁵

It seems that the Workers' Art Guild came very close to being classified an 'unlawful body' under the National Security Act.

After Victor Arnold's departure 'amidst much beer and good wishes', the Guild was reportedly now 'struggling along again' — '[u]pon sobering up we settled down to steady organisation.'⁸⁶ In August 1941, Guild member Gavin Casey referred to difficulties in staging Guild productions due to 'the usual shortage of actors, and generally bad conditions of the Dramatic Section of the Guild', although the writers' group, Casey reported, 'hangs together reasonably well, though it has not done much work lately':

> It shows signs of revival having recruited one or two men willing to act as secretary, delegate to managements committee.⁸⁷

John Lunghi had become a central figure in the writers' group and Victor Williams, recently enlisted in the Army, maintained some involvement while he was in Perth in August undergoing his military training.⁸⁸

The Guild began to host regular monthly Saturday-night cabarets to raise funds for its draining coffers, but a few months later Guild secretary Gwen Duggan wrote to Brisbane's Unity Theatre that its efforts 'seem hopeless' and sought 'advice regarding organisation'.[89]

Guild activities struggled through the fog of war. It had been many months since the Guild had staged a substantial theatre production. Laboured preparations continued on a reprise of the Workers' Art Club's first major play, Clifford Odets's *Till the Day I Die*, which the Guild hoped would have 'a vitalising effect'.[90] Rehearsals overseen by Phyllis Harnett, rehabilitated after Victor Arnold's departure, began in August 1941. Arnold reappeared briefly a short time before the play's opening in October, and helped Axel Poignant and John Lunghi with technical and design preparations. The play was to be performed within quite a different political context from that of its 1936 premiere. New South Wales had just rescinded a five-year ban on the play's performance, Australia was now at war with Germany and there seemed to be little reason to object to the play. Given that the play's forewarning about the horrors of the Nazi regime in Germany had by now been horribly realised, it was now an echo rather than a prelude, though still potent, stinging and powerful.

Henry Cuthbertson's younger brother Allan, a principal actor with the Repertory Club who would later build a steady career as a character actor in some notable British and American films, made his Guild debut in this production of *Till the Day I Die*.[91] He had been full of admiration for Harnett's dramatic work at the Five Arts Club and was keen to appear in a production of the play directed by Harnett.

Ruth Pettersen also played a role, albeit unreliably. Since her arrival from Sydney she had helped out around the Guild, typing scripts and doing 'odd jobs which' — as she put it — 'prove I'm not the degenerate sometimes painted',[92] but her mental state was deteriorating. She was drinking a good deal and arrived at performances after the pub's closing swill, which only heightened the enmity between herself and Harnett, who later recalled:[93]

> I would be dressed in her clothes [for the performance] three times out of four when she arrived at the theatre. But on the last night of *Till the Day I Die*, she arrived just in time to get on [but] she hadn't got her prop, [which] was a letter. There was no letter, and I had in my pocket a letter, which I found it *very* hard to give her because I feared the worst. My girlfriend at school ... had got out of Belgium into France and was under the dryer in the hairdressers when the Germans walked into Paris, and she'd written a letter to her mother

describing all these things and her mother had lent it to me and I was going to post it back to *my* mother the next day. Never got it back from Ruth — and I hated Ruth! I knew she was going to do it when I handed it over ... because she had some extraordinary objection to me that was causing trouble all around the place.[94]

Harnett, by her own admission, was apt to 'go on a moral rant about this time', which only served to isolate her more from many of her peers in the Guild. She had become 'disapproving of everybody's affairs ... not that they weren't fairly alarming!'[95]

Some of the original 1936 cast of *Till the Day I Die* — Howard Smith, Ian Smith, Maurie Lachberg and Louis (Lou) Conto — reappeared in the 1941 production, Lachberg and Conto reprising their earlier roles. Ric Throssell, having inherited the tall, athletic good looks of his father and his mother's gentle piercing eyes, cut a fine figure on stage in this production. He appreciated Harnett's skills as a director, though he conceded that she was less demanding and less meticulous in her preparations for the play than Keith George had been.[96]

Harnett did not attempt to emulate George's distinctive 1936 production of the play. As good a director as she was, she was bound to suffer in comparison with George and she had spent far less time in preparation than George had. She felt ostracised by many of the Guild principals, and was reluctant to give the production her full attention. 'In this awful coldness the production came to an end,' she recalled later.[97] Nevertheless, the season was a popular success and *The West Australian*, despite some criticisms, praised the performances of Throssell, Howard Smith, Gwen Duggan, Lachberg and Cuthbertson.[98]

The Repertory Club, given the greater patriotic fervour of its members, faced a more pronounced crisis. There had been mass membership resignations in early 1941 due to military enlistment, and the adoption of the Club's new policy, at the end of 1938, of admitting the general public to performances had also led to the departure of members, this break from elitism having offended many within the Club.[99] When a Repertory Club production of *Quiet Night*, by Melbourne playwright Dorothy Blewett, was staged for the 1941 West Australian Drama Festival in September, the cast of fourteen was drawn from the Repertory, Garrick, Marlowe, Shakespeare and Pleiades Clubs, as well as from the Workers' Art Guild.[100] Players included Betty Hamill, May Hollands, Howard Smith and Kevin Caporn, who had made his debut in the 1936 Workers' Theatre performances of *Till the Day I Die* and *Bury the Dead*.[101] *Quiet Night* was the winning entry of the forty full-length plays submitted to the 1941 Drama Festival competition, and the only play staged at the festival that year. A comedy set in a Melbourne hospital ward, it was by no means a polemic play and was later widely performed among Australian repertory theatre groups. It required no scenery changes and, 'on this score alone, when lack of manpower [was] a pressing consideration with repertory clubs, the play [had] much to commend it.'[102]

The Repertory Club dedicated a lot of its work during the War years to the support of various 'patriotic bodies', and its members 'were all out to do what they could for the War'.[103]

The Repertory Club secretary had resigned in November 1941, and an executive meeting in early December discussed a new appointment to the paid position, during which:

> [Repertory Club member Walter Poole-Johnson] wished to know whether the Sub-Committee had considered Mr. Keith George as a possible Secretary for the Club. It was pointed out that Mr. George's appointment to the position would be a means of placing the services of a producer of distinct merit at the Club's disposal, and in this way help the Club over a considerable number of difficulties.[104]

Consideration was deferred.

Within days, America declared war on Japan. The following day Curtin announced that Australia was also at war with Japan, and Keith George submitted his formal application for the position of Repertory Club secretary, requesting 'that in addition to his work as Secretary he should be also given at least two productions each year and that he should also supervise the remaining productions when required to do so'.[105] Two days later, Germany and Italy declared war on America, and Keith George was advised that he had been appointed secretary on his terms, to start in January 1942. Three days before Christmas, the first American troops arrived on Australian soil.

In early January 1942, CIB inspector Stanley Read was notified that a Midland Junction police officer had 'recently investigated the matter of a report concerning signalling' in the hills above Perth.

> He is of the opinion that signalling did take place from Mrs. Throssell's house at Greenmount at 11.20 am on 23 Dec. 41. He is in possession of what he describes as a signalling lamp ... it is desired that he be contacted and the matter further investigated.[106]

Prichard was not at Greenmount at the time. She was on her lecture tour of the eastern states, and was staying with her sister in Frankston, south of Melbourne, at the time of the reported signalling. A neighbour of Prichard's had notified police of his suspicions of signals coming from Prichard's home, and he later took a policeman to Prichard's property to investigate the source. Many more police visits determined that the house had 'not been occupied for some considerable time', that it was too far from the alleged source of the 'signals' to have been involved, and that no 'apparatus ... capable of throwing a light strong enough to be seen by daylight' had been found.[107]

The 'signals' turned out to be sunlight reflecting off an empty tin sitting on a tree stump. When Prichard returned home in late January 1942, she found that her house had been broken into by police and left open. She heard what had happened through neighbourhood gossip, and wrote a derisive letter of complaint to police.

> Needless to say, if the house was used for any improper purpose, during my absence, I am only too anxious to co-operate with the authorities in discovering any source of danger to our troops or the defence of Australia. If there was any indication of the house being so used, I think I should be informed, also, for my own protection ... Under the circumstances I would value an explanation.[108]

In December 1941, Prichard had dined in Canberra with then federal attorney-general and minister for external affairs 'Doc' Evatt. When she began to discuss her lecture tour, he interrupted, telling her:

> You needn't tell me. I've been kept informed by the Security lads of all your movements; had an almost hourly report on where you were going and what you've been saying.[109]

It seems, however, that the Perth CIB had been kept out of the loop.

The Workers' Art Guild limped into 1942 while, conversely, Keith George's livelihood in the theatre appeared to have been resurrected. In January 1942, at the age of forty-one, George took up his salaried appointment as secretary of the Repertory Club. He was also to direct a planned February Repertory Club production of Frederick Lonsdale's play *Canaries Sometimes Sing*, having worked on a 1933 production of the play at the Five Arts Club.[110] He also planned to direct productions of German farce

Are You a Mason? in April, Pirandello's *Henry IV* in June and Molière's *The Hypochondriac* in October.

George quickly stamped his authority on the Repertory Club, applying the rigid control and discipline that had been a hallmark of his work with the Guild. He set up a stage committee to oversee seven separate stage departments, and appointed overseers. He also proposed the introduction of a number of innovations that he had introduced to the Guild, including a Saturday-afternoon children's theatre class that included dance and music tuition.[111]

Indications of the Workers' Art Guild's effective demise came when, on 4 February 1942, Howard Smith was elected to the membership of the Repertory Club. The Repertory Club's executive meeting on 17 January had 'resolved that the sum of £5 be expended on purchase of Wardrobe from Workers' Art Guild'.[112] In February the Club registered under the *War Funds Regulation Act 1939* (WA) and Keith George announced that its net profits for the year would be 'devoted to patriotic purposes', with regular shows three nights a week to augment its funds. He busied himself with preparations required for a wartime 'blackout' during a Saturday-night performance, but in that prevailing state of universal flux, his tenure with the Repertory Club was short-lived.[113]

A few days prior to the Repertory Club's three-night season of *Canaries Sometimes Sing*, Keith George accepted an appointment as a special lecturer on Australian drama at the University of Western Australia. A week later, at the end of February 1942, less than two months into his appointment and having directed only one Repertory Club production, he was granted 'leave of absence' from the Repertory Club 'for the duration of the War' after being called up for military service. It was a 'serious blow'[114] to the Repertory Club to lose him.[115]

The War was now on Western Australia's doorstep. In March 1942, at least seventy people were killed in the state's north-west by Japanese air strikes on the towns of Broome and Wyndham, and in July Japanese aircraft bombed Port Hedland, further to the south.

At the end of June 1942, Keith George married dancer Linley Wilson and moved out of his Kenwick farmhouse. Wilson was a pioneer of ballet in Western Australia, whose ballet companies were considerable cultural institutions in Perth in the 1930s. She hailed from a respectable and affluent family, her father Frank Wilson having twice served as premier of Western Australia. She had studied dance in London in the early 1920s and, on her return to Perth, opened her own ballet school; she also formed

Western Australia's first ballet company in the 1930s and helped set up the Royal Academy of Dancing throughout Australia. She was a member of the Repertory Club and regularly gave public lectures on dance.[116]

A number of people who knew Keith George were surprised when he married. Of his choice of bride, Ric Throssell summed up the feelings of many in saying, 'a more odd pair you never imagined'.[117] Another commentator observed:

> Wilson was a quietly spoken West Perth snob and that era's equivalent of a jet-setter. George was a loud unaffected man who had grown up in the country and had never been anywhere else. Wilson was immaculately groomed and her wardrobe included designer dresses bought in Paris. George held up his trousers with a neck-tie and wore meal-stained shirts.[118]

A week after George's wedding, Thomas Bath, president of the Repertory Club, wrote a testimonial:[119]

> I have known Mr. Keith George for many years as a director and organiser of dramatic and other forms of entertainment. He has earned a first-class reputation in this class of work. In view of the great need for providing entertainment for the military forces of the various arms of the services, there is a niche in the Army for the organisation of such entertainment which Private Keith George is able to fill in admirable fashion.[120]

In July, Prichard delivered an address on Australian drama at the University of Western Australia. She referred 'posthumously' and with great affection to the playwriting achievements of the Workers' Art Guild, singling out *I Am Angry*, *The Lyons Bungles*, *Hold Your Wheat* and *Feed The Sheep* for particular praise.[121] In October 1942 she left Perth for Sydney, where she was to serve as a member of the CPA's central committee through the War. The CPA in Western Australia had undergone 'reorganisation', with official positions filled temporarily. Paddy Troy had joined the secretariat but 'his permanent handicaps — irregular working hours and heavy domestic responsibilities' ruled him out 'as a possible leader'. Leah Healy was struggling as acting state secretary and Maurie Lachberg was being groomed for the position.[122]

The CPA was still an illegal organisation and continued to conceal its activities until John Curtin lifted the ban on it a week before Christmas

1942, acknowledging that the Soviet Union had helped in the defeat of the Nazis. Little more than two years later, Curtin was dead, his life undoubtedly shortened by the burden of administering the War and sending Australian troops to their death from his lonely outpost in Canberra.

By year's end, nearly all of the Workers' Art Guild's major players had enlisted. Most were moved to the eastern states to be trained and accommodated in the AIF. The core of the Guild had left the state, many never to return. The exodus was to have an adverse effect on the cultural life of Perth well beyond the War. Western Australian culture retreated back to the orthodox, Western Australian art to the comforting landscape.

Academic Fred Alexander described his return to Perth in early 1941, from a Rockefeller Scholarship in the United States, as 'a very rude shock'. He was struck by the changes that had occurred in Perth during his year abroad, most notably 'the absence of the exciting public interest in world affairs which had characterised the late 1930s'.[123]

By 1943, national membership of the CPA had reached a peak of around 23,000 before beginning its decline.[124] In April 1943, Bill Irwin wrote in a letter to a friend:

> Everything's nep here. Johnny Hep's in Papua. Bugs [Burgoyne] is Gunner Burgoyne just training. Phil [sic] Harnett's expecting illegit child in S.A. and very happy about same … Everyone you knew except me (manpowered) is in the Forces … Keith George in Infantry.[125]

The term 'manpowered' referred to being assigned to what were deemed essential employment roles in support of the war effort.

The War had engulfed Western Australia, and when the tide receded it had washed away virtually all imprints of the iconoclastic 1930s. The experiment was over, and the West returned to provincialism.

Ben Chifley succeeded John Curtin as Labor prime minister after the War, and the formidable National Security Act, ostensibly created to maintain civil order during the War, was not repealed until December 1947.[126]

In 1949, CPA general secretary Lawrence ('Lance') Sharkey was convicted of sedition after making pro-Soviet remarks over the phone to a journalist from Sydney's *The Daily Telegraph* and sentenced to three years' imprisonment. Kevin Healy was also charged with sedition after endorsing Sharkey's comments to another journalist, but was acquitted of the charge before a jury. Reflecting on the poor state of the CPA and on general political apathy in Australia after the War, Sharkey is said to have declared that 'more Australian comrades will die from eating Sargents pies than ever will die on the barricades.'

In the 1950s, CPA speakers on the Esplanade were again intimidated and attacked, as they had been two decades earlier.

In April 1954, Menzies — now serving a second stint as prime minister, which would ultimately see him become the nation's longest-serving head — broke off diplomatic relations with the USSR and the Cold War began. It would last for almost forty years.

APPENDIX

AFTER THE WAR

The hope for a safer world was widely shared, but the form that better world should take was bitterly contested. And the conflict between those contending visions ... poisoned the political and intellectual life of Australia for the next four decades.[1]

Victor Arnold (c. 1907–1982)[2] never returned to Sydney New Theatre in any official capacity. He remained in Adelaide, on and off, until 1943 and then joined the Armed Forces Entertainment Unit, serving in Australia and New Guinea. In 1946 he was appointed artistic director of Melbourne's New Theatre and directed the bulk of its plays until 1950. In the early 1950s he became involved with Melbourne's Realist Film Association, a subsidiary of New Theatre. In 1958 he was elected secretary of the Victorian branch of what was then the Actors' and Announcers' Equity Association of Australia. In that role he did much to improve the working conditions of Australian actors and helped to establish an Australian content quota on Australian television. He remained active in the Communist Party into the 1960s but started to drift away from the Party, like many others, around the time of the CPSU's 20th Congress in 1956, when Stalin's crimes were exposed by Khrushchev. He retired from his position as secretary of (what by then was known as) Actors' Equity in 1982, and died later that year.

Maurice Benn (1917–1975) enlisted in the Navy in 1941 and served during the War. He was an outstanding scholar with a particular interest in German studies. In 1945 he enrolled as a postgraduate student at the University of Western Australia, and later moved to London to undertake a master's degree. He returned to Perth in 1952 and established a reputation as one of Australia's most distinguished German-language scholars. In April 1964 he was found guilty of the wilful murder of his son and sentenced to hang. He had shot his severely disabled son and then turned himself in to police. The incident led to national public recognition of the inadequacy of disability care and support services in Australia. A public outcry over the severity of Benn's sentence led to the Western Australian government commuting his sentence. He was released, having served only four-and-a-half years of his commuted sentence, and returned to the University of Western Australia.

Gordon ('Bugs') Burgoyne (1911–1993) and **Hope Bath** became involved with New Theatre on their arrival in Sydney in 1940. Later that year they moved to Darwin, where Burgoyne was appointed editor of North Australian Workers' Union journal the *Northern Standard*. The following year he passed the job on to John Hector, and returned with Hope Bath to Sydney. In 1942 Burgoyne took up a post in the Canberra office of the ABC's new independent news service. He was called up for active service soon afterwards and was discharged as 'Gunner Burgoyne' from the Darwin Coastal Artillery in December 1945. He resumed his employment with the ABC's news department in Canberra, where he remained until retirement, having served as senior journalist in the parliamentary press gallery. He likely served as Canberra correspondent for *The Tribune* on an ad-hoc basis, and remained within the sights of intelligence agencies.

> Burgoyne has always been a hard man to get to know. He is one of those deep, silent men, who refuses to have anything to do with A.B.C. office intrigue, but reportedly always takes a big interest in industrial matters. He seems to stand highly with the talks section of the A.B.C. particularly. As you know that section is reportedly supposed to contain some fellow travellers.[3]

The Gordon Burgoyne Memorial Prize for Journalism is today awarded annually to the most outstanding young journalism student at the University of Canberra.

Gavin Casey (1907–1964), who was also a successful short story writer, took over the presidency of the Western Australian branch of the Fellowship of Australian Writers in 1942. In 1945 he moved to New York to administer the Australian News and Information Service, later working as a journalist in Sydney and Canberra with the Australian News and Information Bureau.

> A gregarious personality, Casey became a popular member of Sydney's journalistic scene.[4]

John Curtin (1885–1945) died in office in July 1945 at the age of sixty. At his state funeral, 100,000 people turned out to pay their respects. Percy Trainer, Curtin's old mate from his days on the *Westralian Worker*, was a pallbearer. Curtin is buried in Perth's Karrakatta Cemetery.

Allan Cuthbertson (1920–1988) served in New Guinea and after the War's end he sailed to London where he resumed performing in repertory theatre. He went on to appear in Old Vic productions and major West End plays, and later established a steady career as a staple character actor in British and Hollywood films, his appearance little changed from his days on the Perth stage in the 1930s. He appeared in films including *Carrington VC* (1954), *The Man Who Never Was* (1956), *Room at the Top* (1959), *The Guns of Navarone* (1961), *Bitter Harvest* (1963), *Performance* (1970), *The Railway Children* (1974), *The Sea Wolves* (1981) and *Edge of Darkness* (1986). He also appeared in television episodes of *Fawlty Towers*, *The Avengers*, *The Saint* and *The Goodies*, and performed as a foil to British comedian Tommy Cooper.[5]

Keith George (1900–1972) was classified 'unfit' for military service outside Australia.[6] He was employed by the Australian Army Education Service (AAES) during the War and consulted by Fred Alexander, then in charge of the AAES in Western Australia, 'on some of the early experimental work of Army Education in performing arts fields'.[7] George was a proponent for the introduction of theatre into the armed forces through the formation of an Army repertory company as a means of education, relaxation and propaganda. He proposed Living Newspaper dramatisations of war news. He recommended that the director responsible for the Army's drama company 'should be a capable producer with a knowledge of amateur work and above all a sound knowledge at least of the New York Theatre Guild, the New Theatre League, the New York Mercury Theatre, the pro-Nazi German Theatre and the Russian Theatre'. He was inarguably the perfect candidate.[8] He was discharged from the Army's 19th Garrison Battalion in November 1944 and resigned from his position as secretary of the Repertory Club, from which he had been on leave of absence through the War. He bought a small farm at Gooseberry Hill in the Darling Range outside Perth, where he settled with his wife, Linley Wilson. In 1945, Fred Alexander recruited George to take charge of drama classes at UWA's Adult Education Board Summer School, which George continued to do until the summer of 1947 and intermittently for a few years thereafter. He ran a 'producers' course for the Summer School, but declined the position of drama tutor in-residence over the summer of 1948 due to his 'advancing years and declining physique', although the Summer School did implement what it called 'Keith George's Five-Year Plan'.[9] George's professional involvement in the theatre became limited to working in his wife's dance company—teaching drama to the dancers, lighting the shows and managing the dance school and company tours, as well as managing 'Linley Wilson's Australian Caravan Ballet', which travelled throughout Western Australia in the 1940s and 1950s. George's services were also sought in helping to set up country theatre groups, and he gave regular lectures on drama. He was instrumental through the late 1940s in the push to establish an Australian national theatre company. He worked on the 1948 Drama Festival and was stage director for the 1949 Drama Festival, and 'came out of self-imposed retirement to make the last assault upon the comfortable sensibilities of the local critics' to direct Ric Throssell's anti-war play *Valley of the Shadows* at the Repertory Club Theatre in November 1949.[10] His highly stylised direction of the play was misunderstood by critics and not loved by audiences, but Paul Hasluck attended a performance and sang its praises.[11] George then 'abandoned the theatre', according to Throssell:

> He would occasionally be coaxed along to see something, but walk out after the first scene because it was never up to his standard. Discarded like that, a great mistake.[12]

He again came under ASIO scrutiny in the 1950s because of his continuing association with Katharine Susannah Prichard.[13] On their retirement in the late 1960s, Keith George and Linley Wilson moved to Pinjarra, eighty-five kilometres south of Perth, where George became active as a local historian. He developed diabetes, which led to the amputation of a leg. In 1969 he was appointed honorary historian of the Shire of Murray to compile a history of the Shire and Pinjarra for its centenary, helped by his 'two old friends' Bill Irwin and Fred Alexander; delayed by illness, it was published in 1971.[14] George and Prichard remained lifelong friends. In November 1971 he wrote to Prichard's son Ric:

> Since I last wrote I have had a second [leg] amputation. A rather more traumatic experience than the first and I am losing much of my contact with the past and the future.[15]

On 18 February 1972, Keith George died in Perth aged seventy-one. His obituary appeared in *The West Australian* the following day, under the headline 'Theatre, Ballet Pioneer Dies':

Mr George, a lawyer whose heart was in the theatre, was known among his friends as a conversationalist, bon viveur and cook … He was a producer with the radical Workers' Art Guild in the early thirties. There he introduced new techniques of staging and brought many famous plays to Perth for the first time … Yesterday Professor Fred Alexander described Mr George as a theatrical producer of quality who was much respected by professional ballet people. Mr Howard Smith, of the National Theatre at the Playhouse, said that Mr George was one of the best and most thorough producers he had known. 'He could take a raw amateur and produce a top class performance,' Mr Smith said. Mr George, who had no children, left a widow.[16]

As a mark of respect for his work in political theatre, an obituary was also published in Sydney CPA newspaper The *Tribune*:

Keith George … played a notable part in the development of a strong Left theatre movement in Perth in the late 'thirties. He was the central figure in the Workers' Art Guild, which produced a series of notable plays and ran first-rate classes in writing and painting … His production of the Clifford Odets play 'Till the Day I Die' did much to alert the public to the horrors of nazism. The production, which played to packed houses, was warmly reviewed by 'Polygon', theatre critic Paul Hasluck of 'The West Australian' and the present Governor-General. 'Waiting For Lefty' was another powerful and famous play produced by Mr. George, and later his production of Ernst Toller's powerful anti-war play 'Hinkemann' was a theatrical sensation. Sectarian concepts within the Guild led to a break with Mr. George, but his service to the anti-fascist movement at a critical time should be put on record.[17]

Shortly after George's death, Ric Throssell wrote in a condolence letter to Linley Wilson:

Keith taught me all I know, all I ever will know, I think, about the theatre. He really had the touch of genius … I will miss my old master.[18]

Phyllis Ophel (formerly Harnett) wrote of George after his death:

Keith meant so much to all of us who knew him in my Perth days and his last letter brought back all the feeling of his directiveness in theatre, an influence which none of us cared to wholly outgrow.[19]

Elizabeth (Betty) Hamill (1917–2007) moved to Melbourne during the War and spent many years working in adult education. In 1946 she published a book of literary criticism titled *These Modern Writers*. After the War she wrote radio drama scripts on post-war reconstruction, and married painter Danila Vassilieff. She painted under the pseudonym 'Vassilieva' and lectured on the history of modern literature and modern art at the Victorian Council of Adult Education. Her political activities intensified in the early 1950s. She organised gatherings of leading left-wing writers, including George Farwell, Roy and Nadine Dalgarno, and Vance and Nettie Palmer, at 'Stonygrad', the house Vassilieff built in Warrandyte outside Melbourne.[20] In the early 1950s she was a literary critic, an English lecturer for the University of Melbourne Extension Board and an associate editor of literary journal *Meanjin*. In 1952 she attended the World Peace Conference in Vienna and a peace conference in Peking as the delegate of the Victorian Branch of the Fellowship of Australian Writers, closely tailed by ASIO officers who fell short in 'the art of concealing their occupation'.[21] In 1953 she published an account of her 1952–1953 travels to Vienna, the Soviet Union and China in *Peking Moscow Letters*. On her return from this trip she came under the Menzies government's 'passport ban'. She later remarried and moved to Sydney.

Paul Hasluck's (1905–1993) high praise of Workers' Art Guild theatre, he later wrote, led 'some of my right-wing friends to express concern that I was becoming a communist'.

> After Abyssinia and after the Spanish Civil War there were more people who could not understand how a man who had staunch Roman Catholic friends could also hob-nob with the Workers' Art Guild.[22]

Hasluck left journalism in 1941 and his friendship with John Curtin enabled his transfer to a position in the Department of External Affairs in Canberra. Curtin had encouraged Hasluck to work in the Commonwealth public service rather than enlist and, with Curtin's accession to prime minister, Hasluck worked as a policy advisor to minister for external affairs 'Doc' Evatt.[23] Hasluck was a member of the Australian delegation that accompanied Evatt to the 1945 San Francisco conference that led to the establishment of the United Nations in April of that year; in 1946 Hasluck attended the first session of the UN General Assembly as an official. From 1946 to 1947 he was the Australian representative to the UN Mission in New York, also serving as the Australian representative to the UN Security Council. He maintained his interest and activities in theatre. During the War, he became active in the Canberra Repertory Society with Ric Throssell. In 1948 he returned to Perth as a reader in history at UWA. In 1949 he was elected as the first member for the new federal parliamentary seat of Curtin in Perth, named after his old friend, which he held until 1969. Hasluck's portfolios in successive Menzies governments included Territories (1951–1963), Defence (1963) and External Affairs (1964–1969). When Menzies retired in 1966, Hasluck was very nearly elected deputy leader of the Liberal Party and deputy prime minister, but his lack of ambition saw him defeated in the party room ballot by William McMahon, who went on to become prime minister. After Harold Holt's death, Hasluck was Menzies's preferred candidate for leader of the Liberal Party and the post of prime minister, but a lack of lobbying by Hasluck saw John Gorton take the position. In 1969 Hasluck was knighted and appointed governor-general. When his term expired in 1974, then prime minister Gough Whitlam encouraged him to stay on but Hasluck declined. He was succeeded in July 1974 by John Kerr and returned to Perth. Political history may have unfolded very differently had Hasluck remained governor-general through 1975.[24] Despite their parliamentary stoushes, Whitlam acknowledged Sir Paul Hasluck as a man of decency, and said of Hasluck when he retired:

> In the brief periods when he was not making history, he was teaching it or writing it.[25]

After **John Hector** (1914–1991) and **Kathleen Beechey** (1917–?) arrived in Sydney in 1940 they worked with New Theatre for a short time before moving to Brisbane, then Darwin in October 1941, where Hector took over as editor of trade union newspaper *The Northern Standard* from Gordon Burgoyne. Hector also served as a roving Darwin press correspondent. He and Beechey intended to spend two years in Darwin, but four months after their arrival the Japanese bombed Darwin and their home took a direct hit. Hector was the only correspondent in Darwin at the time. He subsequently enlisted and served in New Guinea with the Australian Army Education Service (AAES), producing a daily news-sheet,

Jungle News, for the troops. On his return from active service he moved to Melbourne where he wrote a foreign affairs column for distinguished AAES journal *SALT*, of which he became a subeditor and later assistant editor. Between 1946 and 1950, Hector was employed by the Department of Defence as an Australian correspondent on a daily newspaper produced for the Commonwealth Occupation Force in Japan. He was a vocal AJA activist and, as such, found many newspaper doors closed to him. He worked on various trade magazines, including a stint as editor of the poultry producers' journal, a defacto CPA organ. Beechey had to wait on Hepworth's return from active service before she was able to divorce him in 1946 (after Hepworth had 'obligingly committed bigamy') and marry John Hector.[26] One of their sons would later work with John Hepworth on the journal *Nation Review*.

John Hepworth (1921–1995) served with the AIF in the Middle East, Ceylon and New Guinea under the alias 'John Hale Davidson'.

> I served for five years as a private soldier, and maintained my rank with considerable difficulty.[27]

He was discharged from 2/2nd Battalion of the Australian Infantry in November 1945 and returned to Sydney New Theatre. He was arrested on a charge of bigamy and received a two-year good behaviour bond. In 1947 he wrote *The Long Green Shore*, a war novel set in New Guinea, which won second prize and a commendation in the 1949 *Sydney Morning Herald* literary competition. UK publisher Macmillan rejected it, perhaps because there was little taste at the time for novels about the War so recently ended. In the early 1950s Hepworth lived in Newcastle in New South Wales with his wife Oriel Gray (1920–2003) and their two children, while working as an ABC news roundsman. The Attorney-General's Department and ASIO again made enquiries into his activities because:

> it is claimed that during the recent coal strike news supplied by Hepworth to the ABC bore a distinct Communist bias. It is said also, that his superiors in the Commission are aware of his activities but cannot take action because of possible repercussions from the Australian Journalists Association.[28]

Hepworth left the CPA during the 1949 coal strike. He was extremely critical of the CPA's divisive tactics designed to disrupt the Chifley Labor government during the strike. This followed his censure by the CPA in 1947 for 'lacking faith' in the central committee.[29] ABC management seems also to have pressured Hepworth to curb his political activities.[30] In 1952 he transferred to Melbourne as a general reporter and subeditor with the ABC, and joined Melbourne New Theatre. In 1958 he played in the Melbourne New Theatre production of his wife Oriel Gray's play *The Torrents* — joint winner, with Ray Lawler's *Summer of the Seventeenth Doll*, of the 1955 Playwrights' Advisory Board best play. Hepworth wrote material for Melbourne New Theatre and was involved in its 'mobile theatre' unit taking performances to the suburbs. He spent twenty years working for the ABC news department, mainly as a subeditor, after which he began what he later described as a 'splendid decade' as a staff writer on the journal *Nation Review*, where he became known for his 'Outsight' column.[31] In 1974 he received a Literature Board Fellowship and returned to Perth, on his way to London, where he sought out old Workers' Art Guild colleagues.

Plays written by John Hepworth include *The Beast in View* (1959), *The Last of the Rainbow* (1962) and *My Aunt the Unicorn* (1966). In 1978, he published *John Hepworth ... His Book*, in which Morris Lurie described him as a 'genuine Australian original' and a 'national treasure'. Hepworth also wrote a number of children's books including *Little Australian Library* (1983), *Paper Boy* (with Bob Ellis, 1985; later made into a film), *Colonial Capers* (1986), *Multitude of Tigers* (1990) and *Big Wish* (1990) (with playwright Steve J. Spears). His children's book *Birds and Beasties of Australia* sold 150,000 copies. He also co-wrote (with John Hindle) *Boozing Out in Melbourne Pubs: An Occasional History and Sociological Study of Melbourne as Seen through the Bottom of a Glass* (1980) and *Around the Bend* (1983), which documented a raft trip down the Murray River undertaken by the pair with ABC producer Patrick Amer. Hepworth was also a contributing writer for television programs including *Prisoner*, *House Rules* and *Liftoff* (1992), and co-wrote screenplays with Bob Ellis and with his son Peter Hepworth.

John Hepworth again remarried and was forced to give up the bottle when his health deteriorated in the mid-1980s. In November 1994 *The Age* reported that 'at the age of 73, and after 100 years spent living life to the full, John Hepworth is dying. It's cancer that will take away this journalist, gadfly and man-about-town.'[32] Hepworth — enfant terrible, journalist, author, playwright and poet — died of lung cancer in Melbourne in January 1995 at the age of seventy-three. The publication of his novel *The Long Green Shore* was announced a few days before his death. This was the great novel he had planned to write when he had moved to Sydney in the 1940s, and it was received with deserved acclaim. His obituary in *The Age*, published the day after his death, reported that 'he turned dying into an art form ... Theatrical by inclination, he was determined to die in his own bed with his hat on ... Hepworth was splendid while dying. Dressed in a magnificent nightshirt, and wearing a Victorian smoking cap, he entertained the friends who had come to say goodbye.'[33] He had arranged his own BYO funeral to be held on the front garden of his Toorak home, at which his pre-recorded valedictory speech was played to the assembled mourners, self-eulogising beyond the end.[34] He was well known, loved and loathed in Australian journalism and bohemian literary circles, and his death was widely reported in publications from metropolitan newspapers to populist magazines.[35] Following a 2001 report in Hollywood film journal *Variety* that *The Long, Green Shore* was being planned for a major film production to be produced and directed by Russell Crowe, a rush of orders led to a reprint of the novel by Pan Macmillan.

Edward (Bill) Irwin (1908–1995) enlisted in March 1942 but was 'manpowered' out of military service, serving instead in the Volunteer Defence Corps. He retained his position as chief subeditor and leader writer on the *Daily News* through most of the War.[36] He was a leading member of the Anti-Fascist League in Western Australia. In 1944 he took up a three-year appointment to the New York office of Australian Associated Press, a posting arranged by Geoffrey Burgoyne (Gordon Burgoyne's father). In November 1947 he returned to Perth with his wife **Dorothy Irwin** (1897–1988) to write *A Geographical Survey of Central Australia*, and in 1948 he was appointed to Melbourne's *The Herald* and as the Melbourne correspondent for Perth's *Daily News*. He remained in Melbourne until 1965.

Bill and Dorothy Irwin were frozen out of the CPA in 1956. The couple were shaken by Khrushchev's denunciation of Stalin at the 20th Congress, and deliberated over a crisis of conscience about leaving the Party.[37] Bill's friend and long-time Party member Ken Gott was expelled from the CPA for distributing Khrushchev's 'secret' speech and criticism of Soviet forays into Poland and Hungary. Bill Irwin and prominent Australian Communist academic Ian Turner denounced the Party's treatment of Gott, for which Turner was expelled from the CPA. Irwin was interviewed three times by the CPA's control commission, castigated for publicly supporting Gott and subsequently ostracised by the Party.[38] Twenty years later, Irwin wrote to Gott of the shock of that time when many political idealists were shaken by the

Khrushchev revelations, 'the disenchantment of the Communists — storming heaven, to find death camps — was something without precedent in scope and horror'.[39] In 1966 Irwin travelled to Europe and worked on London's Fleet Street as a reporter for Reuters. He returned to Perth in 1968 and was appointed as an editorial consultant for West Australian Newspapers. He retired from newspapers in March 1972 after forty-five years in journalism, mainly in the employ of West Australian Newspapers.

The Irwins' wide circle of friends included Wilfred Burchett, Leslie Rees, Bernie Taft, Frank Hardy, Vance and Nettie Palmer and Dorothy Hewett. Bill was a prominent member of Amnesty International and was made an honorary life member of the Fellowship of Australian Writers. After Dorothy's death, Bill became more involved in the political struggles of Indigenous Western Australians. Although frail and blind for the last few years of his life, he remained politically active until his death in Perth at the age of eighty-six.[40]

Alexander (Alec) King (1904–1970) was a member of the editorial board of *Westerly* until 1966. He left UWA in 1965 after thirty-five years as a lecturer and reader in the English Department, and took up an appointment to the English Chair at Monash University in Melbourne. He retired in 1969. He was well known as a radio broadcaster and literary critic.

Herbert McClintock (1906–1985) shifted to social realist art during the War. He continued his work as a cartoonist on the CPA's *The Tribune* and trade union publications. In 1943 he was appointed an official war artist alongside William Dobell. He was a founding member (with John Oldham and Hal Missingham) of the Studio of Realist Art (SORA) in 1945 — a political breakaway from the Contemporary Art Society.[41] McClintock was a regular arts contributor to CPA journals until the early 1970s, and for several years he produced banners for May Day marches. He remained a member of the Communist Party for the rest of his life and served on the CPA central committee in the 1950s. A major retrospective exhibition of his work was held in Melbourne in 1980.

Harold (Hal) Missingham (1906–1994) moved to Sydney in 1941 where he worked as a graphic designer and film director. In 1944 he co-founded SORA in Sydney with John Oldham and Herbert McClintock.[42] After his discharge from the AIF in 1945 he was appointed director of the Art Gallery of New South Wales, a post he held for twenty-six years until his retirement in 1971. He continued to practise as a photographer and his writing was published widely. In 1973 he and his wife Esther moved back to Darlington in the Perth hills, and he published his autobiography, *They Kill You in the End*. He was awarded the Order of Australia in 1978. In 1986 his Darlington studio was destroyed in a bushfire and with it his life's work in photography, comprising more than 10,000 negatives. He was shattered and subsequently suffered a series of strokes that left him blind. He died in Perth aged eighty-eight.[43]

Wilfred (Bill) Mountjoy (born 1901) was sacked from the CPA central committee 'for liberalism and lack of vigilance in his leadership of the W.A. Party organisation'.[44] On his return to Sydney in 1940 he worked as a brickmaker in the North Sydney brickworks and was the Canberra correspondent for *The Tribune* in the mid-1940s.

Francis (Frank) O'Grady (1910–?) continued to perform with the Repertory Club in Perth before serving with the AIF's Field Ambulance in Malaya. He was taken prisoner when Singapore fell to the Japanese in February 1942 and sent to the notorious Changi prison camp, where he would spend the long remaining years of the War. He was recovered from Changi in September 1945, a few days before the official surrender of the Japanese Army at Singapore. His old friend Dorothy Rowe wrote of meeting him on his return to Sydney:

> I will never forget the wait on the wharf, the searching for his face among all those emaciated, hopeful men lined up on deck, and the quiet excitement of the nervous crowd of the men's families on the wharves, who seemed to be holding their breath. At last Frankie came ashore and after the first shock of his ravaged appearance, and his weird yellow boots, we bore him off to our friend's place. He stood in the dining room and glanced at the food, but his fingers touched the afternoon tea cloth and he said 'Lace, a lace cloth' and his eyes filled with tears.[45]

O'Grady returned to Western Australia where he was hospitalised for a few months and discharged from the Army in December 1945.[46] He again trod the boards with Dorothy Rowe in the eastern states but died within a few years, his health ravaged by his imprisonment at Changi.

John Oldham (1907–1999) was a member of the Contemporary Art Society in Sydney and a member (in 1944) of The Constructivists group of artists that included Grace Crowley, Frank Hinder, Gerald Ryan and Ralph Balson. He was a foundation member, with Hal Missingham and Herbert McClintock, of SORA in Sydney in 1945, and was elected president of SORA in 1948. Oldham and his wife Ray were elected to CPA body the People's Council for Culture, and were peripherally involved in Sydney New Theatre. In 1943, Nugget Coombs, a confidant of then prime minister Ben Chifley, invited Oldham to join the new Ministry of Post-War Reconstruction, which Coombs headed, as a housing and town planning consultant. By 1945 Oldham had moved into the lucrative position of exhibitions officer in the Ministry of Post-War Reconstruction and he designed a number of exhibitions praised by his political masters, including Chifley. Oldham was appointed to the Joint Coal Board to help stimulate coal production and plan improvements in the amenities and conditions of coal miners, but his proposals were not heeded. The federal government failed to honour its promises to the miners and Oldham resigned in protest before Chifley sent troops into the coalmines to break a major strike in 1949.

In the early 1950s Oldham joined the Snowy Mountains Hydro-Electric Authority, then undertaking the massive project of building dams and power stations in the New South Wales snowfields, where Oldham oversaw the Snowy Mountains Scheme architectural drawing office in Cooma. Isolated from the CPA, the Oldhams drifted away from the Party.[47]

In 1954 the Oldhams returned to Perth, where John became Australia's first full-time landscape architect. In 1956 he took up the government position of State Landscape Architect, working on a number of major government projects. He designed the landscaping for the Narrows Bridge interchange on the Kwinana Freeway and for the Serpentine Dam. In 1959 he was appointed a member of the Grand Council of the International Federation of Landscape Architects, and served as vice-president of the Australian branch from 1973 until 1977. His honours include an Order of Australia Medal, citations from the Australian Institute of Landscape Architects and the International Federation of Landscape Architects, and membership of the prestigious American Society of Landscape Architects. He was founding president of the Conservation Council and led a push to save many of Perth's historically significant buildings from demolition. John and Ray Oldham were the authors of three books on landscape and colonial architecture. John Oldham is represented in the collection of the Art Gallery of Western Australia.[48] In 2000, John Oldham Park in Perth was named in his honour.

After her return to Perth in 1954, **Ruby (Ray) Oldham** (1911–2005) initiated the preservation of the state's notable historic buildings, and co-wrote with her husband John an evaluation of Western Australian colonial architecture titled *Western Heritage: A Study of the Colonial Architecture of Perth, WA*. She continued her career as a journalist, being appointed the architecture and Perth society correspondent for *Vogue, Australia Today* and *The West Australian*. She was also a regular columnist for Perth's Murdoch-owned *Sunday Times* newspaper, and penned the newspaper's architecture column for a decade. She was a qualified landscape architect and both she and her husband John were foundation members in 1956 of the Western Australian branch of the National Trust. Ray Oldham was a long-term council member of the Royal Western Australian Historical Society (serving as president from 1983 to 1985) and a member of the Western Australian branch of the Fellowship of Australian Writers.[49] She was also awarded an Order of Australia.

Kathleen Phyllis (Phyl) Ophel (formerly Harnett) (1907–2000) became inactive in Communist Party circles during the War and lived in relative isolation in South Australia as a childcare nurse.[50] She moonlighted in radio drama in Adelaide where she helped form a theatre company. After the War she moved to Melbourne, where she remarried. She joined the Arts Theatre in Carlton and was involved with Melbourne New Theatre from the late 1940s into the 1960s as an actor and director. She directed and performed in a 1947 Melbourne New Theatre production of Ric Throssell's adaptation of 1939 Soviet play *The Ordinary Man* by Russian dramatist Leonid Leonov, but became critical of Melbourne New Theatre's concentration on polemical theatre and left. She also left the CPA in the mid-1960s — or, more accurately, it left her. She was a friend to many of the leading lights of the art and theatre world, including infamous Sydney eccentric 'Bee' Miles (1901–1973). One of the legendary stories about Miles is of her catching a taxi from Sydney to Perth and back to visit Ophel. Ophel appeared as pub owner 'Ivy' in Australian film *Sunday Too Far Away*, alongside Jack Thompson (John and Pat Thompson's adopted son). She also appeared in episodes of the television series *Bellbird* in which her son, Gerard Kennedy, was a regular cast member. Ophel acted in the ABC television series *Lucky Colour Blue* and played bit parts in *Homicide*, as well as performing in the theatre. She was a bright, exuberant and fascinating person until her death at the age of ninety-two.

Irene Osterberg (formerly Keiller) (1910–1997) moved to Sydney in 1940 with her husband **Albert Osterberg** (1897–1974). Her daughter

Katherine, named after Katharine Susannah Prichard, wrote of Irene Osterberg after her death:

> Later, on a trip to Ireland, she visited the place where the Irish poet Thomas Moore, b. 1779, had written his poem, 'The Meeting of the Waters', and recalled her volume of Moore's poetry, seized in the police raid of 1940 and never returned. At the end of her life, when other memories were dimming, she still spoke of her time with the Workers' Art Guild in Perth, and the people she had known there, with great fondness and pleasure.[51]

(Harold) Axel Poignant (1906–1986) made an early colour film on Western Australia's Canning Stock Route in 1942. He joined a camel expedition to check the wells along the stock route, a trek undertaken as a precautionary measure after the bombing of Darwin by the Japanese, in the event of stock having to be moved south following a possible Japanese invasion of the north. It was on this trek that he encountered Aboriginal people working on the cattle stations, and they were to become the central subjects of his photography.[52] Poignant left the expedition when it reached Lake Disappointment and returned to Perth, where he married Ruth Petterson.[53] He then enlisted in the Army, and the couple moved to Sydney. He spent two years in the Army processing radar film before his release towards the end of the War to work as an assistant cameraman on *The Overlanders*, a feature film shot in the Northern Territory, produced by the British Ealing studios. Poignant worked for the Commonwealth Department of Information as a movie photographer in the 1940s and 1950s. In 1948 he worked as the stills photographer on Harry Watt's film *Eureka Stockade*, and published his first book, *Bush Animals of Australia*. He travelled widely throughout Australia as a freelance photographer for Australian and American clients and journals, including *Life* magazine, *Encyclopaedia Britannica* and the Department of Information, and his photographs were published regularly in prestigious journal *U.S. Camera*.[54] In 1952, with the help of Paul Hasluck, then federal minister for territories, Poignant undertook a long photographic study of a group of Aboriginal people from Arnhem Land that produced a wealth of material including a children's book, *Piccaninny Walkabout* (1957), which was named Australian Children's Picture Book of the Year.[55]

Poignant and Petterson divorced in 1953. Poignant remarried and moved to London in 1956, where he worked as picture editor for *The Times* and as a freelance photographer for a number of English newspapers and for BBC television. In the 1970s Poignant published another two children's books. A retrospective exhibition of his photography was held at the Art Gallery of New South Wales in 1982, and he died in London four years later. An extensive posthumous exhibition of his work was held in Stockholm in 1988–1989. His photography is represented in a number of collections and major art galleries in Australia, England and Germany. In 1996 a book of Poignant's photographs of Aboriginal people from the Northern Territory, *Encounter at Nagalarramba (1952)*, was published. He is probably now best known for his iconic 'Swagman' photograph.

Katharine Susannah Prichard (1883–1969) was elected to the CPA central committee in June 1943.[56] She moved to Sydney and lived in a flat in Darlinghurst from 1943 until 1946, when she resigned from the central committee and returned to Perth. A number of prominent writers were then living in and around the Kings Cross area, including Mary Gilmore, Marjorie Barnard and Flora Eldershaw, and Prichard's time in neighbouring Darlinghurst was a welcome contrast to her isolation at Greenmount.

The instalments of her goldfields trilogy of novels were published in 1946, 1948 and 1950, respectively, the initial volume being her first serious novel in a decade. In the early 1950s she began work on her autobiography, which was eventually published in 1964 under the title *Child of the Hurricane*. In 1956, having returned to Greenmount and recuperating from a heart attack she had suffered earlier that year, Prichard wrote nostalgically to her friend Spencer Brodney about their discussions on drama and literature in earlier times in London:

> There I was, sitting on my verandah, under a trellis of vines, with jacarandas and le laurier rose in bloom alongside, thinking back to those days when it didn't seem possible that our dreams would come true. So many of mine have, I'm mostly grateful for the wonderful experiences life has given me. First of all being part of this country and its people, then, politically, having 'seen the light' so long ago, and in my husband and son found such marvellous understanding and companionship. Unbelievable, that my work has had such a success d'estime also! The novels published in twelve of the languages of Europe, and I've just heard of short stories being translated into Chinese which I'm thrilled about. Of course, I'm not approved of in the U.S.A. just now, but that does not grieve me. Three of the early novels were published in New

> York and had a good press, but nothing sensational in the way of sales. Not that I've ever been interested in sales so much as doing in writing what I wanted to — although it has always been necessary to earn a crust. The crusts, these days, in foreign royalties, have been very pleasant ... How can we be tired of politics? They are so much a part of our lives. Philosophy, psychology, cosmology, dependant [sic] on the right to think and work for the best and highest purposes in life. So much better to live in the breakers than to let the waves throw you up on the beach with driftwood ... a little tired sometimes and ready for the long farewell. [57]

Six months earlier, artist Noel Counihan had visited Prichard at Greenmount and written of her as 'an idealistic and lonely figure here, not understood by those who should be helping her'.[58] In 1960 Prichard was awarded the Joliot-Curie peace medal. Her health improved and she resumed a characteristically busy routine. In 1962 a mutual friend, Isla Marsh, wrote to Spencer Brodney that she had stayed for a few days with Prichard at Greenmount and 'spent hours over cups of tea and a wood fire, digging up the past'.

> The house is old, unpretentious and personal — full of books, and pictures that have been given to her. Katharine is white-haired and delicate — she suffers from high blood pressure. But she is remarkably active and independent — lives by herself up there which of course she should not do. Her mind is very alert and flexible, her voice young, and her memory extraordinarily good. She goes out to various meetings and sometimes speaks in public.[59]

Living alone at Greenmount became more difficult for Prichard as she became increasingly frail and in 1965, a companion and helper joined her there.[60] She continued to quietly support writers, artists, political figures and others, including pianist David Helfgott. The 'long farewell' came to its conclusion on 2 October 1969, two months before Prichard's eighty-sixth birthday. She died at the moment her son's flight from the eastern states touched down at Perth airport, having listened for its descent over the hills above her home on his return home to see her. The following day, CPA secretary Laurie Aarons paid tribute:

> Her death removes a towering figure from Australia's literature. She had a great influence on Australian writing and the socialist and communist movements in Australia.[61]

Prichard's ashes were scattered on the Greenmount hillside where she had lived, almost uninterrupted, for fifty years.

Katharine Susannah Prichard's Greenmount property has been preserved as the Katharine Susannah Prichard Writers' Centre for writers and artists. The hedge where she hid her tin trunk full of potentially incriminating material during the CPA's illegal period still remains. The trunk itself is still stored at the house. The writing shed, with its shelves carefully labelled in Prichard's hand, also remains. Prichard insisted that her unpublished writing be destroyed on her death. 'I do not like to be seen in déshabillé even in manuscript,' she wrote. Her son Ric Throssell somewhat reluctantly carried out her wish, destroying virtually all her personal papers, though fortunately some material survived.

George Ronald (Ron) Richards (1904–1984) was seconded in 1942 to the Commonwealth Security Service overseeing Western Australia. After the War he returned to routine police duties, but his reputation saw him rapidly rise up the ranks. In 1949 he was appointed to establish the Western Australian branch of the Australian Security Intelligence Organisation (ASIO), and in 1950 he was employed as an ASIO officer. Richards was promoted from his position as regional director of ASIO's Perth office to director of operations in ASIO's New South Wales office, from there to NSW regional director and then, in 1954, to director of operations and deputy director-general of ASIO, effectively making him operational head of the peak intelligence organisation. As such, he took charge of the Petrov case.

Vladimir Petrov and his wife Evdokia were middle-ranking officials in the Soviet Embassy in Canberra. In a series of secret meetings over six weeks, Richards gained Vladimir Petrov's confidence and together they planned Petrov's defection to Australia, which took place in April 1954. Documents Petrov furnished to ASIO named three members of the staff of the Department of External Affairs overseen by 'Doc' Evatt, then leader of the federal Labor opposition, as being Soviet informers.[62] This led to a split in the ALP, which kept the Party out of federal government for seventeen years. The report of the Petrov Royal Commission in October 1955 stated that two Soviet spies had been operating from inside the Department of External Affairs between 1945 and 1948. The Venona cables later released confirmed this. Richards's reputation as a 'ruthless ASIO spymaster' saw him awarded an OBE in 1957.[63] He continued to thwart the Throssell family, impeding Ric Throssell's attempts at promotion in the Commonwealth public service. Richards resigned as deputy director of ASIO in 1965 but remained with ASIO in an advisory role. He retired in 1969 and returned to Perth, where he died aged eighty. He is buried at Karrakatta Cemetery.[64] The character of 'Sergeant Ron Redmond' in Frank Hardy's semi-biographical novel *Power without Glory* was based on Ron Richards.[65]

Arthur Rudkin (1908–1994) was appointed to the committee of the Western Australian division of the Australian Association of Scientific Workers (AASW), and in the late 1940s was elected as a federal AASW council delegate. In 1945, Rudkin moved to Melbourne to take up a position in the laboratory of the Forest Products division of CSIR (the Council for Scientific and Industrial Research — precursor to CSIRO), and he remained active in the Communist Party.[66] In March 1947 the minister responsible for CSIR, John Dedman, was questioned in federal parliament about Rudkin's employment, given his involvement with the CPA and his earlier jailing in Perth. Rudkin was accused in federal parliament of treachery and described as 'a bad security risk'. The Chifley government was pressured to set up a security review of CSIR. CSIR was involved in highly sensitive atomic energy research with the United States, and a rumour took hold that the United States government would not entrust certain classified information to the Australian government given United States concerns that CSIR was not sufficiently under Australian government control and accusations that there were 'fifth columnists' in its scientific ranks. The government relieved CSIR of much of its sensitive work and Rudkin, in spite of his reputation as 'a brilliant chemist', was blacklisted in 1948 and dismissed from CSIR.[67] It was not until some thirty years later that he learned of the political motive for his dismissal.[68]

In 1950 the Rudkin family moved to Sydney, where Arthur joined the Sydney New Theatre choir. He also left the CPA at that time, for reasons he never disclosed.[69] His loyalty to the Communist Party had probably come at too great a cost. Cold War political prejudice again led to his forced resignation from the Sydney Metropolitan Water Board. He remained active within Sydney New Theatre for the rest of his life, performed in many of its plays between 1953 and 1978, was elected to its committee of management and became president in the early 1960s. He also played roles in a number of television dramas, including *Matlock Police*, as well in feature films, including *The Great McCarthy* (1975) and *Mad Dog Morgan* (1976). Rudkin retired from the Physics Department of the University of New South Wales in 1984, and was invested with honorary life membership of Sydney New Theatre.

In 1946, **Josiah (Joe) Skinner** (1891–?) married **Rose Dvoretsky (Atkinson)**, who was the model for the main character of Elodie Blackman in Katharine Susannah Prichard's 1937 novel *Intimate Strangers* (Dvoretsky's former husband Les Atkinson was the model for the character of Greg Blackman). Joe and Rose Skinner opened the Skinner Galleries in Perth in October 1958 and became significant patrons of the fine arts in Western Australia.[70]

Howard Smith (1913–1985) married the Workers' Art Guild's Marjorie Berry. He joined the Repertory Club in 1942, where he continued to perform and direct, and was elected to the committee of the Repertory Club in the late 1940s. He was later a member of professional theatre group Company of Four, precursor to the National Theatre in Perth, and he served on the board of the Playhouse Theatre. He was inaugural chairman of the Western Australian Arts Orchestral Foundation and a devoted supporter of community theatre. Following his death in 1985, his obituary in *The West Australian* noted that he 'kept such a low profile that no public honour was bestowed on him, but community theatre companies will cherish his memory'.[71]

Richard (Ric) Throssell (1922–1999) enlisted for overseas service with the AIF in 1942 and fought during the infamous battle against Japanese forces at Milne Bay in New Guinea later that year. He was discharged from active service in 1943, partly facilitated by his mother, to take up a position at the Department of External Affairs in Canberra as a diplomatic staff cadet, where he renewed his association with John Curtin and Paul Hasluck. Throssell's mother did what she could to shift her son away from active service to a diplomatic posting and was helped by her contacts within the Curtin government, particularly by her close relationship with attorney-general and minister for external affairs 'Doc' Evatt. Her motives were, presumably, simply those of a mother concerned about the welfare of her only child, but they were later suspected of being something altogether more sinister, given that Prichard had lobbied to have Ric posted to the Australian Embassy in Moscow after his release from the Army. As it turned out, these suspicions were found later to have been misplaced. Prichard had told Australian Soviet agent Walter Clayton that she wanted Throssell posted to Moscow, but Clayton had thought it would be more advantageous to the Communist Party if he were posted to Europe.[72] It seems Throssell's posting to Moscow itself had little to do with his mother, but may instead have been organised to expose Throssell to the horrors of Soviet life in an attempt to dissuade him from Communist activism.

Towards the end of the War, Throssell, Curtin and Hasluck worked together in drafting Australia's post-War geopolitical strategic plans, with Hasluck serving as Throssell's supervisor in the Post-Hostilities Planning Division of the Department of External Affairs. Throssell and Hasluck were also active members of the Canberra Repertory Society, formed in 1944, until Throssell took up a Moscow posting in 1945. From 1944, the British MI5 security service had detected security leaks from Canberra to Moscow that they believed originated from a spy ring within the Department of External Affairs, and Ric Throssell quickly came under suspicion. In the late 1940s, MI5 and the CIA, decoding cables sent between Canberra and Moscow, uncovered the identities of figures mentioned in the cables. The cables revealed that Soviet agents had abandoned attempts to recruit Ric Throssell, probably because he was the son of such a prominent Communist. British and American spy-catchers pressured then prime minister Ben Chifley to establish a security intelligence organisation to deal with the security threat. ASIO was established and its immediate priority was to expose the members of the Canberra spy ring. Throssell was initially cleared of suspicion by ASIO; however, when Menzies won the federal election on a pledge to quell the perceived Communist threat within Australia, Throssell again became a pawn in the game. Ron Richards, by then a senior ASIO figure, was tasked with uncovering this suspected espionage ring and nothing would dispel his suspicions that his old foes, the Prichard–Throssell family, were involved. Richards suspected that Prichard had deliberately orchestrated Ric's appointment to the Department of External Affairs (which was indeed true) and that she had then used her influence to have Ric posted to Moscow. ASIO began a thorough investigation of Ric Throssell, and his fate was sealed. He was from that point on, as *The West Australian* later put it, 'one of the walking dead'.[73]

From 1945 to 1946, Throssell, recently married, served as third secretary to the Australian Legation in Moscow, where his wife died of polio. He returned to Canberra in 1946, resumed his association with the Canberra Repertory Society and remarried in 1947. In 1948 the Canberra Repertory Society staged Throssell's play *Valley of the Shadows*, and between 1948 and 1953 Throssell wrote other plays including *Highly Confidential, Babes At Arms* and *Standing Room Only*. He was posted to the Australian Embassy in Rio de Janeiro from 1949 until 1952, but after Menzies returned to office in 1949, Throssell had his security clearance restricted by the Commonwealth Investigation Service.[74] There were still firmly held suspicions that he was active in an Australian spy ring reporting to Soviet agents. ASIO officers interviewed him in 1949 and reported that he was not a threat to national security. Extensive investigations in 1951 found nothing to incriminate Throssell, but Richards recommended that 'while there is not sufficient evidence to debar him from employment, it is certainly evident that he should not have access to anything of even a secret nature'.[75] In 1953 Throssell was again put under ASIO surveillance and interviewed by ASIO officers, who concluded that he was 'neither a communist nor pro-Russian in outlook'.[76] Throssell was aggressively grilled by ASIO again in July 1954, and he continued to deny that he had ever been a member of the CPA or involved in any criminal activity. Richards remained unconvinced. A 1954 ASIO report described Throssell as 'most unlike what one would expect from a member of the diplomatic corps':

> He wore a cheap, badly fitting pale blue suit. His hair, collar and tie and shoes were most untidy [and] he was not wearing a black tie as other members of the department were on the account of the period of mourning of the death of Queen Mary.[77]

When Vladimir Petrov defected in April 1954, Richards was assigned as his minder, confidant and inquisitor. Petrov and his wife unconvincingly identified Throssell as an 'agent of the Soviet Union'. Petrov fell for the charms of Richards, as had many others before him, and Richards's obvious interest in implicating Throssell led Petrov, seemingly, to embellish Throssell's involvement in the KLOD Soviet spy ring. Throssell subsequently endured another week of questioning by ASIO. A month after Petrov's defection, Throssell was barred from direct access to secret material within the Department of External Affairs, which put paid to his chances of promotion and effectively barred him from working in policy formulation areas within the department. Throssell appeared before the 1954–1955 Petrov Royal Commission, which dismissed allegations of spying against him as 'hearsay', but the allegations would shadow him until his death. His appearance before the Royal Commission received widespread media coverage and, despite his exoneration, his public reputation was irrevocably tarnished and his career dramatically affected by enduring speculation. He was to be continually denied the high security clearance he required for promotion within the ranks of the Department of External Affairs and later the Department of Foreign Affairs. Throssell described the thirty years that followed the Petrov Royal Commission as 'real Kafka country':

> I was fighting shadows right until the time I retired. I tried every turn I could to answer it — they wouldn't tell you what the charges were against you ... you were blocked at every turn.[78]

Having been repeatedly passed over for significant promotion since 1955, Throssell sought the help of Hasluck, then the federal minister for external affairs. Hasluck made enquiries but was unable to provide any satisfaction for Throssell.[79] Throssell applied for promotion forty-four times during his career, and for forty years ASIO blocked his promotion.

In the early 1970s, Whitlam government attorney-general Lionel Murphy contacted Throssell to say he was disturbed by what he saw as injustices visited on Throssell and he promised to look into the case, but Throssell heard no more of it. Alan Renouf, head of the Department of Foreign Affairs, then attempted to have the documents pertaining to Throssell's case furnished to Ric, but was warned by ASIO that the release of the documents would be a major breach of national intelligence and would compromise Australia's relationship with allied governments. Renouf told Throssell that he was an 'intelligence pawn and a victim of it', but was able to reassure Throssell that the offending documents that had interminably impeded Throssell's career and smeared his reputation did not reflect on Throssell's integrity.[80] During a 1972 interview with ASIO, Throssell was told that 'the case would never be completely closed against him'.[81] This was as much, and as little, as Throssell would know of the case against him for another twenty-four years.

At the end of his career, Throssell served as assistant secretary in charge of the cultural relations branch of the Department of Foreign Affairs, and in 1980 he was appointed director of the Commonwealth Foundation in London, a post he held until his retirement from the Department of Foreign Affairs in 1983.

Throssell, a protégé of Keith George, was a theatre director and a prolific playwright whose work was produced by Australian and overseas theatre companies. His plays include *The Day Before Tomorrow* (1956), a cautionary tale reflecting the fears of the atomic age, and *For Valour*, which loosely depicts his father's decline after returning home from the First World War; the latter won the 1959 Mary Gilmore Award and was described by Keith George as 'one of the finest pieces of dramatic writing Australia has produced'.[82] Throssell was awarded a Commonwealth Literary Fund Fellowship in 1958.

Throssell also wrote a number of pieces for television, and published four novels: *A Reliable Source*, *In a Wilderness of Mirrors*, *Tomorrow* and

Jackpot. In 1975 he wrote a biography of his mother titled *Wild Weeds and Wind Flowers*, and in 1989 he published *My Father's Son*, a moving account of his father and a chronicle of his own life and his attempts to clear his name.

In 1996 the mystery of Throssell's thwarted attempts at promotion was revealed when the US government released the Venona decryption cables — the records of Soviet radio communications between Moscow and its overseas diplomatic missions — in which Throssell was named on three occasions, relatively innocuously.[83] Hysterical media speculation again followed the release of the intelligence cables. Throssell's photo appeared alongside that of infamous British spies Burgess and Philby on the front page of *The Courier-Mail*, and the newspaper labelled him a 'suspected Russian agent'.[84] His photograph was also published on the front page of *The Australian* under the headline 'Confirmed: Our Soviet Spies', despite the fact that the newspaper reported that Throssell was 'not suspected of spying'.[85] The cables clearly show that the Soviets were interested in recruiting Throssell, but there is no evidence of his collusion with the Soviets. Throssell had never been a member of the CPA, and he believed that the release of the Venona cables vindicated him. 'The Cold War is generally thought to have ended,' *The Canberra Times* reported in December 1996, 'but not for Ric Throssell'.[86] An updated edition of Throssell's book *My Father's Son*, subtitled *The Last Knot Untied*, was published in 1997 after the release of the Venona cables.

The publication in 1998 of Desmond Ball and David Horner's controversial intelligence exposé *Breaking the Codes: Australia's KGB Network 1944–1950* rekindled speculation that Throssell had passed information to the Soviets. Again he had to endure slurs and gossip.[87] Throssell claimed he was an unwitting victim of a paranoid intelligence organisation, but he never publicly expressed any bitterness about it.

In April 1999, Throssell's wife died after a long illness. Like his father before him, Ric Throssell took his own life, in line with an arrangement the couple had made.[88] He was seventy-six.

The day after Throssell's death, senator Kate Lundy, addressing the federal senate, described the intelligence campaign against Throssell as a 'witch-hunt'.[89] The Throssells' combined obituary in *The Age*, written by the newspaper's deputy editor, was titled 'Lives of Grace under Fire':

> Their lives were a microcosm of Australian history, from greatness to tragedy. They were haunted by a smear from the time of the Petrov Royal Commission … Left behind is a remarkable

Australian family story, one with an unequal share of tragedy, but also bravery, intrigue, political passion, astonishing creative flair, and old-fashioned, mulish stubbornness.[90]

Throssell's obituary in Melbourne's *Herald Sun* appeared under the heading 'Petrov Spy Figure Dies'.[91]

Harald Vike (1906–1987) shunned the art establishment, but the craft of painting 'absolutely sustained' him until his death.[92] In 1945 he was employed as a newspaper cartoonist on the *Australasian Post*. He befriended artist and art critic Alan McCulloch (1907–1992) and artist Len Annois (1906–1966), and the trio frequently undertook painting trips. From 1949 to 1950, Vike drew caricatures for the Melbourne *Argus* (then edited by George Johnston, author of *My Brother Jack*), and between 1949 and 1955 he worked as a set designer for Melbourne's Luna Park and Palais and Princess theatres. In the mid-1950s, artist Lina Bryans gave Vike the use of her expansive studio in East Melbourne.[93] Vike was employed as a scenic artist at television station HSV-7 in Melbourne from 1958 to 1965, and again from 1967 to 1971.[94] In the intervening period he travelled around Australia on a painting trip. He and Joan Vike had separated in 1956, and he remarried in 1965. After his retirement he moved to Adelaide, and later to Brisbane. In 1983 he joined the Franklin River blockade in Tasmania, where he sketched and painted protesters. He returned to Perth in 1986, where he died of cancer soon afterwards.

Vike held a number of solo exhibitions around Australia from the 1940s onwards. His work is held in the collections of the Australian National Gallery, the Art Gallery of Western Australia, the Tasmanian Museum and Art Gallery, the National Gallery of Victoria and the University of Western Australia, as well as in the Holmes à Court and overseas collections. He left behind more than 2000 artworks purchased in 1988 by Kingstream Fine Art in Perth for $1.5 million. Major retrospectives of Vike's art have been held since his death, including a 1990 exhibition at the Art Gallery of Western Australia.

Jerold Wells (1908–1999) returned to Sydney New Theatre where he continued to direct plays until 1948. He later became a successful film and television character actor in England, appearing in films including Joseph Losey's *The Criminal* (1960), Terry Gilliam's *Jabberwocky* (1977) and *Time Bandits* (1981), and Lars von Trier's *The Element of Crime* (1985). He also appeared in episodes of *The Benny Hill Show* and *Hancock's Half-Hour*.

Victor (Vic) Williams (1914–2011) served with the AIF in Darwin, New Guinea and New Britain during the War. After the War he joined the New Theatre Group of Western Australia. His poem 'Harvest Time' won the 1945 W.J. Miles poetry prize. He published three books of verse — *Harvest Time* (1946), *Hammers and Seagulls* (1967) and *Three Golden Giants* (1977) — and his political poetry appeared in published anthologies. He also wrote a biography of waterside union leader Jim Healy.[95]

Williams was employed as a waterside worker from 1952 and spent twenty-four years on the Fremantle wharves, active in the Waterside Workers Federation. He also became caught up in the Petrov dragnet. Vladimir Petrov had issued Williams with a visa and some money to cover expenses before a visit Williams made to Russia in 1952, as a guest of the Soviet Writers' Union. During the preparations for the 1954 Petrov Royal Commission, Petrov described a meeting with Williams at the Soviet Embassy and a highly classified Royal Commission file on Williams was prepared, though he was not implicated in any misdemeanour.[96] Williams served on the Literature Board of the Australia Council for three years, and remained active in left-wing politics well into his nineties, overseeing the Western Australian branch of the CPA until his death in Perth at the age of ninety-seven.

The building that housed the **Workers' Art Guild** in Hay Street West was demolished in the 1960s to make way for the construction of the Mitchell Freeway.

ENDNOTES

INTRODUCTION: 'THAT MAD LITTLE ERA' IN THE WEST
1. Peter Cowan, 1989, *The Hills of Apollo Bay*, Fremantle Arts Centre Press, p. 18. (This statement is made about Perth by a character in the novel.)
2. 'Dissonance is a good word for that mad little era [the 1930s], I think. It was a time of dissonance' (George Johnston, 1964, *My Brother Jack*, The Reprint Society, London, p. 201).
3. Betsey Linton, interview with Andrew Hyde, 30 June 1997.
4. *Fremantle Arts Review*, vol. 2, no. 2, February 1987, p. 18.
5. John Graham, 1962, *Perth and the South-West*, The Jacaranda Press, Queensland, pp. 53–54.
6. E.W. Irwin and Ivan Goff, 1934, *No Longer Innocent*, Angus & Robertson, Sydney, p. 6.
7. ibid., pp. 6–7.
8. George Johnston, *My Brother Jack*, pp. 199–200.
9. ibid., p. 200.
10. William Butler Yeats, 1916, 'Easter, 1916'.
11. Veronica Brady, 1982, 'Place, Taste and the Making of a Tradition: Western Australian Writing Today', *Westerly*, no. 4, p. 107.
12. Ted Snell, 1991, *Cinderella on the Beach: A Source Book of Western Australia's Visual Culture*, UWA Press, Nedlands.
13. Michael Heyward, 1993, *The Ern Malley Affair*, University of Queensland Press, St Lucia, p. 43.
14. Ted Snell, op. cit.
15. Lenore Layman and Julian Goddard, 1988, *Organise!: A Visual Record of the Labour Movement in Western Australia*, Trades and Labour Council of Western Australia, East Perth, p. 19.

1: THE RED WITCH OF GREENMOUNT
1. Alfred Deakin, 24 May 1888, 'Clue' 240, Papers of Alfred Deakin, MS 1540, NLA.
2. Katharine Susannah Prichard, 1963, *Child of the Hurricane: An Autobiography*, Angus & Robertson, Sydney, p. 125.
3. ibid.
4. Frank Moorhouse, 1999, 'Introduction', in Walter Murdoch, *Alfred Deakin*, Bookman Press, Melbourne.
5. Susan Bradley Smith, 2001, 'Girl Meets Tractor: Socialist Desire in Prichard's Suffrage Plays', *Overland*, no. 164, Spring, p. 72.
6. Katharine Susannah Prichard, interview with Ian Turner, 29 February 1960, Canberra, MS 8888, MSB 440, La Trobe Library, SLV, Melbourne; Katharine Susannah Prichard, c. 1957, *Why I Am a Communist*, Current Book Distributors, Sydney, p. 8.
7. Prichard wrote her first novel, *The Wild Oats of Han*, in 1908 but it was not published until 1928. *The Pioneers* was her first published novel. It was twice

adapted as a feature film, first in 1916 and again in a 1926 production directed by Raymond Longford. Prichard was also soliciting the adaptation of her writings for film in Hollywood as early as 1932, and certainly into the war years. The Sydney New Theatre League staged a production of *The Pioneers* in January 1944.

8 John Hamilton, 2012, *The Price of Valour: The Triumph and Tragedy of a Gallipoli Hero, Hugo Throssell, VC*, Pan Macmillan Australia, p. 227.
9 Throssell's Victoria Cross was awarded 'for most conspicuous bravery and devotion to duty during operations on the Kaialij Aghala (Hill 60) in the Gallipoli Peninsula on 29th and 30 August 1915', in which he was badly wounded.
10 Katharine Susannah Prichard, *Why I Am a Communist*, p. 8.
11 Katharine Susannah Prichard, *Child of the Hurricane*, p. 239.
12 ibid.
13 For more information on Bill Earsman and the formation of the CPA, see Stuart Macintyre, 1998, *The Reds: The Communist Party of Australia from Origins to Illegality*, Allen & Unwin, Sydney, pp. 19–22.
14 The cottage, known as Rose Charman's Cottage, still stands today in a picturesque valley two kilometres north of Emerald.
15 Investigation Branch of the Attorney-General's Department, NAA, A6119, item 42, 24 November 1919; and Noel Butlin Archives, N57/282, ANU, Canberra.
16 Isla Marsh, letter to 'Leon Spencer' (Spencer Brodney), 29 September 1962, Papers of Spencer Brodney, MS 6069, 1286/6, MS 5805, La Trobe Library, SLV, Melbourne.
17 Vance Palmer, letter to Nettie Palmer, n.d. (c. May 1930), Papers of Vance and Nettie Palmer, MS 1174/1/3554-3556, NLA.
18 Drusilla Modjeska, 1981, *Exiles at Home: Australian Women Writers, 1925–1945*, Sirius Books, Sydney, p. 88.
19 Katharine Susannah Prichard, letter to Spencer Brodney, 25 May 1930, Brodney Papers, MS 6069, 1286/6, MS 57859, La Trobe Library, SLV, Melbourne. Spencer Brodney (born Leon Brodzky; 1883–1973) was an Australian journalist, drama critic and playwright then living in New York. In 1904 he founded the Australian Theatre Society in Melbourne — a group, like William Moore's Annual Drama Nights and Esson's Pioneer Players, devoted to the production of Australian drama and influenced by W.B. Yeats's Irish national theatre, the Abbey Theatre in Dublin. The names in this letter are references to friends of Prichard's: poet, playwright and journalist Louis Esson (1878–1943), Melbourne writers Vance Palmer (1885–1959) and Nettie Palmer (1885–1964), Melbourne writer and illustrator Hugh McCrae (1876–1958), and cartoonist and caricaturist Will Dyson (1880–1938).
20 For accounts of Lawrence's visit to Western Australia, see Robert Darroch, 1981, *D.H. Lawrence in Australia*, Macmillan, Melbourne, p. 16; and *The West Australian*, 'Big Weekend', 14 October 1995, pp. 1–2. Prichard was unable to meet him at the time, but she and Lawrence began a long-term correspondence after his visit.
21 John Curtin was also president of the WA branch of the Australian Journalists' Association during the 1920s, of which he remained a member for the rest of his life.
22 David Day, 1999, *John Curtin: A Life*, HarperCollins, Sydney; and Ron Davidson, 1994, *High Jinks at the Hot Pool: Mirror Reflects the Life of a City*, Fremantle Arts Centre Press, Fremantle, pp. 45–46.
23 Curtin had been a member of both the Victorian Socialist Party and the ALP for most of his adult life up until his time in Perth.
24 *The Red Star*, 14 September 1934, p. 3. The term 'social fascism', attributed to Stalin, had been used by the international communist movement to describe the alliance of left-wing political parties, including the ALP. It was a pejorative term used to

describe left-wing bodies that did not adhere to the Communist International (Comintern) line.
25	Janet McCalman, 1993, *Journeyings: The Biography of a Middle-class Generation, 1920–1990*, Melbourne University Press, pp. 219–220.
26	John Hepworth, interview with author, 18 June 1994.
27	*The Age*, 'Good Weekend', 26 August 1995, p. 39.
28	A 1935 Investigation Branch report observed that during her 1912 sojourn in England, Prichard 'took an interest in communal kitchens, etc. and usual socialist movements' (NAA, A6119/23, item 367, folio 14).
29	The Investigation Branch of the Attorney-General's Department differed from the Special Bureau, which was a branch of the state police with responsibility for intelligence gathering to aid the Investigation Branch.
30	The United Australia Party gained office in the 1932 federal election with a mandate to deal with the perceived communist threat in Australia, and imposed a severe legislative crackdown on the CPA including the banning of communist publications and a broader implementation of the *Crimes Act 1914* (Cth) against the CPA. It saw the CPA as a threat to national security, given its loyalty to the Comintern. Surveillance of Prichard began in 1912 but remained fairly dormant in the decade from 1922 to 1932. 'The authorities' kept a close watch on her travel movements in the 1930s.
31	Peter Cowan, letter to author, 24 October 1995.
32	Robert Cooksey (ed.), 1969, The Great Depression in Australia, *Labour History*, no. 17, Australian Society for the Study of Labour History, p. 89.
33	Stevens's arrest and conviction, and character evidence given by Prichard on his behalf, were reported in Melbourne's *The Sun News-Pictorial* (3 July 1931, p. 2) and *The Sydney Morning Herald* (3 July 1931, p. 11). Prichard compared Stevens's character to that of Jesus Christ, and stated that 'he was similarly persecuted'. For further reading on this period, see Geoffrey Bolton, 1969, 'Unemployment and Politics in Western Australia', Robert Cooksey (ed.), The Great Depression in Australia, *Labour History*, no. 17, Australian Society for the Study of Labour History, p. 89; Stuart Macintyre, 1984, *Militant: The Life and Times of Paddy Troy*, Allen & Unwin, Sydney, p. 37; and *The Workers' Star* (formerly *The Red Star*), 25 June 1937, p. 3.
34	The supply of warm surplus army coats and other military clothing to the unemployed, as well as the provision of accommodation in unused military camps through the winter, was instigated by then federal defence minister Ben Chifley.
35	The Labor Party of Western Australia was usually referred to at that time, in that state, as the Labour Party, as it was also known in Britain. For the purposes of consistency, it is referred to in this book as the Labor Party.
36	Geoffrey Bolton, 1972, *A Fine Country to Starve In*, UWA Press, Nedlands, p. 19.
37	ibid.
38	*The West Australian*, 19 April 1933, p. 8.
39	Katharine Susannah Prichard, letter to Hugh McCrae, 1 October 1932, McCrae Family Collection, MS 12831, 3607/16, (i), La Trobe Library, SLV, Melbourne.
40	Katharine Susannah Prichard, letter to Nettie Palmer, August 1931, Palmer Papers, MS 1174/1/3806, NLA.

2: THE FIVE ARTS CLUB
1	Peter Cowan, *The Hills of Apollo Bay*, p. 59.
2	Henrietta Drake-Brockman, 1935, 'Small Theatre Movement in Perth', *The Playbill*,

no. 1, March. According to James Quinn, who was involved through the 1930s with a number of Perth's amateur theatre groups, 'It was suggested that there were two reasons for this proliferation of clubs at this time. One was that a lot of people were out of work and therefore had the time to be able to do this, and secondly, the living conditions were so bad during the Depression years, it was kinder and better to live in a make-believe world than it was in reality.' (James Quinn interview, 17 May 1976, OH 131, Battye Library, SLWA, Perth.)

3   Dorothy Rowe was known variously as Betty, Dorothea, Dolly and, in later years, Thea. In Perth in the early 1930s she was best known as Betty.
4   One of the stated aims of the Five Arts Club was to give 'prominence to the works of local artists and writers'. The Five Arts Club also conducted 'producers' and 'dramatic art' classes (*Aims and Objects of the Playbox*, n.d. held in Dorothy Rowe's scrapbook, in the possession of Phil Young, Glebe, NSW).
5   The Adelphi Hotel now occupies the site where the Playbox Theatre once stood at 130 Mounts Bay Road.
6   Dorothy Rowe stated in her memoirs that Keith George 'quickly removed me from the ardours of producing [directing] and "took over"' (Phil Young, 2005, *Thea Rowe: Parts of Her Life Story*, unpublished manuscript, in the possession of Phil Young, Glebe, NSW). Phyllis Ophel (nee Harnett) also recalled that 'Keith George longed to get his own way and [direct] what he wanted in the way he wanted and the Repertory Club wasn't giving him full scope and he would more or less twist Doll [Rowe] around his little finger because she did admire him very much' (Phyllis Ophel, interview with author, 11 September 1996). Keith George was given much of the credit for the Playbox performances (*Music and the Drama*, vol. 1, no. 2, 10 September 1933, p. 4).
7   Phyllis Ophel, interview with author, 29 January 1997. American actor James Cassius (J.C.) Williamson and his wife Maggie Moore established an entertainment promotion and management company in the late nineteenth century that would dominate the Australian theatre industry for nearly a century. Such was its monopolisation of theatre in Australia that it became known as 'The Firm'. It promoted many overseas artists and bankrolled many overseas productions on the Australian circuit, to the detriment of native theatre.
8   Born Keith Merkin George, he later changed his name to Keith Merlin George (Don Batchelor, 1995, *The Context of Australian Playwriting 1939–1968: A Case Study of the Theatre Career of Ric Throssell*, PhD thesis, Department of English, University of Queensland, p. 19).
9   The University Dramatic Society was founded in 1917. Professor Edward Shann was its inaugural director and stage manager.
10 Keith George's farmhouse, known as the Yule Brook Homestead, remained in the hands of the extended George family until 1957. Its original address was Harris Road, Kenwick, but it is now listed as 69 Horley Road, Beckenham. When I visited the property in early 1996, the old farmhouse (and its chickens) still stood next to the narrow Yule Brook, overhung by weeping willows. The Canning River, on which George punted, flows along the bottom of the property. The historic farmhouse has since been renovated by the state government and now serves as the office of the South East Regional Centre for Urban Landcare, though it is no longer as tranquil as it once was as it now sits beside a major traffic arterial.
11 Philip Parsons and Victoria Chance (eds), 1995, *Companion to Theatre in Australia*, Currency Press, Sydney, p. 172.
12 Tom Wignall recalled a visit he and a friend made to George's house during which George offered to make them curried pigeon. George pulled his carbine out of a

cupboard, loaded it with shot and walked outside; the sound of gunshots followed soon after and George reappeared with pigeons in hand, which he duly curried and served with his favourite Frontignac (Tom Wignall, interview with author, 17 October 1994).

13. Patricia Thompson, 1988, *Accidental Chords*, Penguin Books, Ringwood, pp. 164–165.
14. Tom Wignall, interview with author, 17 October 1994; and Joan Vike, interviews with author, 4 December 1994 and 26 March 1995.
15. Keith George was an articled clerk in the Children's Court (Lynne Margaret Fisher, 1992, *Dance Class: A History of Professional Dance and Dance Training in Western Australia from 1895–1940*, MA thesis, History Department, UWA, Perth, pp. 313–314).
16. Ray Oldham, interview with author, 11 October 1994. John Hepworth, whose social circle was wide, remembered George as 'one of the most fascinating and intellectually stimulating people I've ever met' (John Hepworth, interview with author, 18 June 1994). Hepworth described George as 'a real Renaissance man — except for the bit about the athletic combination of things' (Don Batchelor, *The Context of Australian Playwriting 1939–1968*, p. 20).
17. Phyllis Ophel, interview with author, 19 June 1994.
18. The Repertory Club was formed in 1919 and initially housed in the basement of the august Palace Hotel on St George's Terrace, before moving to rooms in King Street and, in 1921, to a rented cottage in Pier Street, next to the St Andrew's Hall (later renamed the Assembly Hall), where it performed until 1923. The early activities of the Repertory Club were predominantly social until it began to concentrate seriously on the production of drama in the 1930s. High on its initial agenda was the formation of the Ladies' House Committee to organise bridge afternoons. Repertory Club plays were chosen by a committee and the Club engaged theatre directors on an ad-hoc basis. Another point of difference between the Playbox and the Repertory Club was the Playbox's use of 'naturalist' set design rather than the traditional painted backdrops used by the Repertory Club and most other dramatic groups at that time. The Repertory Club and the Playbox shared the distinction, in the 1930s, of being the only two drama groups in Perth that had their own theatre venue. In 1933 the Repertory Club moved to Newspaper House on St George's Terrace (Henrietta Drake-Brockman, 'Small Theatre Movement in Perth'). In 1935 the Repertory Club formed a playwriters' circle and an acting class, and began annual performances of a local three-act play with regular performances of local one-act plays on Club nights (which seems to have been an initiative of the Five Arts Club a few years earlier; see Drake-Brockman's column in *The Playbill*, July 1935). The Repertory Club held weekly play readings, lunchtime talks on literary and drama topics, and monthly musicales (also an earlier Five Arts Club practice). Documents relating to the Repertory Club are held in the records of the Western Australian Theatre Company, MN 891, ACC 615A, Battye Library, SLWA, Perth.
19. Phyllis Ophel, interview with author, 21 July 1995. Havelock Ellis was an English sexual psychologist whose best-known work was probably *Psychology of Sex* (a synthesis of his earlier writings on the subject), published in February 1933. Ostensibly a text for medical students, it found a very widespread readership in the 1930s and 1940s and received a commendation from Bertrand Russell. For a brief biography of Kathleen Phyllis Ophel, see her obituary in *The Age*, 27 July 2000.
20. Harnett was asked to read for a part in a Doris Fitton play, which may well have made her reputation, but she left for Perth before the audition. Fitton (1897–1985)

formed the Independent Theatre in 1930 to promote Australian drama, and it continued until 1977 (Judith Gadaloff, 1991, *Australian Drama*, The Jacaranda Press, Queensland, p. 36). For further information on Fitton, see Doris Fitton, 1981, *Not Without Dust and Heat: My Life in Theatre*, Harper & Row, Sydney. Phyllis Harnett had also been a sculpture student at East Sydney Technical College.

21   Kathleen Hector (nee Beechey), interview with author, 22 March 1997. For further information on Brian Penton, see Bridget Griffen-Foley, 2000, *Sir Frank Packer: The Young Master*, HarperCollins, pp. 118–122 and 142–144.

22   Phyllis Ophel, interview with author, 19 June 1994. This is most likely a reference to the demonstration of 6 March 1931. For further information on this demonstration, see Justina Williams, 1976, *The First Furrow*, Lone Hand Press, Willagee, WA, p. 120. This demonstration is also recorded in J.M. Harcourt, 1986 reprint, *Upsurge: A Novel*, UWA Press, Nedlands. Phyllis Harnett must have arrived in Perth by June 1931 at the latest, as her son, Gerard, was born in March 1932.

23   'Phyl was famous for her housekeeping — or lack of it' (Mairi McKenzie [nee Wignall], interview with author, 13 October 1994).

24   Phyllis Ophel, interview with author, 1 November 1997.

25   Phyllis Ophel, interview with author, 11 September 1996.

26   Phyllis Ophel, interview with author, 7 February 1996.

27   The Australian accent was then acceptable on radio, though not encouraged on the stage.

28   Phyllis Ophel, interviews with author, 19 June 1994 and 11 September 1996. Clem Kennedy was, in the latter 1930s, the principal of The Studio of Arts (above the Booklovers' Library), a school of dramatic art, stagecraft, interpretive rhythm, drawing, painting and sculpting.

29   'I still think that someone can train themselves for theatre by reading Ibsen's directions' (Phyllis Ophel, interview with author, 11 September 1996).

30   *The Playbill*, no. 1, March 1935.

31   Peter Fitzpatrick, 1995, *Pioneer Players: The Lives of Louis and Hilda Esson*, Cambridge University Press.

32   Anne Filippini also guest-conducted the Perth Symphony Orchestra. The Filippinis spent two periods in Perth: 1926, and 1928–1932. In a letter written in July 1930, Prichard mentions 'the almost certain crash of my poor friends, the Filippinis' and their company. Although the Filippinis struggled financially, their reputation kept them afloat during the difficult days of the Depression, and in 1932 the company left Perth to tour Tasmania, after which the Filippinis opened a singing studio in Melbourne. Ercole Filippini died in 1934.

33   The Filippinis had two children, one of whom, Josephine, was Ric Throssell's age. The two formed a mischievous friendship playing together around the Throssell home in Greenmount. Josephine Filippini is the mother of Australian singer-songwriter Paul Kelly, who bears a striking resemblance to his grandfather Ercole. For information on the Filippinis, see Anne Beeching, 1988, *Nancy Takes the Stick: Autobiography of Contessa Filippini, Australian Opera Pioneer, 1896–1987*, published by C. Tonti-Filippini, Imscan Technologies, Melbourne; and *Australia's Italians: 1788–1988*, 1988, published by the Italian Historical Society and SLV.

34   Phyllis Ophel, interview with author, 7 February 1996.

35   Lotte Lehmann discovered Sydney-Smith during her 1937 Australian tour and, with Lehmann's help, Sydney-Smith moved to Vienna in 1937 where she studied singing under Lehmann and others. She became a principal mezzo-soprano with the Vienna State Opera and secured an engagement with the Berlin State Opera,

cancelled at the outbreak of the Second World War, and was interned by German authorities through the War. After the War she returned to Vienna where she became a star. She was later known as Lorna Sydney.

36 Keith George, letter to Ric Throssell, November 1971, Papers of Ric Throssell, MS 8071, series 4, box 13, folder 93, NLA. George directed and played a lead role in the Five Arts Club production of *Ghosts*.

37 Thorndike and Casson did perform in Perth, but only played *Ghosts* in east-coast capitals.

38 Phyllis Ophel, interview with author, 7 February 1996. Kenneth Seaforth Mackenzie (1913–1955) went on to author two novels set in Perth — *The Young Desire It* (1937) and a semi-autobiographical account of his 'complicated encounters' in Perth at that time, *The Chosen People* (1938) — both published by Prichard's London publisher, Jonathan Cape. Mackenzie also moved to Sydney in 1934 at the suggestion of his friend Norman Lindsay. *The Young Desire It* won the Australian Literary Society Gold Medal for Mackenzie at the age of twenty-four. His later publications included poetry and the novels *Dead Men Rising* (1951) and *The Refuge* (1954). His novels were initially published under the pseudonym Seaforth Mackenzie. See also 'The History of the Playbox Theatre', *Music and the Drama*, vol. 1, no. 2, 10 September 1933.

39 *The Playbill*, no. 1, March 1935; and *Music and the Drama*, vol. 1, no. 2, 10 September 1933, p. 5.

40 Harnett directed occasional plays for the Little Theatre. For reflections on the Playbox and Little Theatre, see transcript of James Quinn interview, 17 May 1976.

41 Katharine Susannah Prichard, letter to Ric Throssell, 13 August 1946, after the death of Throssell's wife, quoted in Katie Holmes, *A Decent Privacy? Personal Revelation and History*, <http://www.nla.gov.au/events/history/papers/Katie_Holmes.html>.

42 Ric Throssell, 1997, *My Father's Son: The Last Knot Untied* (revised edition), Em Press, Melbourne, p. 140.

43 Janet McCalman, *Journeyings*, pp. 153–154.

44 A Victoria Cross won by another Australian soldier at Lone Pine, Gallipoli, in August 1915 sold for a million dollars at public auction in July 2006.

45 Katharine Susannah Prichard, letter to Spencer Brodney, 5 September 1933.

46 The Radical Bookshop was situated at 264 William Street (between Aberdeen and Francis Streets), Perth. On 5 April 1935 *The Red Star* reported that a branch of the Radical Bookshop had also opened at 45 High Street, Fremantle.

47 A March 1935 issue of *The Red Star* advertised Radical Bookshop sales of 'Working-Class Periodicals & Newspapers; Communist Theoretical Works; Pamphlets on the Trade Union Movement; Soviet Novels & Accounts of Socialist Construction in the USSR'.

48 John A. McKenzie, 1993, *Challenging Faith*, Fremantle Arts Centre Press, Fremantle, p. 71.

49 Katharine Susannah Prichard, letter to Hugh McCrae, 10 September 1933, McCrae Papers, MS 12831, 3607/16, SLV, Melbourne.

50 For references to Prichard's visit to the Soviet Union, see Betty Roland, 1989, *Caviar For Breakfast*, Imprint, Sydney, pp. 65–68, 72, 86–87 and 98–99; and Jeff Sparrow, 2007, *Communism: A Love Story*, Melbourne University Press, pp. 199–202 and 213. Roland described Prichard as 'very much persona grata' in the Soviet Union, 'being taken to a lot of interesting places and is meeting important people … She is tremulous with happiness. Here is the fulfilment of her dreams' (p. 68). But it seems

she saw things that also unsettled her. The Stalin terror was taking hold and signs of it could not be entirely hidden from Prichard.
51 One-quarter of Perth's male population was unemployed by 1933 and another quarter was working only part time, according to C.T. Stannage, 1979, *The People of Perth: A Social History of Western Australia's Capital City*, Perth City Council, Perth.
52 Janda Gooding, 1987, *Western Australian Art and Artists 1900–1950*, AGWA, Perth.
53 There was a significant downturn in the Western Australian building industry in 1930, according to Robyn Dianne Taylor, 1993, *An Investigation into the Nature of Modernism and Modernity During the 1930s in Perth, Western Australia, Through the Study of Specific Buildings and Related Art and Design Forms*, PhD thesis, Department of Fine Arts, UWA, p. 99.
54 Poster Studios was located in Perth's landmark AMP Building — as was the office of Oldham, Boas & Ednie-Brown. The AMP Building had been designed by Charles Lancelot Oldham and Alfred Cox; it was demolished in 1972. For further information on Poster Studios, see Taylor (above), pp. 383–387.
55 Esther Missingham, interview with author, 20 January 1996.
56 John Oldham, interview with Jane Fleming, 29 September 1981, OH 1800, SLWA, Perth.
57 John Oldham, interview with author, 11 October 1994. Oldham's 'bible' in the 1930s was Moholy-Nagy's *The New Vision* (originally published in New York in 1930).
58 Contrary to some sources, John Oldham did not design the Lawson Flats in Perth nor the Swanbourne Hotel. Oldham's renderings were greatly influenced by English architectural illustrator Cyril Farey, who entered a 'typical Farey' rendering to the UWA Crawley design competition (John Oldham, interview with author, 17 January 1996).
59 John Oldham, interview with author, 11 October 1994.
60 Jenny Gregory, 1990, 'Western Australia Between the Wars: The Consensus Myth', Jenny Gregory (ed.), Western Australia Between the Wars 1919–1939, *Studies in Western Australian History*, issue 11, June, Centre for Western Australian History, Department of History, UWA, Perth, p. 8.
61 Francisco Vanzetti, 1934, 'The Quality of Art: Students' Display Opened', *The West Australian*, 13 November.
62 John Oldham, interview with author, 17 January 1996.
63 The Chelsea Flats were built in 1934. Information on Joe Skinner comes from the records of the Skinner Galleries, MN 1320, ACC 4043A, Battye Library, SLWA, Perth; Joan (aka Justina) Williams, letter to author, 17 May 1995; John Oldham, interview with Jane Fleming, 29 September 1981; and various other interviews with the author.
64 John Oldham, interview with Jane Fleming, 29 September 1981.
65 John Oldham, interview with author, 17 January 1996. See also John Oldham in *The West Australian*, 25 August 1986, p. 5; and Jenny Gregory and Robyn Taylor, 1992, '"The Slums of Tomorrow"? Architects, Builders and the Construction of Flats in Interwar Perth', Frank Broeze (ed.), Private Enterprise, Government and Society, *Studies in Western Australian History*, issue 13, Centre for Western Australian History, Department of History, UWA, Perth, pp. 78–91).

3: KISCH AND THE POPULAR FRONT
1 Peter Cowan, *The Hills of Apollo Bay*, p. 27.
2 Ray Oldham, letter to author, 1 March 1995.
3 ibid.

4   Ray Oldham, interview with author, 11 October 1994; Leah Healy (nee Marks), interview with author, 18 September 1996; Ruth Rudkin, interview with author, 21 March 1997; and Olive Lachberg, interviews with author, 14 October 1994 and 21 January 1996. McClintock and Holland had been members of the University Dramatic Society with Keith George. Dorothy Tangney (1911–1985), first female member of the Australian Senate, was also part of Holland and McClintock's social set (Ray Oldham, letter to author, 1 March 1995).

5   Janet McCalman, *Journeyings*, p. 191.

6   Phyllis Ophel, interview with author, 21 July 1995.

7   Kalgoorlie, though extremely isolated, was home to a vibrant intellectual population, hosting an active debating club and one of the most active dramatic societies in Australia.

8   UWA established its Irwin Street campus in 1913. In 1930 it opened its purpose-built campus at Crawley, on the banks of the Swan River.

9   Ray Oldham, interview with author, 1 October 1994.

10   Ray Oldham, interview with author, 17 January 1996. McClintock's article on women writers was published in *The West Australian* on 26 October 1934, p. 8, as part of a fortnightly series by McClintock in the paper on prominent Australian women. McClintock was a particularly erudite champion of women's issues.

11   Paul Hasluck, 1977, *Mucking About: An Autobiography*, Melbourne University Press, Melbourne, p. 87. Hasluck worked on *The West Australian* for many years.

12   Justina Williams, 1993, *Anger and Love*, Fremantle Arts Centre Press, Fremantle, p. 48.

13   *Fremantle Arts Review*, vol. 2, no. 2, February 1987, p. 19.

14   John Oldham gatecrashed a party at Mouse Cottage in order to meet Ray McClintock (John Oldham, letter to author, 19 February 1995; Ray Oldham, letter to author, 1 March 1995; and Phyllis Ophel, interview with author, 21 July 1995).

15   'Walking was only just becoming a popular sport then. We had this thing at the university called the "Wanderers Club" and we used to go for hikes up in the hills ... walking quite a considerable distance' (Ray Oldham, interview with author, 11 October 1994).

16   Gordon Burgoyne, letter to Ric Throssell, May 1972, MS 8071, box 12, folder 91, folio 72, NLA.

17   Justina Williams, *Anger and Love*, p. 65.

18   The Playbox had performed a one-act play written by Burgoyne in September 1932. Entitled *Anzac Day*, it portrayed 'the rebellion of forthright youth against the old conventions of a sentiment encrusted age', a typical theme of the 1930s. A boy chooses, against his parents' wishes, to attend a picnic with his friends rather than an Anzac Day memorial service (newspaper clipping dated 3 October 1932 in Dorothy Rowe scrapbook).

19   Geoffrey Burgoyne went on to become editor of the *Daily News* during the War, with the notorious *West Australian* journalist Victor Courtney later describing him as a 'picturesque personality in Western Australian journalism' (Victor Courtney, 1962, *Perth – and All This!: A Story About a City*, Halstead Press, Sydney, pp. 305–306; and Geoffrey Burgoyne obituary in *The West Australian*, 11 January 1969, p. 9).

20   Gordon Burgoyne, letter to Ric Throssell, May 1972. The 'personal tone' and 'vividly descriptive and emotive, even poetic' language of Prichard's political speeches and political writing was a sometimes stark contrast 'with that of much of the other CPA propaganda of the time, which was often dryly polemical or overlaid with cliched revolutionary rhetoric' (Julie Wells, 1985, 'Katherine [sic] Susannah Prichard: The Writer as Communist Activist', *Melbourne Historical Journal*, vol. 17, p. 72).

21 Gordon Burgoyne, letter to Ric Throssell, May 1972.
22 Ric Throssell wrote of Prichard's deeply painful suspicion of her husband's enactment of the suicide in *Wild Weeds and Wind Flowers* (Ric Throssell, 1975, 'Intimate Strangers' in *Wild Weeds and Wind Flowers: The Life and Letters of Katharine Susannah Prichard*, Angus & Robertson, Melbourne).
23 McCrae Papers, MS 12831, 3607/16, SLV, Melbourne.
24 Bernard Smith, 1993, *Noel Counihan: Artist and Revolutionary*, Oxford University Press, Melbourne, pp. 286–287. The series started in *The Herald* on 14 April 1934.
25 *The Red Star*, 5 October 1934, p. 3. Despite the fact that, according to Betty Roland, some aspects of Soviet society had shocked Prichard on her visit there in 1933, there are no such reports in Prichard's supposedly candid account of her visit in *The Real Russia* (Betty Roland, *Caviar for Breakfast*, p. 78; and Jeff Sparrow, *Communism*, p. 200). Expedience dictated otherwise.
26 As a Liberal-Country League candidate, Florence Cardell-Oliver (1876–1965) won the Legislative Assembly seat of Subiaco in 1936 by one vote, and in 1947 became the first woman cabinet minister in Australia when she was elected an honorary minister in WA's McLarty government. She was minister for supply and shipping in two successive governments, and was a member of the Legislative Assembly between 1936 and 1956. Cardell-Oliver was made a Dame Commander of the Order of the British Empire in 1951.
27 Frank Brennan and Maurice Blackburn had been vocal critics, from the opposition benches, of the Bruce–Page government's censorship of books, pamphlets and films.
28 Phyllis Ophel, interview with author, 7 February 1996.
29 ibid. For a more substantial reading of the Kisch visit to Australia, see Heidi Zogbaum, 2004, *Kisch in Australia: The Untold Story*, Scribe Publications, Melbourne. The ban by Menzies came about after a flawed reading of rather vague information on Kisch from British Intelligence. The Australian and British governments viewed those associated with the Movement Against War and Fascism with grave suspicion.
30 Walter Murdoch (uncle of newspaper proprietor Sir Keith Murdoch and great-uncle of Rupert Murdoch) would later become vice-president of the Council for Civil Liberties. Though the moral product of his Presbyterian upbringing, he was labelled by some a 'liberal humanist'. He showed some interest in Australian literature, but his passion was nineteenth-century English literature. In 1904 he was appointed Lecturer in English Literature at the University of Melbourne, where he taught until 1911. It was here that he became friendly with a number of prominent contemporary and later writers, including Nettie Palmer with whom he remained lifelong friends, and Prichard, who as a student was greatly influenced by him. She had enormous respect for Murdoch and they also remained lifelong friends (see Sydney CPA newspaper *The Tribune*, 6 July 1960, p. 11). In 1912 Murdoch was appointed foundation Professor of English at the newly founded UWA, a position he held until his retirement in 1939. He became a regular columnist with *The Argus*, the *Melbourne Herald* and *The West Australian*, gave regular radio talks in the 1930s, and counted H.G. Wells, George Bernard Shaw and Heidelberg School painter Arthur Streeton among his friends.
Professor Frank Reginald Beasley was listed in the Security file 'Communists in Western Australia — List of Persons Known to be Associated with Communism in 1940', NAA, A6122/40, item 292, folio 10. He was also a member of the Spanish Relief Committee and was central to the establishment of the Council for Civil Liberties in Perth.

31   *The West Australian*, 19 July 1939, p. 14.
32   John A. McKenzie, *Challenging Faith*; and Fred Alexander, 1987, *On Campus and Off: Reminiscences and Reflections of the First Professor of Modern History in the University of Western Australia, 1916–1986*, UWA Press, Nedlands, p. 11.
33   Janet McCalman, *Journeyings*, pp. 164–165.
34   ibid., p. 155.
35   Peter Cowan, letter to author, 24 October 1995. For some personal recollections of student and staff life at UWA in the 1930s, see John A. McKenzie, *Challenging Faith*.
36   The W.A. Council Against War held its first annual conference in July 1934.
37   According to Stuart Macintyre, the Council Against War was formed from the League Against Imperialism in late 1933 (Stuart Macintyre, *The Reds*, p. 268).
38   Katharine Susannah Prichard, *Recollections on Kisch*, typed manuscript in Papers of Katharine Susannah Prichard, MS 6201, box 17, folder 15, NLA.
39   Heidi Zogbaum, *Kisch in Australia*.
40   Devanny, like Prichard, spoke in glowing terms of life in the Soviet Union after her visit there. Addressing a meeting at a factory gate in Sydney on her return, Devanny spoke of the joys to be experienced in the workers' state. 'And comrades, in the Soviet Union sexual intercourse is wonderful,' she told the gathering, to which one of the assembled waterside workers is said to have responded, 'It's not too bloody bad here either, lady!' (Carole Ferrier, 1999, *Jean Devanny: Romantic Revolutionary*, Melbourne University Press, Carlton, Vic., p. 129).
41   A workers' theatre had been formed in Sydney prior to the formation of the WIR workers' art and theatre group and Workers' Art Club. In early 1932, a group known as the Socialisation Drama and Art Group (SDA) formed the Theatre of the Hammer in Newtown. An article in the May 1932 issue of *The Socialisation Call* (a newspaper published by the Socialisation Committee and 'Socialist Units' of the NSW branch of the ALP, formed in response to the Scullin federal Labor government's dramatic economic policies instituted during the Depression) titled 'The First Workers' Theatre in Australia' announced the formation of the Theatre of the Hammer. Its first production was to be Ernst Toller's *Masses and Man*.
42   *The Sydney Morning Herald*, 6 August 1932.
43   *Workers' Art* (official organ of the Workers' Art Club, Sydney), vol. 1, no. 1, April 1933 (Noel Butlin Archives, ANU, Canberra).
44   For a concise history of the Sydney Workers' Art Club and its latter incarnation as New Theatre, see Mona Brand, 1986, 'A Writer's Thirty-six Years in Radical Theatre: New Theatre's Formative Years 1932–1955 and Their Influence on Australian Drama', *Australian Drama 1920–1955: Papers Presented to a Conference at the University of New England, Armidale, September 1–4, 1984*, UNE, Armidale. The publication includes a paper given by Ric Throssell titled 'Paths Towards Purpose: The Political Plays of Katharine Susannah Prichard and Ric Throssell' (pp. 28–38).
45   The Victorian Workers' Theatre Group's first public production was a performance of *Waiting for Lefty* in August 1936. This followed a small-scale performance of two short sketches written by Betty Roland and an extract from the play *Love on the Dole*.
46   George Wignall, interview with Julie Wells, 8 August 1984.
47   Ray Oldham, letter to author, 1 March 1995.
48   *The Red Star*, 29 March 1935, p. 3.
49   See *The Red Star*, 1 February 1935. Yugoslavs accounted for a large proportion of CPA members in WA, and the Yugoslav Workers' Cultural and Educational Club in Perth (The Oreski Club) was a consistently reliable donor to the state branch.
50   Stuart Macintyre, *The Reds*, p. 354.

51 *The Red Star*, 29 March 1935, p. 3.
52 Ric Throssell, *Wild Weeds and Wind Flowers*, pp. 78–79. Kisch's own written account of his trials in Australia (Egon Erwin Kisch, 1937, *Australian Landfall*, translated from the German by John Fisher and Irene and Kevin Fitzgerald, Secker & Warburg, London) is not an entirely accurate account of his Australian visit.
53 See NAA, A6126/25, item 388, folio 11. The name change to the Council Against War and Fascism had certainly occurred by March 1935. It appears that the W.A. Council Against War changed its name to the W.A. Council Against War and Fascism at the same time as the national body of the CAW changed its name to the Movement Against War and Fascism. However, the state bodies of the MAWF continued to be known as CAWFs for some time. By late 1935 the WA branch was known as the Movement Against War and Fascism. See David Rose, 1980, 'The Movement Against War and Fascism: 1933–1939', *Labour History*, no. 38, May, Australian Society for the Study of Labour History.
54 *The Red Star*, 15 March 1935, p. 1.
55 *The West Australian* (12 March 1935, p. 16) reported on Kisch's visit to Perth. See also Egon Erwin Kisch, *Australian Landfall*.
56 Jean Devanny, 1986, *Point of Departure: The Autobiography of Jean Devanny*, Carole Ferrier (ed.), University of Queensland Press, St Lucia, p. 180; and *The Red Star*, 8 November 1935.
57 A Western Australian branch of the Writers' League was not formed until early 1936. That year the League became the Writers' Association and in 1937, the FAW and the Writers' Association joined forces to form the Central Cultural Council 'to co-ordinate the activities of various literary, dramatic and cultural societies in matters of common concern' relating to literature. In 1938 the FAW and the Writers' Association amalgamated under the name Fellowship of Australian Writers, in which communist writers were prominent.
58 The United Front was sometimes found confusing in the far-flung outposts of the international communist movement. Arthur Rudkin said of Perth: 'I remember on one occasion we set up an organisation, complete with Secretary, known as the "United Front", and called upon members of the CP and ALP and non-Party workers to join it'; however, the Central Committee 'pointed out our mistake', informing the group that 'the United Front was not a permanent organisation but a tactic' ('History of Communist Movement in W.A. 1929–1939' in a letter written by Arthur Rudkin, 2 April 1945, NAA, A6119/1, item 44, part 1, folio 6). The ALP's antagonism to any sort of united front partnership with the CPA is illustrated by the fact that the ALP twice expelled prominent federal Labor member Maurice Blackburn for supporting the Movement Against War and Fascism and for later supporting 'Aid for Russia'.
59 Bill and Dorothy Irwin, interview with Don Grant and John McLaren, 10 August 1985, Papers of Kenneth Davidson Gott, MS 13047, box 3765/7, SLV, Melbourne. The CPA orders were also 'to try and not have the same people' in all of these United Front organisations (Phyllis Ophel, interview with author, 21 July 1995).

4: THE 'LIVING THEATRE': FORMATION OF THE PERTH WORKERS' THEATRE

1 *The Red Star*, 20 April 1934, p. 4.
2 John Baker, 1938, *The Right Theatre is Left*, s.n., Adelaide. Baker formed a left-wing theatre collective in Adelaide in 1937, and wrote a number of articles about theatre during 1937–1938 for Adelaide newspaper *Workers' Weekly Herald*, including 'The

Right Theatre is Left', 6 May 1938. His theatre essays were also published in John Baker, 1937, *The Sit-Down Theatre*, s.n., Adelaide, and *Workers' Theatres of the World* (a copy of which is held in the SLV).
3   Unity Theatre, a major left-wing theatre group, also formed in London around this time from the amalgamation of the Rebel Players and a number of smaller workers' theatre groups. See also Richard Haese, 1982, *Rebels and Precursors: The Revolutionary Years of Australian Art*, Allen Lane, London, p. 156.
4   Keith George, letter to Ric Throssell, November 1971.
5   Gregan McMahon (1874–1941) began as a stage actor and went on to establish the Melbourne Repertory Theatre Company in 1911 and the Sydney Repertory Theatre Society in 1920.
6   Keith George, letter to Ric Throssell, November 1971.
7   Phyllis Ophel, interview with author, 21 July 1995.
8   Keith George, letter to Ric Throssell, November 1971.
9   Phyllis Ophel, interview with author, 7 February 1996.
10 Ric Throssell, interview with author, 3 November 1995.
11 Phyllis Ophel, interview with author, 19 June 1994.
12 Keith George, letter to Ric Throssell, November 1971.
13 Gordon Burgoyne, letter to Ric Throssell, May 1972. The first mention found of the Perth Workers' Theatre (under the caption 'Workers' Art Club') is in *The Red Star*, 10 May 1935, p. 2, apart from references in *The Red Star* in April 1934 to the proposed formation of a 'Workers' Club' in Perth. The early Victorian Socialist Party also organised what were called 'workers' clubs' (David Day, *John Curtin*, p. 91). The local branch of the CPA and *The Red Star* initially viewed the proposed Workers' Art Club with hysterical suspicion as perhaps a rival Trotsky faction 'workers' party' planned by 'agents of the bourgeoisie'. It seems probable that the proposed Workers' Club, then the subject of 'gossip on street corners', referred to the formation of the Workers' Art Club rather than a body of 'counter-revolutionary renegades' and *The Red Star* subsequently backed away from its initial broadside and gave its tacit support to the idea of a 'non-party club' devoted to social support 'for relief workers'. See *The Red Star*, 'Communist Renegade', 20 April 1934, p. 4; and 'Workers' Club', 27 April 1934, p. 2.
14 Harry Gould, a respected CPA theorist and cadre, was the author of a report titled *Suggestions to Party re Literary, etc., Artists, on the Need for Self-restraint in Dealing with Them*, in which he wrote, 'I think there are very few leading members of our Party who know how to write; but I fear we do know how to destroy writing' (memo by L.H. Gould, c. 1939, NAA, series A467, item bundle 89, part 2, SF42/81).
15 John and Mairi McKenzie, interview with author, 20 January 1996.
16 Keith George, letter to Ric Throssell, November 1971.
17 *The Playbill*, May 1935, p. 18. A report in *The West Australian*, 6 June 1936, p. 23, referred to the foundation date of the Workers' Theatre as 'a year ago'. For information, though sometimes misleading, on the early formation days of the Perth Workers' Theatre (Workers' Art Club), see David Bromfield (ed.), 1986, *Aspects of Perth Modernism, 1929–1942*, The Centre, Nedlands, WA, pp. 38 and 242; Charles Merewether (ed.), 1984, *Art and Social Commitment: An End to the City of Dreams 1931–1948*, AGNSW, Sydney; Terry Craig, 1990, 'Radical and Conservative Theatre in Perth in the 1930s', Jenny Gregory (ed.), *Western Australia Between the Wars 1919–1939, Studies in Western Australian History*, issue 11, June, Centre for Western Australian History, Department of History, UWA, Perth; and interviews conducted by the author with Angus McGregor (30 December 1996); Ruth Rudkin

(21 March 1997); John Hepworth (18 June 1994 and 21 September 1994); Phyllis Ophel (19 June 1994 and 30 July 1994); John and Ray Oldham (11 October 1994); and Joan Vike (14 December 1994).

18 *The Red Star*, 10 May 1935, p. 2.
19 ibid.
20 A Sydney production of *Who's Who in the Berlin Zoo* was staged by the Christian Democrats Drama Group at the New Theatre League theatre on 25 October 1936.
21 Andrei Zhdanov, speech at the first All-Soviet Congress of Writers, Moscow, 1934.
22 The theme of *The Thief* is similar to that of Prichard's earlier play *The Burglar*. Copies of *The Thief* are held in the Campbell Howard Collection at UNE in Armidale, NSW, and in the Papers of Katharine Susannah Prichard, NLA, MS 6201/6/9 and MS 6021/6/10. A copy was also sent to Unity Theatre in Britain (Unity Theatre Archives, Britain), and Prichard sent a copy to the Soviet Union in 1935.
23 Prichard mentioned in a letter to Frank Huelin in late 1935 that the early plays staged by the Perth Workers' Theatre were *X=O: A Night of the Trojan War* and three subsequent plays but made no mention of *Who's Who in the Berlin Zoo*, *The Thief* or *A Bed-Time Story*, and I can find no record of the production of these plays. In April 1936 she sent the program for the 'second performance' of the Workers' Theatre to the editor of *International Literature* in Moscow, Sergei Dinamov. Presumably this means the group had put on only two performances up to that time and, as there was certainly a performance of *X=O: A Night of the Trojan War* in August 1935 and a performance of the three plays *Captain Pernot's Honour*, *Forward One* and *Calphurnia's Claws* in December 1935, it appears that the planned earlier performance of *Who's Who in the Berlin Zoo*, *The Thief* or *A Bed-Time Story* may not have taken place (Katharine Susannah Prichard, letter to Sergei Dinamov, 19 April 1936, MN 1465, ACC 5835A/2, Battye Library, SLWA, Perth). *The Workers' Star* (26 June 1936, p. 3) refers only to the Workers' Theatre's 'trial performance of four one-act plays' in 1935 (presumably *X=O: A Night of the Trojan War*, *Captain Pernot's Honour*, *Forward One* and *Calphurnia's Claws*). Early Workers' Theatre member Angus McGregor remembers plans for *Who's Who in the Berlin Zoo* (Angus McGregor, interview with author, 30 December 1996), and Maurice Lachberg mentions appearing in this play in *The Western Mail* (28 November 1981, p. 14), so it may have had a 'trial' run.
24 Angus McGregor, interview with author, 30 December 1996.
25 John Hepworth, an early participant, also mentioned that he felt the Workers' Theatre was modelled on the 'New York Guild as much as anything else' (John Hepworth, interview with author, 18 June 1994). Phyllis Ophel said that George thought of *Till the Day I Die* as great melodrama rather than great theatre, though Ophel, once she started work on the play, began to think it was 'extraordinarily good theatre' (Phyllis Ophel, interview with author, 29 January 1997). The Group Theatre in New York performed *Till the Day I Die* on 26 March 1935. Prichard may have been sent the script as early as April 1935, very shortly after it was written, as Angus McGregor remembered a meeting of the Workers' Theatre discussing production of *Till the Day I Die* prior to the group planning to stage *Who's Who in the Berlin Zoo*, which was reportedly in rehearsal in May 1935.
26 Keith George, letter to Ric Throssell, November 1971.
27 Keith George was still president of the CAWF at the beginning of August 1935 when the Workers' Theatre put on *X=O: A Night of the Trojan War*, three months after the formation of the Workers' Theatre.

28 Keith George, letter to Ric Throssell, November 1971.
29 John Oldham, interview with author, 11 October 1994.
30 Phyllis Ophel, interviews with author, 19 June 1994 and 30 July 1994.
31 In a letter to *The West Australian* (13 November 1934, p. 6), George, in his role as acting chairman of the CAWF, slammed critical chatter from unnamed 'official sources' that the Communist Party was 'working secretly behind' the CAWF, claiming 'the part played by the communist party in the work of the Councils Against War has never been concealed'. Despite the fact that George never joined the Communist Party, he did come to the notice of authorities when he started working with the Workers' Theatre. (Strangely, his earlier work with the W.A. Council Against War and the CAWF did not seem to attract much attention.) He was described in an intelligence report as a 'Dangerous type who … took charge of the [Workers' Art Club] and moulded it into a communist "cell"', and he remained under surveillance until at least the early 1950s (NAA, A6126/25, item 388, folio 12).
32 Keith George, letter to Ric Throssell, November 1971. Phyllis Ophel recalled that there was 'another arm' of the Workers' Theatre at Franklin Print (with Hepworth, etc.) (Phyllis Ophel, interview with author, 30 July 1994). I have no other evidence of more than one arm of the group. The next time Angus McGregor attended a Workers' Theatre meeting, after his early meeting at which *Who's Who in the Berlin Zoo* was discussed, was for a reading of *Till the Day I Die* in a hall in William Street, he said, probably at Franklin Print, at which he thought Betsey Currie was also present (Angus McGregor, interview with author, 30 December 1996). This may have been in the lead-up to the move to rooms above Mortlock Motors in Hay Street. If so, this dates preparations for the move to Mortlock's.
33 John Hepworth, interview with author, 18 June 1994. Franklin Print was located at 415 William Street until it moved to 154 Pier Street (corner Moore Street) in August 1935.
34 Keith George, a 'dangerous type [who] took charge of the Guild and moulded it into a communist "cell"', was reported as being 'one of the committee of 3 in connection with the commencement of the Franklin Print' (NAA, A6126/25, item 388, folio 12). The other two committee members were probably James Thomas Woodcock and Ernest Owen Bloomfield, who were joined by Leith Angelo as a business partner in Franklin Print in July 1936. According to an intelligence report dated 10 February 1938, the firm of Franklin Print had an acute shortage of ready cash and was looking into the possibility of receiving finance from a new partner (NAA, A6126/25, item 388, folio 12).
35 The close association between the Workers' Theatre and leading CPA members in Perth generated confusion about the relationship between the CPA and the Workers' Theatre (Workers' Art Club), as reflected in comments of participants on the fringe of the group's formation. Ruth Rudkin, whose husband was certainly an early participant in the Workers' Theatre, was sure that the group 'was set up through the Party' (Ruth Rudkin, interview with author, 21 March 1997). This was echoed by others I spoke to, but is not correct.
36 For example, see *The Workers' Star* issue of 25 March 1938.
37 See *The Workers' Star*, 14 January 1938, p. 1, for details of the early chain of command on *The Red Star*. (Note that *The Red Star* began as a roneoed news-sheet until it became a newspaper in August 1933; in 1936 its name was changed to *The Workers' Star*.)
38 *Workers' Weekly*, 1 June 1934.

39 The use of spies and plants within CPA ranks was a common ploy by police and surveillance authorities in the 1930s.
40 The label of 'social fascism' became an anachronism with the advent of the United and Popular Fronts.
41 Stuart Macintyre, *The Reds*, p. 200. The CPA in WA also stood a candidate in the 1931 Senate elections. The candidate, Finlay McKay, 'polled very poorly but the campaign served to bring forward a lot of activists' ('History of Communist Movement in W.A. 1929–1939', in a letter written by Arthur Rudkin, 2 April 1945).
42 Justina Williams, *The First Furrow*, p.141. The voting figures were published in *The West Australian*, 6 October 1934, p. 17.
43 For further information on Bill Mountjoy, see NAA, A6119/83, items 1528 and 1529.
44 Phyllis Ophel, interview with author, 30 July 1994.
45 'Personal recollections of the Workers' Art Guild by Arthur Rudkin', 1 April 1984, p. 2 (document in the possession of David Milliss, Sydney New Theatre).
46 Arthur Rudkin, 1983, draft article about *The Workers' Star* prepared for the Sydney CPA newspaper *The Tribune*.
47 Arthur Rudkin, interview with Ken Mansell, 7 December 1981 (Oral History section 240/1-46, no. 24, Mitchell Library, SLNSW, Sydney).
48 NAA, A6119/2, item 47, folio 4.
49 Phyllis Ophel, interview with author, 7 February 1996.
50 Olive Lachberg, interview with author, 14 October 1994.
51 Although he was known as a hard and hot-tempered man, there was also a soft and romantic side to Lachberg (Joan Vike, interview with author, 3 June 1995). Joan (writing as Justina) Williams described Lachberg as 'a communist with a gift for vivid, if exaggerated oratory' (Justina Williams, *Anger and Love*, p. 71).
52 John Hepworth, interview with author, 21 September 1994; and John and Ray Oldham, interview with author, 11 October 1994.
53 Information about the constitution of the Perth Workers' Theatre is from an undated 'New Theatre' column in the Records of the New Theatre, 1914–1990, MSS 6244, Mitchell Library, Sydney, henceforth referred to as the New Theatre Archives; and Phyllis Ophel, interview with author, 7 February 1996.
54 Phyllis Ophel, interview with author, 29 January 1997.
55 Dorothy Rowe wrote of Frank O'Grady that 'he was full of enthusiasm and energy, with a great sense of humour, and he was a great asset to the [Playbox]' (Phil Young, *Thea Rowe*).
56 Phyllis Ophel, interviews with author, 19 June 1994 and 7 February 1996.
57 The names 'Workers' Theatre' and 'Workers' Art Club' were often used interchangeably until a further name change to the Workers' Art Guild after the July 1936 production of *Till the Day I Die*. There is some confusion about the precise date of the later name change from 'Workers' Art Club' to 'Workers' Art Guild'. The Guild name was not used in advertising until August 1936, just prior to the production of *Bury the Dead*, despite the program for *Bury the Dead* stating that the Guild had been 'established in February' 1936.
58 Program for Workers' Theatre production of *Till the Day I Die* (Gilchrist Workers' Art Guild manuscript, Papers of John and Roma Gilchrist, 1927–1984, MN 1034, ACC 3255A/52, Battye Library, SLWA, Perth).
59 Sydney New Theatre League brief (NAA, bundle 89, part 2, SF42/81).
60 *The West Australian*, 6 June 1936, p. 23.
61 This was the first time the group performed under the alternative name of the 'Workers' Art Club'. Sydney productions of *X=O: A Night of the Trojan War* were

held in February, March and April 1937. Keith George was obviously a great admirer of the play and returned to it in later years.

62   *The Red Star*, 9 August 1935, p. 4.
63   An article titled 'On the Question of Illegal Work', published in *The Communist Review* (vol. 2, no. 10, October 1935), outlined how the CPA would operate should it be declared an illegal organisation.
64   Katharine Susannah Prichard, letter to Vance Palmer, 10 October 1935, Palmer Papers, MS 1174/1/4862, NLA.
65   Katharine Susannah Prichard, letter to Sergei Dinamov (editor of *International Literature*, Moscow), 19 April 1936.
66   This performance was reviewed in *The Red Star* (13 December 1935).
67   A copy of the play *Forward One* is held in the New Theatre Archives, Mitchell Library, Sydney (box 146X) and in the Campbell Howard Collection (UNE).
68   Another was the later *Women of Spain*, also written by Prichard (Ken Harper, 1984, 'The Useful Theatre: The New Theatre Movement in Sydney and Melbourne 1935–1983', Jack Hibberd (ed.), Performing Arts in Australia, *Meanjin*, vol. 43, no. 1, March, University of Melbourne).
69   Ric Throssell, *Wild Weeds and Wind Flowers*, p. 82. The reference to 'miners' relates to Prichard's later play *Penalty Clause* (also known as *Solidarity*).
70   Keith George, letter to Ric Throssell, November 1971.
71   *The Red Star*, 13 December 1935, p. 4.
72   John Bramwell Miles (1888–1969) was generally known as 'J.B.', sometimes 'Jack'. He was elected CPA general secretary in 1931 and held the position until 1948.
73   Harry Gould, letter to Ric Throssell, Throssell Papers, MS 8071, box 13, folder 94, NLA; and Ric Throssell, interview with author, December 1995. Publicly, Miles praised Prichard's writing. He stated that the CPA was 'proud' to have Prichard, the author, as a member (Carole Ferrier, *Jean Devanny*, p. 141), but privately he was often troubled by her public profile and literary and political pronouncements.
74   Bill Irwin, letter to Ric Throssell, MS 8071, box 13, NLA.
75   Jean Devanny, *Point of Departure*, p. 181.
76   Carole Ferrier, *Jean Devanny*, p. 107.
77   Katharine Susannah Prichard, letter to Frank Huelin, 11 December 1935, NAA, A6119/1, item 42, folio 42.
78   Katharine Susannah Prichard, letter to Sergei Dinamov, 19 April 1936; and Tom Wignall, interview with author, 17 October 1994. Keith George organised a range of classes to train the Workers' Art Club actors, including fencing. Members who attended classes for which instructors were employed paid an additional charge on top of their monthly membership fee, though most Workers' Art Club instructors received little or no payment for their services.
79   Harald Vike Biographical Notes file (AGWA).
80   Bill Irwin, interview with author, 15 October 1994; and Joan Vike, interview with author, 4 December 1994.
81   Angus McGregor, interview with author, 30 December 1996; and Betsey Linton, interview with Andrew Hyde, 30 June 1997.
82   Angus McGregor, interview with author, 30 December 1996.
83   Archibald Bertram (A.B.) Webb (1887–1944), another of Perth's conservative establishment artists who decried the 'degeneration' of art in the latter 1930s, was appointed art master at Perth Technical College in 1932 when Linton retired from the post.
84   The studio was at Tower House, 231 Beaufort Street, Perth.

85 George Pitt Morison (1861–1946) was curator of the Western Australian Art Gallery from 1928 to 1942.
86 Angus McGregor, interview with author, 30 December 1996; 'notes from an interview with Harald Vike', n.d., Harald Vike folio, AGWA Library; and Janda Gooding, *Western Australian Art and Artists 1900–1950*. According to Vike, Dressler ran the initial Workers' Art Club life drawing class. Dressler gave private art tuition to Harald Vike in Vlase Zanalis's studio in Barrack Street, Perth.
87 *The West Australian*, 15 November 1933.
88 Vike was recruited to the CPA in 1935 or 1936 (assuming the Party name Comrade Low) and drew political cartoons under the pseudonym Rau, meaning Red. In October 1935 *The Red Star* published a cartoon by Vike satirising Mussolini's 'peaceful' penetration of Abyssinia; it was later reproduced in the *Christian Science Monitor* in the US.

5: 'A MAN OF ENTERPRISE': KEITH GEORGE AND THE WORKERS' ART CLUB

1 Paul Hasluck, referring to Keith George in his review of *Till the Day I Die* in *The West Australian*, 20 June 1936, p. 21.
2 A more temperate British art exhibition than London's mid-year Surrealist show arrived in Perth late in 1936 on the first stop of its national tour. The British Masters from London's National and Tate Galleries, known also as the Empire Loan Exhibition, was the first international exhibition of original art works seen in Perth.
3 Constantine FitzGibbon, 1965, *The Life of Dylan Thomas*, J.M. Dent, London, pp. 215–216. When Dalí was being fitted for the suit he was asked how deep he intended to dive. 'Into the depths of the unconscious,' he is said to have replied.
4 Workers' Art Club program for *Till the Day I Die*.
5 The Repertory Club Theatre was in the West Australian Chambers Building on St Georges Terrace, near the Palace Hotel.
6 N.Y. Purves, 1962, *The Growth and Development of the Perth Repertory Club and National Theatre*, Teachers' Higher Certificate thesis, Graylands Teachers College, Perth, p. 40.
7 Peter Cowan referred to the Assembly Hall Salvation Army band in his 1989 novel *The Hills of Apollo Bay*.
8 Keith George, letter to Ric Throssell, November 1971. Bill Irwin also used this metaphor to describe the Workers' Theatre's initial impact on Perth, saying it 'fell like a bomb into the waters of Perth society, which were calmer on the surface than the Swan River' (Bill Irwin, interview with author, 15 October 1994).
9 Walter Poole-Johnson interview, May 1976, OH 128, Battye Library, SLWA, Perth. Poole-Johnson was one of the Workers' Theatre's staple actors.
10 Phyllis Ophel, interview with author, 30 July 1994.
11 Keith George, letter to Ric Throssell, November 1971.
12 Katharine Susannah Prichard, letter to Louis Esson, 26 August 1936, MS 6201, box 16, folder 2, folio 62, NLA; and Papers of Hugh Anderson, MS 6946, box 21, folder 79, NLA.
13 Keith George, letter to Ric Throssell, November 1971.
14 R.H. Packman, Introduction to Léon Moussinac, 1931, *The New Movement in the Theatre: A Survey of Recent Developments in Europe and America*, B.T. Batsford, London, p. 1.
15 Ric Throssell, letter to author, December 1995.

16 Ric Throssell, interview with author, 3 November 1995 (referring to Keith George's production of Ric Throssell's play *Valley of the Shadows*).
17 *The West Australian*, 20 June 1936, p. 21.
18 ibid.
19 Bill Irwin, interview with author, 8 March 1995.
20 Robert Porter, 1993, *Paul Hasluck: A Political Biography*, UWA Press, Nedlands, p. 15.
21 ibid., p. 9.
22 Paul Hasluck, *Mucking About*, p. 91.
23 ibid., p. 96.
24 ibid., pp. 97–98.
25 ibid., p. 98.
26 Katharine Brisbane and John McCallum in *Companion to Theatre in Australia*, p. 173.
27 Walter Poole-Johnson, interview, May 1976.
28 *The West Australian*, 20 June 1936, p. 21.
29 ibid.
30 Phyllis Ophel, interview with author, 30 July 1994.
31 ibid.
32 *The West Australian*, 20 June 1936, p. 21.
33 Keith George's work at the Playbox Theatre informed his theatre design. It was written of the Playbox that, because space was limited, 'stage setting becomes extraordinarily important, and the designer becomes an artist playing on the minds of the audience, concentrating on what will be seen and noticed and cutting out as far as possible all that would be unseen or not significant.' (*Music and the Drama*, vol. 1, no. 2, 10 September 1933, p. 5).
34 *Daily News*, 9 July 1936, p. 2.
35 'Jews Deplore Theatre's Omission Of Anthem', *Daily News* (citing *The Westralian Judean*), 9 July 1936, p. 2.
36 *The West Australian*, 20 June 1936, p. 21.
37 Clifford Odets, 1935, *Till the Day I Die*. (These are the stage directions at the end of Scene 1.)
38 Ric Throssell, letter to author, December 1995.
39 Katharine Susannah Prichard, letter to Louis Esson, 6 August 1936, MS 6201, box 10, folder 2, folio 62, NLA.
40 Ric Throssell, interview with author, 3 November 1995.
41 *The West Australian*, 20 June 1936, p. 21; *The Workers' Star*, 26 June 1936, p. 3; and *Daily News*, 12 December 1936, p. 9.
42 Phyllis Ophel, interview with author, 7 February 1996.
43 Beryl Hearder (nee Seward), interview with author, 23 January 1996.
44 Keith George, letter to Ric Throssell, November 1971.
45 ibid.
46 Linley Wilson, interview with Ric Throssell (from Ric Throssell's research notes for *Wild Weeds and Wind Flowers* [1972], MS 8071, NLA).
47 Katharine Susannah Prichard, letter to Louis Esson, 26 August 1936. The term 'producer' was used then to describe the director of a theatre production.
48 Keith George, letter to Ric Throssell, November 1971.
49 *The Daily Telegraph* (Sydney), 23 July 1936, p. 2.
50 Annette Bain, 1980, 'Brighter Days', in Jill Roe (ed.), *Twentieth Century Sydney: Studies in Urban and Social History*, Hale & Ironmonger, Sydney.

51 George Wignall, interview with Julie Wells, 8 August 1984.
52 Phyllis Ophel, interview with author, 7 February 1996.
53 George Wignall, interview with Julie Wells, 8 August 1984.
54 Joan Williams, interview with author, 16 October 1994; and Bill Irwin, interview with author, 8 March 1995.
55 *Daily News*, 25 June 1936, p. 2.
56 Katharine Susannah Prichard, letter to Louis Esson, 6 August 1936; and Bill Irwin, interview with author, 8 March 1995.
57 *The West Australian*, 20 June 1936, p. 21.
58 Phyllis Ophel, interview with author, 7 February 1996.
59 Ric Throssell, letter to author, December 1995.
60 Phyllis Ophel, interviews with author, 19 June 1994 and 30 July 1994; and Joan Vike, interview with author, 26 March 1995.
61 Tom Wignall, interview with author, 17 October 1994.
62 John Hepworth, interview with author, 18 June 1994.
63 NAA, A6122/40, item 411, folio 8.
64 ibid.
65 ibid.
66 ibid., folio 7.
67 *The Daily Telegraph* (Sydney), 24 July 1936, p. 6.
68 New Theatre secretary Victor Arnold remembered the police actually coming onto the stage in an unsuccessful attempt to stop the performance; however, this was later disputed by some of the other cast and audience members, who insisted the police remained backstage (Victor Arnold talk on Sydney New Theatre, Mitchell Library Oral History section, SLNSW, Sydney, uncatalogued, n.d., but probably late 1961 or early 1962).
69 ibid. For an extensive examination of the police investigations into the performance of the banned play, see Fiona Capp, 1993, *Writers Defiled: Security Surveillance of Australian Authors and Intellectuals 1920-1960*, McPhee Gribble, Ringwood, Victoria.
70 For photographs of this private Sydney New Theatre performance of *Till the Day I Die*, see *Pix*, vol. 6, no. 10, 7 September 1940, p. 26.
71 *The West Australian*, 14 September 1936, p. 4.

6: THE WORKERS' ART GUILD AND THE PARTY LINE

1 An old proverb, notably used by former prime minister Paul Keating to describe moving on and 'getting on with things'.
2 Bill Darbyshire was, according to Phyllis Ophel, politically 'our way, but not *of* us' (Phyllis Ophel, interview with author, 21 July 1995).
3 Letter from Victor Arnold, Perth, to Unity Theatre, Brisbane, titled 'Agit Prop in W.A.', c. 1940 (NAA, series A6335/1, item 21, ff. 26-27).
4 Phyllis Ophel, interview with author, 7 February 1996.
5 Australians also qualified for the Group Settlement Scheme, an extension of the Soldier Settlement Scheme to repatriate returned World War One servicemen onto the land.
6 John Philip Gabbedy, 1988, *Group Settlement, Part 2, Its People: Their Life and Times — An Inside View*, UWA Press, Nedlands.
7 Phyllis Ophel, interview with author, 21 July 1995.
8 Victor Arnold, 'Agit Prop in W.A.'.
9 Phyllis Ophel, interview with author, 21 July 1995.

10   ibid.
11   John Hepworth, 1990, 'Love and the Party Line', *G.H.*, April, p. 78. National CPA official Harry Gould sought to address this common curse within the Communist Party in a report he wrote pleading for more official tolerance of Party writers and writing. The report contained policy recommendations to the Party in this area, including the 'allowance by the Party of very wide liberty in the field of art' and 'determined rejection by the Party only of what is directed against the revolutionary aims of the working class' (L.H. Gould, *Suggestions to Party re Literary, etc., Artists, on the Need for Self-restraint in Dealing with Them*). Despite its decrees on most matters political and industrial, it seems the CPA did not adopt any set 'cultural' policies until the 1940s.
12   Prominent local CPA member Gus Stagg was secretary of the MAWF state branch, was employed on the *Workers' Star* and played a role in the Workers' Art Guild production of *Till the Day I Die* in 1936. He was later elected to the CPA's state committee.
13   NAA, A6126/25, item 810.
14   John Hepworth, interview with author, 18 June 1994.
15   John Hepworth, 'Love and the Party Line', p. 76. A number of prominent CPA members attended the International Lenin School in Moscow. Oriel Gray, who would later marry and divorce John Hepworth, wrote that had he been sent to Moscow, 'the Communist Party of the Soviet Union might have been in for an earlier and bigger shock than Khrushchev's denunciation of Stalin!' (Oriel Gray, 1985, *Exit Left: Memoirs of a Scarlet Woman*, Penguin Books, Ringwood, p. 58).
16   This boarding house is the partial setting for Hepworth's play *Yellow Ticket*. Hepworth's mother also taught dance classes to teenagers at the boarding house in the mid-1930s; Tom Wignall (Jnr) was a student of hers (Tom Wignall, telephone conversation with author, 5 February 1995).
17   Kathleen Hector, interview with author, 22 March 1997.
18   Paul Hasluck, *Mucking About*, p. 101; and Peter Conole, 2002, *Protect and Serve: A History of Policing in Western Australia*, Western Australia Police Service, p. 227.
19   John Hepworth, interview with author, 21 September 1994. The Trades Hall Flats, built into the new Trades Hall building in 1934, were located on the second and third floors of the three-storey building at 60 Beaufort Street, wedged between the old Trades Hall building and the Court Hotel, both of which still stand today, on the site of what is now Curtin House. The building was converted into the Trades Hall Annexe in the late 1940s (*The West Australian*, 18 April 1975, p. 7).
20   The Court Hotel was then run by Bartholomew Cornelius O'Brien, who in 1901 was the first Labor member elected to the Western Australian Legislative Council. He served twice in the state parliament, and was publican of the Court Hotel from 1905 to 1938.
21   Olive Lachberg, interview with author, 14 October 1994.
22   Herbert McClintock, interview with Ken Mansell, 6 May 1983, Oral History section 202/1–74, no. 12, Mitchell Library, SLNSW, Sydney.
23   ibid. Eric Thake was one of the first Australian artists to exhibit surrealist work, in 1932.
24   McClintock was art editor of *Strife*.
25   Charles Merewether (ed.), *Art and Social Commitment*.
26   The vagrancy charge was later dropped.
27   Katherine Perrin (daughter of Albert and Irene Osterberg), letter to author, 27 August 1997.

28   Osterberg later adopted the Party pseudonym of 'Comrade Henry Morgan-Jones' (after his maternal grandfather).
29   Phyllis Ophel, interview with author, 30 July 1994. Osterberg worked at the Midland Railway Workshops from 1936 to 1940, where a strong CPA branch was established.
30   An article in *The Workers' Star* on 17 July 1936 still referred to the 'Workers' Art Club', while a letter from Katharine Susannah Prichard to Louis Esson dated 26 August 1936 notes the name change to Workers' Art Guild.
31   Private Keith M. George, 'Report on the Formation of Army Repertory Companies', held in the Perth Theatre Trust Archives, His Majesty's Theatre, Perth. Keith George's admiration for the New York Theatre Guild was also mentioned by Phyllis Ophel in an interview with the author, 19 June 1994.
32   Phyllis Ophel, interview with author, 19 June 1994.
33   ibid. Although James W.R. Linton was not particularly conservative (according to Betsey Linton he was significantly more socially and culturally progressive than most of his arts peers and decidedly Labor; Betsey Linton, interview with Andrew Hyde, 30 June 1997), he was of the older generation then being swept aside.
34   The Linton Institute of Art building still stands. In 1938 Linton gave up teaching and moved to his property, Hovea, at 1445 Falls Road in Hovea in the Perth hills, with his assistant and long-time companion Betsey Currie, whom he later married.
35   Joan Vike, interview with author, 26 March 1995.
36   ibid.
37   George Wignall, interview with Julie Wells, 8 August 1984.
38   Kathleen Hector, interview with author, 22 March 1997.
39   Kathleen Hector, telephone conversation with author, n.d.
40   Phyllis Ophel, interview with author, 30 July 1994; and Workers' Art Guild theatre programs.
41   According to a police report, a portion of the Sydney New Theatre's audience comprised 'a particularly vicious type of young thug and the homo-sexual … There is [sic] probably more followers of the New Theatre, who are homo-sexuals, than the number evident at other legitimate theatre in Sydney. But more important is the type; and he (the female aspect is almost non-existent) is the most degenerate breed of homo-sexual — the one possessing low intelligence' (NSW police report on Sydney New Theatre, NAA, A6122/40, item 411, folio 89).
42   The wider Australian New Theatre movement was dominated from its initial formation through to virtually the present day by women writers and other practitioners.
43   Phyllis Ophel, interviews with author, 19 June 1994 and 21 July 1995; and John Hepworth, interview with author, 21 September 1994.
44   John Hepworth, interview with author, 21 September 1994.
45   John Hepworth, interview with author, 18 June 1994.
46   Bruce Harris, letter to author, 14 July 1993.
47   John Hepworth, interview with author, 21 September 1994.
48   Phyllis Ophel, interview with author, 7 February 1996.
49   Phyllis Ophel, interviews with author, 19 June 1994 and 7 February 1996. Ophel attributed George's decision to eventually leave the Guild to this battle.

7: 'BURY THE DEAD'
1   Workers' Art Guild poster for the production of *Bury the Dead*.

2   Nettie Palmer, letter to Vance Palmer, October 1936 (Palmer Papers, MS 1174/1/5129-5131, NLA).
3   Augustus (Gus) Stagg had previously been secretary of the W.A. Council Against War, was at one time secretary of the state branch of Friends of the Soviet Union, served on the CPA state committee and in 1940 would become manager of local CPA newspaper *The Workers' Star*. He had a slightly disconcerting appearance: having a partly paralysed face, a wire connected to his ear held his bottom lip up (Tom Wignall, interview with author, 13 January 1996). Stagg had been expelled from the CPA by Bill Mountjoy in 1932 for 'an irresponsible petty-bourgeois approach and political unreliability' during a factional brawl arising from the Party's inaugural state conference in October 1931, but was soon readmitted (Justina Williams, *The First Furrow*, pp. 139 and 156; and 'History of Communist Movement in W.A. 1929–1939' in a letter written by Arthur Rudkin, 2 April 1945).
4   Ray Oldham, interview with author, 17 January 1996.
5   John Oldham, interview with Jane Fleming, 29 September 1981.
6   Phyllis Ophel, interview with author, 30 July 1994; John Oldham, interview with author, 17 January 1996; and John Oldham, interview with Jane Fleming, 29 September 1981.
7   Ray Oldham, interview with author, 17 November 1996.
8   Ray Oldham, letter to author, 1 March 1995. John Oldham had been greatly influenced by László Moholy-Nagy's 1930 treatise *The New Vision*.
9   John Oldham, interview with author, 11 October 1994.
10 John Oldham, interview with Jane Fleming, 29 September 1981.
11 Ray Oldham, letter to author, 1 March 1995, and interview with author, 11 October 1994. Ray Oldham regretted giving in to her husband and donating her personal library. The books were never returned to her. 'I have never really forgiven John for his persuading me to give all my books to the W.A. Guild' (Ray Oldham, letter to author, 1 March 1995). 'When the Workers' Art Guild folded up, of course the books just disappeared' (Ray Oldham, interview with author, 11 October 1994).
12 Ray Oldham, interview with author, 11 October 1994.
13 Phyllis Ophel, interview with author, 19 June 1994.
14 John McKenzie, interview with Chris Jeffery, 4 July 1982, TRC 2404, interview 6014, NLA.
15 Phyllis Ophel, interview with author, 19 June 1994.
16 Dorothy Hewett, 1990, *Wild Card: An Autobiography 1923–1958*, McPhee Gribble, Ringwood, pp. 87–88. Hewett also wrote of this experience in Dorothy Hewett, 1982, 'The Garden and the City', *Westerly*, no. 4, December, p. 101.
17 A security file on Alec King is held at NAA, A6119/84, item 1941.
18 Francis King, letter to author, 8 May 1995. Alec King was political enough to hold the position of Secretary of the University Teachers' Association at UWA in 1940.
19 Phyllis Ophel, interview with author, 19 June 1994.
20 Léon Moussinac, *The New Movement in the Theatre*, p. 12.
21 *The West Australian*, 13 November 1936, p. 19.
22 Workers' Art Guild poster for the production of *Bury the Dead*.
23 John Hepworth, interview with author, 18 June 1994. Hepworth acted in the play, while his mother was business manager of the production and his father in charge of props.
24 Phyllis Ophel, interview with author, 21 July 1995. New York's Group Theatre had also used a constructivist set and Vike was probably aware of this, as theatre journals allowed him to keep up with theatre design overseas. Herbert McClintock

had also recently experimented in constructivist painting, and this may also have influenced Vike's set.
25 Gordon Craig, Foreword to Léon Moussinac, *The New Movement in the Theatre*.
26 ibid., pp. v–vi.
27 A.D. White, 1972, 'Brecht's Quest for a Democratic Theatre', *Theatre Quarterly*, vol. 2, no. 5, January–March, London, pp. 66–67.
28 Keith George, quoted in *The West Australian*, 11 October 1937, p. 10.
29 Phyllis Ophel, interview with author, 21 July 1995.
30 Phyllis Ophel, interview with author, 7 February 1996.
31 Oriel Gray, *Exit Left*, p. 41. The Workers' Art Guild had sent photos of its *Bury the Dead* set to Sydney's New Theatre (captioned, it appears, by Vike himself). Edmund Allison constructed the Sydney set for the play and described it as 'a lot of platforms' with the 'projection' of six dead soldier figures in a graveyard in the background. Although Allison denied that Sydney's New Theatre used Vike's set design — he stated that the set was worked out between himself and the play's director, Jerold Wells — it appears in all likelihood that the set he used was that which had been designed by Vike, with Allison's description of the Sydney set sounding strikingly similar to Vike's set. Freda Brown (nee Lewis), then centrally involved in Sydney's New Theatre, recognised photos of Vike's set as that which the New Theatre had used (Edmund Allison, interview with author, 29 January 1995; and Freda Brown, interview with author, 22 March 1997). There had also been an earlier Sydney New Theatre production of *Bury the Dead*, with a different set.
32 *The West Australian*, 13 November 1936, p. 19.
33 The absence of any interval did create problems for the actors forced to remain on stage for the entirety of the play. One of the actors playing a corpse had to relieve himself on stage (Phyllis Ophel, interview with author, 19 June 1994).
34 Phyllis Ophel, interviews with author, 19 June 1994 and 21 July 1995.
35 Katharine Susannah Prichard, letter to Louis Esson, 6 August 1936.
36 Arthur Rudkin, 1984, written recollections of the Workers' Art Guild sent to David Millis at Sydney's New Theatre.
37 *The West Australian*, 13 November 1936, p. 19.
38 Phyllis Ophel, interview with author, 7 February 1996.
39 These were executed by John Jeffery, a CPA member, pharmacist, music enthusiast and talented amateur photographer.
40 Tom Wignall, letter to author, 4 September 1995. Descriptions of lighting from interviews with Phyllis Ophel, Tom Wignall and Olive Lachberg; Tom Wignall, telephone conversation with author, 10 July 1995 and letter to author, 4 September 1995; Ruth Rudkin, interview with author, 21 March 1997; Arthur Rudkin, written recollections of the Workers' Art Guild, 1984; Oriel Gray, *Exit Left*, p. 3; and *Daily News* and *The Mirror* reviews of the play.
41 Tom Wignall, telephone conversation with author, 5 February 1995.
42 Phyllis Ophel, interview with author, 7 February 1996.
43 Arthur Rudkin, written recollections of the Workers' Art Guild, 1984. For further descriptions of the Guild production of *Bury the Dead*, see Justina Williams, *Anger and Love*, p. 66 and John A. McKenzie, *Challenging Faith*, p. 83.
44 Author interviews with Phyllis Ophel, Tom Wignall and Ric Throssell; newspaper reviews; and Tom Wignall, letter to author, 4 September 1995.
45 Author interviews with Bill Irwin (8 March 1995), Tom Wignall (17 October 1994 and 13 January 1996) and Phyllis Ophel. Ophel clearly remembered that this climax 'frightened the audience to death … some people ran out crying' (Phyllis Ophel,

interview with author, 7 February 1996). Keith George circulated photograph(s) of an audience member who had fainted during a performance.

46   Tom Wignall, letter to author, 4 September 1995. Those who played the corpse roles were John Hepworth (Private Driscoll); Herbert Ende (Private Schelling); George Hunt (Private Morgan); Maurie Lachberg (Private Webster); Louis Conto (Private Levy); and Tom Wignall (Private Dean). Marjorie Smith, who had also performed in *Forward One*, played the prostitute in *Bury The Dead* (under her married name of Marjorie [May] Robson).
47   *The Mirror*, 14 November 1936.
48   *Daily News*, 12 November 1936, p. 5.
49   Memo from Paul Hasluck, dated 23 November 1936, Papers of Sir Paul Meernaa Caedwalla Hasluck, MN 1184, ACC 3499A, Battye Library, SLWA, Perth.
50   The Guild's financial concerns after the production of *Bury the Dead* are evident in a letter written by Keith George to Louis Esson, dated 29 December 1936 (Anderson Papers, MS 6946, series 15, box 21, folder 79, NLA).
51   Phyllis Ophel, interview with author, 19 June 1994. John and Ray Oldham do not remember these 'enormous' tram ads. John recalled that there were only small press ads, with his posters simply pasted 'on any available prominent surfaces' (John Oldham, letter to author, 19 February 1995); Ray added that the ads 'were put inside trams, below the roof and above the seats' (Ray Oldham, letter to author, 1 March 1995). However, Phyllis Ophel's recollections are generally very reliable and such an extensive advertising campaign was certainly possible after the financial success of *Till the Day I Die*.
52   Tom Wignall, letter to author, 4 September 1995. Chalking contemporary political slogans on footpaths and roads was a common CPA practice in Perth.
53   John Oldham, telephone conversation with author, 10 March 1998, and interview with author, 17 January 1996. Tom Wignall recollects that the Guild's art section was responsible for all advertising of Guild plays (Tom Wignall, letter to author, 4 September 1995).
54   John Oldham, interview with author, 11 October 1994. Oldham's poster for *Bury the Dead* is now held in the AGWA collection (accession number 985/OOQ6).
55   Lenore Layman and Julian Goddard, *Organise!*, p. 184.
56   *The Workers' Star*, 11 December 1936, p. 2.
57   *The West Australian*, 12 December 1936, p. 17.
58   It was not until late 1942 that the world would learn of the Holocaust. The full extent of the Nazi persecution of Jews was not widely known until the end of the Second World War.
59   Phyllis Ophel, interview with author, 7 February 1996.
60   Phyllis Ophel (recounting Tom Wignall's reporting of the incident), interview with author, 11 September 1996.
61   ibid. Nevertheless, observed Ophel, 'It was ridiculous to ever talk of the Communist Party as a Jewish party — that was ludicrous — but the Jews were grateful for something in the Communists which didn't turn out to be there. I mean when Russia became a Communist country, she bloody well belted into the Jews like everybody else'.
62   *Daily News*, 12 December 1936, p. 9.
63   *The West Australian*, 12 December 1936, p. 17.
64   Joan Vike, interview with author, 4 December 1994.
65   Peter Cowan, letter to author, 18 August 1995.
66   ibid.

67 Ric Throssell, interview with author, 3 November 1995.
68 John Oldham, interview with author, 11 October 1994.
69 Bill Irwin, interview with author, 15 October 1994.
70 Ric Throssell, *My Father's Son*, p. 9.
71 Katharine Susannah Prichard, letter to Louis Esson, 26 August 1936.
72 Katharine Susannah Prichard, letter to Hugh McCrae, 1 August 1936, McCrae Papers, 3706/16, (X), La Trobe Library, SLV, Melbourne.
73 Prichard's greatest love as a writer was material for the theatre, according to Ric Throssell, 'Paths Towards Purpose', p. 28.
74 George Wignall interview with Julie Wells, 8 August 1984.

8: SPAIN, MOSCOW AND 'THE SOUTHERN CROSS'

1 Bill Irwin and Ivan Goff on meeting Groucho Marx at a Hollywood restaurant in the early 1930s (E.W. Irwin and Ivan Goff, *No Longer Innocent*, p. 249).
2 The Spanish Civil War began on 18 July 1936 and ended on 1 April 1939. The left-wing Loyalist–Republican coalition was made up of the Communists (PSUC), the Socialists (POUM) and the Anarchists or Anarcho-Syndicalists (CNT), each with their own political agendas, which fractured the coalition.
3 *The Workers' Star*, 8 April, 11 March and 15 April 1938.
4 Ray Oldham, letter to author, 1 March 1995.
5 Lee Edwards (ed.), 1999, *The Collapse of Communism*, Hoover Institution Press, Stanford, California, p. 182.
6 The fifty or so Australian International Brigadiers (*The West Australian*, 8 February 1939, p. 21) comprised a modest proportion of the approximately 50,000 who made up the International Brigade. The Australian Division of the International Brigade was known as the Eureka Brigade. Some eighteen Australians were killed in Spain during the Civil War and another ten Australian volunteers died when the ship on which they were travelling to Spain, the *City of Barcelona*, was torpedoed off the coast of Valencia by an Italian submarine in early 1937.
7 Gordon Burgoyne, letter to Ric Throssell, May 1972.
8 *The Workers' Star*, 23 September 1938, featured a photo of one of five £300 ambulances purchased for the Spanish Government by the Australian Spanish Relief Committee.
9 *The West Australian*, 22 June 1937, p. 14; and *The Workers' Star*, 18 June 1937, p. 2, and 25 June 1937, p. 5.
10 *The Workers' Star*, 8 October 1937, p. 1.
11 This right-wing ALP faction broke away in 1955 to form the Democratic Labor Party (DLP).
12 *Daily News*, 3 July 1937, p. 15.
13 Lockwood would later join the CPA and become involved with Sydney's New Theatre. He was also a friend of Bill Irwin's.
14 For more about Stevens's death, see *The Workers' Star*, 14 January 1938, and Katharine Susannah Prichard's tribute to him in *The Workers' Weekly*, 28 January 1938, p. 2.
15 Bill and Dorothy Irwin, interview with Don Grant and John McClaren, 10 August 1985. Irwin's initial feature was published in the *Daily News* on 24 July 1936, p. 4.
16 Irwin was integral to the formation of both the Young Labor League (YLL) — the youth arm of the ALP established under a socialist plank in May 1935 — and the Young Communist League (YCL), which was formed in 1934 to recruit young

people to the Left in general and the CPA in particular (Bill Irwin, interview with author, 8 March 1995; and Ray Oldham, interview with author, 17 January 1996). John and Ray Oldham were prominent members of the YLL, as were the Wignalls and Ric Throssell. The CPA attached a lot of importance to the YCL as a recruiting ground for the Party (J.B. Miles was titular national president of the YCL), though most YCL members were the children of existing CPA members. The YCL later became the Eureka Youth League, of which Bill Irwin was elected president in 1943.

17   Bill and Dorothy Irwin, interview with Don Grant and John McClaren, 10 August 1985; Ron Davidson, *High Jinks at the Hot Pool*, p. 185; Justina Williams, *Anger and Love*, p. 58; and author interviews with Kathleen Hector, Ray Oldham and Bill Irwin. Under Jim McArtney's stewardship the *Daily News* became a more progressive liberal publication than its predecessor. It carried pro-Republican reports on the Spanish Civil War by Vance, Nettie and Aileen Palmer. Jim McArtney would eventually become managing director of West Australian Newspapers.

18   E.W. Irwin and Ivan Goff, *No Longer Innocent*, pp. 6–8.

19   John McLaren, 2003, *Free Radicals: On the Left in Postwar Melbourne*, Australian Scholarly Publishing, Melbourne, p. 144.

20   Anne Beeching, *Nancy Takes the Stick*.

21   Katharine Susannah Prichard, letter to Guido Baracchi, 13 April 1965, Prichard Papers, series 10, folder 17, NLA.

22   ibid. Prichard continued: 'I feel grateful to you always for having introduced me to Marxism, and an understanding of communist principles. My life has been illuminated by them. Despite shocks and vicissitudes along the way I have been able to hold to the fundamental principles. It seems that you have been more susceptible to changes in the political atmosphere' (ibid., quoted in Jeff Sparrow, *Communism*, pp. 286–287).

23   *The Roaring Nineties* was published in 1946. Prichard had been undertaking research for her goldfields novels during visits to the goldfields over a number of years. The country had impressed itself upon her from the time she and Hugo had camped at Larkinville, south of Kalgoorlie, in 1930.

24   Drusilla Modjeska, *Exiles at Home*, p. 141.

25   Katharine Susannah Prichard, 1934, *The Real Russia*, Modern Publishers, Sydney, p. 248.

26   *Woman Today*, February 1937, vol. 1, no. 7, p. 2. *Woman Today* had replaced CPA monthly national journal *Working Woman* in 1936.

27   Katharine Susannah Prichard, letter to Louis Esson, 26 August 1936, Anderson Papers, MS 6946, box 21, folder 79, NLA. Prichard in fact sent a copy of *The Southern Cross* to Sergei Dinamov, editor of *International Literature* in Moscow, in October 1936 and ask that he 'forward the play to the proper quarters, with a view to production' (Katharine Susannah Prichard, letter to Sergei Dinamov, 30 October 1936, MN 1465, ACC 5835A/2, Battye Library, SLWA, Perth).

28   Ric Throssell, interview with author, 25 March 1997.

29   Keith George, letter to Ric Throssell, November 1971.

30   Katharine Susannah Prichard, letter to Louis Esson, 26 August 1936. Prichard also wrote in October that year that the Guild 'will produce the play next year, and later also, I hope, The Theatre Guild of Sydney' (Katharine Susannah Prichard, letter to Sergei Dinamov, 30 October 1936).

31   Keith George, letter to Louis Esson, 29 December 1936.

32   Katharine Susannah Prichard, letter to Louis Esson, 26 August 1936.

33 Leslie Rees, 1973, *The Making of Australian Drama: A Historical and Critical Survey from the 1830s to the 1970s,* Angus & Robertson, Sydney, p. 136.
34 Katharine Susannah Prichard, letter to Louis Esson, 26 August 1936.
35 Peter Fitzpatrick, *Pioneer Players,* p. 309. *The Southern Cross* was published soon after Louis Esson's death, in Louis Esson, 1946, *The Southern Cross and Other Plays,* Robertson & Mullens, Melbourne. In her introduction to the book, Hilda Esson wrote that its publication was an effort to 'rescue' Esson's work from 'Oblivioni Sacrum' (p. ix).
36 Keith George, letter to Louis Esson, 29 December 1936.
37 ibid. It is not clear what 're-organisation' was being referred to; perhaps the planned changing of the guard at the Guild on George's departure.
38 John Oldham, interview with author, 11 October 1994.
39 Keith George, letter to Ric Throssell, November 1971.
40 Dorothy Rowe and Keith George hosted a reception at the Playbox for Sybil Thorndike and Lewis Casson in early 1933, and Thorndike praised the Playbox for encouraging local playwriting. Lorna Sydney Smith sang at the reception, and a play and readings were performed. Phyllis Ophel remembered performing for Thorndike at this event, and Hugo Throssell and Ray McClintock also reportedly attended. (Phyllis Ophel, interview with Zoe Ackroyd Curtis, n.d.; and undated newspaper clippings in Dorothy Rowe scrapbook). When she returned to England, Thorndike told an Australian journalist, 'That little Playbox Theatre in Perth seemed to me to be doing some extraordinarily forward work' (undated newspaper clipping in Dorothy Rowe scrapbook).
41 Phyllis Ophel, interviews with author, 19 June and 30 July 1994.
42 ibid.
43 Phyllis Ophel, interview with author, 30 July 1994.
44 John Oldham, interview with author, 11 October 1994.
45 Phyllis Ophel, interview with author, 7 February 1996.
46 Ray and John Oldham, interview with author, 11 October 1994; and John Oldham letter to author, 19 February 1995.
47 Tom Wignall, interview with author, 17 October 1994.
48 George Wignall, interview with Julie Wells, 8 August 1984.
49 Phyllis Ophel, interview with author, 7 February 1996.
50 Phyllis Ophel, interview with author, 11 September 1996.
51 John Oldham, interview with author, 11 October 1994; and Ray Oldham, letter to author, 1 March 1995.
52 Ray Oldham, letter to author, 1 March 1995.
53 John Oldham, interview with author, 17 January 1996.
54 Ray Oldham, interview with author, 11 October 1994.
55 Ric Throssell, interview with author, 3 November 1995. Some powerful figures in the CPA, friends included, tried to convince Prichard to introduce a revolutionary hero into the second novel of her goldfields trilogy, *Golden Miles* (published in 1948), along socialist-realist lines, when, as Prichard defiantly and correctly stated, there was none and she would not falsify history by inventing one. This caused a temporary rift between Prichard and the CPA hierarchy. Throssell noted that the Soviet Writers' Union criticised the novel for the same reason.
56 Phyllis Ophel, interview with author, 7 February 1996.
57 New Theatre members also regularly attended 'cultural committee' meetings at the CPA's Marx House in Sydney, home to the CPA Central Committee, with senior members of the Central Committee including J.B. Miles (Oriel Gray, interview with

author, 7 August 1995). Freda Brown, a leading Sydney New Theatre official, stated that there was 'very, very strong' Party control over Sydney New Theatre (Freda Brown, interview with author, 22 March 1997). See also Angela O'Brien, 1989, *The Road Not Taken: Political and Performance Ideologies at Melbourne New Theatre, 1935–1960*, PhD thesis, Monash University, Melbourne; Paul Herlinger, 1980, *New Theatre: The Pre-war Years, 1932–1939*, MA Qual., University of Sydney; and Paul Herlinger, 1989, *A History of New Theatre, 1939–1953*, MA Hons thesis, University of Sydney.

58 CPA influence in the Guild was insignificant during most of Keith George's tenure. He left the Guild in 1939, reportedly because of the increasing influence of the CPA on Guild affairs, but there is not a lot of evidence, apart from a small increase in agitprop work and an increase in Popular Front cooperation with trade unions, that the CPA had any marked influence on the repertoire of the Workers' Art Guild after his departure. The declaration of War in September 1939, however, brought any possibility of a stronger Party line to an abrupt halt.

59 *The Workers' Weekly*, Sydney, 12 March 1937, p. 3.

60 George Wignall, interview with Julie Wells, 8 August 1984.

61 The family's 'official' surname was Blundell-Wignall, but both generations tended simply to use the surname Wignall; for this reason the surname Wignall is used throughout this book.

62 Mairi McKenzie, interview with author, 13 October 1994.

63 Beryl Hacker, 1994, *Rosa: A Biography of Rosa Townsend*, UWA Press, Nedlands, p. 34.

64 Mairi McKenzie, interview with author, 13 October 1994.

65 Justina Williams, *Anger and Love*, pp. 136–137. The family patriarch, Tom Wignall Snr, according to his son, was a member not of the ALP but of a union affiliated with the ALP. Tom Wignall Snr and Prichard had a very close relationship, to the point of romantic attachment.

66 Franklin Print bought its own linotype machine on hire purchase in late 1937 or early 1938 (NAA, A6119, item 1528).

67 Joan Vike, interview with author, 4 December 1994.

68 Ron Davidson, *High Jinks at the Hot Pool*, p. 179.

69 *The West Australian*, 29 July 1937.

70 *The Workers' Star*, 19 December 1937. This was, nevertheless, a significant increase from the 2700 national members in mid-1936 (Stuart Macintyre, *The Reds*, p. 351). Western Australian membership numbered 219 in mid-1937 (Marx House 'Statistical Return for W.A. District C.P. of A. to 30/6/38', NAA, A6119, item 1529).

71 Peter Coleman, 1974, *Obscenity, Blasphemy, Sedition: 100 Years of Censorship in Australia*, Angus & Robertson, Sydney. The federal government established the Literature Censorship Board to replace the temporary Book Censorship Board (1933–1937).

72 Joyce Stevens, 1987, *Taking the Revolution Home: Work Among Women in the Communist Party of Australia: 1920–1945*, Sybylla Press, Fitzroy, p. 66–67. The Modern Women's Club was at Chancery House at 3–5 Howard Street in Perth.

73 *The Workers' Star*, 29 April 1938, p. 3. Concern for the plight of Aboriginal people was considered grounds for suspicion, surveillance and sometimes character assassination in Australia at this time.

74 Special Bureau, Criminal Investigation Branch report, August 1941 (NAA, A6119/84, item 1944, folio 14). The Modern Women's Club was dissolved in July 1958.

75   Bill Irwin, interview with Melony Hyde, 8 March 1995.
76   *The West Australian*, 5 July 1937, p. 2.
77   *The Mirror*, 3 July 1937, p. 4.
78   *The West Australian*, 2 July 1937, p. 11.
79   *Daily News*, 2 July 1937, p. 10.
80   ibid.
81   A Sydney New Theatre performance of *Where's That Bomb?*, directed by Jerold Wells, took place in October 1937.
82   George Wignall, interview with Julie Wells, 8 August 1984.
83   John Oldham, interview with Jane Fleming, 29 September 1981.
84   John Oldham, interview with author, 11 October 1994, and letter to author, 19 February 1995; Ray Oldham, letter to author, 1 March 1995; and Bruce Harris, letter to author, 14 July 1993. 'Money Power' was a pejorative expression of Capitalism.
85   Guild performances of *Where's That Bomb?* took place at Midland Junction and the Victoria Park Literary Institute (under the auspices of the Adult Education Board of UWA study group), as well as at Trades Hall and other trade union functions and meetings (*The Workers' Star*, 18 June 1937, p. 5).
86   Terry Craig, 'Radical and Conservative Theatre in Perth in the 1930s', pp. 109–111.
87   *The West Australian*, 21 June 1937, p. 16. For further reports on the UWA ban on the play, see also *The West Australian*, 1 July 1937, p. 24, and 8 July 1937, p. 23; *Daily News*, 19 June 1937, p. 2; and *The Workers' Star*, 25 June 1937, p. 4.
88   *The Workers' Star*, 13 August 1937, p. 4.
89   Phyllis Ophel, interview with author, 19 June 1994.
90   A Sydney Workers' Art Club production of *Waiting For Lefty*, directed by Jerold Wells, was staged in late January 1936, and by its antecedent, the New Theatre League, in late February 1936.
91   John Hepworth, interview with author, 18 June 1994.
92   *The Workers' Star*, 9 July 1937, p. 4.
93   Joan Williams, interview with author, 16 October 1994.
94   Keith George, letter to Ric Throssell, November 1971.
95   *The West Australian*, 2 July 1937, p. 11.
96   Paul Herlinger, *A History of New Theatre, 1939–1953*, p. 66.
97   Peter Cowan, letter to author, 18 August 1995.
98   Peter Cowan, *The Hills of Apollo Bay*, pp. 40–41.
99   See Richard Nile's introduction to J.M. Harcourt, *Upsurge: A Novel*.
100 Peter Cowan, letter to author, 24 October 1995.
101 Arthur Rudkin, interview with Ken Mansell, 7 December 1981.
102 Phyllis Ophel, interviews with author, 30 July 1994 and 21 July 1995.
103 The Bunbury CPA branch had been established by late October 1937. Angelo appears to have been relieved by Gus Stagg, who took up a full-time position as CPA organiser for Bunbury and surrounding districts in February 1939 (*The Workers' Star*, 10 February 1939, p. 1).
104 Bill Irwin, interview with author, 8 March 1995.
105 *The Collie Mail and W.A. Coalfields Miner*, 23 September 1937. This issue includes a review of the Guild performance.
106 George Wignall, interview with Julie Wells, 8 August 1984.
107 Paul Hasluck, *Mucking About*, p. 245.
108 N.Y. Purves, *The Growth and Development of the Perth Repertory Club and National Theatre*, p. 39; and *Music and the Drama*, vol. 5, no. 3, 10 September 1937, Perth.

109 James Quinn interview, 17 May 1976. Quinn was secretary of the Five Arts Club in 1932 and also directed Playbox plays.
110 Dorothy Krantz, interview with author, 16 October 1994; and Joyce Riley interview, March 1976, OH 125, Battye Library, SLWA, Perth.
111 *Music and the Drama*, vol. 5, no. 3, 10 September 1937, Perth, p. 2.
112 ibid.
113 Plays for the Drama Festival competition were required to be submitted under a pseudonym, and Harnett chose 'Yalden', her third given name (after Thomas Yalden, 1671–1736, an ancestor who was an English poet of some renown in the Middle Ages).
114 In a lecture on Australian drama in 1942, Katharine Susannah Prichard nominated Harnett's *I Am Angry* as one of the best Australian plays written up to that time.
115 *Music and the Drama*, vol. 5, no. 4, 10 October 1937, Perth, pp. 4–5.
116 Phyllis Ophel, interview with author, 21 July 1995.
117 *The West Australian*, 6 October 1937, p. 21. *I Am Angry* bore some resemblance to Prichard's early play *Her Place*, which was a similar social critique of the idle rich.
118 Hepworth's play *We Are Hungry* was mistakenly placed among the radio play entries.
119 John Hepworth, introduction to his play *Yellow Ticket* (written under the pseudonym 'Reeve'). Copy of script in author's possession.
120 ibid.
121 Phyllis Ophel, interviews with author, 21 July 1995 and 7 February 1996. A Laurence Olivier–Lionel Barrymore–Boris Karloff film with the same title (and on the same topic) had been made in 1931.
122 Phyllis Ophel, interviews with author, 21 July 1995 and 7 February 1996. It was assumed that the last copy of *Yellow Ticket* was 'destroyed by enemy action' during the Japanese bombing of Darwin in February 1942 while Hepworth was serving there. It apparently led Oriel Gray, Hepworth's later wife, to remark at the time that she had 'never realised before what perceptive literary critics the Japanese are'. A copy of the play, originally typed for Hepworth by Kathleen Hector, turned up in Hector's house in Sydney in the late 1990s, a copy of which is in the author's possession.
123 Kathleen Hector, interview with author, 22 March 1997.
124 Gordon Burgoyne, letter to Ric Throssell, May 1972. Joan Vike also said that Hepworth was frequently 'fussed over' at the Guild (Joan Vike, interview with author, 4 December 1994).
125 Hepworth recalled later that McClintock 'was going through a Dada-ist period at the time, so I joined him' (John Hepworth, interview with author, 18 June 1994). Hepworth later described McClintock, who apparently hated joining 'anything', as the Workers' Art Guild's 'most prominent non-member' (John Hepworth, interview with Julian Goddard, n.d).
126 John Hepworth, interviews with author, 18 June 1994 and 21 September 1994.
127 John Hepworth, interview with author, 18 June 1994.

9: 'OFFENSIVE EPITHETS'
1 Keith George, introducing the Workers' Art Guild production of *Hinkemann*, 1937.
2 *Music and the Drama*, vol. 5, no. 3, 10 September 1937, Perth, pp. 7–11.
3 *The West Australian*, 5 October 1937, p. 24.
4 Undated clipping from *The West Australian*, Gilchrist Papers, MN 1034, ACC 3255A/5, Battye Library, SLWA, Perth.

5   *Music and the Drama*, vol. 5, no. 3, 10 September 1937, Perth, pp. 7–11.
6   *Music and the Drama*, vol. 5, no. 4, 10 October 1937, Perth, p. 5.
7   Undated newspaper clipping, Gilchrist Papers, MN 1034, ACC 3255A/16, Battye Library, SLWA, Perth.
8   *The West Australian*, 7 October 1937, p. 17. The Guild program for *Hinkemann* incorrectly credited Howard Smith as the play's director.
9   Phyllis Ophel, interview with author, 19 June 1994.
10 Phyllis Ophel, interview with author, 7 February 1996.
11 ibid.
12 *Music and the Drama*, vol. 5, no. 3, 10 October 1937, Perth, p. 5.
13 *The West Australian*, 7 October 1937, p. 17.
14 *The West Australian*, 8 October 1937, p. 28.
15 Phyllis Ophel, interview with author, 19 June 1994.
16 ibid.
17 Joan Vike, interview with author, 26 March 1993.
18 Nicholas Hern, 1972, 'The Theatre of Ernst Toller', *Theatre Quarterly*, vol. 2, no. 5, January–March, London, pp. 81–83.
19 Bill Irwin, interview with author, 8 March 1995.
20 *Music and the Drama*, vol. 5, no. 3, 10 October 1937, Perth, p. 5.
21 *The Mirror*, 9 October 1937, p. 4.
22 Phyllis Ophel, interview with author, 7 February 1996.
23 *Music and the Drama*, vol. 5, no. 3, 10 October 1937, Perth, p. 14.
24 Justina Williams, *The First Furrow*, p. 154, and *Anger and Love*, p. 66.
25 Phyllis Ophel, interview with author, 7 February 1996.
26 Phyllis Ophel, interview with author, 1 November 1997. See also Rolf Harris interview, July 1997, OH 226, Battye Library, SLWA, Perth.
27 Tom Wignall, interview with author, 17 October 1994.
28 Katharine Susannah Prichard, letter to Mollie Skinner, 12 October 1937, Papers of Mary Louisa Skinner, MN 186, ACC 3490A/16/1, Battye Library, SLWA, Perth.
29 *The West Australian*, 13 October 1937, p. 18.
30 Letter to the editor, *The West Australian*, 9 October 1937, p. 24.
31 *The West Australian*, 13 October 1937, p. 18.
32 *Daily News*, 5 October 1937, p. 6. The 'volume of one-act plays' then just published in Sydney was William Moore and T. Inglis Moore (eds), 1937, *Best Australian One-Act Plays*, Angus & Robertson, Sydney. Plays by Western Australians in the book included *Pioneers* (Katharine Susannah Prichard), *Dampier's Ghost* (Henrietta Drake-Brockman), *Hester Siding* (Alexander Turner) and *Sub-Editor's Room* (Leslie Rees).
33 *The West Australian*, 11 October 1937, p. 10.
34 *Music and the Drama*, vol. 5, no. 3, 10 September 1937, Perth, p. 7.
35 *The Sydney Morning Herald*, 11 October 1937, p. 13.
36 Undated newspaper clipping, Gilchrist Papers, MN 1034, ACC 3255A/5, Battye Library, SLWA, Perth.
37 *The Lyons Bungles* was also known as *The Lyons Review*. George Wignall recalled that it was primarily written (with some help) by Bill Irwin (George Wignall, interview with Julie Wells, 8 August 1984). Alec King was likely also involved in oversight of the Guild writers' group at this time. A copy of the script of *The Lyons Review* can be found in box 127 of the New Theatre Archives, Mitchell Library, SLNSW, Sydney.
38 Victor Arnold, 'Agit Prop in W.A.'.

39 *The Workers' Star*, 22 October 1937, p. 4. *The Lyons Bungles* may have been written in response to an article by John S. Baker titled 'Elections Theatre', published in Adelaide's *Workers' Weekly Herald* in mid-October 1937. Baker, who had formed a theatre group in Adelaide in 1937, probably sent a copy of this article (prior to publication) to the various left-wing Australian theatre groups. In it he 'called for the dramatization of issues which would expose to both industrial and rural workers the hypocrisy of the Lyons Federal Government' and that elements of fascist suppression were evident in some decisions of the Lyons government (Peter Douglas, 1994, *Origins: A History of the Adelaide New Theatre Movement 1937 to 1950*, BA Hons, Dip. Ed., Flinders University, Adelaide, pp. 22 and 79). The appearance of the *Lyons Bungles* shortly after Baker's article was published, and the striking similarities between what Baker wrote of the Lyons government's record and those events dramatised by the *Lyons Bungles* — including caricatures of 'the farmer' and 'the factory worker' — appear to be more than coincidental. The following year, Baker published a book on the history of the international left-wing theatre movement, titled *The Right Theatre is Left*.

40 F.K. Crowley (ed.), 1974, *A New History of Australia*, Heinemann, Melbourne, p. 448.

41 Freer was eventually allowed into the country eight months later, after her case was taken to the High Court. Her Australian soldier was by then in another relationship.

42 George Wignall, interview with Julie Wells, 8 August 1984.

43 Victor Arnold, 'Agit Prop in W.A.'.

44 *The Workers' Star*, 29 October 1937, p. 3.

45 *The Workers' Star*, 22 October 1937, p. 4; and George Wignall, interview with Julie Wells, 8 August 1984.

46 In an issue of *The Workers' Star* just prior to the election, Prichard wrote an article urging the 'Middle Class' to vote Labor (*The Workers' Star*, 22 October 1937).

47 Note written by Katharine Susannah Prichard in 1942 (MS 6201/7/4, NLA). The UWA address was given on 21 July 1942.

48 The old Trades Hall in Beaufort Street was opened in 1912. The Unity Theatre, a large hall at the rear of the building, seated 1500 people and was designed as a theatre and general entertainment venue to help offset the Trades Hall's costs, but it was predominantly used for ALP conferences, union mass meetings and social functions, and the occasional boxing bout. The Unity Theatre closed in 1967 (*The West Australian*, 18 April 1975, p. 7). The building still stands, next to Curtin House in Beaufort Street.

49 Arnold Zable, 1998, *Wanderers and Dreamers: Tales of the David Herman Theatre*, Hyland House, Melbourne; Israel Cohen, 1943, *Vilna*, Jewish Publication Society of America, Philadelphia, pp. 372–373 and 444–445; and interviews with Arnold Zable and David Waislitz (son of Jacob Waislitz).

50 Phyllis Ophel, interview with author, 21 July 1995.

51 The play was made into a film in the USSR that year (1937), for which the screenplay was co-written by Friedrich Wolf. It was the first feature-length Soviet film seen in Australia when it screened some years later (Justina Williams, *Anger and Love*, p. 106).

52 Phyllis Ophel, interview with author, 21 July 1995.

53 The title *Yellow Spot* referred to the star insignia worn by Jews in Nazi Germany. This play is also known as *Yellow Patch*. In Jewish mythology, a *dybbuk* is a pernicious possessive spirit thought to be the soul of a dead person.

54 Arnold Zable, *Wanderers and Dreamers*, p. 40.
55 Hilary L. Rubinstein, 1991, *The Jews in Australia, Volume 1*, William Heinemann, Melbourne.
56 There was also a rival Yiddish theatre in Perth in the 1930s under the control of Oscar Thau, as well as the Jewish United Dramatic Society and the Hebrew Dramatic Society (David Mossenson, 1990, *Hebrew, Israelite, Jew: The History of the Jews of Western Australia*, UWA Press, Nedlands, p. 132; and *Jewish Communal Directory*, Perth, 1935).
57 In the three years prior to the Second World War, the relatively small intake of Jews into Western Australia comprised 123 from Germany and Austria, fifty-three from Poland and nine from Italy (David Mossenson, *Hebrew, Israelite, Jew*, pp. 142 and 145).
58 Don Watson, 1975, 'Anti-Communism in the Thirties', *Arena*, no. 37, pp. 40–51. Many Jewish immigrants were members of the Communist Party in opposition to European fascism.
59 David Mossenson, *Hebrew, Israelite, Jew*, p. 129.
60 The Masel homes were all named Java Head, after Joseph Hergesheimer's book of the same name. Harold Krantz designed the Masels' Peppermint Grove home, Java Head 2. The Masels' Nedlands home, Java Head 3, was adjacent to the Osborne Steps in Claremont and to the steep slope down to a spectacular broad reach of the Swan River.
61 Phyllis Harnett was, according to a police report, 'reported to have been an active member of the Communist Party in W.A., 1937–1943' (NAA, A6119/8, item 1944).
62 Phyllis Ophel, interviews with author, 21 July 1995 and 7 February 1996.
63 Phyllis Ophel, interview with author, 30 July 1994.
64 See, for example, 'Left Book Club Explains', *Daily News*, 19 February 1941, p. 6.

10: STANDING GUARD FOR THE PARTY

1 Peter Cowan, *The Hills of Apollo Bay*, pp. 61–62.
2 William Moore and T. Inglis Moore (eds), *Best Australian One-Act Plays*, p. xxiv. William Moore had worked in the theatre with Prichard and the Essons on the Annual Drama Nights in Melbourne twenty-five years earlier.
3 Paul Herlinger, *New Theatre, 1932–1939*.
4 At that time, Western Australia commemorated Labour Day in early May.
5 *The Workers' Star*, 6 May 1938.
6 *Daily News*, 4 May 1938.
7 *The West Australian*, 1 October 1937, p. 24.
8 ibid.
9 Vike's shift from landscape to urban art was inspired, in part, by a touring exhibition of contemporary Canadian art shown at AGWA in 1937. A few weeks after his solo exhibition, Vike was represented in a major showing of some 150 works of Western Australian Art at AGWA, the first major survey of Western Australian art ever held.
10 Leah Healy, interviews with author, 18 September 1996 and 26 November 1996.
11 ibid.; and Joan Vike, interviews with author, 4 December 1994, 3 June 1995 and 3 June 1999.
12 Joan Vike, interview with author, 14 December 1994.
13 Bill Irwin remembers Hope Bath as 'the only real secretary' of the Guild 'that was worthy of the name' (Bill Irwin, interview with author, 15 October 1994). When Phyllis Harnett took over the role after her position as manager of the CPA

Radical Bookshop came to an end, she was paid double the wage she had earned at the Radical Bookshop (Phyllis Ophel, interview with author, 21 July 1995). CPA 'functionaries' "sustenance" was nominally about 20% more than the dole, but there was hardly ever enough in the kitty to pay even this in full' (Arthur Rudkin, draft article prepared for *The Tribune*). Harnett remained a paid Guild official until Victor Arnold took over the reins in late July 1940.

14   Keith George, letter to Ric Throssell, November 1971.
15   ibid.
16   ibid.
17   ibid
18   Katharine Susannah Prichard, letter to Mikhail Apletin, 3 July 1938, Papers of Katharine Susannah Prichard, ACC 5835A/3, folio 30, Battye Library, SLWA, Perth.
19   *The Workers' Star*, 27 May 1938. Prichard's plays *Women of Spain* and *Forward One* also reflected her concern with the plight and universal rights of women (Drusilla Modjeska, *Exiles at Home*, p. 147; and Henrietta Drake-Brockman, 1967, 'Katharine Susannah Prichard', in Geoffrey Dutton (ed.), *Australian Writers and Their Work*, Oxford University Press, Melbourne, p. 10).
20   Jack Bedson and Julian Croft (eds), 1993, *The Campbell Howard Annotated Index of Australian Plays, 1920–1955*, Centre for Australian Language and Literature Studies, UNE, Armidale.
21   Ric Throssell, *Wild Weeds and Wind Flowers*, pp. 82 and 254.
22   Justina Williams, *Anger and Love*, p. 65.
23   Ric Throssell, 'Paths Towards Purpose', p. 32.
24   *The Workers' Star*, 2 September 1938, p. 1. Copies of the play *Women of Spain* are held in the Campbell Howard Collection, UNE, Armidale; in the Prichard Papers, NLA, Canberra; and in the Melbourne New Theatre Archives, Performing Arts Department, University of Melbourne.
25   *The Workers' Star*, 27 May 1938, p. 4.
26   *The Workers' Star*, 24 June 1938, p. 4.
27   Workers' Art Guild program for *Inga*.
28   ibid.
29   *The West Australian*, 28 May 1938, p. 6. See also Paul Hasluck's review of *Inga* in *The West Australian*, 18 June 1938, p. 21.
30   Workers' Art Guild program for *Inga*.
31   Phyllis Ophel, interview with author, 7 February 1996.
32   Phyllis Ophel, interview with author, 21 July 1995.
33   Phyllis Ophel, interview with author, 7 February 1996. Betty Campbell also played a leading role in Beryl Seward's production of Phyllis Harnett's *I Am Angry* during the 1937 Drama Festival.
34   *The West Australian*, 18 June 1938, p. 21.
35   Bill Mountjoy, letter to Katharine Susannah Prichard, 12 April 1938, NAA, A6119/83, item 1529, folio 114.
36   According to Joan Williams, Mountjoy 'resented Mrs. Throssell's wide influence, possibly because she was a woman, but mostly because she frankly expressed disapproval of his drinking' (Justina Williams, *The First Furrow*, p. 139). Mountjoy possibly also resented Prichard's close personal connections with members of the CPA's central committee. Despite this, Lindsay Mountjoy suggested that she and her husband had a close personal relationship with Prichard (Ric Throssell, *Wild Weeds and Wind Flowers*, pp. 235–236). It seems that it certainly soured in the latter 1930s: Prichard wrote to the central

committee complaining about Mountjoy's drinking and 'unreliability', but the committee did not intercede (Stuart Macintyre, *The Reds*, p. 354).
37   Ric Throssell, *My Father's Son*, p. 118.
38   C. Hartley Grattan, 1949, *Introducing Australia*, Angus & Robertson, Sydney.
39   Katharine Susannah Prichard, letter to Hartley Grattan, 27 June 1938, cited in Laurie Hergenhan, 1995, *No Casual Traveller: Hartley Grattan and Australia*, University of Queensland Press, St Lucia, p. 132.
40   Peter Cowan, *The Hills of Apollo Bay*, pp. 61–63.
41   Cecil W. Davies, 1972, 'The Volksbühne: A Descriptive Chronology', *Theatre Quarterly* (London), vol. 2, no. 5, January–March, pp. 57–59.
42   *The Workers' Star*, 1 July 1938.
43   *The Workers' Star*, 12 March 1938, p. 4.
44   ibid.
45   *The West Australian*, 8 August 1938, p. 18.
46   Sydney Ure Smith (ed.), 1939, *Australian Art Annual 1939*, Ure Smith Pty Ltd, Sydney, p. 20.
47   ibid.
48   Phyllis Ophel, interview with author, 19 June 1994.
49   *The West Australian*, 20 August 1938, p. 10.
50   Humphrey McQueen, 1979, *The Black Swan of Trespass: The Emergence of Modernist Painting in Australia 1918–1944*, Alternative Publishing, Sydney, p. 80.
51   AGWA Trustees purchased a 'Max Ebert' painting in July 1940.
52   Herbert McClintock, interview with Ken Mansell, 6 May 1983. See also *The West Australian*, 15 June 1936, p. 14; and Alec King's article on surrealism in the *Black Swan*, April 1937. Charles Merewether wrote in *Art and Social Commitment* that 'in the late Thirties [McClintock] became a notorious figure when surrealism became the subject of great debate. It received high praise and utter condemnation' and he 'loved it' (p. 100).
53   Herbert McClintock, interview with Ken Mansell, 6 May 1983. McClintock believed he was the first Australian surrealist. He probably was the country's first overtly surrealist painter, though James Cant had referred to the surrealist form in his painting *The Fig Trees* as early as 1932 (this painting is now in the Agapitos/Wilson Collection of Australian surrealist art). Other early examples of the surrealist influence on art in Australia included Max Dupain's and George Finey's surrealist-inspired photographs, exhibited in 1937, and James Gleeson's poem drawings of 1938–1939. Surrealism also influenced Albert Tucker's landscape paintings of 1939 and the Sidney Nolan collages of 1936–1939. The first heralded exhibition of surrealist paintings by Albert Tucker and James Gleeson was held in 1939, and the inaugural Contemporary Art Society exhibition at the National Gallery in Melbourne in June 1939 included surrealist works by Tucker, Gleeson and Eric Thake.
54   Notes for an exhibition of Australian surrealist art from the Agapitos/Wilson Collection at Heide Gallery in 2002–2003.
55   Harald Vike's 1938 painting *Western Australian Museum Looking towards Perth Boys School* was displayed in this exhibition under the title *The Old Museum*. It is now a part of the Janet Holmes à Court collection and is on display at AGWA.
56   *The West Australian*, 6 September 1938, p. 9.
57   Der Blaue Reiter ('the Blue Rider') was a pre–First World War German expressionist art group, of which Franz Marc was a key member.

58 Drama Festival subcommittee member Bill Darbyshire complained of the difficulties for Australian playwrights in a radio talk he gave during the 1938 festival.
59 *The Workers' Star*, 19 August 1938, p. 4.
60 See also Drusilla Modjeska's interview with Betty Roland in *Australasian Drama Studies*, no. 8, April 1986, pp. 66–74.
61 Betty Roland, letter to Paul Hasluck, 19 August 1938, 3499A/8/12, Battye Library, SLWA, Perth.
62 ibid. Roland found many aspects of Soviet society disturbing, and more so later when she learned the full extent of Stalin's 'terror' and the fate of her friends and acquaintances caught up in it. Like Prichard, she chose to keep her disquiet relatively confidential for some time after her return, but she would soon leave the Party she had only recently joined because of her concerns about events within the Soviet Union.
63 *Music and the Drama*, October 1938, p. 8.
64 *Music and the Drama*, August 1938, p. 16.
65 Leslie Rees, *The Making of Australian Drama*, p. 188. The Sydney premiere of *Are You Ready, Comrade?* was in March 1939.
66 Dorothy and Harold Krantz, interview with author, 16 October 1994.
67 *The West Australian*, 10 October 1938, p. 10.
68 ibid.
69 *Music and the Drama*, October 1938, p. 8.
70 *The Workers' Star*, 14 October 1938, p. 2.
71 Phyllis Ophel, interview with author, 19 June 1994.
72 Beryl Hearder, interview with author, 23 January 1996.
73 *The West Australian*, 27 January 1939, p. 22.
74 *Man Gets House* was probably written by Gordon Burgoyne (Bill Irwin, interview with author, 8 March 1995).
75 Second inaugural address of Franklin Delano Roosevelt, 20 January 1937, the Capital, Washington D.C.
76 *The Workers' Star* regularly reported on the shortcomings of the Workers' Homes Board (see, for example, *The Workers' Star*, 10 March 1939, p. 1).
77 Gordon Burgoyne, letter to Ric Throssell, May 1972.
78 Tom Wignall, interview with author, 17 October 1994.
79 Victor Arnold, 'Agit Prop in W.A.'
80 *Socko* was probably written by Bill Irwin (Bill Irwin, interview with author, 8 March 1995).
81 Victor Arnold, 'Agit Prop in W.A.'
82 *The Workers' Star*, 17 March 1939, p. 4.
83 Performances of *Man Gets House* and *Socko* may also have taken place elsewhere other than on the back of a truck. Victor Arnold, referring to performances of the agitprop plays, seemed to differentiate 'the street presentations on a lorry' from other 'street presentations' (Victor Arnold, 'Agit Prop in W.A.').
84 Tom Wignall, interview with author, 17 October 1994.
85 Kathleen Hector, interview with author, 22 October 1995.
86 Letter from Melbourne New Theatre secretary to CPA District Committee, 13 January 1939 (New Theatre League [Victoria], vol. 1, A6122/2, NAA).
87 Phyllis Ophel said that when the 'call came' for the Guild to amalgamate with the New Theatre, the proposal was met with horror by some in the Guild. The amalgamation did not go ahead (Phyllis Ophel, interview with author, 30 July 1994).

88 Paul Hasluck in *The West Australian*, 31 March 1939, p. 21.
89 Ironically, it was Mussolini who later put a stop to the German military annexation of Austria.
90 Austrian fascists later assassinated Dollfuss during an occupation of parliament in an unsuccessful coup attempt in July 1934.
91 Phyllis Ophel, interview with author, 7 February 1996. Ophel remembered *Floridsdorf* as a 'marvellous political education ... for us ... You began to hear of German politics which you would never have heard of otherwise' (ibid.).
92 Ben Kidd, interview with author, 21 March 1995; and Phyllis Ophel, interviews with author, 30 July 1994 and 7 February 1996.
93 Phyllis Ophel, interview with author, 30 July 1994.
94 Phyllis Ophel, interview with author, 21 July 1995.
95 Stanley (Stan) Wilbur, who also performed in the play, was a playwright who had acted with the Repertory Club and was an early member of the Playbox Theatre. He was related by marriage to Harnett's husband Clem Kennedy. Another actor in *Floridsdorf* was William (Will) King, an accountant who, according to police, was a 'leading' CPA member (in the Victoria Park branch). He apparently joined the CPA in the month before *Hinkemann* was performed and was secretary of the Friends of the Soviet Union and treasurer of the 1940 anti-conscription committee as well as a member of the Russian Aid Committee in 1941 (NAA, A6122/40, item 125, folio 36). Pat O'Keefe, who was in charge of props for *Floridsdorf*, had worked as an effects technician on *Where's That Bomb?* and *Waiting For Lefty*, and was later a membership secretary for the Guild. Joan Kidd performed with the Guild's music section orchestra during the performance of *Floridsdorf*.
96 Bruce Bennett (ed.), 1979, *The Literature of Western Australia*, UWA Press, p. 117.
97 Phyllis Ophel, interview with author, 19 June 1994; Joan Williams, interview with author, 16 October 1994; and Joan Williams, letter to author, 17 May 1995.
98 Kathleen Hector, interview with author, 22 March 1997.
99 Paul Hasluck in *The West Australian*, 31 March 1939, p. 21.
100 *The Workers' Star*, 7 April 1939, p. 4.
101 Kathleen Hector, interview with author, 22 March 1997.
102 Kathleen Hector, interview with author, 22 October 1995.
103 Phyllis Ophel, interview with author, 21 July 1995.
104 Stuart Macintyre, *The Reds*, pp. 113–114.
105 Jack Blake, 1971, 'The Early Thirties', *Arena*, no. 25.
106 CPA records (NAA A6119/83, item 1529, folio 66); and Stuart Macintyre, *The Reds*, p. 354.
107 Norman Bartlett, a Perth journalist of the time, wrote later that the citizens of Perth 'were not political automatons — the climate forbade it' (Norman Bartlett, 1977, 'Perth in the Turbulent Thirties', *Westerly*, no. 4, December).

11: LEADING THE REVOLUTION ON A WHITE HORSE

1 Excerpt from letter to the editor of *The Workers' Star*, 5 May 1939, p. 4.
2 *The West Australian*, 13 July 1939, p. 18.
3 *The West Australian*, 13 July 1939, p. 16.
4 John A. McKenzie, *Challenging Faith*, p. 91. For other reports of the incident, see Justina Williams, *Anger and Love*, p. 82; and *The Mirror*, 15 July 1939, p. 13.
5 Phyllis Ophel, interview with author, 21 July 1995.
6 *The West Australian*, 13 July 1939; *The Workers' Star*, 14 July 1939, p. 1; and Leah Healy, interview with author, 18 September 1996.

7   *The Workers' Star*, 2 June 1939.
8   John Oldham, interview with author, 11 October 1994.
9   Workers' Art Guild theatre program notes for *Cannibal Carnival*.
10 Julian Goddard, talk on the Workers' Art Guild, November 1990, transcript held in Battye Library, SLWA, Perth.
11 Workers' Art Guild theatre program notes for *Cannibal Carnival*, 1939.
12 Letter to the editor, *Daily News*, 18 July 1939, p. 24.
13 ibid.
14 Bill Irwin, interview with Melony Hyde, 8 March 1995.
15 Ric Throssell, interview with author, 3 November 1995. Many years later Ric Throssell directed *Antony & Cleopatra* for the Canberra Repertory Club as an anti-war play and he presented the character of Antony as 'a real slob' (Ric Throssell, letter to Keith George, November 1971). For another version of the Keith George *Antony & Cleopatra* clash, see Don Batchelor, *The Context of Australian Playwriting 1939–1968*, p. 23.
16 Bill Irwin, interview with Melony Hyde, 8 March 1995.
17 Keith George, letter to Ric Throssell, November 1971.
18 Joan Vike (nee Kidd), interview with author, 3 June 1995.
19 *The West Australian*, 15 July 1939, p. 4. The poster for *Cannibal Carnival*, incorrectly credited to John Oldham, is now held in the collection of the AGWA (accession number 985/OOQ7). Oldham had no involvement with the production given he was no longer in Perth (John Oldham, interviews with author, 11 October 1994 and 17 January 1996). Irene Keiller or Leith Angelo may have designed the poster. AGWA records for Workers' Art Guild posters also incorrectly state that they were made by stencil/screen-print. John Oldham stated categorically to the author that he never used screen-printing for these posters, they were linocuts, but as Oldham did not produce the poster for *Cannibal Carnival*, it may have been paper-stencilled and silk-screened.
20 *Daily News*, 15 July 1939, p. 17.
21 Phyllis Ophel, interview with author, 21 July 1995.
22 Patricia Thompson, *Accidental Chords*, p. 164.
23 Roslyn Poignant, interview with author, 13 October 1994. Poignant also came into fleeting contact with Phyllis Harnett outside a Sydney theatre where he worked as a theatre commissionaire at this time, and they struck up a casual acquaintance.
24 Roslyn Poignant, 1993, 'The Photographic Witness?', *Continuum*, vol. 6, issue 2, p. 180.
25 ibid.
26 Poignant and Chase were not divorced until 1941.
27 Axel Poignant, 1978, 'Axel Poignant' in Laurence Le Guay (ed.), *Australian Photography: A Contemporary View*, The Globe Publishing Company, Sydney, pp. 8–11.
28 Some of Poignant's films — including Linley Wilson's dance performances, at least one Greenmount picnic and the 1939 Labour Day parade — are held in the National Film and Sound Archive, Canberra.
29 'Lumpers' were waterside workers, or 'wharfies'. For a history of the Fremantle Lumpers' Union and a report on the Lumpers' Union celebration, see *The Westralian Worker*, 7 July 1939, p. 1.
30 Letter to the editor of *The Workers' Star*, 5 May 1939, p. 4. Detective Ron Richards, a senior member of the West Australian police force, described Lachberg leading the Labour Day procession as a 'Red on a white horse' (*The West Australian*, 11 June 1941, p.3)

31 *Westralian Worker*, 17 March 1939, p. 9.
32 *The West Australian*, 25 April 1939, p. 5. For information on Harald Vike's trade union banners, see Ann Stephen and Andrew Reeves, 1985, *Badges of Labour, Banners of Pride*, Allen & Unwin, Sydney; Lenore Layman and Julian Goddard, *Organise!*; and David Bromfield, 'A Dream of New York' in *Aspects of Perth Modernism 1929–1942*, p. 12.
33 *Westralian Worker*, 17 March 1939, p. 9; and *The West Australian*, 26 May 1939, p. 13. A copy of the 1939 Labour Day parade film by Axel Poignant and Keith George is held in the National Film and Sound Archives in Canberra.
34 Keith George, letter to Ric Throssell, November 1971.
35 Bill Irwin, interview with author, 15 October 1994.
36 Tom Wignall, interview with author, 17 October 1994.
37 Phyllis Ophel, interview with author, 19 June 1994.
38 Mairi McKenzie, interview with author, 13 October 1994.
39 Arthur Rudkin, c. 1984, 'Reminiscence of the Perth Workers' Art Guild', held in the Sydney New Theatre archives (courtesy David Milliss).
40 Ric Throssell, interview with author, 3 November 1995.
41 Phyllis Ophel, interview with author, 19 June 1994.
42 Bill Irwin, interview with Melony Hyde, 8 March 1995.
43 'The committee won, and defiantly Keith retired to his farm' (Ric Throssell, *My Father's Son*, p. 156).
44 Keith George, letter to Ric Throssell, November 1971.
45 Bill Irwin, interview with author, 15 October 1994.
46 Ric Throssell, interview with author, 3 November 1995.
47 Keith George, letter to Ric Throssell, November 1971.
48 ibid.
49 Phyllis Ophel, interview with author, 7 February 1996.
50 Tom Wignall, interview with author, 17 October 1994.
51 Phyllis Ophel, interview with author, 19 June 1994.
52 *The West Australian*, 20 May 1939, p. 21.
53 *The Workers' Star*, 26 May 1939, p. 4.
54 ibid.
55 *The West Australian*, 20 May 1939, p. 21.
56 Phyllis Ophel, interview with author, 29 January 1997.
57 Phyllis Ophel, interview with author, 19 June 1994.
58 See also *The Australian Quarterly*, vol. 12, no. 1, March 1940, pp. 24–30; and *The Age*, 'Review' supplement, 24 January 2004, pp. 1–2.
59 *The West Australian*, 23 August 1939, p. 14.
60 ibid.
61 Phyllis Ophel, interview with author, 11 September 1996.
62 John Gilchrist, 'Recollections of the Workers' Art Guild', Gilchrist Papers, MN 1034, ACC 3255A/16, Battye Library, SLWA, Perth.
63 Keith George, letter to Ric Throssell, November 1971.
64 *The Workers' Star*, 2 June 1939, made reference to the exciting new agitprop work of the Workers' Art Guild.
65 Keith George, letter to Ric Throssell, November 1971.
66 ibid.
67 Gordon Burgoyne, letter to Ric Throssell, May 1972.
68 ibid.

12: THE WAR, AND 'BLOOD ON THE MOON'

1. Peter Cowan, *The Hills of Apollo Bay*, p. 67.
2. This was the Herald Exhibition of French and British Contemporary Art, sponsored by Melbourne's *Herald and Weekly Times*. For more information on this exhibition, see Eileen Chanin and Steven Miller, 2005, *Degenerates and Perverts: The 1939 Herald Exhibition of French and British Contemporary Art*, Miegunyah Press, Melbourne.
3. C. Hartley Grattan, *Introducing Australia*, pp. 175–176.
4. James Stuart MacDonald, cited in *The Weekend Australian*, 20–21 November 1999, 'Review', p. 18.
5. Janda Gooding, 1985, *Herbert McClintock's Years in Perth 1934–1940*, unpublished manuscript, AGWA Archive.
6. *The West Australian*, 15 August 1939, p. 14, and 16 August 1939, p. 15.
7. *Daily News*, 11 August 1939, p. 21.
8. *Approximate Portrait in a Drawing Room*, a Freudian image symbolising the fear of castration, was painted in 1938 and its setting was the banks of Perth's Swan River.
9. *Daily News*, 14 October 1939, p. 5.
10. Despite this, the *Daily News* did not cover the Guild's 'Modern Art' lectures.
11. *Daily News*, 16 August 1939, p. 24. William Hatfield was the pseudonym of Australian author Ernest Chapman (1892–1969), who gave a lecture at the Workers' Art Guild rooms in July 1939 on 'The Geography of Capitalism'.
12. Vike's painting *Perth Roofs (Suburban Perth)* (1939) is now held in AGWA's permanent collection. The exhibition included Colin Colahan's portrait of John and Pat Thompson. Colahan had introduced the pair in London.
13. Herbert McClintock, interview with Janda Gooding, 17 August 1984, AGWA Archive. McClintock was 'a frightfully nervous bloke on stage [and] always found it difficult' to speak publicly. He said of this lecture: 'I got the shock of my life. I was sitting there scribbling it out, writing something, looked up and there was a huge mob of people' (Herbert McClintock, interview with Ken Mansell, 6 May 1983).
14. Dr 'Kurt Rodgers' (a pseudonym) was a local German Jew and art expert later interned as a German alien during the war.
15. Phyllis Ophel, interview with author, 7 February 1996.
16. A.J.P. Taylor, 1996, *The Origins of the Second World War*, Simon & Schuster, New York, p. 246.
17. Arthur Rudkin, draft article prepared for *The Tribune*.
18. *The Workers' Star*, 6 October 1939.
19. *The Workers' Star*, 29 September 1939.
20. Phyllis Ophel, interview with author, 19 June 1994.
21. *The West Australian*, 25 September 1939, p. 11.
22. *The Australian Quarterly*, 'The Drama' column, September 1939.
23. Phyllis Ophel, interview with author, 19 December 1997.
24. Katherine Perrin, letter to author, 27 August 1997.
25. Phyllis Ophel, interview with author, 21 July 1995.
26. Peter Conole, *Protect and Serve*, p. 230.
27. Western Australian Police report, 'W.A. Art Club Alleged to Be Run by Aliens', NAA, A6335/1, item 21.
28. ibid.
29. ibid.
30. ibid.
31. ibid.

32 ibid.
33 ibid.
34 ibid. A footnote to the report stated that the Guild 'is well known in the amateur theatrical circles'. See also the *Daily News*, 3 October 1939, p. 7, for an abridged version of events.
35 Phyllis Ophel, interviews with author, 21 July 1995 and 7 February 1996.
36 ibid.
37 *The West Australian*, 25 September 1939, p. 11.
38 *The Workers' Star*, 6 October 1939, p. 4. The Guild musical quartet's accompaniment to *Blood on the Moon* from the theatre's orchestra pit included Max Bruch's mournful Jewish standard, *Kol Nidrei* (Op. 47). George and Thomas Benn accompanied Joan Kidd on violin, without Maurice Benn who had recently sailed to London where he arrived a short time after the declaration of war. Patricia Darragh was responsible for the play's musical arrangements.
39 Phyllis Ophel, interview with author, 21 July 1995.
40 Phyllis Ophel, interview with author, 19 December 1997; and *The Workers' Star*, 13 October 1939, p. 4.
41 *Daily News*, 7 October 1939, p. 7. See also *The West Australian*, 7 October 1939, p. 17.
42 Repertory Club brochure, c. June 1939, held in the records of the Western Australian Theatre Company, SLWA, Perth. This reference to 'bitterness' probably telegraphs the political differences between the Repertory Club and the Guild. The indication that *No More Peace* was not as didactic a play as previous Toller works may also have been a means of allaying the fears of members who were concerned about the Club's shift to a more left-wing drama repertoire.
43 *The West Australian*, 23 September 1939, p. 15.
44 *The West Australian*, 4 September 1939, p. 13.
45 N.Y. Purves, *The Growth and Development of the Perth Repertory Club and National Theatre*, pp. 40–41.
46 *The Workers' Star*, 8 September 1939, p. 4.
47 ibid.
48 *The Workers' Star*, 15 September 1939.
49 *The West Australian*, 23 September 1939, p. 15.
50 Phyllis Ophel, interview with author, 21 July 1995.
51 Phyllis Ophel, interview with author, 1 November 1997.
52 'Backseat', in *The Workers' Star*, had praised *Juno and the Paycock* as 'probably the most interesting play' of the 1938 Drama Festival after *Are You Ready, Comrade?* (7 October 1938, p. 3).
53 The Repertory Club staged the 1936 Broadway Comedy *Stage Door* by Edna Ferber and George S. Kaufman in March 1939 (directed by Dorothy Mark), J.B. Priestley's *When We Are Married* and Eugene O'Neill's 1936 play *Ah! Wilderness* in August 1939 (directed by Beryl Seward), and George Bernard Shaw's *The Millionairess* (directed by Jerold Wells), slightly more politically acerbic than the others, in October 1939.
54 Bill Dunstone, 1979, 'Drama', in Bruce Bennett (ed.), *The Literature of Western Australia*, UWA Press, Nedlands, p. 186.
55 George Mulgrue, letter to Repertory Club, June 1939, records of the Western Australian Theatre Company, SLWA, Perth.
56 Repertory Club membership in December 1939 was 783 and its revenue was £1150. Given that Australia was by this time at war, the Club was certainly not in a parlous state.

57 *The Workers' Star*, 4 August 1939 and 8 September 1939, p. 4.
58 *The Workers' Star*, 4 August 1939, p. 4.
59 *The West Australian*, 14 August 1939, p. 13.
60 N.Y. Purves, *The Growth and Development of the Perth Repertory Club and National Theatre*, p. 40.
61 Although this was an increase from the seven plays presented at the previous year's Drama Festival, the 1937 Drama Festival had presented seventeen plays.
62 *The West Australian*, 3 July 1939, p. 21.
63 ibid.
64 Arts academic Julian Goddard has gone so far as to suggest that the Guild became 'a bourgeois institution' at this time (synopsis of talk by Julian Goddard on the Workers' Art Guild, November 1990). However, it was only a few months since the Guild's CPA fraction had dispensed with Keith George. It is more plausible to say that the War and the fact of the USSR becoming a Western ally made the Communist Party and allied institutions more respectable to the liberal middle class, who had previously feared association with such groups. The taste for adventurous art and theatre also diminished with the onset of the War, and Guild productions reflected this.
65 Janda Gooding wrote of this time, 'The Second World War abruptly terminated this surge of interest and openness. The desire for national purity and self-preservation that dominated Australian society throughout the war and immediately after it caused Western Australians to retreat from Internationalism. For many years ... art was relegated to the social pages of the press' (Janda Gooding, *Herbert McClintock's Years In Perth 1934–1940*, p. 9).
66 John McKenzie, letter to author, May/June 1995.
67 Jean Devanny, letter to Katharine Susannah Prichard, 9 January 1940, NAA, A6119/1, item 42, ff. 91–92.
68 ibid.
69 *The Workers' Star* appealed to its readers on 15 December 1939 to 'see that your Union or other organisation sends its greetings to Comrade Stalin next Thursday'.

13: 'THE FERVENT YEARS'

1 Victor Arnold later described the 1930s in New Theatre as 'the fervent years'. This is also the title of a history of the New York Group Theatre in the 1930s (Harold Clurman, 1945, *The Fervent Years: The Story of the Group Theatre and the Thirties*, Alfred Knopf, New York).
2 Victor Williams, 1939, 'Human Drought', a poem about the wheat farmers' strike that Williams also documented in his Living Newspaper *Hold Your Wheat*. 'Human Drought' was first published in *The West Australian Wheatgrower* on 19 December 1940, p. 7, and later in Victor Williams, 1966, *Hammers and Seagulls: Poems by Victor Williams*, Australasian Book Society. Williams later wrote of 'Human Drought' and the wheat dispute: '["Human Drought"] was written in 1939 in the immediate influence of the West Australian wheat farmers strike, or refusal to cart their wheat to the bins at the sidings, taking on the Menzies' Government that had commendeered [sic] all their wheat at 2/2d a bushel ... it plowed [sic] deep into my country and my consciousness' (Victor Williams, letter to Robert Fitzgerald, 10 December 1966, Papers of Robert D. Fitzgerald, MS 7334/140-145, NLA). The 'ten thousand fists' were those of the wheat farmers pitted against the government.
3 Arthur Rudkin, interview with Ken Mansell, 7 December 1981.

4   Bill Irwin, interview with author, 8 March 1995.
5   Arthur Rudkin, interview with Ken Mansell, 7 December 1981. Alcohol was not Mountjoy's only vice. His wife also 'lamented [his] philandering with party women.' (Stuart Macintyre, *The Reds*, p. 238).
6   Peter Conole, *Protect and Serve*, p. 232.
7   Stuart Macintyre, *Militant*, p. 59.
8   Arthur Rudkin, draft article prepared for *The Tribune*.
9   Ric Throssell, interview with author, 25 March 1997.
10 Arthur Rudkin, interview with Ken Mansell, 7 December 1981.
11 Rudkin described McLernon as a 'really vicious bigot' who conducted such thorough raids 'that [they] destroyed every public manifestation of the Communist Party' (Arthur Rudkin, interview with Ken Mansell, 7 December 1981).
12 Paul Hasluck, *Mucking About*, p. 102.
13 Stuart Macintyre, *Militant*, p. 60.
14 *The West Australian*, 'Good Weekend', 14 December 1996, p. 12.
15 Leah Healy, interview with author, 18 September 1996.
16 Phyllis Ophel, interview with author, 1 November 1997.
17 Jean Devanny, letter to Katharine Susannah Prichard, 9 January 1940.
18 Arthur Rudkin, draft article prepared for *The Tribune*.
19 *Star*, 26 April 1940 and 10 May 1940.
20 Arthur Rudkin, draft article prepared for *The Tribune*.
21 Bill and Dorothy Irwin, interview with Don Grant and John McClaren, 10 August 1985.
22 *Star*, 19 April 1940.
23 *The Spark* (CPA state committee circular, Perth), no. 7, 17 April 1940, Q324.29402/06, Mitchell Library, SLNSW, Sydney.
24 CPA W.A. State Committee Circular 25, 27 April 1940, NAA, A6122/40, item 134.
25 Jean Devanny, letter to Katharine Susannah Prichard, 9 January 1940.
26 The *Daily News*, 23 April 1940, p. 8.
27 *The Workers' Star*, 23 February 1940 and 15 March 1940.
28 Victor Williams, interview with author, 18 January 1996.
29 Bernard Heinz, 1971, 'A Theatre for Lefty: USA in the 1930s', *Theatre Quarterly*, vol. 1, no. 4, October–December, London, p. 55; and Arthur Arent, 1971, 'The Techniques of the Living Newspaper', *Theatre Quarterly*, vol. 1, no. 4, October–December, pp. 57–59.
30 Victor Williams, interviews with author, 16 October 1994 and 18 January 1996; and Victor Williams, 1988, 'Why I Am a Communist and a Poet', *Papers in Labour History*, no. 2, October, Australian Society for the Study of Labour History, Department of Industrial Relations, UWA, Perth, pp. 25–26.
31 *The Workers' Star*, 1 January 1937.
32 NAA, A6119, item 1954, folio 8. Williams encouraged the establishment of the Farm Labourers' Union in an impassioned letter to *The West Australian Wheatgrower* on 4 January 1940, p. 5. See also *The West Australian Wheatgrower*, 11 January 1940, p. 2 for an editorial on the proposed Farm Labourers' Union.
33 Williams stated that he had 'a vague utopian socialist kind of line, [but] it was only with the contact with the Workers' Art Guild that I came into the Communist Party' (Victor Williams, interview with author, 16 October 1994).
34 Dorothy Hewett, *Wild Card*.

35 Victor Williams, interviews with author, 16 October 1994 and 18 January 1996; Phyllis Ophel, interview with author, 21 July 1995; and Ric Throssell, interview with author, 25 March 1997.
36 Victor Williams, 1966, introduction to *Hammers and Seagulls*.
37 Victor Williams, 'Why I Am a Communist and a Poet', pp. 25–26.
38 *The Workers' Star*, 18 August 1939.
39 *The Red Star*, 23 February 1934.
40 Victor Williams contributed articles on rural issues to both *The West Australian Wheatgrower* and *The Workers' Star*.
41 Victor Williams, interview with author, 18 January 1996.

14: 'ART AS A WEAPON IN THE PEOPLE'S FIGHT'
1 Peter Cowan, *The Hills of Apollo Bay*, p. 39.
2 *Daily News*, 2 April 1940, p. 8.
3 Phyllis Ophel, interview with author, 21 July 1995.
4 Oriel Gray, interview with author, 7 August 1995.
5 *Daily News*, 2 April 1940, p. 8.
6 Phyllis Ophel, interview with author, 21 July 1995.
7 *Daily News*, 23 April 1940, p. 9.
8 *The Workers' Star*, 12 April 1940, p. 4.
9 *The Workers' Star*, 3 May 1940, p. 2.
10 *The Age*, 4 August 1994, Green Guide, p. 26.
11 *The Workers' Star*, 12 April 1940, p. 4.
12 *Daily News* (Sydney), 2 February 1939, p. 2.
13 Letter dated 29 April 1940, NAA, A6119/1, item 42, folio 98.
14 *Daily News*, 2 April 1940, p. 8.
15 Dorothy Krantz, interview with author, 16 October 1994. Dorothy Powell had married Harold Krantz shortly before the play.
16 Joan Williams, 1988, 'Writing Labor History in Western Australia: My Experience with "The First Furrow"', *Papers in Labour History*, no. 1, January, Society for the Study of Labour History, Department of Industrial Relations, UWA, p. 16).
17 Keith George, letter to Ric Throssell, November 1971.
18 Katharine Susannah Prichard, letter to Bartlett Adamson, 12 June 1940, Papers of Bartlett Adamson, MS 1258/1, folio 199, NLA.
19 Rumours about the sinking of the Oldhams' ship, *Aorangi*, were reported in many Australian newspapers including *The West Australian* (9 September 1939, p. 14).
20 Ray Oldham had known Coombs as a fellow student at UWA, where they had both played an active part in campus politics. Coombs had studied economics under Edward Shann and was remembered by Shann as the 'most brilliant' student he ever taught (Tim Rowse, 2002, *Nugget Coombs: A Reforming Life*, Cambridge University Press).
21 John Oldham, interview with author, 17 January 1996.
22 Arthur Rudkin, interview with Ken Mansell, 7 December 1981.
23 Stuart Macintyre, *Militant*, p. 61.
24 ibid., pp. 60–61.
25 ibid., p. 61.
26 Jean Buckley-Moran, 1986, 'Australian Scientists and the Cold War', in Brian Martin, C.M. Ann Baker, Clyde Manwell and Cedric Pugh (eds), *Intellectual Suppression: Australian Case Histories, Analysis and Responses*, Angus & Robertson, Sydney, pp. 11–23, <www.uow.edu.au/arts/sts/bmartin/pubs/86is/Buckley.html>;

Arthur Rudkin, interview with Ken Mansell, 7 December 1981; Justina Williams, *The First Furrow*, pp. 165–166; John A. McKenzie, *Challenging Faith*, p. 102; *Daily News*, 6 June, 7 June and 10 June 1940; and *The West Australian*, 11 June 1940, p. 9.
27 *Northern Star* (NSW), 8 June 1940, p. 7.
28 *Kalgoorlie Miner*, 11 June 1940, p. 2.
29 W.A. State Committee Circular, 25–27 April 1940, NAA, A6122/40, item 134.
30 *Daily News*, 10 June 1940, p. 1; and *The Canberra Times*, 11 June 1940, p. 2.
31 The Workers' Art Guild had by July 1939 begun conducting classes in 'speech-training' (public speaking), taught by Keith George. Mairi McKenzie remembers George also conducting some classes in public speaking at CPA headquarters (probably in 1939 or thereabouts) because he was very critical of the lack of oratory skills in the Party (Mairi McKenzie, interview with author, 20 January 1996). It seems that George had not entirely cut his ties with the Workers' Art Guild.
32 Justina Williams, *The First Furrow*, p. 166; Arthur Rudkin, interview with Ken Mansell, 7 December 1981; and *Daily News*, 31 May 1940, p. 3.
33 Katharine Susannah Prichard, letter to Timofei Rokotov, 12 June 1940, NAA, A6119/23, item 367, folio 17 and A6119, item 43, ff. 149–150.
34 An article by Katharine Susannah Prichard on Bernard O'Dowd was published in the English-language edition of Moscow's *International Literature* in February 1941, and in a Russian-language edition later that year (Timofei Rokotov, letter to Katharine Susannah Prichard, 6 March 1941, NAA, SP109-3, item 316-10). This was probably the article Prichard sent to the journal in June 1940 that was intercepted and confiscated by authorities.
35 Perth Censor's Office, letter to Chief Publicity Censor, Melbourne, 31 July 1940, NAA, series SP109-3, item 316-10.
36 Timofei Rokotov, letter to Katharine Susannah Prichard, 6 March 1941.
37 MS 6201, box 17, folder 15, folio 39, NLA.
38 'Katharine Susannah Prichard' (Overseas Broadcast VLQ No 333b), written and produced by Irene Greenwood for the Department of Information (Broadcasting Division), went to air on 16 November 1940. An audio recording of the program is held in the Irene Greenwood Collection at Murdoch University, Western Australia. Greenwood joined the CPA in 1942.
39 Ric Throssell, *Wild Weeds and Wind Flowers*, pp. 93–94; and Bill Irwin, letter to Ken Gott, 11 September 1985, MS 13047, 3800/7, La Trobe Library, SLV, Melbourne.
40 Harry Gould, letter to Ric Throssell.
41 Stuart Macintyre, *Militant*, p. 62.
42 NAA, A6119/XR1, item 47. Kevin Healy was sentenced in June 1940.
43 John Oldham, interview with author, 11 October 1994.
44 Joan Williams, interview with author, 18 January 1996.
45 *Star*, 19 April 1940.
46 NAA, A6119/84, item 1942, folio 17.
47 Arthur Rudkin, draft article prepared for *The Tribune*. The 'comrade from the Central Committee' was John Simpson.
48 Arthur Rudkin, interview with Ken Mansell, 7 December 1981.
49 *The Daily Telegraph* (Sydney), 17 June 1940, p. 6.
50 Mooney's Cafe was at 222a William Street, part of the Rechabite Hall building at 222–224 William Street. The building still stands.
51 CIB report, 25 July 1940, NAA, A6119/84, item 1944, folio 8.
52 Some of these notebooks with newspaper extracts are now held in the Prichard Papers at the NLA.

53 Katharine Susannah Prichard ('Throssell'), letter to Ministry of Information, 12 July 1940, NAA, A6119, item 42.
54 ibid.
55 Two of those arrested were given jail sentences of just over two years (seemingly lenient sentences given their crimes, relative to those imposed on CPA members in Western Australia); the other two were interned by the military.
56 NAA, A6119/83, item 1529, folio 81.
57 Justina Williams, *The First Furrow*, p. 170.
58 NAA, A6122/44, item 1492, folio 6.
59 NAA, A6119/79, item 1321, folio 31.
60 Bill Irwin, interview with author, 15 October 1994.
61 ibid.
62 ibid.
63 ibid.; and Bill and Dorothy Irwin, interview with Don Grant and John McClaren, 10 August 1985.
64 NAA, A6119/79, item 1321, folio 31.
65 Arthur Rudkin, draft article prepared for *The Tribune*; and John Oldham, interview with author, 17 January 1996.
66 NAA, A6119, item 1528.
67 Arthur Rudkin, draft article prepared for *The Tribune*; and Bill and Dorothy Irwin, interview with Don Grant and John McClaren, 10 August 1985.
68 Arthur Rudkin, interview with Ken Mansell, 7 December 1981.
69 Arthur Rudkin, draft article prepared for for *The Tribune*.
70 Leah Healy, interview with author, 18 September 1996.
71 'The Kremlin' was on the corner of Salvado Street and Broome Street in Cottesloe. A photograph of it appears in Beryl Hacker, *Rosa*, p. 69. Tenants of 'The Kremlin' through the years included J.B. Miles, Sam Aarons (later Western Australian CPA state secretary) and Gus Stagg. The place was often raided during the time of Menzies's later proposed *Communist Dissolution Act*.
72 Most of the local CPA and Workers' Art Guild records were destroyed or confiscated during the period of CPA illegality. Book stocks in the Radical Bookshop were also confiscated by police or destroyed at the time (Arthur Rudkin, draft article prepared for *The Tribune*).
73 NAA, A6335/1, item 21, folio 15.
74 John Oldham, interview with author, 11 October 1994.
75 NAA, A6335/1, item 21.
76 Bill Irwin, interview with author, 15 October 1994.
77 Harnett's enthusiasm was palpably waning at this time. Prichard had disciplined her for not rehearsing enough for *Blood on the Moon*, and this may have contributed to her dismissal (Phyllis Ophel, interview with author, 19 June 1994).
78 Phyllis Ophel, interview with author, 21 July 1995.
79 Phyllis Ophel, interview with author, 30 July 1994.
80 Phyllis Ophel, Kathleen Hector and Bill Irwin, various interviews with author.
81 *Daily News*, 23 April 1940, p. 8; and Bill Irwin, interview with author, 8 March 1995.
82 Oriel Gray, interview with author, 7 August 1995.
83 Phyllis Ophel, interview with author, 19 June 1994.
84 *The Tribune*, 17 May 1940, no. 72, p. 3.
85 Paul Herlinger, 1986, 'A New Direction for "the New"?', *Australasian Drama Studies*, no. 8, April, p. 98.

86 Oriel Gray, *Exit Left*, p. 33.
87 Victor Arnold, 'Repertory of the Left Theatre' in Paul Herlinger, *A History of New Theatre, 1939–1953*.
88 Victor Arnold, talk on New Theatre, Oral History section, Mitchell Library, SLNSW, Sydney. *War on the Waterfront* was first published in the *Communist Review* in February 1939 (pp. 110–114), and later in *Australasian Drama Studies* no. 8, in April 1986 (pp. 74–76).
89 Victor Arnold, talk on New Theatre.
90 Tom Wignall, interview with author, 17 October 1941.
91 Oriel Gray, interview with author, 7 August 1995.
92 Phyllis Ophel, interviews with author, 21 July 1995 and 19 December 1997; and Esther Missingham, interview with author, 20 January 1996.
93 NAA, A6119/1, item 43, folio 104.
94 Esther Missingham, interview with author, 20 January 1996.

15: 'THE SURREALIST MOB'

1 Peter Cowan, *The Hills of Apollo Bay*, p. 18.
2 'Moonda', 1940, 'The Surrealist Mob', *The West Australian*, 20 July, p. 7.
3 Joan Williams, letter to author, 17 May 1995; and Kathleen Hector, interview with author, 29 December 1996.
4 Justina Williams, *Anger and Love*, p. 64.
5 Kathleen Hector, interviews with author, 22 October 1995 and 29 December 1996.
6 NAA, A6119/84, item 1722, folio 60.
7 Phyllis Ophel, interview with author, 21 July 1995. Hepworth himself said on different occasions that his behaviour led to his sacking and that he was sacked because of police interest in his CPA affairs.
8 Phyllis Ophel, interview with author, 21 July 1995.
9 Charles Merewether, *Art and Social Commitment*; and Alan McCulloch, 1994, *Encyclopedia of Australian Art*, 3rd edition, revised and updated by Susan McCulloch, Allen & Unwin, Sydney.
10 Kathleen Hector, interview with author, 22 October 1995.
11 NAA, A6119/84, item 1944, folio 29.
12 Phyllis Ophel, interview with author, 19 June 1994.
13 *Love on the Dole* was made into a 1941 British feature film starring Deborah Kerr.
14 *The West Australian*, 2 August 1940, p. 10.
15 'W.A. Drama Festivals incorporated still carries on its tradition of encouragement to Australian national drama in spite of … the innumerable difficulties thrown across the track of all arts by war' (*The West Australian*, 23 August 1941, p. 7). The Drama Festivals continued on a much smaller scale through the War until 1943.
16 Copies of the script for *Penalty Clause* (later adapted for a wider audience outside Western Australia and retitled *Solidarity*) are held in the Campbell Howard Collection, UNE, Armidale; Prichard Papers, NLA; and New Theatre Archives, box 112, Mitchell Library, SLNSW, Sydney.
17 *The Workers' Star*, 18 March 1938.
18 *The West Australian*, 8 March 1937, p. 10.
19 Justina Williams, *The First Furrow*, p. 162
20 Details of the incident and its ramifications were reported in *The West Australian*, 17 March 1938, p. 16. See also Stuart Macintyre, *Militant*, pp. 50–53.
21 Paddy Troy, letter to Ric Throssell, 10 December 1975, MS 6201/6/15, NLA.

22   Jack Bedson and Julian Croft (eds), *The Campbell Howard Annotated Index of Australian Plays, 1920–1955*.
23   Esther Missingham, interview with author, 20 January 1996; *The West Australian*, 13 September 1940, p. 16; and *Daily News*, 13 September 1940, p. 9.
24   Written notes by Prichard in a copy of the script for *Solidarity* (formerly titled *Penalty Clause*) sent to Sydney New Theatre, box 112, New Theatre Archives, Mitchell Library, SLNSW, Sydney. See also Dennis Carroll, 1985, *Australian Contemporary Drama 1909–1982: A Critical Introduction*, Peter Lang Publishing, New York, pp. 30–31.
25   Ric Throssell, 'Paths Towards Purpose', p. 32.
26   *The West Australian*, 13 September 1940, p. 16.
27   Keith George, letter to Ric Throssell, November 1971.
28   Gordon Burgoyne, letter to Ric Throssell, May 1972.
29   Katharine Susannah Prichard, letter to Mikhail Apletin, 19 September 1940, Prichard Papers, ACC 5835A/3, Battye Library, SLWA, Perth. Prichard enclosed a copy of *Penalty Clause*, proposing a possible production of the play in the Soviet Union, but expressed concern about a critical Soviet reception to the play. 'In many ways,' she wrote, 'the play may fall short of what you consider it should be. But I was working on actual conditions of a strike which occurred … and anxious not to go beyond the framework of those conditions.' This aesthetic–political conflict between 'an authentic sketch of life' at odds with the 'social significance' of the prescribed Soviet orthodoxy of socialist realism would resurface later that year with the publication of her next novel.
30   *The Red Star*, 6 December 1935. Harmsworth is listed in the security file 'Communists in Western Australia — List of Persons Known to be Associated with Communism in 1940'.
31   *The Red Star*, 7 December 1934, p. 2.
32   *The Red Star*, 6 December 1935.
33   The country known as Yugoslavia did not come into existence until 1929. Herne Hill and Millendon in the Swan Valley (now a major wine-producing region) were at that time centres for Perth's Yugoslav population.
34   Esther Missingham, interview with author, 20 January 1996.
35   Phyllis Ophel, interviews with author, 19 June 1994 and 30 July 1994.
36   Hal Missingham biographical folio, AGNSW Library, Sydney; interviews with Hal Missingham, 1989, OH 2508 and OH 2509, Battye Library, SLWA, Perth; and Esther Missingham, interview with author, 20 January 1996.
37   CIB Special Bureau report, 6 September 1940, NAA A6335/1, item 21, folio 15/17.
38   Constable William Basley's written report on the raid on Lunghi and Arnold, NAA, A6335/1, item 21, folio 16.
39   Record of Basley's interview with Lunghi at Gibbney's (NAA, A6335/1, item 21, folio 15).
40   CIB Special Bureau report, 6 September 1940.
41   Police monitored the major daily newspapers as well as the CPA press.
42   NAA, A6122/40, item 25, ff. 23–27.
43   Report by G. Standen, Perth CIB (Special Bureau), 7 October 1940, NAA, A6335/1, item 21.
44   ibid.
45   Constable William Basley, police report on John Oldham raids, NAA, A6119/79, item 1177, folio 8. John Oldham later said that he 'resented' Basley's 'attitude' during

this raid, which Oldham considered 'aggressive and offensive', and that he 'thought Basley was going to strike' him (*Daily News*, 16 June 1941, p. 7).
46 William Moore and T. Inglis Moore (eds), *Best Australian One-Act Plays*.
47 'Rain came and saved the clash' (Victor Williams, letter to Robert Fitzgerald, 10 December 1966). See also *The West Australian Wheatgrower*, 26 September 1940, p. 2.
48 Victor Williams, letter to Robert Fitzgerald, 10 December 1966.
49 See Stuart Macintyre, *The Reds*, pp. 189–190.
50 Victor Williams, interview with author, 16 October 1994.
51 *The West Australian*, 10 January 1941, p. 8.
52 *The Herald* (Melbourne), 10 January 1941, p. 5.
53 Workers' Art Guild flyer for *This Bondage*.
54 Phyllis Ophel, interview with author, 21 July 1995.
55 ibid. For an analysis of Katharine Susannah Prichard and the suffrage movement, see Susan Bradley Smith, 'Girl meets Tractor'.
56 ibid.
57 *The West Australian*, 23 December 1940, p. 15.
58 Dinan was listed in the Security file 'Communists in Western Australia — List of Persons Known to be Associated with Communism in 1940'. See also NAA, A6119/84, item 1942.
59 Katharine Susannah Prichard, letter to Louis Esson, 16 December 1940, MS 6201, box 10, folder 7, folio 54, NLA. It is unlikely that the Kalgoorlie performance of *Penalty Clause* ever took place. The *Kalgoorlie Miner* newspaper contains no record of a performance in April 1941, and Phyllis Ophel, who played a leading role in the Perth production of the play, said she did not perform in a Kalgoorlie production (Phyllis Ophel, interview with author, 1 November 1997).
60 Katharine Susannah Prichard, letter to Louis Esson, 16 December 1940.
61 Transcript of interview with Ric Throssell, NLA Oral History collection, TRC 2794; and Don Batchelor, *The Context of Australian Playwriting 1939–1968*, p. 24.
62 Ric Throssell, interview with author, 3 November 1995.
63 Katharine Susannah Prichard, letter to Louis Esson, 16 December 1940.
64 Marie Kathleen Fitzgerald, n.d., *History of Perth Theatre*, unpublished monograph held in the Battye Library, SLWA, Perth, p. 25.
65 *The West Australian*, 21 August 1940, p. 3.
66 Ric Throssell, *Wild Weeds and Wind Flowers*, pp. 97–98. *Moon of Desire* would be published by Jonathan Cape in 1941, though both its American publication and film adaptation were shelved.
67 Katharine Susannah Prichard, letter to Louis Esson, 16 December 1940.
68 MS 6201/10/11, NLA.
69 In 1939, after his retirement from the UWA English Department, Emeritus Professor Walter Murdoch (1874–1970) was appointed a trustee of AGWA. He was also Chancellor of UWA from 1943 to 1948. He continued to write regular newspaper commentaries until the late 1960s, including a column opposing the Communist Dissolution Bill in the 1950s. He was knighted in 1964. Western Australia's second university was named in his honour just prior to his death in 1970.
70 Katharine Susannah Prichard, letter to Louis Esson, 16 December 1940.
71 Henrietta Drake-Brockman, letter to Hugh McCrae, September 1937, McCrae Papers, MS 12831, box 3674/1, A–F, La Trobe Library, SLV, Melbourne.
72 Ric Throssell, *Wild Weeds and Wind Flowers*, p. 160.

73 Katharine Susannah Prichard, letter to Mikhail Apletin, 19 September 1940.
74 *The West Australian*, 1 July 1940, p. 5.

16: 'THE FADED YEARS': A RETREAT TO PROVINCIALISM

1   'The faded years' was a term used by Max Harris, editor of Modernist magazine *Angry Penguins*, to describe the years following the Second World War in Australia (*Direction*, 1952, no. 1). Harris would later become subject to infamy when another peripheral participant in the Workers' Art Guild, Brian Elliott, exposed the work of fictitious poet 'Ern Malley' as a hoax in what became known as the 'Ern Malley Affair'.
2   Katharine Susannah Prichard, letter to Keith George, 22 April 1948 Papers of Linley Wilson, MN 1459, ACC 4616A, letter 10, G/42/69, Battye Library, SLWA, Perth.
3   NAA, A6122/40, item 411.
4   Victor Arnold, 'Agit Prop in W.A.'.
5   Howard Smith, letter, April 1941, NAA, A6119/84, item 1938, folio 46 ('Efforts will be made to obtain affiliations with the various unions').
6   ibid.
7   Victor Arnold, 'Agit Prop in W.A.' This ballet and chorus work was limited to the rehearsal of only one or two musical revues that did not make it to performance.
8   Howard Smith, letter, April 1941.
9   George Wignall, interview with Julie Wells, 8 August 1984. Wignall also said of the War, 'It was a turning point. It was an ending or beginning for lots of things.'
10 *The West Australian*, 14 December 1940, pp. 4–5.
11 Victor Arnold, 'Agit Prop in W.A.'
12 Dinan increased the ALP vote from the 1940 election by nine-point-two per cent, receiving 16,729 votes (thirty-seven-point-four per cent of the votes in the by-election). Farmer and former WA senator Thomas Marwick was elected to the seat.
13 David Day, *John Curtin*, pp. 393–394; and Justina Williams, *The First Furrow*, pp. 173–175.
14 *Westralian Worker*, 21 February 1941; and *The West Australian*, 29 May 1941, p. 12.
15 John Oldham, interview with author, 17 January 1996; and NAA, A6119/84, item 1942, folio 17.
16 *The West Australian*, 20 June 1941, p. 2.
17 John Oldham, interview with author, 17 January 1996.
18 *The West Australian*, 29 May 1941, p.12.
19 NAA, A6335/1, item 21, folio 34; and *The West Australian*, 18 June 1941, p. 3.
20 *The West Australian*, 20 June 1941.
21 John Oldham, interview with author, 17 January 1996.
22 *Daily News*, 16 June 1941, p. 10.
23 Justina Williams, *The First Furrow*, p. 170; and Leah Healy, interview with author, 18 September 1996.
24 Intelligence Security report, 16 May 1941, NAA, A6119/84, item 1942, ff. 20-22.
25 ibid.
26 NAA, A6119/84, item 1942, ff. 20–22.
27 NAA, A6119/84, item 1942.
28 ibid.
29 NAA, A6119/79, item 1177, folio 93; and John Oldham, interview with author, 17 January 1996.
30 NAA, A6119/79, item 1177, folio 11.

31 ibid. and John Oldham, interview with author, 17 January 1996.
32 NAA, A6119/79, item 1177, folio 11.
33 Letter to the Military Board in Melbourne from the Colonel in charge of Western Command, 4 June 1941, NAA, A6119/79, item 1177, folio 23.
34 NAA, A6119/79, item 1177, folio 26.
35 *The West Australian*, 30 April 1941, p. 13.
36 NAA, A6119/84, item 1942, folio 29. For a report of Simpson's initial trial, see *The West Australian*, 30 April 1941, p. 13.
37 *The West Australian*, 7 May 1941, p. 15.
38 John Oldham, interview with author, 17 January 1996.
39 Military Intelligence report, 23 July 1941, NAA, A6119/84, item 1942, folio 29.
40 Joan Vike, interview with author, 4 December 1994.
41 Harald Vike, note to Joe Skinner, records of the Skinner Galleries, MN 1320, ACC 4043A, item 5, Battye Library, SLWA, Perth.
42 Papers of Miles Franklin, MS 364, vol. 21, p. 216, Mitchell Library, SLNSW, Sydney.
43 Katharine Susannah Prichard, letter to Timofei Rokotov, May 1941, Prichard Papers, Battye Library, SLWA, Perth: MN 1465, ACC 5835A/4.
44 Katharine Susannah Prichard, letter to Mikhail Apletin, 25 June 1941, NAA, A6119/23, item 367, folio 17.
45 Military Intelligence report dated 23 July 1941, NAA, A6119/84, item 1942, folio 29.
46 It appears the production was later cancelled.
47 Anonymous letter addressed to 'Detective Richards, C.I.D, Perth', dated 12 June 1941, NAA, A6119/1, item 43, ff. 12–15. It seems Richards and the police service likely cultivated the informant against the CPA.
48 Phyllis Ophel, interviews with author, 21 July 1995 and 28 April 1996.
49 Katharine Susannah Prichard, letter to Timofei Rokotov, 6 August 1941.
50 Security report (c. 1941) on Katharine Susannah Prichard, NAA, A6119/23, item 367, folio 17.
51 David Day, *John Curtin*, pp. 408–409.
52 Australian poet Judith Wright later said of the period: '[N]ot to have Marx on your bookshelf was the sign of a fool in those days' (Veronica Brady, 1998, *South of My Days: A Biography of Judith Wright*, Angus & Robertson, Sydney, p. 56).
53 Ric Throssell, *My Father's Son*, pp. 162–163.
54 Katharine Susannah Prichard, letter to *International Literature*, Moscow, 12 July 1941, NAA, A6119/1, item 43, folio 149.
55 NAA, A6119/84, item 1944, folio 24.
56 *The Mirror*, 22 July 1939, p. 9.
57 Olive Lachberg, interview with author, 14 October 1994; and Joan Vike, interview with author, 3 June 1995. Vike was to haul nearly every picture he had ever painted around Australia with him on his travels for the rest of his life.
58 Paul Hasluck, 1970, 'Brisbane Line', in Paul Hasluck, *The Government and the People, 1939–1945*, Australia in the War of 1939–1945, vol. 2, Australian War Memorial, Canberra, pp. 711–717, <www.awm.gov.au/articles/encyclopedia/homefront/brisbane_line>.
59 Joan Vike, interviews with author, 4 December 1994 and 3 June 1995.
60 For a review of this exhibition, see *The West Australian*, 16 September 1941, p. 6.
61 Hal Missingham, foreword to *Axel Poignant: Photographs 1922–1980* (catalogue from Poignant retrospective exhibition, AGNSW, 1982). See also Hal Missingham and Axel Poignant, 1941, *New Directions in Photography: Catalogue of an Exhibition*, Newspaper House, Perth.

62 Ric Throssell, *Wild Weeds and Wind Flowers*, p. 108; NAA, SP109/3, item 316/10; and Katharine Susannah Prichard, letter to Timofei Rokotov, May 1941.
63 *The Age*, 26 September 1952, p. 1.
64 David Day, 2001, *Chifley*, HarperCollins, Sydney, pp. 240–241 and 245.
65 Katharine Susannah Prichard, letter to Hilda Esson, 16 December 1940, MS 6201/10/7, folio 54, NLA. Hilda Esson was herself then directing plays for Melbourne New Theatre.
66 Freda Brown, interview with author, 22 March 1997.
67 NAA, A6122/2, item 415.
68 Internal Defence Department letter, 15 May 1941, NAA, A6119/784, item 1938, folio 18.
69 ibid.
70 Peter Douglas, *Origins*, p. 37.
71 NAA, A6119/84, item 1938, folio 84.
72 John Hector, letter to Victor Arnold in Adelaide, 15 July 1941 NAA, A6122/2, item 415.
73 Katharine Susannah Prichard, letter to Louis Esson, 16 December 1940.
74 Oriel Gray, *Exit Left*, pp. 58–59. Doug Wilson joined the Air Force shortly afterwards. His plane was shot down over Berlin and he was killed.
75 John Hector, letter to Victor Arnold, 18 July 1941, NAA, A6119/84, item 1938, folio 11.
76 Oriel Gray, *Exit Left*, pp. 58–59. In Sydney after the War, John Hepworth indeed did write an impressive novel that garnered a good deal of attention. Bob Ellis later described Hepworth's wartime novel, *The Long Green Shore*, as 'the finest novel of World War Two'.
77 Freda Brown, interview with author, 22 March 1997.
78 John Hector, letter to Victor Arnold, 18 July 1941.
79 John Hepworth, 1978, *John Hepworth: His Book*, Angus & Robertson, Sydney, pp. 33–34.
80 ibid.
81 ibid.
82 NAA, A6122/2, item 415.
83 Oriel Gray later said that Hepworth and fellow New Theatre actor Peter Finch were 'the two most untidy Australian soldiers' she had ever seen (Oriel Gray, interview with author, 7 August 1995).
84 John Hector, letter to Victor Arnold, 18 July 1941, NAA, A6122/2, item 415. Victor Arnold was very concerned that Hepworth's behaviour would reflect badly on New Theatre.
85 NAA, A6335/1, item 21, folio 35.
86 Letter from a member of the Workers' Art Guild committee to Unity Theatre, Brisbane, NAA, A6335/1, item 21, ff. 46-47.
87 Gavin Casey, letter to Victor Arnold, c. 5 August 1941, NAA, A6122/2, item 415.
88 ibid.
89 Gwen Duggan, letter to Unity Theatre in Brisbane, c. October 1941, NAA, A6335/1, item 21, ff. 46–47 and 52.
90 'Blonde' (Ruth Petterson), letter to Victor Arnold, probably late July 1941, NAA, A6335/1, item 21; and Ruth Petterson, letter to Victor Arnold, 19 September 1941, NAA, A6119/84, item 1938, ff. 23–24.
91 Phyllis Ophel, interview with author, 7 February 1996.
92 Ruth Petterson, letter to Victor Arnold, July 1941.

93 Phyllis Ophel, interview with author, 29 January 1997.
94 Phyllis Ophel, interview with author, 19 December 1997.
95 ibid.
96 Ric Throssell, interview with author, December 1995.
97 Phyllis Ophel, interview with author, 19 December 1997.
98 *The West Australian*, 18 October 1941, p. 8.
99 Records of the Western Australian Theatre Company, SLWA, Perth.
100 *The West Australian*, 5 September 1941, p. 9.
101 Joyce Riley (nee Mortlock), taped interview, OH 125, Battye Library, SLWA, Perth.
102 *The West Australian*, 5 September 1941, p. 9.
103 Beryl Hearder, interview with author, 23 January 1996.
104 Records of the Western Australian Theatre Company, SLWA, Perth. Walter Poole-Johnson had appeared on stage in the Guild productions of *Inga, Ghosts, Are You Ready, Comrade?, Floridsdorf, Awake and Sing!, Cannibal Carnival* and *Blood on the Moon*.
105 Records of Repertory Club executive meeting, 10 December 1941, Records of the Western Australian Theatre Company, SLWA, Perth, item 2(I), p. 96.
106 NAA, A6119, item 43, folio 132.
107 NAA, A6119/1, item 43, folio 144.
108 ibid., folio 84.
109 Desmond Ball and David Horner, 1998, *Breaking the Codes: Australia's KGB Network 1944–1950*, Allen & Unwin, Sydney, pp. 236–237.
110 *Canaries Sometimes Sing* was staged at the Repertory Club Theatre on 19–21 February 1942. See *The West Australian*, 20 February 1942.
111 Repertory Club Papers, His Majesty's Theatre Archives, Perth.
112 Records of the Western Australian Theatre Company, SLWA, Perth.
113 ibid.
114 ibid.
115 ibid. Keith George had enlisted for military service on 15 January 1942 (NAA Defence Records, series B884, item number W21370). On his oath of enlistment he had refused to swear allegiance to the King, instead replacing 'swear' with 'solemnly sincerely declare and affirm' and striking the words 'So help me God' from the oath.
116 For more information on Linley Wilson (1898–1990) see Wilson Papers, SLWA, Perth; and Ursula Yellard, 1963, *A History of the Development of Ballet in West Australia*, monograph held in the Battye Library, SLWA, Perth.
117 Ric Throssell, interview with author, 25 March 1997.
118 Lynne Fisher, cited in Don Batchelor, *The Context of Australian Playwriting 1939–1968*, p. 20.
119 Keith George must have won him over, as Thomas Bath had been the only Repertory Club committee member to dissent on the vote to appoint George to the Club's Secretarial position six months earlier. Thomas Henry Bath (1875–1956) was a leading business and political figure in Western Australia. He had served as a state Labor minister and leader of the opposition until 1914.
120 Repertory Club Papers, His Majesty's Theatre Archives. For information on the Army entertainment units, see Philip Parsons and Victoria Chance (eds), *Companion to Theatre in Australia*, pp. 58–60.
121 Prichard Papers, MS 6201/7/4, NLA.
122 CPA WA district committee, letter to CPA central committee in Sydney, 21 September 1942, NAA, A6119/84, item 1942, folio 72.
123 Fred Alexander, *On Campus and Off*, p. 15.

124 West Australian CPA members numbered 791 in February 1944, almost double its membership of May 1939, just before the CPA ban.
125 Bill Irwin, letter to Frank Maybank, General Secretary of the Mine Workers Union in Northern Rhodesia, shortly after Maybank's enforced deportation from Northern Rhodesia (NAA, A6119/84, item 1944, folio 31).
126 Bobbie Oliver, 1997, *Peacemongers: Conscientious Objectors to Military Service in Australia, 1911–1945*, Fremantle Arts Centre Press, Fremantle, p. 76.

APPENDIX: AFTER THE WAR

1 Janet McCalman, *Journeyings*, p. 219.
2 There is some dispute about Victor Arnold's precise date of birth, due probably to his lying about his age when entering the Army (Joan Arnold, letter to author, 22 May 1995).
3 NAA, A6119/83, item 1529, folio 63.
4 William Wilde (with Joy Hooton and Barry Andrews), 1985, *The Oxford Companion to Australian Literature*, Oxford University Press, Melbourne, p. 146.
5 *The West Australian*, 11 May 1963, p. 12.
6 NAA Defence Records (Service and Casualty Form), series B884, item number W21370.
7 Don Batchelor, *The Context of Australian Playwriting 1939–1968*, p. 24; and Fred Alexander, *On Campus and Off*, p. 34.
8 Private Keith M. George, 'Report on the Formation of Army Repertory Companies'.
9 UWA Adult Education Board Twentieth Annual Summer School program, pp. 2–4 (PR2881/43).
10 Ric Throssell, *My Father's Son*, p. 255.
11 Ric Throssell, *My Father's Son*; Ric Throssell, interview with author, 3 November 1995; and Don Batchelor, *The Context of Australian Playwriting 1939–1968*, p. 33.
12 Ric Throssell, interview with author, 3 November 1995.
13 NAA, A6126/25, item 388, folio 11.
14 Linley Wilson, letter, 8 April 1972, Wilson Papers, SLWA, Perth.
15 Keith George, letter to Ric Throssell, November 1971.
16 *The West Australian*, 19 February 1972, p. 10.
17 *The Tribune*, no. 1745, 916 March 1972.
18 Ric Throssell, letter to Linley Wilson, 29 February 1972, Wilson Papers, SLWA, Perth, box 2.
19 Phyllis Ophel, letter to 'Linley George', Wilson Papers, SLWA, Perth, box 2. For more information on Keith George, see NAA, A6126/25, item 388; Wilson Papers, SLWA, Perth; Lynn Margaret Fisher, *Dance Class*; and Keith George Papers, His Majesty's Theatre Archives, Perth.
20 Felicity St. John Moore, 1982, *Vassilieff and His Art*, Macmillan Art, Melbourne.
21 Elizabeth Vassilieff, 1953, 'First Cultural Report from Delegation for Peking', *Mary's Own Paper*, October, p. 17.
22 Paul Hasluck, *Mucking About*, p. 327.
23 David Day, *John Curtin*, p. 394.
24 A former adviser to Gough Whitlam later speculated that had Hasluck taken over leadership of the Liberal Party, Whitlam would not so easily have won the 1972 federal election.
25 Robert Porter, *Paul Hasluck*.
26 Kathleen Hector, interview with author, 29 December 1996.
27 Extract from John Hepworth's obituary, *The Australian*, 25 January 1995, p. 16.

28   NAA, A6119/84, item 1722, folio 3.
29   John Hepworth, 'Love and the Party Line'.
30   NAA, A6119/84, item 1722, folio 17.
31   Richard Walsh, 1993, *Ferretabilia: Life and Times of Nation Review*, University of Queensland Press, St Lucia.
32   *The Age*, 25 November 1994, p. 2.
33   *The Age*, 25 January 1995.
34   *The Australian*, 25 January 1995, p. 16; and *The West Australian*, 26 January 1995, p. 36.
35   See, for example, *Who* magazine, 13 February 1995, p. 60.
36   NAA, A6119/79, item 1319, ff. 3–4.
37   Bill and Dorothy Irwin, interview with Don Grant and John McClaren, 10 August 1985.
38   The CPA took a hard line against wavering Party members after the 1956 Khrushchev speech to stem the potentially massive haemorrhaging from the Party that could have resulted. Many who left the Communist Party at the time, including the Irwins, felt that the Party had left them. Loyal friends, such as Prichard, refused to adhere to the Party embargo on relations with the Irwins, and some Party members resigned from the CPA over Ian Turner's expulsion. Despite her support of the Irwins, their break with the CPA at this time caused Prichard grief for many years and some degree of estrangement, which she attempted to heal towards the end of her life when she wrote to the Irwins: 'Let us contend no more.' (Ric Throssell, *Wild Weeds and Wind Flowers*, p. 231; and Bill and Dorothy Irwin, interview with Don Grant and John McClaren, 10 August 1985).
39   Bill Irwin, letter to Ken Gott, 22 March 1976, MS 13047, box 3765/7, La Trobe Library, SLV, Melbourne.
40   See obituaries of Bill Irwin in *The West Australian*, 9 June 1995, p. 32 and *The Australian* 27 June 1995, p. 18. See also NAA, A6119/79, item 1321, folio 31.
41   Richard Haese, *Rebels and Precursors*, p. 172. Other artists involved in SORA were Roy Dalgarno, William Dobell, James Cant, Noel Counihan, Yosl Bergner, George Finey, Sali Herman, Lionel Jago, Vic O'Connor, Margaret Preston and Jeffrey Smart.
42   Interview with Hal Missingham, OH 2508, Battye Library, SLWA, Perth.
43   Hal Missingham's papers are held in the Manuscripts section, NLA, MS 3940.
44   L.L. Sharkey, 1943, *Congress Report on the Work of the Central Committee from the 12th to the 13th Party Congress*, Dimitrov Press, Sydney. Sharkey went as far as calling Mountjoy a 'police informer'.
45   Phil Young, *Thea Rowe*.
46   Defence Records for Francis Ellsmere O'Grady, NAA, B883, item WX16359.
47   John and Ray Oldham, interview with author, 11 October 1994.
48   *The Architect* (Western Australia), Spring 1999, p. 15.
49   *Fremantle Arts Review*, vol. 2, no. 2, February 1987, pp. 18–19; Margaret A. Sacks, 1980, *The Way 79 Who is Who: Synoptic Biographies of Western Australians*, Crawley Publishers, Nedlands, WA; and *History West*, Royal Western Australian Historical Society, vol. 44, no. 2, March 2005, p. 4.
50   Phyllis Ophel, interview with author, 21 July 1995; Phyllis Harnett (Kennedy), letter to CPA secretary in South Australia, August 1943, NAA, A6119/84, item 1944, folio 38; Bill Irwin, letter to Frank Maybank, April 1943; and Phyllis Ophel, interview with Zoe Ackroyd Curtis, n.d.
51   Katherine Perrin, letter to author, 4 May 2006.

52 The Depression-era American Farm Security Administration photographs were a great influence on Poignant's Canning Stock Route photography.
53 Roslyn Poignant, interview with author, 18 September 1996.
54 NAA, A452, item 1952/21.
55 See 'Axel Poignant Proposed visit to Arnhem Land re Pictorial Record, NAA, A452, item 1952/21. *Piccaninny Walkabout* was later retitled *Bush Walkabout*.
56 Prichard was elected to the central committee along with Walter Clayton, who would later be implicated as leader of the KLOD Soviet spy network in which Prichard was said to be active.
57 Katharine Susannah Prichard, letter to Spencer Brodney, 12 December 1956, MS 1286/6, La Trobe Library, SLV, Melbourne. Although many of Prichard's novels were published in Eastern Bloc countries, she received little income from this.
58 Bernard Smith, *Noel Counihan*, p. 304.
59 Isla Marsh, letter to Spencer Brodney, 29 September 1962.
60 Prichard's house companion was Joan Williams's mother (Victor Williams's mother-in-law).
61 *The Australian*, 4 October 1969.
62 Evatt believed Petrov's defection and the Royal Commission that followed were a conspiracy designed by Menzies, the head of ASIO and B.A. Santamaria to deny Evatt the prime ministership in the election that followed the Royal Commission. Evatt subsequently went into mental decline.
63 *The West Australian*, 'Good Weekend', 14 December 1996, p. 12.
64 Ron Richards profile in *Police News*, February 2002; and Peter Conole, *Protect and Serve*.
65 This information came from a typed list of the book's characters and the real-life figures on which they were based, however loosely, that Frank Hardy sent to Katharine Susannah Prichard, with a copy of *Power without Glory*, in August 1950. Hardy was unsuccessfully sued for criminal libel the following year over his supposed representation of powerful Melbourne figure John Wren in the novel.
66 Ruth Rudkin, interview with author, 21 March 1997.
67 Jean Buckley-Moran, 'Australian Scientists and the Cold War', in Brian Martin, C.M. Ann Baker, Clyde Manwell and Cedric Pugh (eds), *Intellectual Suppression*, pp. 11–23.
68 Arthur Rudkin, interview with Ken Mansell, 7 December 1981.
69 Ruth Rudkin, interview with author, 21 March 1997.
70 Joan Williams, letter to author, 17 May 1995.
71 *The West Australian*, 18 April 1985.
72 Nigel West, 1999, *Venona: The Greatest Secret of The Cold War*, HarperCollins, London, p. 107.
73 *The West Australian*, 'Big Weekend', 14 December 1996, p. 2.
74 In late 1949, Throssell was identified as the figure code-named 'Ferro' in Venona intelligence decrypt, though this was not to come to his nor public attention until shortly before his death.
75 NAA, CRS A6119/XR1, item 97.
76 ibid.
77 NAA, CRS A6119/XR1, item 97, folio 28.
78 Bernice Morris, 1988, *Between the Lines*, Sybylla Co-operative Press, Collingwood, p. 43.
79 Ric Throssell, *My Father's Son*, p. 378.
80 *The Canberra Times*, 5 December 1996.

81 *The West Australian*, 'Big Weekend', 14 December 1996, p. 2.
82 Don Batchelor, *The Context of Australian Playwriting 1939–1968*, p. 233.
83 The first was a reference to his being Prichard's son and being posted to Moscow in 1945; the second mentioned the possibility of his being cultivated as a possible KLOD spy ring member; and the third was a cable enquiring as to his address. The Venona cables also indicated that Prichard had had a conversation with Australian Soviet agent Walter Clayton in which she discussed Throssell's posting to Moscow.
84 *The Courier-Mail*, 3 October 1996.
85 *The Australian*, 4 October 1996.
86 *The Canberra Times*, 5 December 1996. *The Canberra Times* ran a consistently sympathetic line on Ric Throssell while many other national newspapers published reports about Throssell with a rather accusatory and hysterical 'Cold War' rhetoric.
87 See *The Age*, 8 August 1998, p. 12.
88 *The Australian*, 22 April 1999, p. 3; *The Weekend Australian*, 24 April 1999, p. 7; *The Age*, 22 April 1999, p. 2; *Herald Sun*, 22 April 1999, p. 9; *The Age*, 30 April 1999; *Muse* (Canberra Arts Monthly), May 1999, p. 3; *The Canberra Times*, 22 April 1999; and the extensive obituary of Throssell in *The Canberra Times*, 27 April 1999, p. 11.
89 Senator Kate Lundy in extract from Senate Hansard, 21 April 1999, p. 4080.
90 *The Age*, 30 April 1999.
91 *The Herald Sun*, 22 April 1999, p. 9.
92 Joan Vike, interview with author, 4 December 1994.
93 See Lina Bryans and Gillian Forwood (curator), 1995, *The Babe Is Wise: Lina Bryans and Her Portraits*, University of Melbourne, Museum of Art; and Lina Bryans Papers, La Trobe Library, SLV, Melbourne.
94 Barry Dickins wrote of working with Vike in the scenery department of Channel Seven in his autobiography (Barry Dickins, 1991, *I Love to Live: The Fabulous Life of Barry Dickins*, Penguin Books, Ringwood, pp. 78–80). The pair also worked with The Loved Ones vocalist Gerry Humphries.
95 For a description of Williams's politics and activities after the War, see Victor Williams, letter to Robert Fitzgerald, 10 December 1966.
96 See NAA, A6119/84, item 1954, ff. 100–105 and 143.

BIBLIOGRAPHY

BOOKS, ARTICLES AND THESES

Alexander, Fred, 1987, *On Campus and Off: Reminiscences and Reflections of the First Professor of Modern History in the University of Western Australia, 1916–1986*, UWA Press, Nedlands.

Anderson, Roderick, 1986, *Western Australian Art: A Selection of Early Works from the Robert Holmes à Court Collection*, Heytesbury Holdings, Perth.

Arent, Arthur, 1971, 'The Techniques of the Living Newspaper', *Theatre Quarterly*, vol. 1, no. 4, October–December.

Bain, Annette, 1980, 'Brighter Days', in Jill Roe (ed.), *Twentieth Century Sydney: Studies in Urban and Social History*, Hale & Ironmonger, Sydney.

Baker, John, 1938, *The Right Theatre is Left*, s.n., Adelaide.

Ball, Desmond & Horner, David, 1998, *Breaking the Codes: Australia's KGB Network 1944–1950*, Allen & Unwin, Sydney.

Bartlett, Norman, 1977, 'Perth in the Turbulent Thirties', *Westerly*, no. 4, December.

Batchelor, Don, 1995, *The Context of Australian Playwriting 1939–1968: A Case Study of the Theatre Career of Ric Throssell*, PhD thesis, Department of English, University of Queensland.

Bedson, Jack and Croft, Julian (eds), 1993, *The Campbell Howard Annotated Index of Australian Plays, 1920–1955*, Centre for Australian Language and Literature Studies, UNE, Armidale.

Beeching, Anne, 1988, *Nancy Takes the Stick: Autobiography of Contessa Filippini, Australian Opera Pioneer, 1896–1987*, published by C. Tonti-Filippini, Imscan Technologies, Melbourne.

Bolton, Geoffrey, 1986, 'Newspapers for a Depression Child', *Westerly*, no. 4, December.

——1977, 'A Local Identity: Paul Hasluck and Western Australian Self Concept', *Westerly*, no. 4, December.

——1972, *A Fine Country to Starve In*, UWA Press, Nedlands.

——1969, 'Unemployment and Politics in Western Australia', Robert Cooksey (ed.), The Great Depression in Australia, *Labour History*, no. 17, Australian Society for the Study of Labour History.

Brady, Veronica, 1998, *South of My Days: A Biography of Judith Wright*, Angus & Robertson, Sydney.

——1989, 'A Postmodernist City', in Michael Denholm and Andrew Sant (eds), *First Rights: A Decade of Island Magazine*, Greenhouse Publications, Elwood.

——1982, 'Place, Taste and the Making of a Tradition: Western Australian Writing Today', *Westerly*, no. 4.

——1981, 'Katharine Susannah Prichard and the Tyranny of History: Intimate Strangers', *Westerly*, no. 4.

Brand, Mona, 1986, 'A Writer's Thirty-six Years in Radical Theatre: New Theatre's Formative Years 1932–1955 and Their Influence on Australian Drama', *Australian Drama 1920–1955: Papers Presented to a Conference at the University of New England, Armidale, September 1–4, 1984*, UNE, Armidale.

Brett, Judith, 2017, *The Enigmatic Mr Deakin*, Text Publishing, Melbourne.

Buckley-Moran, Jean, 1986, 'Australian Scientists and the Cold War', in Brian Martin, C.M. Ann Baker, Clyde Manwell and Cedric Pugh (eds), *Intellectual Suppression: Australian Case Histories, Analysis and Responses*, Angus & Robertson, Sydney.

Burchill, Sandra, 1988, 'The Early Years of Katharine Susannah Prichard: The Growth of Her Political Conscience', *Westerly*, no. 2, June.
Capp, Fiona, 1993, *Writers Defiled: Security Surveillance of Australian Authors and Intellectuals 1920–1960*, McPhee Gribble, Ringwood, Vic.
Carroll, Dennis, 1985, *Australian Contemporary Drama 1909–1982: A Critical Introduction*, Peter Lang Publishing, New York.
Chanin, Eileen and Miller, Steven, 2005, *Degenerates and Perverts: The 1939 Herald Exhibition of French and British Contemporary Art*, Miegunyah Press, Melbourne.
Clurman, Harold, 1945, *The Fervent Years: The Story of the Group Theatre and the Thirties*, Alfred Knopf, New York.
Cohen, Israel, 1943, *Vilna*, Jewish Publication Society of America, Philadelphia.
Coleman, Peter, 1974, *Obscenity, Blasphemy, Sedition: 100 Years of Censorship in Australia*, Angus & Robertson, Sydney.
Conole, Peter, 2002, *Protect and Serve: A History of Policing in Western Australia*, Western Australia Police Service, Perth.
Cooksey, Robert, 1969, 'Editorial', Robert Cooksey (ed.), The Great Depression in Australia, *Labour History*, no. 17, Australian Society for the Study of Labour History.
Courtney, Victor, 1962, *Perth – and All This!: A Story About a City*, Halstead Press, Sydney.
Cowan, Peter, 1989, *The Hills of Apollo Bay*, Fremantle Arts Centre Press, Fremantle.
Craig, Terry, 1990, 'Radical and Conservative Theatre in Perth in the 1930s', Jenny Gregory (ed.), Western Australia Between the Wars 1919–1939, *Studies in Western Australian History*, issue 11, June, Centre for Western Australian History, UWA, Perth.
Crowley, F.K. (ed.), 1974, *A New History of Australia*, Heinemann, Melbourne.
Davidson, Alistair, 1969, *The Communist Party of Australia: A Short History*, Hoover Institution Press, Stanford, California.
Davidson, Ron, 1994, *High Jinks at the Hot Pool: Mirror Reflects the Life of a City*, Fremantle Arts Centre Press, Fremantle.
Davies, Cecil W., 1972, 'People's Theatre in Germany', *Theatre Quarterly*, vol. 2, no. 5, January–March, London.
——1972, 'The Volksbühne: A Descriptive Chronology', *Theatre Quarterly*, vol. 2, no. 5, January–March, London.
Davis, Annette, 1990, 'Good Times For All? Popular Entertainment and Class Consciousness in Western Australian Society between the Wars', Jenny Gregory (ed.), Western Australia Between the Wars 1919–1939, *Studies in Western Australian History*, issue 11, June, Centre for Western Australian History, UWA, Perth.
Day, David, 2001, *Chifley*, HarperCollins, Sydney.
——1999, *John Curtin: A Life*, HarperCollins, Sydney.
Devanny, Jean, 1986, *Point of Departure: The Autobiography of Jean Devanny*, Carole Ferrier (ed.), University of Queensland Press, St Lucia.
Douglas, Peter, 1994, *Origins: A History of the Adelaide New Theatre Movement, 1937 to 1950*, BA Hons, Dip. Ed., Flinders University, Adelaide.
Drake-Brockman, Henrietta, 1967, 'Katharine Susannah Prichard', in Geoffrey Dutton (ed.), *Australian Writers and Their Work*, Oxford University Press, Melbourne.
——1935, 'Small Theatre Movement in Perth', *The Playbill*, no. 1, March.
Dunstone, Bill, 1979, 'Drama', in Bruce Bennett (ed.), *The Literature of Western Australia*, UWA Press, Nedlands.
Edwards, Lee (ed.), 1999, *The Collapse of Communism*, Hoover Institution Press, Stanford, California.

Esson, Louis, 1946, *The Southern Cross and Other Plays*, Robertson & Mullens, Melbourne.
Famous Plays of 1936, 1936, Victor Gollancz, London.
Famous Plays of 1937, 1937, Victor Gollancz, London.
Famous Plays of 1938–1939, 1939, Victor Gollancz, London.
Ferrier, Carole (ed.), 1992, *As Good as a Yarn with You, Letters between Miles Franklin, Katharine Susannah Prichard, Jean Devanny, Marjorie Barnard, Flora Eldershaw and Eleanor Dark*, Cambridge University Press, Oakleigh, Vic.
Ferrier, Carole, 1999, *Jean Devanny: Romantic Revolutionary*, Melbourne University Press, Carlton, Vic.
Fisher, Lynne Margaret, 1992, *Dance Class: A History of Professional Dance and Dance Training in Western Australia from 1895–1940*, MA thesis, History Department, UWA, Perth.
Fitton, Doris, 1981, *Not Without Dust and Heat: My Life in Theatre*, Harper & Row, Sydney.
FitzGibbon, Constantine, 1965, *The Life of Dylan Thomas*, J.M. Dent, London.
Fitzpatrick, Peter, 1995, *Pioneer Players: The Lives of Louis and Hilda Esson*, Cambridge University Press.
Gabbedy, John Philip, 1988, *Group Settlement, Part 2, Its People: Their Life and Times — An Inside View*, UWA Press, Nedlands.
Gadaloff, Judith, 1991, *Australian Drama*, The Jacaranda Press, Qld.
Gentilli, Joseph, 1988, *The Unbent Poplar: Francesco Vanzetti and His Times*, Department of Geography, UWA, Perth.
Goddard, Julian, 1990, *Harald Vike*, Kingstream Fine Art, Perth.
——1990, 'Urban Themes: The Art of Harald Vike', *Art and Australia*, vol. 27, no. 3, March.
Godfrey, Lauren, 1993, 'Communists, Catholics, and the Labor Party: Western Australian Accounts of the Spanish Civil War', Charlie Fox (ed.), *Papers in Labour History*, no. 11, June, Australian Society for the Study of Labour History, Deptartment of Industrial Relations, UWA, Perth.
Gooding, Janda, 1987, *Western Australian Art and Artists 1900–1950*, AGWA, Perth.
Graham, John, 1962, *Perth and the South-West*, The Jacaranda Press, Qld.
Grattan, C. Hartley, 1949, *Introducing Australia*, Angus & Robertson, Sydney.
Gray, Anne, 1986, *Line, Light and Shadow — James W.R. Linton: Painter, Craftsman and Teacher*, Fremantle Arts Centre Press, Fremantle.
Gray, Oriel, 1985, *Exit Left: Memoirs of a Scarlet Woman*, Penguin Books, Ringwood.
Gregory, Jenny, 1990, 'Western Australia Between the Wars: The Consensus Myth', Jenny Gregory (ed.), Western Australia between the Wars, 1919–1939, *Studies in Western Australian History*, issue 11, June, Centre for Western Australian History, UWA, Perth.
Gregory, Jenny & Taylor, Robyn, 1992, '"The Slums of Tomorrow"? Architects, Builders and the Construction of Flats in Interwar Perth', Frank Broeze (ed.), Private Enterprise, Government and Society, *Studies in Western Australian History*, issue 13, Centre for Western Australian History, UWA, Perth.
Griffen-Foley, Bridget, 2000, *Sir Frank Packer: The Young Master*, HarperCollins.
Gullan, Roger & Roberts, Buckley, 1937, *Where's That Bomb? A Comedy in Two Acts*, Lawrence and Wishart, London.
Hacker, Beryl, 1994, *Rosa: A Biography of Rosa Townsend*, UWA Press, Nedlands.
Haese, Richard, 1982, *Rebels and Precursors: The Revolutionary Years of Australian Art*, Allen Lane, London.

Hamilton, John, 2012, *The Price of Valour: The Triumph and Tragedy of a Gallipoli Hero, Hugo Throssell, VC*, Pan Macmillan Australia.
Harcourt, J.M., 1986 reprint, *Upsurge: A Novel*, UWA Press, Nedlands.
Hardy, Frank, 1972, *Power Without Glory: A Novel*, Lloyd O'Neil, Hawthorn.
Harper, Ken, 1984, 'The Useful Theatre: The New Theatre Movement in Sydney and Melbourne 1935-1983', Jack Hibberd (ed.), Performing Arts in Australia, *Meanjin*, vol. 43, no. 1, March, University of Melbourne.
Hasluck, Paul, 1977, *Mucking About: An Autobiography*, Melbourne University Press, Melbourne.
—— 1970, 'Brisbane Line', in Paul Hasluck, *The Government and the People, 1942-1945*, Australia in the War of 1939-1945, vol. 2, Australian War Memorial, Canberra.
Heinz, Bernard, 1971, 'A Theatre for Lefty: USA in the 1930's', *Theatre Quarterly*, vol. 1, no. 4, October-December, London.
Hepworth, John, 1995, *The Long Green Shore*, Picador, Sydney.
—— 1978, *John Hepworth: His Book*, Angus & Robertson, Sydney.
Hergenhan, Laurie, 1995, *No Casual Traveller: Hartley Grattan and Australia*, University of Queensland Press, St Lucia.
Herlinger, Paul, 1989, *A History of New Theatre, 1939-1953*, MA Hons, University of Sydney.
—— 1986, 'A New Direction for "the New"?', *Australasian Drama Studies*, no. 8, April.
—— 1980, *New Theatre: The Pre-War Years, 1932-1939*, MA Qual., University of Sydney.
Hern, Nicholas, 1972, 'The Theatre of Ernst Toller', *Theatre Quarterly*, vol. 2, no. 5, January-March, London.
Hewett, Dorothy, 1990, *Wild Card: An Autobiography 1923-1958*, McPhee Gribble, Ringwood.
Heyward, Michael, 1993, *The Ern Malley Affair*, University of Queensland Press, St Lucia.
Hillel, Angela, 1986, 'Against the Stream: New Theatre Melbourne 1936-1986', *50 Years of New Theatre: Melbourne N.T. 1936-86*, New Theatre, Clifton Hill.
Holmes, Katie, n.d., *A Decent Privacy? Personal Revelation and History*, <http://www.nla.gov.au/events/history/ papers/Katie_Holmes.html>.
Hyde, Dylan, 1997, '"We Present this Play Not for Your Entertainment But for Your Chastening": The Workers' Art Guild, 1935-1942', Janis Bailey (ed.), *Papers in Labour History*, no. 18, March, Australian Society for the Study of Labour History, Edith Cowan University.
Irwin, E.W. & Goff, Ivan, 1934, *No Longer Innocent*, Angus & Robertson, Sydney.
Johnston, George, 1964, *My Brother Jack*, The Reprint Society, London.
Kisch, Egon Erwin, 1937, *Australian Landfall*, translated from the German by John Fisher and Irene and Kevin Fitzgerald, Secker & Warburg, London.
Layman, Lenore & Goddard, Julian, 1988, *Organise! A Visual Record of the Labour Movement in Western Australia*, Trades and Labour Council of Western Australia, East Perth.
Le Guay, Laurence (ed.), 1978, *Australian Photography: A Contemporary View*, The Globe Publishing Company, Sydney.
Lemon, Charles, 1939, 'A New Spirit in Perth', *Art in Australia*, 15 February.
Macintyre, Stuart, 1998, *The Reds: The Communist Party of Australia from Origins to Illegality*, Allen & Unwin, Sydney.
—— 1984, *Militant: The Life and Times of Paddy Troy*, Allen & Unwin, Sydney.
McCalman, Janet, 1993, *Journeyings: The Biography of a Middle-class Generation, 1920-1990*, Melbourne University Press.
McCulloch, Allan, 1994, *Encyclopedia of Australian Art*, 3rd edition, revised and updated by Susan McCulloch, Allen & Unwin, Sydney.

McKenzie, John A., 1993, *Challenging Faith*, Fremantle Arts Centre Press, Fremantle.
McLaren, John, 2003, *Free Radicals: On the Left in Postwar Melbourne*, Australian Scholarly Publishing, Melbourne.
McQueen, Humphrey, 1979, *The Black Swan of Trespass: The Emergence of Modernist Painting in Australia 1918-1944*, Alternative Publishing, Sydney.
Merewether, Charles (ed.), 1984, *Art and Social Commitment: An End to the City of Dreams 1931-1948*, AGNSW, Sydney.
Modjeska, Drusilla, 1981, *Exiles at Home: Australian Women Writers, 1925-1945*, Sirius Books, Sydney.
Moore, Felicity St. John, 1982, *Vassilieff and His Art*, Macmillan Art, Melbourne.
Moore, William and Moore, T. Inglis (eds), 1937, *Best Australian One-Act Plays*, Angus & Robertson, Sydney.
Moorhouse, Frank, 1999, 'Introduction', in Walter Murdoch, *Alfred Deakin*, Bookman Press, Melbourne.
Morris, Bernice, 1988, *Between the Lines*, Sybylla Co-operative Press, Collingwood.
Mossenson, David, 1990, *Hebrew, Israelite, Jew: The History of the Jews of Western Australia*, UWA Press, Nedlands.
Moussinac, Léon, 1931, *The New Movement in the Theatre: A Survey of Recent Developments in Europe and America*, B.T. Batsford, London.
O'Brien, Angela, 1989, *The Road Not Taken: Political and Performance Ideologies at Melbourne New Theatre, 1935-1960*, PhD thesis, Monash University, Melbourne.
Odets, Clifford, 1936, *Three Plays by Clifford Odets*, Victor Gollancz, London.
Oldham, John & Oldham, Ray, 1987, 'The 1930s Influence: Ray and John Oldham', *Fremantle Arts Review*, vol. 2, no. 2, February.
Oliver, Bobbie, 1997, *Peacemongers: Conscientious Objectors to Military Service in Australia, 1911-1945*, Fremantle Arts Centre Press, Fremantle.
Parsons, Philip & Chance, Victoria (eds), 1995, *Companion to Theatre in Australia*, Currency Press, Sydney.
Poignant, Roslyn, 1993, 'The Photographic Witness?', *Continuum*, vol. 6, no. 2.
Porter, Robert, 1993, *Paul Hasluck: A Political Biography*, UWA Press, Nedlands.
Prichard, Katharine Susannah, 1963, *Child of the Hurricane: An Autobiography*, Angus & Robertson, Sydney.
——c. 1957, *Why I Am a Communist*, Current Book Distributors, Sydney.
——1934, *The Real Russia*, Modern Publishers, Sydney.
——& Throssell, Ric, 1982, *Straight Left: Articles and Addresses on Politics, Literature, and Women's Affairs Over Almost 60 Years, from 1910-1968*, Wild & Woolley, Sydney.
Purves, N.Y., 1962, *The Growth and Development of the Perth Repertory Club and National Theatre*, Teachers' Higher Certificate thesis, Graylands Teachers College, Perth.
Rees, Leslie, 1973, *The Making of Australian Drama: A Historical and Critical Survey from the 1830s to the 1970s*, Angus & Robertson, Sydney.
Reid, G.S. & Oliver, M.R, 1982, *The Premiers of Western Australia 1890-1982*, UWA Press, Nedlands.
Roland, Betty, 1989, *Caviar for Breakfast*, Collins, Sydney.
Rose, David, 1980, 'The Movement Against War and Fascism, 1933-1939', *Labour History*, no. 38, May, Australian Society for the Study of Labour History.
Rowse, Tim, 2002, *Nugget Coombs: A Reforming Life*, Cambridge University Press.
Rubinstein, Hilary L., 1991, *The Jews in Australia, Volume 1*, William Heinemann, Melbourne.
Sharkey, L.L., 1943, *Congress Report on the Work of the Central Committee from the 12th to the 13th Party Congress*, Dimitrov Press, Sydney.

Smith, Bernard, 1993, *Noel Counihan: Artist and Revolutionary*, Oxford University Press, Melbourne.
Smith, Susan Bradley, 2001, 'Girl Meets Tractor: Socialist Desire in Prichard's Suffrage Plays', *Overland*, no. 164, Spring.
Snell, Ted, 1991, *Cinderella on the Beach: A Source Book of Western Australia's Visual Culture*, UWA Press, Nedlands.
Sparrow, Jeff, 2007, *Communism: A Love Story*, Melbourne University Press.
Stannage, C.T., 1979, *The People of Perth: A Social History of Western Australia's Capital City*, Perth City Council, Perth.
——(ed.), 1981, *A New History of Western Australia*, UWA Press, Nedlands.
Stephen, Ann & Reeves, Andrew, 1985, *Badges of Labour, Banners of Pride*, Allen & Unwin, Sydney.
Stevens, Joyce, 1987, *Taking the Revolution Home: Work Among Women in the Communist Party of Australia: 1920–1945*, Sybylla Press, Fitzroy.
Sydney New Theatre, 1992, *The New Years 1932– : The Plays, People and Events of Six Decades of Sydney's Radical New Theatre*, Newtown.
Symons, Beverley (with Andrew Wells & Stuart Macintyre), 1994, *Communism in Australia: A Resource Bibliography*, NLA, Canberra.
Taylor, A.J.P., 1996, *The Origins of the Second World War*, Simon & Schuster, New York.
Taylor, Robyn Dianne, 1993, *An Investigation into the Nature of Modernism and Modernity During the 1930s in Perth, Western Australia, Through the Study of Specific Buildings and Related Art and Design Forms*, PhD thesis, UWA, Perth.
——1985, 'Stage Props of Modernism — Perth Architecture 1935–1940', *Praxis M*, no. 9, Winter.
'The History of the Playbox Theatre', 1933, *Music and the Drama*, vol. 1, no. 2, 10 September.
'The Origins of the New Theatre Movement', n.d, *Labor Review*, no. 24.
Thompson, Patricia, 1988, *Accidental Chords*, Penguin Books, Ringwood.
Throssell, Ric, 1997, *My Father's Son: The Last Knot Untied* (revised edition), Em Press, Melbourne.
——1986, 'Paths Towards Purpose: The Political Plays of Katharine Susannah Prichard and Ric Throssell', *Australian Drama 1920–1955: Papers Presented to a Conference at the University of New England, Armidale, September 1–4, 1984*, UNE, Armidale.
——1975, *Wild Weeds and Wind Flowers: The Life and Letters of Katharine Susannah Prichard*, Angus & Robertson, Melbourne.
Ure Smith, Sydney (ed.), 1939, *Australian Art Annual 1939*, Ure Smith Pty Ltd,, Sydney.
Walsh, Richard, 1993, *Ferretabilia: Life and Times of Nation Review*, University of Queensland Press, St Lucia.
Watson, Don, 1975, 'Anti-Communism in the Thirties', *Arena*, no. 37.
Wells, Julie, 1985, 'Katherine [sic] Susannah Prichard: The Writer as Communist Activist', *Melbourne Historical Journal*, vol. 17.
——1984, 'Katharine Susannah Prichard: The Artist as Communist Activist 1930–40', *Time Remembered*, no. 6, Murdoch University.
——1984, *The Political Commitment of Katharine Susannah Prichard: Political Activity 1930–1940 and the Writing of the Goldfields Trilogy*, BA Hons, Murdoch University, WA.
West, Nigel, 1999, *Venona: The Greatest Secret of The Cold War*, HarperCollins, London.
White, A.D., 1972, 'Brecht's Quest for a Democratic Theatre', *Theatre Quarterly*, vol. 2, no. 5, January–March, London.
Wilde, William (with Joy Hooton & Barry Andrews), 1985, *The Oxford Companion to Australian Literature*, Oxford University Press, Melbourne.

Williams, Justina, 1993, *Anger and Love*, Fremantle Arts Centre Press, Fremantle.
—1976, *The First Furrow*, Lone Hand Press, Willagee, WA.
Williams, Victor, 1988, 'Why I Am a Communist and a Poet', *Papers in Labour History*, no. 2, October, Australian Society for the Study of Labour History, Department of Industrial Relations, UWA, Perth.
—1966, *Hammers and Seagulls: Poems by Victor Williams*, Australasian Book Society.
—1946, *Harvest Time and Other Poems*, s.n., Melbourne.
Zable, Arnold, 1998, *Wanderers and Dreamers: Tales of the David Herman Theatre*, Hyland House, Melbourne.
Zogbaum, Heidi, 2004, *Kisch in Australia: The Untold Story*, Scribe Publications, Melbourne.

UNPUBLISHED MANUSCRIPTS
Doherty, P.A., n.d., *The History of Amateur Theatre in Perth Since 1920*, unpublished monograph held in the Battye Library, SLWA, Perth.
Fitzgerald, Marie Kathleen, n.d., *History of Perth Theatre*, s.n., unpublished monograph held in the Battye Library, SLWA, Perth.
Gooding, Janda, 1985, *Herbert McClintock's Years in Perth 1934–1940*, AGWA Archive, Perth.
Rowe, Dorothy, n.d. *Aims and Objects of the Playbox*, unpublished manuscript held in Dorothy Rowe's scrapbook, in the possession of Phil Young, Glebe, NSW.
Yellard, Ursula, 1963, *A History of the Development of Ballet in West Australia*, unpublished monograph held in the Battye Library, SLWA, Perth.
Young, Phil, 2005, *Thea Rowe: Parts of Her Life Story*, unpublished manuscript, in the possession of Phil Young, Glebe, NSW.

CATALOGUES
Axel Poignant: Photographs 1922–1980, 1982, AGNSW, Sydney.
Bromfield, David (ed.), 1986, *Aspects of Perth Modernism, 1929–1942: A Catalogue for the Exhibition Organised by Julian Goddard and the Centre for Fine Arts at the University of Western Australia*, Centre for Fine Arts, UWA, Perth.
Missingham, Hal & Poignant, Axel, 1941, *New Directions in Photography*, Newspaper House, Perth.
Poignant, Roslyn, 2011, *Picture Story: Axel Poignant, Photographer, The Formative Years 1929–1942*, The Cross Art Projects, Sydney, February.

ARCHIVAL MATERIALS
Papers of Hugh Anderson, MS 6946, MS ACC 04.186, MS ACC 06.138, NLA, Canberra.
Papers of Spencer Brodney, MS 5805, MS 6066, MS 6069, MS 5805, SLV, Melbourne.
Papers of Robert D. Fitzgerald, MS 7334, NLA, Canberra.
Papers of Miles Franklin, MS364, Mitchell Library, Sydney.
Papers of John and Roma Gilchrist, 1927–1984, MN 1034, ACC 3255A/52, Battye Library, SLWA, Perth.
Papers of Ken Gott, MS 13047, SLV, Melbourne.
Papers of Sir Paul Meernaa Caedwalla Hasluck, MN 1184, ACC 3499A, Battye Library, SLWA, Perth.
Campbell Howard Collection, UNE, Armidale, NSW.
McCrae Family Collection, MS 12831, La Trobe Library, SLV, Melbourne.
Records of the New Theatre (1914–1990), MSS 6244, Mitchell Library, Sydney.
Papers of Vance and Nettie Palmer, MS 1174, NLA, Canberra.

Perth Theatre Trust Archives, His Majesty's Theatre, Perth.
Papers of Katharine Susannah Prichard, MS 6201, NLA, Canberra.
Papers of Katharine Susannah Prichard, MN 1465, Battye Library, SLWA, Perth.
Repertory Club Papers, Western Australian Theatre Company records, MN 891, ACC 615A, Battye Library, SLWA, Perth.
Records of the Skinner Galleries, MN 1320, ACC 4043A, Battye Library, SLWA, Perth.
Papers of Mary Louisa Skinner, MN 186, ACC 3490A, Battye Library, SLWA, Perth.
Papers of Ric Throssell, MS 8071, NLA, Canberra.
Papers of Linley Wilson, MN 1459, ACC 4616A, Battye Library, SLWA, Perth.
W.A. Drama Festivals (inc.) Papers, MN 1184/1, ACC 3499A, Battye Library, SLWA, Perth.
Records of the Western Australian Theatre Company, MN 891, ACC 615A, Battye Library, SLWA, Perth.

ORAL HISTORY INTERVIEWS
As cited in endnotes.

NEWSPAPERS AND OTHER NEWSPAPER ARTICLES
As cited in endnotes.

ABOUT THE AUTHOR

Dylan Hyde has a background in film and television production, and is the nephew of the academic and public figure, Sister Veronica Brady. The son of a scientist and a Classics scholar, he was born in the United States and raised in Perth before emigrating to Melbourne in his late teenage years. He has an ongoing interest in historical research and writing, specifically in the areas of art and political history. His previous writings on the Workers' Art Guild include an article published in *Papers in Labour History* (no. 18, March 1997, Australian Society for the Study of Labour History) and a short piece in the *Historical Encyclopedia of Western Australia* (UWA Press, 2009).

ACKNOWLEDGEMENTS

I am particularly grateful for the help and information provided by the following, who were central players or bore witness to the events described in the book: Joan Arnold, Freda Brown, Peter Cowan, Herbert 'Kitch' Currie, Oriel Gray, Leah Healy, Beryl and Rick Hearder, Kathleen Hector, John Hepworth, Bill Irwin, Ben Kidd, Harold and Dorothy Krantz, Olive Lachberg, Betsey Linton, Angus McGregor, John and Mairi McKenzie, Esther Missingham, John and Ray Oldham, Phyllis Ophel, Roslyn Poignant, Ruth Rudkin, Ric Throssell, Joan Vike, Esther Wignall, Tom Wignall, Joan and Vic Williams.

Many others have assisted in uncovering this shrouded history: Arthur Easton, who was extraordinarily helpful in helping me sort through the treasure-trove of New Theatre records at the Mitchell Library in Sydney; Julian Goddard; Bruce Harris; Nicholas Hasluck; George Hoad and David Milliss from Sydney New Theatre; Ivan King (His Majesty's Theatre, Perth); Francis King; Linn Knuckey; Ric McCracken (formerly of the Perth Trades and Labor Council); Colin Nichol; Julian Ophel; and Katherine Perrin.

Thanks to Helen Anderson for the Perth city map. I would also like to acknowledge the Noel Butlin Archives at the Australian National University; the National Library of Australia; the Mitchell Library; the Axel and Roslyn Poignant Archive, London, through its intermediary Ruark Lewis; and The Cross Art Projects, Sydney for permission to use images for the book.

My thanks go to the wonderful staff in the manuscripts section of the National Library of Australia, where my dear late mother once plied her trade, as well as staff at the National Archives of Australia, the Art Gallery of Western Australia and the State Library of Western Australia.

I am indebted to the SEARCH Foundation in Sydney and the Western Australian History Foundation for their financial support. I am equally grateful to Naama Grey-Smith (Fremantle Press) for being such an enthusiast, to Gail Jones and Dennis Haskell for lending their considerable voices, and to Leila Jabbour for her work as editor.

I want to express my love and gratitude to my siblings Andrew, Dominic and Melony, my late aunt Veronica (Pat) Brady and Arthur O'Neill for their help and wise counsel.

My particular love and gratitude goes to Shaunagh, Charlie and Bridget, who sacrificed quite a lot to indulge me over many years.

INDEX

Notes:
Titles starting with *A* or *The* are filed by the next word (e.g. *The Burglar* files under *Burglar, The* and *A Bed-Time Story* files under *Bed-Time Story, A*).
Surnames starting with Mc or Mac are interfiled as if spelled Mac.

Aboriginal citizenship rights 115
Actresses' Franchise League suffrage theatre 25
Adamson, Bartlett 196
agitprop theatre 29, 43, 59, 114, 116–8, 133, 190–1
  by Prichard 11, 59, 105, 215–7
  by Workers' Art Guild 153–4, 162, 172–3
Agricultural Bank 77
air raid precautions 198
Aldington, Richard, *Death of a Hero* 103
Alexander, Fred 40, 252, 258
All God's Chillun Got Wings (O'Neill) 122
All Soviet Congress of Writers (1st; 1934) 51
All-Australian Congress Against War and Fascism 39
Amalgamated Engineering Union 116, 139, 167
American Group Theatre 30
American League of Workers' Theatres 48
  see also New Theatre League; workers' theatre movement
American Newspaper Guild 191
And Quiet Flows the Don (Sholokhov) 86
Angelo, Leith 57, 62–3, 72, 120
Annand, Douglas 162
Anstey, Frank 15
anti-conscription activities 11, 15, 188
  see also conscription
anti–National Register activities 160–2
anti-Semitism 95, 136, 155–6
Anti-War Day 58
Antony and Cleopatra (Shakespeare) 164–5
Apletin, Mikhail 141, 217, 226, 235
Approximate Portrait in a Drawing Room (McClintock) 175
arbitration 11, 17, 67, 191, 215
Arbitration Court 191, 215
architects and architecture 31–2, 34, 162–3

Are You Ready, Comrade? (Roland) 150–2, 203
  Sydney New Theatre production 151 Workers' Art Guild production (1938) 151–2
Arnold, Victor 74, 133–4, 209–11, 214, 218–9, 223–4, 240–1, 245, 254
Art Deco design 34
Ascent of F6, The (Auden and Isherwood) 183
ASIO *see* Australian Security Intelligence Organisation (ASIO)
Attorney-General's Department 119, 207
  see also Commonwealth Investigation Branch (CIB)
Auden, W.H.
  Ascent of F6, The 183
  Dog Beneath the Skin 110
  On the Frontier 182
Australia First Movement 205
Australian Army Education Service 256, 260
Australian Council Against War 41
Australian Department of Information 201
Australian Imperial Force 189
Australian Journalists' Association 67, 196, 261
Australian Labor Party (ALP)
  aims not entirely divergent to CPA 114–5
  attitude to National Register 160
  Catholic influences in 33, 101–2, 116, 202
  CPA courts 46–7
  Curtin's reform agenda 15
  declares war on CPA 229
  rift over Spanish Civil War 101–2
  Right Wing faction 102, 202
  support from CPA 134
  Workers' Art Guild performances at meetings 167
  see also Labor governments

INDEX

Australian Quarterly, The (journal) 177
Australian Security Intelligence
    Organisation (ASIO) 18, 257, 259,
    261, 271, 274–6
Australian Wheat and Wool Growers'
    Union 192–3, 224
Australian Workers' Union (AWU) 197,
    215–7
Australian Writers' League (AWL) 45–6
Australia-Soviet Friendship Society
    239–40
Awake and Sing! (Odets) 170–1, 242
    Workers' Art Guild production (1939)
    170–1

Baldwinson, Arthur 162
Ball, Desmond, *Breaking the Codes* 277
ballet 44, 166, 228, 250–1, 257–8
Ballets Russes 44
Baracchi, Guido 12, 104, 114, 150
Bartlett, Norman 200
Basley, William 218–9, 220, 230–1, 238
Bath, Hope 140, 178, 196, 203, 214, 255
Bath, Thomas 251
Bauhaus movement 32, 34, 86, 162
Beasley, Frank 40
Beckett, Clarice 175
Bed-Time Story, A (George) 51, 52
Beechey, Kathleen *see* Hector, Kathleen
Bengal, Ben, *Plant in the Sun* 219, 220
Benn, George 140
Benn, Maurice 140, 254–5
Benn, Thomas ('Tom') 140
Benson, George 139
Berinson, Moshe 135–6
Berry, Marjorie 'May' 120, 125, 151, 158,
    196, 223, 273
Black Swan (magazine) 37, 157
Blackboy Hill camp 19–20
Blackburn, Maurice 39
Blewett, Dorothy, *Quiet Night* 247–8
Blood on the Moon (Sifton) 176–80
    Workers' Art Guild production (Sept.
    1939) 176–80, 183
    Workers' Art Guild production (Oct.
    1939) 180
Blueshirts *see* National Socialist (Nazi)
    Party of Western Australia
Boas, Harold 31
bohemianism 36, 113, 208

Bolshevik Revolution *see* Russian
    revolution
Bolton, Geoffrey 20
Book Censorship Board 120
    see also Literature Censorship Board
Booklovers' Library 14
Boretz, Allen, *Room Service* 183
Borich, Yure ('George') 217, 218
Bottomley, John 156
Boulder (town) 121
Boulder (WA political division) 33, 55,
Boy Meets Girl (Spewack) 182
    Repertory Club production (1938) 182
Brackenreg, John 139
Brady, Edwin ('E.J.') 39
Breaking the Codes (Ball and Horner) 277
Brecht, Bertold 69, 89, 216
Brennan, Frank 39
Breton, André, *What is Surrealism?* 149
Brisbane Line 239
Broda, Rudolf 11
Brodney, Spencer 29, 269
Brooks, Harry, *Six Men of Dorset* 109
Bruce, Stanley Melbourne 240
Brumby Innes (Prichard) 105, 140, 226
Budget Protest Committee (BPC) 229–30
Bull, Hilda *see* Esson, Hilda
Burglar, The (Prichard) (1910) 25
Burgoyne, Geoffrey 38
Burgoyne, Gordon ('Bugs') 36, 37–8, 77,
    124, 173, 196, 205, 214, 217, 255
    Heil Jones 83
Bury the Dead (Shaw) 83, 88–94, 90, 140
    Sydney New Theatre production (1936)
    90
    Workers' Art Guild production (1936)
    88–94, 140
Butcher, Joan 196
Buzacott, Nutter 175
Buzolic, Bert 219, 238

Calphurnia's Claws 59
Cameron, Robert 40
Campbell, Betty 143
Canaries Sometimes Sing (Lonsdale) 249,
    250
    Repertory Club production (1942) 250
Cannibal Carnival (Gullan) 163–5
    Workers' Art Guild production (1939)
    163–5

Cape, Jonathan 52
Capek, Karel, *Power and the Glory* 183
Caporn, Kevin 247
Captain Pernot's Honour (play) 59
Cardell-Oliver, Florence 38
Carder case 230, 234, 236, 245
Carder, June 230, 238
Carpenters' and Joiners' Union 56-7, 167
Casey, Gavin 77, 245, 255
Casson, Lewis 27, 109
Catholic Action 187, 189
Catholic Church 101-2, 123
censorship 46, 105, 115, 119-20, 188-9, 197-201, 227
Cézanne, Paul 149
Chaffey, Frank 73
Chase, Muriel 166
Chase, Sandra 166
Chief Censor's Office 227
Chifley, Ben 252, 266
children, Workers' Art Guild activities for 83-4, 101, 158, 250
Christmass, Alfred John *see* Hepworth, John
Churchill, Winston 237
Clarion (newspaper) 189, 198
Clayton, Walter 273
Clovelly frame-up 54
Colahan, Colin 175
Cold War 253
Collie 121-2
Collier, Philip 33
Comintern 30, 35-47, 39, 41, 46, 48, 85, 99, 176
commercial artists 31-2
Commonwealth Investigation Branch (CIB)
  banning of *Upsurge* 119-20
  infiltration of CPA 146, 158, 186-7
  raids on CPA members 21, 204, 208, 213, 218-9, 244, 248-9
  surveillance 11, 18, 30, 158, 202, 204, 237, 245
Commonwealth Literary Fund 226, 237, 276
Communist Party of Australia (CPA)
  'Aid to Russia' campaign 206
  anti-war stance 160, 188, 189, 237
  attitude to bohemianism 36, 43
  attitude to cultural ventures 43-4
  banning of 202, 251-2
  Budget Protest Committee (BPC) 229-30
  candidates in WA elections 55
  censorship of 188-9
  CIB pursuit of 18-21, 146, 158, 235-6
  Crimes Act amendments 58
  formation of 12, 13, 15, 18
  fractions within WA branch 110-2
  membership numbers
    nationally 115, 158-9, 237, 252
    WA branch 45, 158-9
  physical intimidation of WA members 188, 253
  political persecution of 58, 114-5, 186-90, 197-209, 201-2, 240
  relationship with ALP 46-7, 114-5, 134, 229
  relationship with trade unions 47, 110, 202, 231
  Spanish Relief Committee 99, 100-1, 112, 116, 141, 142
  WA branch goes underground 203
  WA branch headquarters 19, 29
  WA branch involvement with Workers' Theatre 50, 53
  see also Militant Minority Movement; Popular Front
Communist Party of the Soviet Union (CPSU) 44, 46, 51, 99-100, 142, 254
Communist Review (journal) 114
Confederation of Labour Unions (Spain) 101
conscription 15, 160-2
constructivism 88, 90, 237, 265-6
Conto, Louis ('Lou') 247
Coombes, Joyce 196
Coombs, Herbert 'Nugget' 17, 197, 266
Corbusier, Le *see* Le Corbusier
Corn is Green, The (Williams) 180-1
  Repertory Club production (1939) 180-1
Council Against War (and Fascism) (CAWF) 39, 41, 50, 53
Country Party 229, 240
Court Hotel 79
Cowan, Peter 18, 120
  Hills of Apollo Bay, The 118-9, 146-7
Coward, Noel 221-2
Cradle Will Rock, The (Living Newspaper) 153

Craig, Gordon 89
Crimes Act 1914 (Cth) 18, 44, 58, 190
Cronin, Bernard 39
Currie, Betsey 81
Curtin government 172, 240, 251–2
Curtin, John 15, 114–5, 160, 167, 229, 240, 251–2, 256
Cuthbertson, Allan 246, 247, 256
Cuthbertson, Henry 83–4

Dadaism 124
Daily News (newspaper) 38, 80, 157
  on banning of CPA publications 189
  on Carder case 230
  on Edward VIII abdication 94
  on McClintock and surrealism 175
  reviews
    Bury the Dead (1936) 93
    Private Hicks 131–2
    Till the Day I Die (1936) 69
    Till the Day I Die reprise (1936) 96
    Waiting For Lefty 116
    Where's That Bomb? 116
  on Spanish Civil War 102
Daily Telegraph (newspaper) 73–4, 203
Dalí, Salvador 64
Dann, George Landen, *No Incense Rising* 183
Darbyshire, Bill 76, 77, 78
Das Kapital (Marx) 24, 227
David Herman Theatre 136
Davidson, John Hale *see* Hepworth, John
Davison, Frank Dalby 114
Deakin, Alfred 10
Dean, William ('Bill') 189, 198–9, 201
Death of a Hero (Aldington) 103
Defence Act 1903 (Cth) 160
demonstration marches 15, 18–9, 24, 41, 113, 160, 214
Dennis, C.J. 38
Depression 16–20, 54, 56, 103
  effect on CPA membership 159
  effect on wheat farmers 191
  financial emergency tax 154
  Group Settlement Scheme 76–7
  sustenance allowance 19–20, 24, 163
Devanny, Jean 42–6, 60, 188, 190
  Paradise Flow 184–5
dictation test 41–2, 133
  see also White Australia policy
Dimitrov, Georgi 46

Dinan, James ('Jim') 223–4, 229
Director-General of Information 208
divorce 114
Dog Beneath the Skin (Isherwood and Auden) 110
Dog Collar Act *see* Transport Workers Act 1928 (Cth)
Dollfuss, Engelbert 155–6
Doyle, John ('Jack') 187, 204, 213
Drake-Brockman, Henrietta 51, 105, 123, 226
  Men Without Wives 153, 181
Dressler, Ernst 62
Drinkwater, John, *X=O: A Night of the Trojan War* 58
Duggan, Gwen 178, 196, 209, 215, 223, 246, 247
Dupain, Max 162
Dybbuk, The (*Der Dibbuk*) 135
Dyson, Bill 14

Earsman, Bill 12, 13
Ebert, Max *see* McClintock, Herbert
Ednie-Brown, Colin 31–2, 34
education intelligentsia 40
Edward VIII, abdication of 94
electoral laws 11
Elliott, Brian 176
Eluard, Paul 64
employment conditions *see* working conditions
Ern Malley poetry hoax 176
Esson, Hilda (nee Bull) 26, 97
Esson, Louis 12, 14, 49
  friendship with Prichard 25–6, 65, 70, 71, 90, 97–8, 105
  Southern Cross, The 105–8
  The Woman Tamer 25–6
Eureka Stockade 105, 106–7
Evatt, Herbert Vere ('Doc') 42, 45, 229, 240, 249, 259–60
Ewers, John K. 200
Exit Left (Gray) 242

Factories and Shops Act 1920 (WA) 59
Fadden, Arthur 229, 240
Farm Labourers' Union 191
fascism 39, 47, 94, 99, 105, 155–6, 159, 212
  see also Franco, Francisco; Hitler, Adolf; Nazi Germany; Spanish Civil War

Federal Theatre Project 163, 191
Feed the Sheep (Williams) 220-1, 251
   Workers' Art Guild production (1940) 220-1
Feint, Adrian 162
Fellowship of Australian Writers (FAW) 45-6, 114, 184, 201, 255
'fifth columnists' 198, 272
Filippini, Anne (nee McParland) 26, 104
Filippini, Ercole 26
Financial Emergency Act 1931 (Cth) 154
financial emergency tax 154
Firebird (Fokine and Stravinksy) 166
First World War 8, 11-2, 15, 126, 160
Fison, Sydney 165
Fitton, Doris 24, 165
Fitzpatrick, Peter 108
Five Arts Club 120, 122
   see also Playbox Theatre
Floridsdorf (Wolf) 155-8
   Workers' Art Guild production (1939) 155-8
Flynn, Maurice 205
Fokine, Michel, *Firebird* 166
For Valour (Throssell) 276
Forward One (Prichard) 59-60, 105, 203, 216, 217
   Sydney New Theatre production (1937) 105
Foy and Gibson 34
Franco, Francisco 99
   see also Spanish Civil War
Franklin, Miles 114, 235
Franklin Print 53, 206-7
Freeland League 171-2
Freer case 133
Freer, Mary 133
Fremantle Lumpers' Union 167
Friends of the Soviet Union (FOSU) 43, 44, 58, 202, 207

Gadfly (journal) 38
gasmasks 198
Gauguin, Paul 149
George, Esmond 122, 149
George, Keith
   artistic versus political drama 49, 109-11
   ASIO scrutiny of 257
   Bed-Time Story, A 51, 52
   death and obituaries 257-8
   as drama tutor 184, 224-5, 250, 256-7
   on Esson 49
   marriage to Linley Wilson 250-1
   military service 250, 256
   on *Penalty Clause* 217
   productions
      Bury the Dead (1936) 89, 90-1
      Floridsdorf (1939) 155-8
      Hinkemann (1937) 126-30
      Inga (1938) 141, 142-4
      Private Hicks (1937) 125
      Till the Day I Die, (June 1936) 64-75
      Till the Day I Die (Dec. 1936) 96
   relationship with Prichard 27, 49-59, 70-1, 105-8, 140-1, 144
   role in CAWF 41, 45, 47, 52-3
   role in Five Arts Club 22-5
   role in Repertory Club 248-50
   role in West Australian Drama Festival 122-3
   role in Workers' Art Club 61, 76
   role in Workers' Art Guild 76, 83, 138, 140-1, 164, 167-70
   role in Workers' Theatre 48-59
   testimonial 251
Ghosts (Ibsen) 27, 147-8
   Workers' Art Guild production (1938) 147-8
Gibbney and Son (printers) 32, 80, 148, 213, 218, 219
Gilchrist, John 122, 156
Glebov, Anatole, *Inga* 142-4
Gledden Building 167
Gloucester, Duke of 35, 39, 166
Goff, Ivan 103
Golden Miles (Prichard) 111, 226, 237
goldfields 31, 52, 159, 215-7, 226-7
   see also Boulder; Kalgoorlie; Wiluna
Gollancz, Victor 137, 165
Gordon, Charles 140
Gorky, Maxim, *Lower Depths* 29
Gott, Ken 263-4
Gould, Harry 201
Gow, Ronald, *Love on the Dole* 211, 214-5
Graham, John 7
Grainger, Percy 166
Grattan, Clinton Hartley 11, 146-7
Gray, Grace 243

Gray, Oriel 90, 195, 210, 242–4, 261
  Exit Left 242
  Torrents, The 262
Great Depression *see* Depression
Great War *see* First World War
Greenmount 13–4
Greenwood, Irene 201
Greenwood, Walter, *Love on the Dole* 211, 214–5
Gropius, Walter 162
Group Settlement Scheme 76–7, 172
Group Theatre (New York) 52
Gullan, Roger
  Cannibal Carnival 163–5
  Where's That Bomb? 115–7
Gunther, John, *Inside Europe* 102

Haldane, J.B.S. 198
Hamill, Elizabeth ('Betty') 175, 196, 211, 247, 259
Harcourt, John Mewton, *Upsurge* 46, 119–20
Hardy, Frank, *Power Without Glory* 272
Harmsworth, Walter 217
Harnett, Phyllis *see* Ophel, Phyllis
Harris, Agnes 83, 117, 129
Harris, Bruce 83
Harris, Rolf 83, 129, 215
Harvest in the North (Hodson) 183
Hasluck, Paul
  on Doyle 187–8
  journalism career 66–9
  lecturer at UWA 200
  public service career 259–60
  reviews
    Are You Ready, Comrade? 151–2
    Awake and Sing! 171
    Blood on the Moon 177, 179–80
    Bury the Dead 88, 90–3
    Cannibal Carnival 165
    Ghosts 148
    Harvest in the North 183
    Hinkemann 127
    Inga 144
    Love on the Dole 215
    Penalty Clause 217
    Private Hicks 125
    Till the Day I Die (1936) 68–9, 72
    Waiting for Lefty 116
    Where's That Bomb? 116

  role in West Australian Drama Festival 122–3
  on Workers' Art Guild 259
Hatfield, William 175
Healy, Kevin 197, 198, 201, 208, 252
Healy, Leah 251
Hearder, Beryl 70
Hector, John 135, 156–7, 180, 194–6, 209–10, 213–4, 241, 243, 255, 260–1
Hector, Kathleen (nee Beechey) 82, 83, 154, 158, 213–4, 241, 260–1
Hedda Gabler (Ibsen) 25
Heidelberg School 62, 79
Heil Jones (Burgoyne) 83
  Workers' Art Guild production (1936) 83
Hepworth, John 78–9, 83, 124, 241–3
  art 124
  books 261–3
  CPA membership 78, 261–2
  death 262–3
  on Depression 16–7
  on Harnett 209
  as John Hale Davidson 244–5, 261
  journalism career 124, 261–2
  later life 261–3
  Long Green Shore, The 261–3
  marriage to Gray 243
  military service 244–5, 261
  Nightmare of a Very Young Egg, The 124
  plays 123, 262
  poetry 101
  police raid on 213
  relationship with Beechey 158, 213
  role in Sydney New Theatre 242–4
  role in Workers' Art Club 35, 73, 77–8
  role in Workers' Art Guild 83, 158, 214
  role in Workers' Theatre 57, 78
  'suicide' 243–4
  on towing the Party line 77–8
  We Are Hungry 123
  writer's group membership 77–8
  Yellow Ticket 123
Herald (newspaper) 38, 102
Herlinger, Paul 118, 138
Herman, David 134
Hewett, Dorothy 87, 192
Heyward, Michael 9
High Court of Australia 41, 42, 45
Hill, John 102

Hinkemann (Toller) 126–30
   Workers' Art Guild production (1937) 126–30, 138
His Majesty's Theatre 8, 26, 95, 97, 122
Hitler, Adolf 21, 64, 155–6, 161, 176–7, 227
Hodge, Herbert, *see also* Gullan, Roger
Hodgson, Agnes 101
Hodson, James Lansdale, *Harvest in the North* 183
Hold Your Wheat (Williams) 190–3, 251
   Workers' Art Guild production (1940) 190–3
Holland, Eleanor 35
Holland, John 35
Hollands, May 247
homosexuality 83
Horner, David, *Breaking the Codes* 277
housing 153–4
Howard, Pat 151, 152, 196
Huelin, Frank 43, 60–1
Hughes, T.J. 230, 234
Hughes, William Morris ('Billy') 202, 240

I Am Angry (Harnett) 123, 251
Ibsen, Henrik
   Ghosts 27, 147–8
   Hedda Gabler 25
immigration 41–2, 76, 133, 135–7, 218
   see also White Australia policy
Immigration Restriction Act 1901 (Cth) 41–2, 133
Independent Players 120, 122
   Ascent of F6, The 183
   Harvest in the North 183
   Power and the Glory 183
Independent Theatre (Perth) 143, 165
Independent Theatre (Sydney) 24
Inga (Glebov) 142–4
   Workers' Art Guild production (1938) 141, 142–4
Inside Europe (Gunther) 102
International Brigades 100–2
International Congress Against War (Amsterdam; 1932) 41
International Exhibition of Surrealism (London; 1936) 64
International Labour Defence (ILD) 41
International Literature (journal) 235
International Theatre (journal) 29

International Women's Day 115
International Workers' Dramatic Union (IWDU) 30
International Workers' Theatre Olympiad (1st; 1933) 30
Intimate Strangers (Prichard) 38, 59, 97–8, 119, 273
Irwin, Edward ('Bill') 191, 196
   on CPA 121, 189, 252
   CPA freezes out 263
   on George 127, 164–5, 169–70
   journalism career 102–3, 189, 194, 206, 263–4
   on Perth in the 1930s 7–8
   police raids on 205–6
   on Workers' Art Club 61
   on Workers' Art Guild 252
Isherwood, Christopher
   Ascent of F6, The 183
   Dog Beneath the Skin 110
   On the Frontier 182
Italo-Australian Grand Opera Company 26

Jasienski, Bruno, *Man Changes His Skin* 86
J.C. Williamson (theatre company) 22, 195
Jewish Freeland League 171–2
Jewish people
   in drama 73, 170–1
   persecution by Nazis 95, 155, 177–8
   in Perth 39–40, 56, 69–70, 95, 96, 135–7, 139, 171
   refugees 171–2
   see also Westralian Judean
Jewish theatres 134–6
Johnston, George 7
Jollie Smith, Christian 41
Jones, Betty 35
Juleff, Francis *see* George, Keith
Juno and the Paycock (O'Casey) 152
   Repertory Club production (1938) 152, 181

Kalgoorlie 31, 36, 55, 121, 223, 237
Katayev, Valentine, *Squaring the Circle* 183
Katharine Susannah Prichard Writers' Centre 271
Keiller, Irene *see* Osterberg, Irene
Keiller, Olive *see* Lachberg, Olive
Kennedy, Clement ('Clem') 25, 27

Kennedy, Gerard 25
Khrushchev, Nikita 254, 263–4
Kidd, Ben 140
Kidd, Bill 92
Kidd, Joan *see* Vike, Joan
King, Alexander ('Alec') 40, 86–7, 157, 175, 192, 212, 220, 264
Kisch, Egon 39–42, 45
Knowles, Eric 197–8
Krantz, Dorothy (formerly Powell) 196
Krantz, Harold 31–2, 34, 197, 218

Labor governments
   federal 10, 11, 15, 39, 240
   WA 33, 64
   see also Australian Labor Party (ALP)
Labor Study Circle of Western Australia 15, 20
Labour Day Committee 113, 167, 202
Labour Day street parades 114, 138–9, 167
Labour Youth Theatre (Adelaide) 241
Lachberg, Maurie 55, 56–7, 61, 79, 80, 251
   acting career 72, 116, 129, 151, 247
   Labour Day Committee 114, 167
Lachberg, Olive (nee Keiller) 80, 196
landscape painting 9
Lawrence, D. H. 14
Le Corbusier 31–2, 88, 162
League of Nations 40
League for Peace and Democracy 184
League of Workers' Theatres 30
Left Book Club 112, 137, 153, 165, 167, 191, 198, 219
Lehmann, 'Lotte' 27
Lenin, Vladimir 11, 39
Lewis, Freda 203, 243
linocuts 32
Linton, James W. R., Sr. 32, 81–2
Linton Art School 81
Linton Institute of Art 62, 81
Literature Censorship Board 115
   see also Book Censorship Board
Little Theatre 27, 120, 122, 143
Living Newspapers 59, 153, 163, 190–1
Lockwood, Rupert 102
London, Jack 10
Long Green Shore, The (Hepworth) 261
Lonsdale, Frederick, *Canaries Sometimes Sing* 249, 250

Lotus Library and Bookshop 95, 120, 122, 137
Love on the Dole (Gow and Greenwood) 211, 214–5
   Workers' Art Guild production (1940) 211, 214–5
Lower Depths (Gorky) 28–9
Lowson, Mary 101
Luce, Clare Boothe, *Women, The* 194–6
Lunghi, John 32, 148, 175, 211, 215, 218–9, 245, 246
Lyons, Joseph 40, 73, 133, 160
Lyons Bungles, The 133–4, 172–3, 203, 251
   Workers' Art Guild production (1937) 133–4, 138

McArtney, James ('Jim') 36, 102, 103, 194
McCalman, Janet 28
McClintock, Albert 36
McClintock, Alexander 79
McClintock, Herbert 32, 79–80, 124, 148–9, 175, 264
   Approximate Portrait in a Drawing Room 175
   as 'Max Ebert' 212, 214
McClintock, Pat 175, 212–3
McClintock, Ruby *see* Oldham, Ruby ('Ray')
McCorkill, George 151
McCrae, Hugh 14, 29, 38, 98
MacDonald, Clifford 151, 156
MacDonald, James Stuart 174
McEwen, John ('Black Jack') 229
McFarlane, May 101
McGregor, Angus 52
Macintyre, Stuart 121, 187
McKenzie, John 161
Mackenzie, Kenneth Seaforth 27
McLaren, John, *Free Radicals* 104
McLernon, Hugh 187, 219
McMahon, Gregan 49
McParland, Anne *see* Filippini, Anne
Making of Australian Drama, The (Rees) 107
Malevich, Kazimir 88
Malleson, Miles, *Six Men of Dorset* 109
Malley, Ern *see* Ern Malley hoax
Malraux, André 100
Maltz, Albert
   Private Hicks 125–6, 131–2, 243
   Rehearsal 220

Man Changes His Skin (Jasienski) 86
Man Gets House 153-4
Manifold, John 95
Mann, Leonard 226
Marc, Franz 149
Marks, Leah 35, 139, 162, 198, 207-8
Marks, Morris 139
Martinez, Rita *see* Prichard, Katharine Susannah
Marx, Groucho 99, 103
Marx, Karl 80
   Das Kapital 24, 227
Marx, Roberto Burle 163
Marxism 12, 16
Masel, Doris 137, 196
Masel family 39-40, 57, 136-7, 180
Masses and Man (Toller) (1932) 43
Matson, Henry 198, 203
Maughan, Jack 43
Maurice, Furnley *see* Wilmot, Frank
May Day celebrations 38, 138
Mein Kampf (Hitler) 227
Melba, Nellie 26
Melbourne New Theatre 138, 154, 262
Meldrum, Max 39
Men Without Wives (Drake-Brockman) 153
   Repertory Club production (1938) 153, 181
Menzies, Robert
   1939 election 229
   banning of CPA and CPA publications 45, 114, 189
   breaks diplomatic ties with USSR 253
   creates National Register 160-2
   declares Kisch illegal immigrant 40, 42
   declares war on Germany 180
   media regulation by 188-9
   on New Theatre League as CPA auxiliary 73
   'Pig-Iron Bob' 167
   as PM 160, 240, 253
   support of Hitler and Mussolini 161
   waterside workers dispute 167, 210
   wheat and wool stock control 192
Meredith, George 10
Meyerhold Academy 237
Meyerhold, Vsevolod 61, 100
MI5 18
Miles, Arthur 22, 24

Miles, John Bramwell (J.B.) 60, 120-1, 158
Militant Minority Movement 39, 47
minimum wage 11
mining industry 215-7
Ministry of Information 204
Mirror (newspaper) 93, 114, 115-6
Missingham, Esther 218
Missingham, Hal 218, 239, 264-5
Mitchell, James 33
Mockeridge, Joan 196, 223
Modern Art Group exhibition (August 1939) 174-6
Modern Women's Club (MWC) 112, 115, 149, 183, 211
Modernism 9, 33, 44, 139, 149, 162, 174-6
Moholy-Nagy, László 32, 86, 88
Moon of Desire (Prichard) 104, 225
Mooney's Cafe 203
Moore, William 138
Morison, George Pitt *see* Pitt Morison, George
Mortlock, Joyce 122
Mortlock Motors 81, 82, 122, 178-9, 219
Moscow News 44
Moscow show trials 99-100
Mountjoy, Wilfred ('Bill')
   anti-National Register protests 162
   as CPA state secretary 85, 186-7, 203
   endorsement of Wells 152
   later life 265
   police raids on 205
   relationship with Prichard 144-6
   relationship with Richards 186-7, 203
   stands for parliament 54-5
Mouse Cottage 35-7
Moussinac, Léon 88
Movement Against War and Fascism (MAWF) 58, 112, 115
   see also League for Peace and Democracy
Moxon, Bert 19
Murdoch, Walter 40, 226
Murphy, Lionel 276
Murray, John, *Room Service* 183
Music and the Drama (journal) 126-7, 128-9, 132, 150
Mussolini, Benito 161
My Father's Son (Throssell) 277

national anthem 69–70
National Gallery Art School (Melbourne) 62, 79
National Gallery of Victoria 174
National Register 160–2
National Register Act 1939 (Cth) 160–2
National Security Act 1939 (Cth) 188, 198, 202, 208, 230, 234, 245, 252
National Security Regulations 227, 235
National Security (Subversive Association) Regulations 234
National Socialism in Germany 21, 155–6
National Socialist German Workers' (Nazi) Party 21
National Socialist Museum of Aryan Art 64
National Socialist (Nazi) Party of Western Australia 71
Nature of the Capitalist Crisis, The (Strachey) 191
Nazi Germany 21, 64, 155–6, 176
Nazi Party (Austria) 155–6
Neughar, Doris 196
Neville, Roy 153, 154, 172
Nevin, Harold 218–9, 220, 230–1
'New Deal' 163
New Theatre (journal) 43
New Theatre League 48, 73, 112, 184, 203, 228, 241
New Way Wins 210
  Sydney New Theatre production (1940) 210
New York Group Theatre 88
New York Theatre Guild 30
Newman, Jack 139
Night Must Fall (Williams) 153
Nightmare of a Very Young Egg, The (Hepworth) 124
No Incense Rising (Dann) 183
  Repertory Club production (1939) 183
Northam 12, 13
Novy Mir (journal) 226

O'Casey, Sean 132
  Juno and the Paycock 152, 181
Odets, Clifford
  Awake and Sing! 170–1, 242
  Till the Day I Die 52, 64–5, 94–6
  Waiting for Lefty 59, 117–9

O'Dowd, Bernard 199, 204
  Poetry Militant 204
Of Mice and Men (Steinbeck) 153
O'Grady, Francis ('Frank') 57, 72, 95, 182, 265
Oldham, Charles Lancelot 31
Oldham, John
  as architect 31–2, 34, 86, 197
  as artist 34, 62–3, 86
  attends 1939 World's Fair 162–3
  later life 265–6
  marriage to Ray McClintock 114
  meets McClintock and Prichard 35, 37
  police raids on 220, 230, 232
  relationship with George 108–11
  role in CPA 85, 220, 229–34
  role in Workers' Art Guild 57, 86, 97, 102, 114, 208
  witness in Carder case 230
Oldham, Ruby ('Ray') (nee McClintock) 35–7, 57, 85–6, 94, 101, 110–111, 114, 157, 162–3, 197, 220, 232–3, 266–7
Oldham, Boas & Ednie-Brown (architects) 31, 220
O'Malley, King 240
On the Frontier (Auden and Isherwood) 182
  Repertory Club production (1939) 182
One-third of a Nation (Living Newspaper) 153
O'Neil, Patrick 220
O'Neill, Eugene, *All God's Chillun Got Wings* 122
opera 26, 27
Ophel, Phyllis (nee Harnett)
  acting career 57, 68, 70–2, 92, 95–6, 109, 117, 129, 143, 196
  on bohemianism 36
  on Five Arts Club 22–7
  friendship with Waislitz 135
  on George 109–10, 111, 259
  I Am Angry 123
  later life 267
  lectures on Modern art 175
  Lotus Library and Bookshop 95, 120
  and Masel family 39–40, 137
  on Pettersen 246–7
  police raid on 203
  relationship with Wells 181
  on Richards 188

Ophel, Phyllis *continued*
   role in anti–National Register protests 161–2
   role in Workers' Art Guild 72, 77, 81, 83–4, 101, 140, 203–4, 209
   West Australian Drama Festival 122, 123
   as Workers' Art Guild director 170–1
      Blood on the Moon (Sept. 1939) 176–80
      Till the Day I Die (1941) 246–7
   on Workers' Art Guild fraction 110–1
Opperman, Hubert 121
Osterberg, Albert 57, 79, 80, 178
Osterberg, Irene (nee Keiller) 79, 80, 178, 267–8
Our Town (Wilder) 225
   Repertory Club production (1940) 225

Page, Earl 229
Palmer, Nettie 12, 14, 21, 85
Palmer, Vance 12, 14, 18, 39, 46, 58
Paradise Flow (Devanny) 184–5
Paris Commune 80
Patch Theatre (Perth) 165
Peace Council 47
Pelican (newspaper) 36
Penalty Clause (Prichard) 215–7
   Workers' Art Guild production (1941) 215–7, 223, 224
penalty clauses 215–7
Penrose, Roland 64
Penton, Brian 24
People's Commissariat for Education 100
Perth
   architecture in 34
   between the wars 118–9
   effect of Depression on 16–20, 30–1
   exposure to theatre 131–2
   as frontier town 7–8
   intellectual isolation 8
   left-wing political groups in 112, 115
   social isolation 8, 14
   social life in 7, 40
Perth Roofs (Suburban Perth) (Vike) 175
Perth Society of Artists 33–4, 148, 175
Perth Technical College 32, 62, 140, 148
Petrov Royal Commission 271, 275, 279
Petrov, Vladimir 188, 272, 275–6
Pettersen, Ruth 211, 246–7, 268

Piccadilly Cinema 167
'Pig-Iron Bob' *see* Menzies, Robert
Pioneer Players 26
Pioneers, The (Prichard) 11, 26
Pitt Morison, George 62, 139
Pius XI (pope), edict against Communism 102
Plant in the Sun (Bengal) 219, 220
   Sydney New Theatre production (1939) 219
   Workers' Art Guild production (1940) 219, 220
Playbill (magazine) 51
Playbox Theatre 22–4, 27, 57
   Ghosts (1931) 27
   Hedda Gabler (1931) 25
Poetry Militant (O'Dowd) 204
Poignant, Axel 165–7, 209, 211, 218, 239, 246, 268–9
police
   as agents of CIB 18, 21
   attacked during protest marches 19
   attacks on protesters by 24
   ignore physical intimidation of CPA members 188, 189
   misinterpret *Blood on the Moon* rehearsals 178–9
   raids on CPA members 21, 188, 189, 197–209, 213, 248–9
   see also Commonwealth Investigation Branch (CIB)
Poole-Johnson, Walter 151
Popplewell, Olive, *This Bondage* 222–3
Popular Front 35–48, 85
Porter, Robert 66–7
Poster Studios 31–2
POUM (Workers Party of Marxist Unification) (Spain) 101
Powell, Dorothy (later Krantz) 151, 178, 196
Power and the Glory (Capek) 183
Power Without Glory (Hardy) 272
Prendiville, Redmond 102
Preston, Margaret 162
Prichard, Katharine Susannah
   agitprop theatre 11, 59, 141–2
   Black Opal 12
   Brumby Innes 105, 140, 226
   Burglar, The 25
   Child of the Hurricane 269

death and obituary 270–1
drama as political tool 49
early life 10–21
For Instance 141
Forward One 59–60, 203, 216, 217
friendship with Anne Filippini 26
friendship with Curtin 15, 240, 273
friendship with Deakin 10
friendship with Essons 25–6, 105
Golden Miles 111, 226
goldfields trilogy 226–7, 237, 269
Great Man, The 26
Greenmount home 13–4, 270, 271
on Hepworth 242
on *Hinkemann* 130
Intimate Strangers 38, 59, 97–8, 119, 273
later life 269–70
lobbies for Ric's diplomatic service 273–4
Modern Women's Club 115
Moon of Desire 104, 225
Penalty Clause 215–7
persecution of by intelligence agencies 11, 21, 30, 188, 235–8, 248–9
Pioneers, The 11, 26
Real Russia, The 38, 105
relationship with Baracchi 104
relationship with George 27, 49–59, 70–1, 90–1, 105–8, 111, 167–70
relationship with Mountjoy 144–6
as Rita Martinez 141
Roaring Nineties, The 104, 226
role in CPA 37–8, 39, 54, 111, 138–9, 185, 199, 238, 269
role in Five Arts Club 25
role in Workers' Art Guild 98, 105, 112, 251
role in Workers' Theatre 48–60
Socialist Realism in drama 51–2, 59, 104
on *Southern Cross, The* 105–8
Thief, The 51–2
Windlestraws 12
Winged Seeds 226
Women of Spain 141–2
Working Bullocks 237
Prichard, Tom 10
Princes Hall 136
Princess Theatre (Melbourne) 26
Private Hicks (Maltz) 125–6, 131–2, 243
  Workers' Art Guild production (1937) 125–6, 138

Professor Mamlock (Wolf) 135
protests 15, 18–9, 41, 113, 160, 214
Quiet Night (Blewett) 247–8
  Repertory Club production (1941) 247–8
Quinn, James 122

Radical Bookshop 29, 38, 44, 53, 56, 78, 137, 189, 198–9, 207
radio plays 23, 24–5
Ragged Trousered Philanthropists, The (1933) 43
Read, Stanley 248
Real Russia, The (Prichard) 38, 104
Rechabite Hall 40–1, 58, 138
Record (journal) 102
Red Army 176–7, 188, 238
Red Star (newspaper) 38, 44, 53–5, 58, 60, 63, 113–4
  see also Workers' Star
Rees, Leslie 151
  Making of Australian Drama, The 107
  Sub-Editor's Room 220
Rehearsal (Maltz) 220
  Sydney New Theatre production 220
  Workers' Art Guild production (1940) 220
Renouf, Alan 276
Repertory Club (Perth)
  directors 122, 149, 152–3, 181–2
  effect of war upon 180–1, 247–8
  financial difficulties 225
  George's involvement in 23, 248–50, 256
  Hasluck's involvement in 68
  Junior Circle 183
  membership 23, 97, 182, 247
  open door policy 182
  political repertoire 182–3
  productions 97, 152–3
    Boy Meets Girl (1938) 182
    Canaries Sometimes Sing (1942) 250
    Corn is Green, The (1939) 180–1
    Juno and the Paycock (1938) 152, 181
    Men Without Wives (1938) 153, 181
    No Incense Rising (1939) 183
    No More Peace 180
    On the Frontier (1939) 182
    Our Town (1940) 225
    Quiet Night (1941) 247–8
    Robert's Wife (1941) 236
    Squaring the Circle (1939) 183
    Valley of the Shadows (1949) 257

Rice, Elmer 191
  Street Scene 152
Richards, George Ronald ('Ron') 186–8, 197, 203, 205–6, 230–1, 233–4, 236, 271–2
Richards, Griff 36
Riley, Cyril 149
Roaring Nineties, The (Prichard) 104
Roberts, Buckley, *Where's That Bomb?* 115–7
Roberts, Russell 162
Robert's Wife 236
  Repertory Club production (1941) 236
Robeson, Paul 132–3
Rodchenko, Aleksandr 44
Rogers, Kurt 176
Rokotov, Timofei 199–200, 235
Roland, Betty 43, 114
  Are You Ready, Comrade? 150–2, 203
  War on the Waterfront 210
  Workers Beware 167
Room Service (Murray and Boretz) 183
Roosevelt, Franklin D. 153, 163, 191
Rowe, Dorothy ('Betty') 22–4, 27
Rudkin, Arthur
  arrest and imprisonment of 198, 201–2
  on George 168–9
  later life 272
  on Mountjoy 186
  police raids on 207
  Richards befriends 187
  role in CPA 55–6, 138, 176, 186–8, 197–8
  role in Workers' Art Guild 86, 90–1, 120
  role on *Workers' Star* 187–8, 198, 201, 207
  role in Workers' Theatre 55
rural unrest 220–1
Russian Ballet Company 166
Russian Revolution 11, 12, 29, 175
Russo-German pact 176

Scullin government 39, 154
Seamen's Union 205
secession referendum (1933) 33
Second World War
  Australia declares war on Japan 248
  Australia enters 180–1
  causes Workers' Art Guild shift to political centre 184
  Germany invades Soviet Union 237
  Germany and Italy declare war on America 248
  Italy enters war 199
  Japanese air strikes in WA 250
  outbreak of 176
Seward, Beryl 137, 209
Shakespeare, William, *Antony and Cleopatra* 164–5
Shakespeare Club 122
Shann, Edward ('Inky') 20
Sharkey, Lawrence ('Lance') 252–3
Shaw, George Bernard 24
Shaw, Irwin, *Bury the Dead* 83, 88–94
shipping reporters 7–8, 103
Sholokhov, Mikhail, *And Quiet Flows the Don* 86
Shop Assistants' Union 59
show trials 99–100, 104
Sifton, Paul and Claire, *Blood on the Moon* 176–80
Simpson, John Spencer ('Jack') 205, 230–1, 232, 233–4
Six Men of Dorset (Malleson and Brooks) 109
Skinner, Joe 34, 208, 234–5, 273
Skinner, Mollie 130
Smith, Christian Jollie *see* Jollie Smith, Christian
Smith, George 178–9
Smith, Howard
  acting career 72, 95, 125, 129, 151, 156, 171, 247
  on attracting trade unions 228
  as director 125, 147–8, 194–5, 196, 223
  on George 168, 258
  later life 273
  role in Repertory Club 250, 273
  role in Workers' Art Guild 220
Smith, Ian ('Bob') 35, 72, 156, 171, 247
Smith, Marjorie 60
Smith, Montaigne ('Monty') 35
Smith, Reginald 45
Smith, Sydney Ure *see* Ure Smith, Sydney
Smith's Weekly (newspaper) 196
Social Democratic movement 156
Social Realism 51
social welfare 11, 17, 19–20

Socialist Realism 51–2, 59, 104, 111, 114, 119, 143
Socko (play) 154
South Australian Grand Opera Company 26
Southern Cross, The (Esson) 105–8
Soviet Union
  art in 44
  diplomatic relations with Australia 238, 240, 253
  German invasion of 237–8
  Prichard's visits to 21, 29–30, 38, 42, 51–2, 104, 173
  Russo–German pact 176
  in Spanish Civil War 101
  Stalinist purges in 99–100, 104
  workers' theatre movement in 29–30
  see also Khrushchev, Nikita; Stalin, Joseph
Soviet Writers' Union 235
Soviets To-day (journal) 44
Spanish Civil War 19, 99, 100–2, 165
Spanish Relief Committee 99, 100–1, 112, 116, 141, 142
Spark, The (newsletter) 197
Spewack, Bella and Samuel, *Boy Meets Girl* 182
Squaring the Circle (Katayev) 183
  Repertory Club production (1939) 183
Stagg, Augustus ('Gus') 40, 45, 78, 85, 188, 198, 203
Stalin, Joseph
  birthday greetings from Prichard 185
  Khrushchev's denunciation of 263
  show trials 99–100, 104
  signs non-aggression pact with Hitler 176
  support of Spanish Civil War 101
  United Front policy 39
  see also Soviet Union
Standen, George 219–20
Stanislavsky, Konstantin 30, 61, 65, 100
Steffens, Lincoln 38
Steinbeck, John, *Of Mice and Men* 153
Steinberg, Isaac 172
Stepanova, Varvara 44
Stevens, John Ernest ('Jack') 19, 102
Strachey, John 137
  Nature of the Capitalist Crisis, The 191
Stravinsky, Igor, *Firebird* 166

Street Scene (Rice) 152
Strife (journal) 79
strike-breaking legislation 18, 58, 167, 215–7
Studio of Realist Art (SORA) 264, 266
Sub-Editor's Room (Rees) 220
  Sydney New Theatre production (1937) 220
  Workers' Art Guild production (1940) 220
Subversive Associations Regulations 202
suffragette movement 11, 222–3
Surrealist movement 64, 124, 148–9, 175, 212
sustenance allowance 19–20, 24, 163
Sydney Morning Herald 42, 79
Sydney New Theatre 138, 167, 195, 203, 210, 228
  Arnold's involvement with 74, 209, 210, 219, 240–1
  CPA association with 112, 154
  police raids on 203
  productions
    Are You Ready, Comrade? 151
    Bury the Dead (1936) 90
    Forward One, The (1937) 105
    New Way Wins (1940) 210
    Plant in the Sun (1939) 219
    Rehearsal 220
    Sub-Editor's Room (1937) 220
    Till the Day I Die (1936) 73–4
    War on the Waterfront (1938) 210
  Wells leaves 149
  writers' group 241–2
Sydney Workers' Art Club 42–3, 210
Sydney-Smith, Lorna 26–7

T.N.T. (newsletter) 36–7
Tangney, Dorothy 79
Tatlin, Vladimir 88
Taylor, A.J.P. 176
Theatres and Public Halls Act 1908 (NSW) 74
Thief, The (Prichard) 51–2
This Bondage (Popplewell) 222–3
  Workers' Art Guild production (1940) 222–3
Thomas, Dylan 64
Thompson, John 176
  What Are We To Do 165

Thompson, Patricia ('Pat') 23, 165, 178, 209
Thorndike, Sybil 27, 109
Thornton, Ernie 230
Throssell, George 13
Throssell, Hugo ('Jim') 11, 12–3, 21, 25, 27–8, 97
Throssell, Ric
  acting career 247
  as author 274–6
  death and obituaries 277–8
  diplomatic service 273–6
  education of 236, 237
  For Valour 276
  on George 23, 66, 169, 169–70, 224, 251, 257, 258
  military service 273
  My Father's Son 277
  persecution of by Richards 188, 271, 274–6
  on Prichard's works 141, 216–7
  tainted by Petrov Affair 275–6
  Valley of the Shadows 257, 274
  and Venona decryption cables 277
  Wild Weeds and Wind Flowers 277
  on Workers' Art Guild audiences 96
Till the Day I Die (Odets)
  Sydney New Theatre production (1936) 73–4
  Workers' Art Club production (1936) 52, 53, 57, 62–75, 76, 140
  Workers' Art Guild production (1936) 94–6
  Workers' Art Guild production (1941) 246–7
Toller, Ernst 180, 184
  Hinkemann 126–30
  Masses and Man 43
  No More Peace 180
Tolpuddle Martyrs 109
trade unions 11, 43, 46–7, 67–8, 110, 117–8, 160, 202, 228, 231
  see also names of unions (e.g. Australian Workers' Union)
Trades Hall Flats 63, 78–9
Trainer, Percy 231
Transport Workers Act 1928 (Cth) 58, 167
Tribune, The (newspaper) 210, 242, 258, 264, 265

Trotsky, Leon 39
Troy, Patrick ('Paddy') 197–8, 203, 215–7, 251

unemployed workers
  during Depression 17–8, 79
  group camps for 19–20
  Workers' Arts Club as hub for 57–8
Unemployed Workers' Movement (UWM) 54
unemployment benefits *see* sustenance allowance
unemployment rate 17–8, 31, 33, 64
United Australia Party 40, 229, 240
United Front 39, 41, 46
Unity Theatre (London) 116, 118, 132–3
Unity Theatre (Perth) 134
University Art Club 212
University Dramatic Society 23
University Labour Club 36, 116
University of Western Australia
  Adult Education Board 174, 256–7
  bans Prichard lectures 199–200
  English Department 86–7, 192
  Irwin Street campus 31, 36
  Summer School 224–5
Upsurge (Harcourt) 46, 119–20
Ure Smith, Sydney 148

Valley of the Shadows (Throssell) 257, 274
  Repertory Club production (1949) 257
Vanzetti, Francesco 33–4
Venona decryption cables 277
Victorian Workers' Theatre Group 43
Vike, Harald 79, 134
  acting career 57, 72, 140, 157
  as artist 32, 57, 139, 148, 149, 167, 175
  declared an alien 239
  elopes to Melbourne with Kidd 238–9
  financial hardship 234–5
  later life 278
  Perth Roofs (Suburban Perth) 175
  role in Workers' Art Club 72
  role in Workers' Art Guild 82, 88–90, 157
  role in Workers' Theatre 57, 61–3
  set design work 88–90, 94, 120, 129, 165, 178–9, 215
Vike, Joan (nee Kidd) 140, 165

Vilna Troupe 134–5
Voigts Linotype Press 113–4

'W.A. First' campaign posters 32, 37, 94
wages 11, 17
  see also working conditions
Waislitz, Jacob (Yankev) 134–6
Waiting for Lefty (Odets) 59, 115, 117–9, 243
  Workers' Art Guild production (July 1937) 115–9, 138
  Workers' Art Guild production (Sept. 1937) 121–2
War Funds Regulation Act 1939 (WA) 250
War on the Waterfront (Roland) 210
  Sydney New Theatre production (1938) 210
Waten, Judah 79
waterside workers 167, 279
We Are Hungry (Hepworth) 78, 123
Webb, A.B. 62
Wells, H.G. 132
  Shape of Things to Come, The 94
Wells, Jerold 149, 152–3, 180–3, 209, 225, 278
West Australian Council Against War (and Fascism) 29, 40, 41, 45
West Australian Drama Festival
  1937 78, 122–3
  1938 149–52, 183
  1939 176–81, 183–4
  1940 215–7
  1941 247–8
  1948 and 1949 257
West Australian Grand Opera Company 26, 27
West Australian (newspaper)
  on art 33–4, 139, 212
  Hasluck at 67, 116
  on immigration 172
  on language in *Where's That Bomb?* 116–7
  letters to the editor 74–5, 149
  on National Register protests 161
  on Nazi invasion of Soviet Union 238
  obituary for George 258
  Ray McClintock (Oldham) at 37–8, 114
  reviews
    Awake and Sing! 171
    Blood on the Moon 177

Floridsdorf 157
Hinkemann and *Private Hicks* 127, 130–1
Inga 143, 144
Till the Day I Die (1936) 96
Till the Day I Die (1941) 247
  on show trials 100
  on Spanish Civil War 102–3
  on Stalinist purges 44, 100
  theatre column 66, 67, 68, 96
West Australian Society of Arts 33–4, 62–3, 148
West Australian Wheatgrower (newspaper) 193
Western Australian Railways Department 207
Western Command Military Intelligence 202, 208, 232–3, 234, 236, 241
Western Mail (newspaper) 103
Westralian Judean (newspaper)
  on omission of national anthem 69–70
  see also Jewish community
Westralian Worker (journal) 15, 229, 230
What Are We To Do (Thompson) 165
What is Surrealism? (Breton) 149
wheat farmers 190, 192–3
Where's That Bomb? (Gullan and Roberts) 115–6
  Workers' Art Guild production (1937) 115–7, 138
White Australia policy 41–2, 76, 136, 218
Who's Who in the Berlin Zoo 51, 52
Wignall, Donald 129
Wignall, George 71, 78, 98, 112–4, 122, 129, 133, 151, 215
Wignall, Gordon 122, 129
Wignall, Mairi ('Molly') 113, 129, 168
Wignall, Tom, Jr. 82, 95, 110, 113, 129–30, 168, 209, 215
Wignall, Tom, Sr. 57, 113, 202
Wild Weeds and Wind Flowers (Throssell) 277
Wilder, Thornton, *Our Town* 225
Willcock, John 167
William Moore's Annual Australian Drama Nights (Melbourne) 25–6
Williams, Emlyn
  Corn is Green, The 180–1
  Night Must Fall 153
Williams, Joan 142, 157, 213

Williams, Victor 162, 191–3, 209, 245, 279
  Farmers' Way Forward 192
  Feed the Sheep 220–1
  Hold Your Wheat 190–3
Wilmot, Frank 101
Wilson, Douglas 242
Wilson, Frank 250
Wilson, Linley 250–1, 256–7
Wilson, Una 101
Wiluna 31, 121, 139
Windlestraws (Prichard) 12
Winged Seeds (Prichard) 226
Wolf, Friedrich
  Floridsdorf 155–8
  Professor Mamlock 135
  Yellow Spot 135
Woman Tamer, The (Esson) 25–6
Woman Today (journal) 105, 114, 141
women
  in Workers' Art Guild positions 83
  working conditions 59–60, 105
Women of Spain (Prichard) 141–2
  Workers' Art Guild production (1938) 141–2
Women, The (Luce) 194–6
  Workers' Art Guild production (1940) 194–6
Workers' Art Club (Perth)
  agenda 58
  dramatic section 61, 68
  fine arts section 61
  formation of 35, 57–63
  as hub for unemployed 57–8
  literary section 76–8
  name change to Workers' Art Guild 80
  subsumes Workers' Theatre 57
  Till the Day I Die (1936) 52, 53, 57, 62–75, 76, 140
  see also Workers' Art Guild
Workers' Art Clubs 42–3, 58
Workers' Art Guild
  Catholic Church opposition to 102
  children's theatre wing 83–4, 101, 158
  CIB raid on 208
  CIB surveillance of 245
  corporate sponsorship 195
  demise of 250
  effect of war upon 184, 194, 229, 246, 252
  fine arts wing 139
  generational change in 168–70
  George's departure from 167–70, 184
  left-wing group affiliations 112
  library 86
  membership 82–3, 112, 190, 194, 228
  musical section 139
  origins 80–4
  plastic and graphic arts section 83, 94
  premises 81, 82
  productions
    Are You Ready, Comrade? (1938) 151–2
    Awake and Sing! (1939) 170–1
    Blood on the Moon (Sept. 1939) 176–80, 183
    Blood on the Moon (Oct. 1939) 180
    Bury the Dead (1936) 88–94, 140
    Cannibal Carnival (1939) 163–5
    Feed the Sheep (1940) 220–1
    Floridsdorf (1939) 155–8
    Ghosts (1938) 147–8
    Heil Jones (1936) 83
    Hinkemann (1937) 126–30, 138
    Hold Your Wheat (1940) 190–3
    Inga (1938) 141, 142–4
    Love on the Dole (1940) 211, 214–5
    Lyons Bungles, The (1937) 133–4, 138
    Penalty Clause (1941) 215–7, 223, 224
    Plant in the Sun (1940) 219, 220
    Private Hicks (1937) 125–6, 138
    Rehearsal (1940) 220
    Sub-Editor's Room (1940) 220
    This Bondage (1940) 222–3
    Till the Day I Die (1936) 94–6
    Till the Day I Die (1941) 246–7
    Waiting for Lefty (July 1937) 115–9, 138
    Waiting for Lefty (Sept. 1937) 121–2
    Where's That Bomb? (1937) 115–7, 138
    Women of Spain (1938) 141–2
    Women, The (1940) 194–6
    Workers Beware 167
  relationship with ALP 153, 154
  relationship with CPA 101, 110–2, 114, 153, 154–5
  relationship with trade unions 228
  relationship with University Labour Club 116–7
  Saturday-night cabarets 246

writers' group 76–7, 110, 133, 162, 192, 228
see also Workers' Art Club (Perth); Workers' Theatre (Perth)
Workers Beware (Roland) 167
  Workers' Art Guild production 167
Workers' International Relief (WIR) 29–30, 42
Workers' Star (newspaper)
  on abdication of Edward VIII 94
  circulation of 113, 159, 187
  on CPA membership 115
  illegal issues of 206–7
  on Menzies' limit on wheat growers 192–3
  police target staff of 188–9, 198, 205–6
  renamed *Clarion* 189
  renamed *Star* 189
  reviews of Independent Players' performances 183
  reviews of Workers' Art Guild productions 117, 133–4, 142, 147–8, 150, 152, 154, 157, 162, 171, 179–81, 195
  on Russo-German pact 176
  on Soviet show trials and purges 100
  on Spanish Civil War 102–3
  see also Clarion; Red Star
workers' theatre movement 29–30, 42, 46, 48, 112
Workers' Theatre (Perth) 35, 48–61, 50, 57
Working Bullocks, (Prichard) 237
'working class culture' 50, 58
working conditions 11, 17, 59, 123, 215–7
World Movement Against War 39, 41
World War One *see* First World War
World War Two *see* Second World War
World's Fair (New York; 1939) 162–3
Wright, Frank Lloyd 162
Writers International 46
Writers' League for the Defence of Culture 105

X=O: A Night of the Trojan War (Drinkwater) 58, 224
xenophobia 185

Yalden, Thomas 24
Yeats, W. B. 8
Yellow Ticket (Hepworth) 123

Young Communist League 113
Young Labour League 38, 113, 134
Yugoslav community 217–8

Zanalis, Vlase 62
Zhdanov, Andrei 51–2

ALSO AVAILABLE FROM

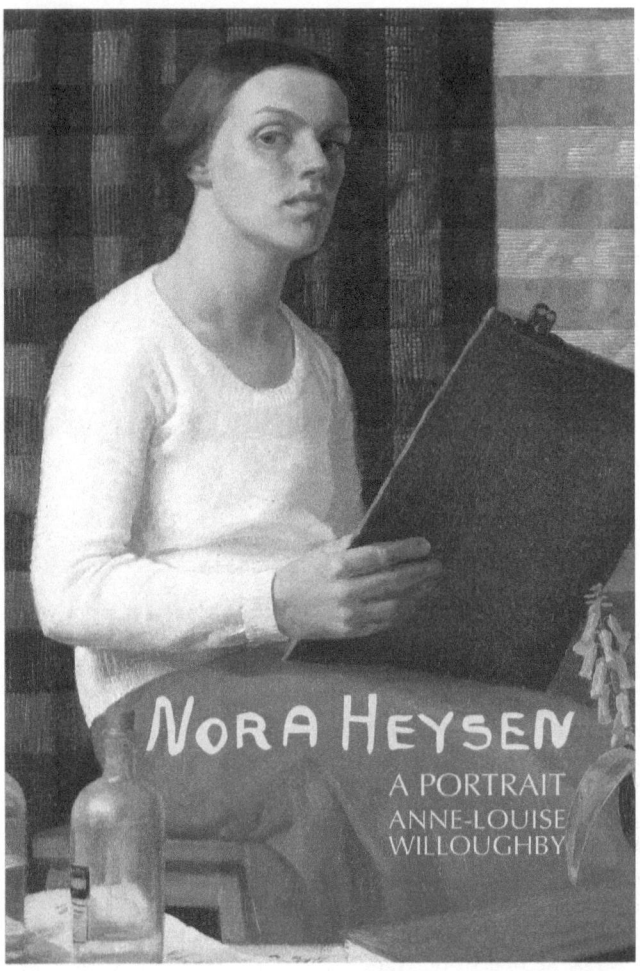

The life of artist Nora Heysen was defined by an all-consuming drive to draw or paint. The first woman to win the Archibald Prize, and Australia's first female painter to be appointed an official war artist, Heysen's post-war portraiture and still lifes sustained a lifelong career.

In 1989, aged seventy-eight, after years of artistic obscurity, she re-emerged on the Australian art scene, and the nation's major art institutions restored her position as a significant Australian artist.

Extensively researched, and containing artworks and photographs from the life of Nora Heysen, this story of a driven, optimistic and resilient painter is a celebration of that restoration.

FREMANTLEPRESS.COM.AU

FREMANTLE PRESS

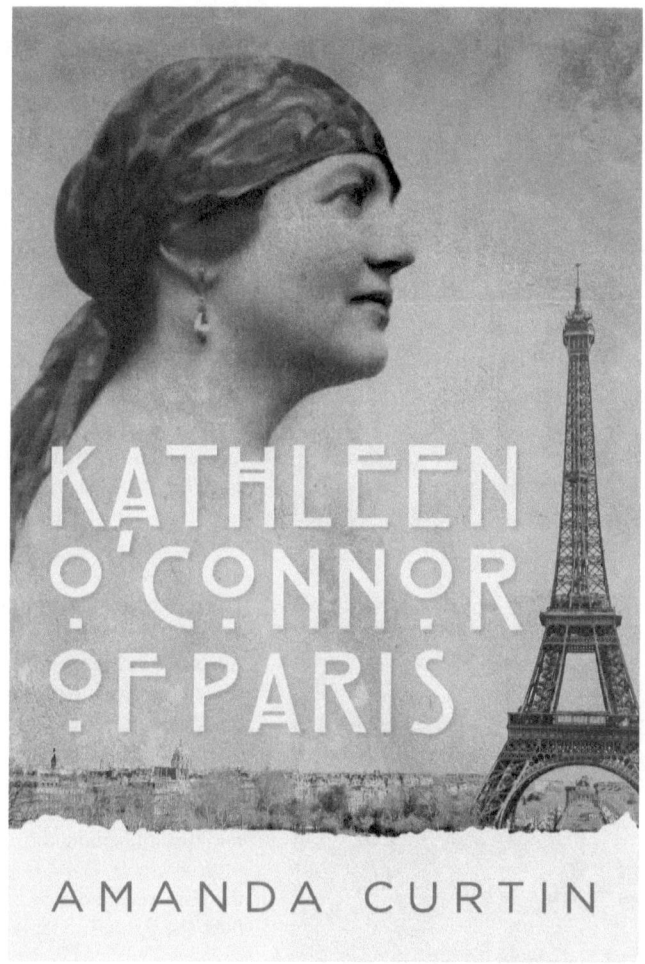

What does it mean to live a life in pursuit of art?

In 1906, Kathleen O'Connor left conservative Perth, where her famous father's life had ended in tragedy. She had her sights set on a career in thrilling, bohemian Paris. More than a century later, novelist Amanda Curtin faces her own questions, of life and of art, as she embarks on a journey in Kate's footsteps.

Part biography, part travel narrative, this is the story of an artist in a foreign land who, with limited resources and despite the impacts of war and loss, worked and exhibited in Paris for over forty years. Kate's distinctive figure paintings, portraits and still lifes, highly prized today, form an inseparable part of the telling.

AND ALL GOOD BOOKSTORES

MORE WESTERN AUSTRALIAN HISTORY

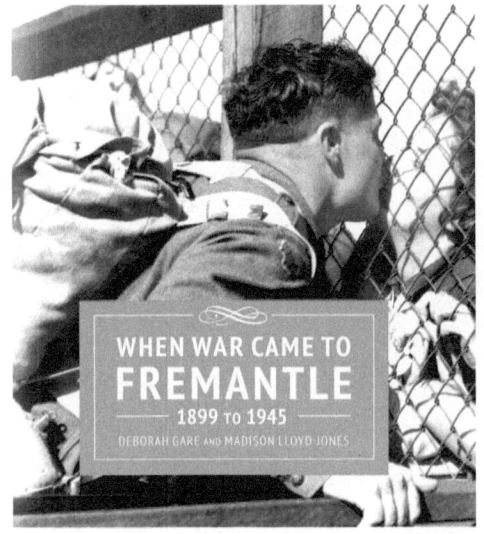

As one of Australia's largest wartime ports, Fremantle played a unique role in the nation's story. Featuring extraordinary photographs, this volume is a fascinating account of our homefront during the Boer War, World War I, World War II and more. It records our history of departure and reunion, victory and celebration, grief and loss, and dissent and activism.

'This is a fascinating local history tracking the evolution of a community against the backdrop of several decades of international conflict.' *The West Australian*

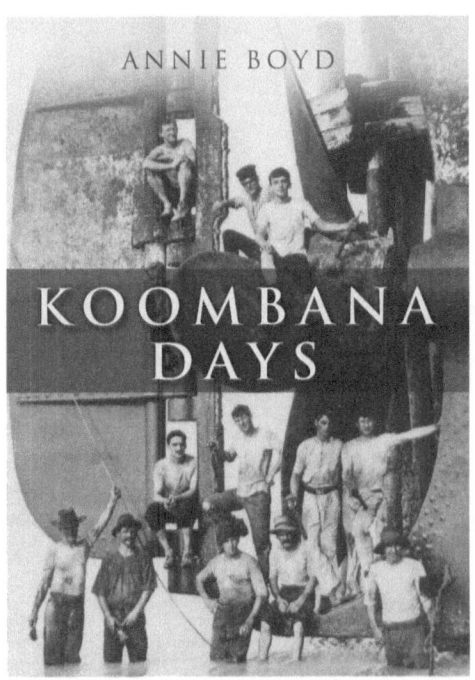

The elegant, ultra-modern S.S. *Koombana* arrived in Western Australia in March 1909. After only three years of Nor'-West service, the ship and her entire complement disappeared in a late-summer cyclone off the Pilbara coast. The vessel has never been found and the tragedy remains unexplained.

Koombana Days is the story of the ship and of the people in whose lives she figured so large.

'It's a fascinating mix that adds up to a work of social history that is engaging and readable for a wide general audience. [Four stars out of five]' *Books+Publishing*

FROM FREMANTLE PRESS

www.ingramcontent.com/pod-product-compliance
Lightning Source LLC
Chambersburg PA
CBHW031606210526
45464CB00004B/1451